T0321779

Healthcare 4.0

The main aim of *Healthcare 4.0: Health Informatics and Precision Data Management* is to improve the services given by the healthcare industry and to bring meaningful patient outcomes by applying the data, information and knowledge in the healthcare domain.

Features:

- Improves the quality of health data of a patient
- Presents a wide range of opportunities and renewed possibilities for healthcare systems
- Gives a way for carefully and meticulously tracking the provenance of medical records
- Accelerates the process of disease-oriented data and medical data arbitration
- Brings meaningful patient health outcomes
- Eradicates delayed clinical communications
- Helps the research intellectuals to step down further toward the disease and clinical data storage
- Creates more patient-centered services

The precise focus of this handbook is on the potential applications and use of data informatics in healthcare, including clinical trials, tailored ailment data, patient and ailment record characterization and health records management.

Healthcare 4.0
Health Informatics and Precision Data Management

Edited by
Lalitha Krishnasamy
Rajesh Kumar Dhanaraj
Balamurugan Balusamy
Munish Sabharwal
Poongodi Chinnasamy

CRC Press
Taylor & Francis Group
Boca Raton London New York

CRC Press is an imprint of the
Taylor & Francis Group, an **informa** business

A CHAPMAN & HALL BOOK

First edition published 2023
by CRC Press
6000 Broken Sound Parkway NW, Suite 300, Boca Raton, FL 33487-2742

and by CRC Press
4 Park Square, Milton Park, Abingdon, Oxon, OX14 4RN

CRC Press is an imprint of Taylor & Francis Group, LLC

ISBN: 978-1-032-10860-5 (hbk)
ISBN: 978-1-032-42262-6 (pbk)
ISBN: 978-1-003-21743-5 (ebk)

DOI: 10.1201/9781003217435

Typeset in Palatino
by SPi Technologies India Pvt Ltd (Straive)

Contents

Preface

Health records in the electronic format are increasing day by day and to analyze these massive records with heterogeneous data sets, informatics and data analysis are obligatory. This book reveals an enigmatic assembly of diverse biomedical data types which comprise clinical data, data from electrocardiogram, genomic data, etc. Biomedical data are notorious for their diversified scales, dimensions, and volumes and requires interdisciplinary technologies for visual illustration and digital characterization. Various computer programs and servers have been developed for these purposes by both theoreticians and engineers. The healthcare industry today is notorious to feel pain from heterogeneous and uneven data, delayed clinical communications, and disparate workflow tools due to the lack of identification of proper disease, lack of interoperability caused by vendor-locked healthcare systems, and security/privacy concerns regarding data storage, sharing, and usage.

Apart from data informatics, which is of paramount importance for improving quality of health data of a patient, there is also a wide range of opportunities and renewed possibilities for healthcare systems to influence the categories of health data. This powerful and breakthrough information system paves a way for carefully and meticulously tracking the provenance of medical records, accelerating the process of disease-oriented data and medical data arbitration, connecting alike patient populations to clinical trials, and creating more patient-centered services.

The precise focus of this handbook will be on the potential applications and use of data informatics in area of healthcare, including clinical trials, tailored ailment data, patient and ailment record characterization, and health records management.

Organization of this Book

Chapter 1 presents the big data era; the healthcare informatics need exploration of the health records to identify the hidden patterns. Machine learning and deep learning techniques provide classification, clustering, and prediction tasks. Healthcare data processed in the centralized architecture pose single point of failure and it is difficult to collaborate with different distribution of data to design a robust system. This chapter identifies the current challenges in the healthcare informatics and addresses those issues with enabling technologies that explore the healthcare informatics with application of artificial learning and security mechanisms.

Chapter 2 investigates the state-of-the-art research solutions for the complete range of healthcare data, analyzes the data, and provides guidance for future progress in healthcare practice. It highlights the developments in using blockchain technology in healthcare domain, emphasizing the need for healthcare data to be shared among various healthcare entities. It then summarizes modern and emerging technologies such as cloud and fog computing in healthcare industry for classifying illness and segmentation, with an emphasis on deep learning and AI and machine learning architectures that have already been established as the standard methodology.

Chapter 3 presents the recent advances in computer storage systems, processing power, and data-analysis algorithms in the modern Clinical Information Systems that made the above task easier. Bioinformatics addresses these problems and aims to create integrated storage systems and analysis tools to convert the biological data into meaningful information. This helps to predict the disease and paves the way for drug discovery in precision medicine.

Chapter 4 discusses how to purchase medicines online that are rarely available in the market. In the COVID period, people suffered a lot to get the recommended medicine from an authorized agency through online. Many fake images were posted and patients received different medicines than expected. Clinical information system analysis is explored with image processing techniques to predict the disease and the correct drug identification and discovery.

Chapter 5 focuses primarily on two strategies for using MATLAB software simulations to segment bone tissues and then adopting the most effective segmentation approach based on iImage pre-processing, edge and boundary detection, and other related tasks. The graph cut technique, which is known for its smoothness and energy economy, has been more popular in the image processing and analysis disciplines in recent years.

Chapter 6 presents that the hospital has planned to maintain the patient history in the form of electronic data. The patients do not prefer to maintain the patient history in the distributed network due to security concerns. Therefore, blockchain technique is evolved to securely maintain the patient's history in the distributed networks.

Chapter 7 briefly introduces sepsis, a life-threatening emergency medical condition and is one of the leading causes of death in patients who are being treated at the intensive care unit (ICU) of hospitals. It is the extreme response shown by the body in response to infection. Sepsis arises due to the excessive quantity of infective microbes in the blood which are in a state of active replication. Here, a novel sepsis detection system using machine learning techniques has been presented. The system would predict if the patient would develop sepsis using a range of clinical parameters like blood pressure, temperature, oxygen saturation, heart rate, and other biochemical investigations.

Chapter 8 discusses oral sickness. Two-thirds of the population has been suffering from oral sickness in Asia for the past three decades, and the ailment is particularly prevalent in low- and middle-income nations, according to the World Health Organization. A neural network-based oral cancer detection system that makes use of a range of image processing methodologies is presented here.

Chapter 9 explores deep learning and is used to identify lungs illness. According to the Globe Health Organization, lung illnesses would be the third most important cause of demise in the world by 2030. Lung infection is a common occurrence all around the globe. The foundation of lung infection diagnosis is the ease with which it may be accomplished.

Chapter 10 proposes that brain–computer interfaces (BCI) circumvent the body's normal neuromuscular controls and are intended to act as a backup mechanism for communication and control in the case of a neuronal or muscle failure. The chapter discusses the effects of BCI on cognition, sensors, machine learning, neurophysiology, psychology, signal detection and processing, source localization, pattern recognition, clustering, and classification of signals, as well as signal detection and processing in general.

Chapter 11 highlights segmentation and feature extractions to diagnose the skin condition at an early stage. Text-based features are extracted with the help of CNN and an image processing technique that incorporates symmetry detection, border detection, and color. A major development in healthcare 4.0 is also occurring in the treatment of aging skin.

Chapter 12 presents the technology and or approach utilized to precisely identify patients, thorough design of the care processes using blockchain will ensure effective patient identification prior to any medical intervention and result in safer care with fewer errors. In healthcare, patient information is shared with healthcare experts using electronic health record (EHR) where patient's information is shared among the healthcare experts with the help of patient/healthcare expert's identity.

Chapter 13 discusses that IoT is a significant improvement in intelligence to the current societal issues. There is no way to classify the subjective pain associated with such an active communication network as something that is outside of artificial intelligence, and we are certainly not outside of artificial intelligence. It is possible to analyze, combine, and prioritize the data collected in this way if it is required. When physicians work with algorithms, they may change therapy while also delivering more cost-effective healthcare, which has a more positive result for patients.

Chapter 14 focuses on developing a secure and privacy-preserving health chain system based on blockchain technology. The system ensures data security and patient privacy by giving full authority of the data to the patient. It also regulates that the data are updated by the skilled healthcare professional, only with the permission of the patient. It will automate the process throughout the chain and contribute toward robustness of the healthcare information sharing environment.

Editor Biography

Dr. Lalitha Krishnasamy is an Associate Professor in the Department of Information Technology, Kongu Engineering College, Erode, Tamil Nadu. She received her B.Tech degree in Information Technology from Anna University, Chennai in 2005 and an M.Tech degree in Information Technology from Anna University of Technology, Coimbatore in 2009 and completed a Ph.D. in Wireless Sensor Networks from Anna University, Chennai in 2019. She has contributed 40+ articles in international journals and conferences. She has conducted various programmes in the area of Wireless Sensor Networks, Internet of Things and Artificial Intelligence Algorithms and Machine Learning. Her research areas of interest include wireless sensor networks, artificial intelligence, and internet of things. She has published three book chapters and obtained four patents. She is a Lifetime member of CSI and IAENG.

Dr. Rajesh Kumar Dhanaraj is a Professor in the School of Computing Science and Engineering at Galgotias University, Greater Noida, UP, India. He received a B.E. in Computer Science and Engineering from the Anna University Chennai, India in 2007 and an M.Tech from the Anna University Coimbatore, India in 2010 and a Ph.D. degree in Computer Science from Anna University, Chennai, India, in 2017. He has contributed over 35+ Authored and Edited books on various technologies, 21 Patents and 68 articles and papers in various referred journals and international conferences and contributed chapters to the books. His research interests include Machine Learning, Cyber-Physical Systems and Wireless Sensor Networks. He is a Senior Member of the Institute of Electrical and Electronics Engineers (IEEE), member of the Computer Science Teacher Association (CSTA); and International Association of Engineers (IAENG). He is serving as an Associate Editor and Guest Editor for reputed journals. He is an Expert Advisory Panel Member of Texas Instruments Inc USA.

Prof. Balamurugan Balusamy has served as Associate Professor in his stint of 14 years of experience with VIT University, Vellore. He completed his Bachelors, Masters, and Ph.D. degrees from top premier institutions from India. His passion is teaching and adapts different design thinking principles while delivering his lectures. He has published 30+ books on various technologies and visited 15+ countries for his technical course. He has several top-notch conferences in his resume and has published over 150 quality journal, conference, and book chapters combined. He serves in the advisory committee for several startups and forums and does consultancy work for industry on industrial IOT. He has given over 175 talks in various events and symposium. He is currently working as a professor at Galgotias University and teaches students and does research on blockchain and IOT.

Dr. Munish Sabharwal is Professor and Dean of the School of Computing Science and Engineering, Galgotias University, Greater Noida (UP), India. He is also Adjunct Professor – Faculty of Digital Technologies at Samarkand State University, Samarkand, Uzbekistan. He has a Ph.D. in Computer Science and Ph.D. in Management and also has a PGDM (International Trade) from Symbiosis Institute of Management Studies, Pune, an M. Tech (Computer Science) from IASE University, Sardarshahr, and a B.E. (Computer Technology) from Nagpur University, Nagpur.

He has 12+ years of research experience and has published more than 83+ research papers in reputed conferences and journals indexed in Web of Science, Scopus etc. He is board member as well as reviewer for a number of leading indexed research journals and has several books to his credit. He is guiding 12 Ph.D. Scholars and his current research interests include data sciences (AI & ML), biometrics, and e-banking. He has more than 12 Professional Memberships and Research Associations with organizations like Life Members – IAENG, TAEI, CSI, AIMA, YHAI, Senior Member – ACM, IEEE, IACSIT, IRED, and Member – ASI, AAAI, AIS etc. He has special fondness for teaching, with 18+ years.

Dr. Poongodi Chinnasamy is Professor of the Department of Information Technology in Vivekanandha College of Engineering for Women, Tiruchengode, Namakkal District and has 20 years of teaching experience. She obtained her B.E. in Electronics and Communication Engineering from Bharathiar University, Coimbatore in 2001, M.E. in Computer Science Engineering from Bharathiar University in 2002 and obtained a Ph.D. in Information and Communication Engineering from Anna University, Chennai, during 2013. She has published more than 40 papers in international conferences and in international journals. She has obtained one Patent. She has been occupying herself as a Journal Reviewer nationally and internationally since 2015. She has acted as co-chair for various International conferences. Her research areas include Internet of Things, Wireless networks and Delay Tolerant Networks.

List of Contributors

Dr. Shailendra S. Aote
Shri Ramdeobaba College of Engineering
  and Management
Nagpur, India

N. Archana
Chennai Institute of Technology
Chennai, Tamil Nadu, India

V. Aruna Devi
Madras Institute of Technology,
  Anna University
Chennai, India

Dr. K. S. Arvind
Jain University
Bangalore, India

Dr. Balamurugan Balusamy
Galgotias University
Greater Noida, India

K. Balasamy
Bannari Amman Institute of Technology
Erode, India

S. Bhuvaneswari
Chennai Institute of Technology
Chennai, Tamil Nadu, India

S. M. J. Blessy Regina
Chennai Institute of Technology
Chennai, Tamil Nadu, India

Dr. Rajesh Kumar Dhanaraj
Galgotias University
Greater Noida, India

Dhanasekar J
Sri Eshwar College of Engineering
Coimbatore, India

M. K. Dharani
Kongu Engineering College
Perundurai, India

J. Eric Clapten
Chennai Institute of Technology
Chennai, Tamil Nadu, India

S. Gowrishankar
Dr. Ambedkar Institute of Technology
Bengaluru, India

Hakkem Babu
Hindustan Institute of Technology
Coimbatore, India

Jai Jaganath Babu Jayachandran
Chennai Institute of Technology
Chennai, India

J. Jenita Hermina
Er. Perumal Manimekalai College
  of Engineering
Hosur, India

Kalpana Kasilingam
Hindustan Institute of Technology
Coimbatore, India

Dr. Amit Khaparde
G. B. Pant DSEU Okhla – I Campus
New Delhi, India

Dinesh Komarasamy
Kongu Engineering College
Perundurai, India

Adesh Kotgirwar
Shri Ramdeobaba College of
  Engineering and Management
Nagpur, India

Dr. Lalitha Krishnasamy
Kongu Engineering College
Erode, Tamil Nadu, India

P. M. Lakshmi Prabha
Chennai Institute of Technology
Chennai, Tamil Nadu, India

R. Menaka
Chennai Institute of Technology
Chennai, Tamil Nadu, India

S. Mohana Saranya
Kongu Engineering College
Erode, Tamil Nadu, India

S. Mohanapriya
Kongu Engineering College
Erode, Tamil Nadu, India

Aayush Muley
Shri Ramdeobaba College of
    Engineering and Management
Nagpur, India

Dr R. Nedunchezian
Coimbatore Institute of Technology
Coimbatore, India

K. Oviya
Chennai Institute of Technology
Chennai, Tamil Nadu, India

R. Pandimeena
Chennai Institute of Technology
Chennai, Tamil Nadu, India

Varalakshmi Perumal
Madras Institute of Technology
Anna University, Chennai

Sakthi Jaya Sundar Rajasekar
Melmaruvathur Adhiparasakthi Institute
    of Medical Sciences & Research
Chengalpattu, Chennai

Ramya S
Hindustan Institute of Technology
Coimbatore, India

D. Sandhiya
Chennai Institute of Technology
Chennai, Tamil Nadu, India

V. Seethalakshmi
KPR Institute of Engineering and
    Technology
Coimbatore, India

M. B. Sharada
Chennai Institute of Technology
Chennai, Tamil Nadu, India

Lalita Sharma
Shri Ramdeobaba College of Engineering
    and Management
Nagpur, India

A. Sivabalan
Chennai Institute of Technology
Chennai, Tamil Nadu, India

M. Sridhar
Chennai Institute of Technology
Chennai, Tamil Nadu, India

K. S. Suganya
KCG College of Technology
Chennai, Tamil Nadu, India

S. Suganyadevi
KPR Institute of Engineering and
    Technology
Coimbatore, India

M. Swetha
Chennai Institute of Technology
Chennai, Tamil Nadu, India

A. Tamilselvi
Chennai Institute of Technology
Chennai, Tamil Nadu, India

K. Tamilselvi
Kongu Engineering College
Erode, Tamil Nadu, India

K. Tamil Selvi
Kongu Engineering College
Erode, Tamil Nadu, India

Teresa V V
Sri Eshwar College of Engineering
Coimbatore, India

R. Thamilselvan
Kongu Engineering College
Erode, Tamil Nadu, India

A. Veena
Dr. Ambedkar Institute of Technology
Bengaluru, India

N. Vidhya
KPR Institute of Engineering and
    Technology
Coimbatore, India

S. Vignesh
Chennai Institute of Technology
Chennai, Tamil Nadu, India

Atharva Uplanchiwar
Shri Ramdeobaba College of Engineering
    and Management
Nagpur, India

1

Privacy-preserving Healthcare Informatics using Federated Learning and Blockchain

K. Tamil Selvi and R. Thamilselvan

Kongu Engineering College, Erode, India

CONTENTS

DOI: 10.1201/9781003217435-1

1.1 Introduction

Real-world healthcare data with its application in artificial intelligence modes like machine learning and deep learning tasks suffer from many practical challenges like distributed nature of data, privacy concerns, computational complexity, constraints on resource utilization, and so on. Application of learning tasks from diverse resources improves the quality of the healthcare provision. Mostly, healthcare data are present in silos and disruptive techniques are in need to apply analytics to mine the insight patterns [1]. The major concern in healthcare information is privacy issues. To preserve the privacy contents of the patients, the critical information is available in a centralized manner and prone to less extraction of features and patterns and single point of failure for the analytic process. Data from diverse applications are prohibited due to regulatory norms like US Health Insurance Portability and Accountability Act (HIPAA) [2], European General Data Protection Regulation (GDPR) [3], and information protection policies. Hence, there is a need for a distributed in-house analytical model for improved efficiency of healthcare informatics and application. To address these issues, Federated learning (FL) allows the construction global healthcare analytical model from diverse distributed silos healthcare local data models without sharing the healthcare raw data.

Differential privacy [4] is a theoretical model for privacy preservation of healthcare information of the user. It ensures addition or removal of the data does not affect the performance of the analytical model. However, computational complexities arise which are leveraged by the FL techniques. Blockchain, a peer-to-peer network for data storage and network tracking, is independent of a trusted third party. The information in the blockchain is distributed with hash values. To protect the privacy of the blockchain, differential privacy is applied. So blockchain with differential privacy [5] can be a fruitful technique in healthcare 4.0 with the integration of wide applications. The sensitivity of the healthcare data is preserved by the addition of noise to preserve the privacy in differential privacy. The data pooling requirement of the current bigdata with complex computation is overcome by the FL. However, many challenges have to be addressed by privacy preservation with the intended data and its associated task in healthcare informatics. Though FL is privacy-preserving mechanism, there may be security attacks like inference attacks and data poisoning attacks. To make the medical data more reliable for the learning models and preservation of the patients' privacy information, blockchain-based FL systems can be applied [6]. It enables the participation in two layers in a decentralized manner for the trusted participation between the distributed models and the gateway or the centralized global model. The generalized view of the integration of blockchain with the distributed learning model is shown in Figure 1.1. The healthcare systems are connected to the distributed network with the learning models and their associated parameters. The blockchain enhances the communication of patient data in a trusted way among the healthcare domains using the consensus protocol and chain-based protocols.

Healthcare data are diverse in nature in the aspect of dimensions, modalities, data acquisition, and demographic properties. These data heterogeneity leads to non-identical and independent data distribution systems with aggregation in global the local medical learning models. Thus, need for the domain adaptation of the data in the FL system with an optimal solution through local data models and its gradients. Generally, federated averaging or max/min averaging among the models is used for updating the gradients of the learning models. At the maximal optimization, bio-inspired optimization approaches are

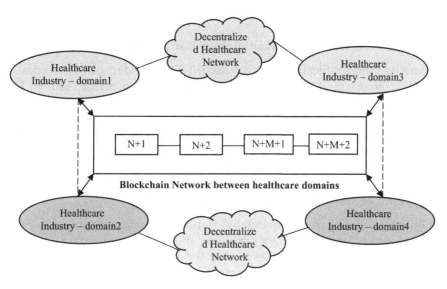

FIGURE 1.1
Blockchain-based distributed healthcare system.

also embedded with the secure transaction of the biomedical patient information. FL can be applied as vertically or horizontally based on the feature sets of data and the domain of interest. Mostly in healthcare information systems, vertical FL can be applied for the identification of insights and pattern mining among the available medical relevances. Horizontal FL contributes to the identification of diverse factors for the learning models with particular augmentations. In certain cases, the data may not fit either into the feature space or the sample space. In such scenarios, federated transfer learning can also apply to derive insights into the unlabeled poor-quality data.

The security attacks that can be possible in healthcare systems are enlisted as model poisoning with adversarial effects on the learning models. Normally, it can be targeted or non-targeted adversarial attacks. These attacks cannot be detected with the federated aggregation for the correctness of the local model updates. This may increase or decrease the convergence aspect of the model and affects accuracy of the model. To address this, Generative Adversarial Network (GAN) is used for the inclusion of noise data in the training phase of the healthcare information systems. The privacy records of the patients are attacked with inferring attack for the record tracing and hence depreciation of the security of the systems. All the aforementioned security flaws are overcome by various methods like homomorphic encryption, locality-sensitive hashing, and secure multi-party computations. These techniques incur large and complex computational costs and communication inefficiency. The best known solution for preserving electronic healthcare information is through the distributed chain of ledgers among the communicating parties. The main advantages of using blockchain in healthcare informatics are the network is secured at all levels, and all the communicating parties are verified and authenticated with identity and authorization uniformity among the access of the information. It also provides real-time monitoring of the healthcare data and its transmission among the distributed environment. It promotes the transparency of the healthcare transaction with the consent management process.

1.2 Electronic Health Record Management and Informatics

The data derived from the Electronic Health Record (EHR) find its place in clinical research informatics [7], the union of biomedical informatics, and biomedical research. The EHRs contain heterogeneous data, and the data quality is assessed by the multi-dimensional completeness and its correctness. With the heterogeneity data, it poses challenges to the identification of clinical conditions like diseases and major complications. To address this, EHR phenotyping provided operational definitions of the healthcare data in different contexts.

1.2.1 Information Retrieval System for Healthcare Informatics

Information retrieval (IR) and its associated technologies can be applied to explore the hidden knowledge of healthcare data which are at a high growing pace and a large collection of data availability. IR focuses to find the most relevant document among the available large collection of medical documents based on the user query on search. The user query is reformulated using query expansion technique which improves the efficiency of the IR systems. The overall structure of the IR process is shown in Figure 1.2 [8].

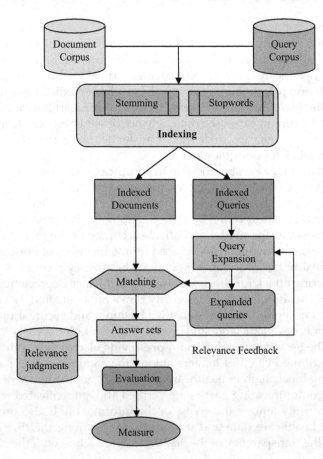

FIGURE 1.2
Information retrieval process.

The two main phases of IR are indexing and matching. The document is preprocessed during the indexing process, and the similarity between the documents is identified during the matching phase.

MEDLINE is the public medical document corpora; Medical Subject Headings (MeSH) is used for indexing and consists of a controlled vocabulary of biomedical and healthcare-related documents. It consists of a hierarchical structure with a set of terms, names, and descriptors for search with various specific levels. After indexing the documents, the documents have to be ranked based on the relevance to the query with functions like the BM25 weighting algorithm. The probabilistic function with the document weight of the search terms is assigned based on its search frequency in the medical document and the given query. It is denoted in Equation 1.1.

$$W_i = SJ \cdot \frac{(P_1+1) \cdot doc_{freq}}{P_1 \cdot \left[(1-b)+b \cdot (1+l_{avg})\right]+doc_{freq}} \cdot \frac{(P_2+1) \cdot query_{freq}}{P_2+query_{freq}} \tag{1.1}$$

SJ is the Robertson Spark Jones weight which is dependent on the number of relevant documents and shown in Equation 1.2. P_1, b, and P_2 are query and datastore parameters. The frequency of the terms in the document is denoted by doc_{freq} and in query by $query_{freq}$. l denotes the length of the document, and the average length is given by l_{avg}.

$$SJ : log \frac{\left(\frac{(r+0.5)}{(R-r+0.5)}\right)}{\frac{(n-r+0.5)}{(N-n-R+r+0.5)}} \tag{1.2}$$

In Equation 1.2, R denotes the number of relevant documents to the given title, r represents the count of document with the relevant terms with a total collection of documents (N) and n for the count of documents containing the given term. The most common measure used statistically to find the relevance of a term to the queried document is given by termed frequency (TF) and inverse document frequency (IDF). As per the BM25 weighting algorithm, IDF is given by Equation 1.3.

$$idf = log \; log\left(\frac{n}{N}+1\right) \tag{1.3}$$

Similarly, the document frequency and query frequency for the term is based on Equation 1.1 and given in Equations 1.4 and 1.5.

$$term_{doc} = \frac{P_1 \cdot doc_{freq}}{doc_{freq} + P_1 \cdot \left(1-b+b \cdot \left(\frac{l}{l_{avg}}\right)\right)} \tag{1.4}$$

$$term_{query} = \frac{P_1 \cdot query_{freq}}{query_{freq} + P_1 \cdot \left(1-b+b \cdot \left(\frac{query\; len}{l_{avg}}\right)\right)} \tag{1.5}$$

The weight of the term is based on inverse document frequency, document term frequency, and term frequency of the query. It is shown in Equation 1.6.

$$W_i = term_{doc} \cdot term_{query} \cdot idf^2 \tag{1.6}$$

Query expansion reformulates the given original user query for the efficient retrieval of the documents for the IR system. Various methods like query-specific terms, corpus-specific terms, and language-specific terms can be applied. Assuming to retrieve m documents for the given query Q, the expanded Q' query is given by Equation 1.7. δ is a parameter and N total number of documents $\{d_1, d_2, \ldots d_m\}$ retrieved for the given query.

$$Q' = Q + \frac{\delta}{N} \sum_{i=1}^{N} d_i \tag{1.7}$$

The various measures used to evaluate the IR system are average precision, mean average precision, and R-precision. The average precision determines the rank of the document with which it is retrieved in line with the relevance of the document. To obtain mean average precision, multiple queries are taken into account for finding the rank of the document. R-precision provides the effectiveness of the IR system after R documents have been retrieved. The average precision is given by Equation 1.8. $P(r)$ represents the precision for the given rank r, and $rel(r)$ denotes relevance of the rank by binary function for N retrieved documents.

$$Average\ Precision = \frac{\sum_{r=1}^{N} \left(P(r) \times rel(r) \right)}{C_r} \tag{1.8}$$

1.2.2 Privacy and Security in E-health Records

The Bigdata of healthcare information demands the need for cloud services and on-demand service provisions. This leads to security breaches, thus violating the security and privacy of the EHRs. There are various security attacks like Denial-of-Service attack (DoS), disclosure of information, collusion attack, spoofing, and so on [9]. The access of healthcare data can be controlled with different access control mechanisms embedded to protect the data. They are based on an attribute, role, and identity-based control of access mechanisms. Most of the access controls are non-cryptographic mode, and it is dependent on the level of access control for the hierarchical healthcare data. For privacy preservation in the distributed environment, the data are stored using encryption, and the normal query does not apply to it. Search encryption can be applied to query the encrypted data. To access data in the multi-cloud environment, searchable symmetric encryption is used which works based on keyword search across the encrypted cloud data.

Cryptographic approaches are used for securing bioinformatic data with the use of keys. Symmetric key and public key encryption are the most commonly used cryptographic mechanisms. The common key is shared in a symmetric key cryptosystem to secure the EHRs. The additional complexity of effective sharing of EHRs poses difficulties. The widely used symmetric key algorithm is Advanced Encryption Standard (AES) and Data Encryption Standard (DES). The main attributes of symmetric key cryptosystems are integrity, confidentiality, authentication, and non-repudiation. The EHR is encrypted using the symmetric key and can be accessed based on the user's role in time-bound constraints.

This ensures the spatial capabilities and temporal capabilities with restriction on access to the sensitive bioinformatics data. For the encrypted data on the cloud, searchable symmetric encryption based on the keyword search can be incorporated. It can further be enhanced with the AES algorithm for encryption of EHRs, and the keys are shared based on attributes of the healthcare industry.

The public key cryptosystem employs two keys: public and private keys. The public key cryptosystem is less efficient due to its slower operation and larger size of the key. Hence, it can be combined with symmetric key encryption. The symmetric key system is used to encrypt the EHRs, and the public key cryptosystem is used for the secure sharing of the symmetric keys among the trusted entities. To maximal requirements of the cryptosystems, public key infrastructure can be embedded to meet the diverse security requirements. The EHRs encrypted with a symmetric key with a public key infrastructure that binds the public key with the user id consisting of a digital certificate. There are some security issues with encryption like the cooperation among the trusted parties, and the confidentiality of EHRs is compromised by the initial data issuing authority and trustworthiness. All these issues can be addressed by using the enhanced security architecture, Trusted Virtual Domain for the electronic healthcare infrastructure as depicted in Figure 1.3.

The essential and needed privacy domains can be created and maintained on-demand with the requirement of the user and the regulations. These virtual domains are essentially virtual machines sharing common security policies. The latest usages like homomorphic encryption, and probabilistic algorithms can be used for encryption and key generation. The proxy re-encryption provides encryption in an end-to-end manner for confidential access of data among the trusted parties. This technique allows the intermediate proxy server to decrypt the cipher data using the user's public key. All the above-said methods have their own merits and demerits with the compensation of the existing deployment of e-health infrastructure. To limit these, Blockchain can be deployed for distributed healthcare information access. The consensus protocol with smart contracts promotes the integrity of the data and verifies the ownership of healthcare informatics. Each piece of information is stored as transactions with the hash values in the blockchain infrastructure.

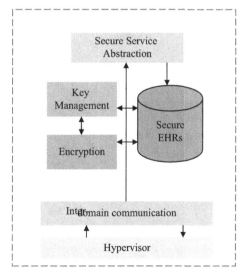

FIGURE 1.3
Trusted virtual domain for e-healthcare system.

TABLE 1.1

Privacy Preservation in Healthcare Systems

Privacy challenges	Privacy preservation mechanisms
EHRs re-identification	Suppression of personal identification and quasi-identification with data aggregation
Notification and consent	Informed consents promote transparency with public views
Data Anonymity	Encryption of EHRs provides data sanitization
Micro aggregation	Statistical measures like standard deviation, mean for aggregated data

The privacy of healthcare information has to be preserved without the loss of information. It can vary from techniques like De-identification to micro aggregation. In de-identification, the identity of the information is removed during the disclosure of the EHRs. The statistical methods like the harbor method can be used to replace the original content with the codes. Data anonymization also preserves the privacy of the EHRs. In micro aggregation, the group of EHRs is linked with each other without revealing the identity of the user. The grouping can be made based on statistical measures like mean, standard deviation, frequencies, and so on. Table 1.1 provides an overview of the privacy challenges and its associated prevention techniques.

1.2.3 Healthcare Informatics and Bigdata

The huge size and multi-dimensional healthcare data help healthcare workers to have bigdata analytics. This provides real-time insight into clinical informatics to derive new possibilities and services in healthcare 4.0. The salient characteristics of bigdata (6 V's) are Volume, Variety, Velocity, Value, and Veracity as shown in Figure 1.4. Volume represents a large amount of EHRs and their associated data. A variety of data in healthcare informatics

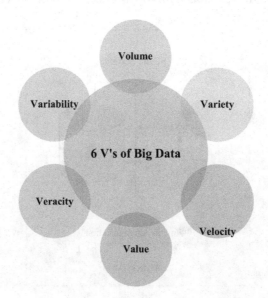

FIGURE 1.4
6 V's of Bigdata.

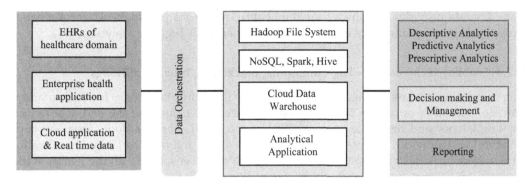

FIGURE 1.5
Bigdata architecture in healthcare informatics.

like structured, unstructured, and semi-structured data must be handled. Velocity refers to the rest values or static values of EHRs. The data values of EHRs can be prescription, X-ray images, diagnostic values, and so on represents Value. Veracity provides insight into the reliability and understandability of EHRs with the diagnosis of healthcare information.

Bigdata analytics tries to abstract valuable information from diverse sources in different formats and attributes. Some of the preprocessing mechanisms like cleansing of data, modeling, and transforming to the preparatory bigdata. Most of the analytics of bigdata fall under three categories: Descriptive analytics, predictive analytics, and prescriptive analytics [10]. The bigdata is condensed into meaningful information with descriptive analytics. The future of the model is predicted with reduced analytics using machine learning and neural network techniques. The predictive analytics that performs actions to provide business services is called prescriptive analytics. The collected healthcare information is preprocessed with extract, load, and transform processes. Then, data transformation is performed using bigdata tools like Map reduce, yarn, and many more. The output can be reports, queries, and data mining floors based on the application. The generalized bigdata architecture is shown in Figure 1.5.

Mostly, in bigdata context, healthcare informatics is used for healthcare administration and policy, health insurance and decision making, and smart healthcare services with security and privacy preservation [11]. Integrated healthcare analysis with heterogeneous bigdata allows precise diagnosis and healthcare promotion. Bigdata mining and deep learning also provide non-linear prediction in the knowledge discovery in healthcare informatics [12]. Some of the emerging paradigms like Medical Internet of things, Complex event processing and cloud computing with bigdata enable advanced medical processing. All these emerging technologies improve the healthcare service efficiency and proposal of optimal solutions with minimal delay. In the bigdata frameworks tools like Apache Hadoop, Spark, Hive, Zookeeper and cloud-based environments like Azure, AWS, and many other web-based cloud services.

The advantages of using bigdata in healthcare 4.0 are summarized as follows: It helps to explore the insights into the uncovered healthcare data. The exploitation of association and correlation helps to improve the quality of healthcare for the patients. Bigdata provides business intelligence strategy for healthcare providers on a diverse volume of data. The bigdata with genomic medicine helps to cure discrete diseases that are dependent on hidden patterns. The early stage of the disease can be easily diagnosed using predictive analytics. In order to discover the unknown correlation and hidden styles among the healthcare data, bigdata provides a pathway for the healthcare service providers. The exponential growth of bioinformatics data can be handled efficiently by bigdata analytics.

1.2.4 Enabling Technologies – Fog Computing, Blockchain, Internet of Things

Fog computing is a low-latency architecture with edge computing nodes for computation, storage, and other purposes. It adds a layer between the cloud and the end user device for low latency and resilience against cloud services [13]. Wireless Body Area Network (WBAN) [14] provides an interface with human sensor interaction. Ubiquitous healthcare system provides precision medicine and analysis of sensor data on the health of the patients. Healthcare system is a highly time-sensitive application for real-time monitoring of patient health conditions. Semantic medical access helps to discover the semantics and ontological contexts of medical information. Data security and user privacy are a big challenge in the healthcare industry. This can be overcome by a trusted distributed ledger for each transaction using blockchain.

The decentralized nature of blockchain [15] helps to address the challenges like security, privacy, and maintenance. Approaches like encryption, private smart contract, anonymization, and differential privacy are used to solve privacy issues. The blockchain provides easy backtracking, non-interference of other channels, secure transaction with transparent log, decentralized peer-to-peer distributed network, and digital transaction with timestamps provides a non-ambiguous update of records. Certain security and privacy attacks are also possible in a blockchain-based healthcare system. The fog layer provides an interface between the edge node and the cloud servers. Real-time monitoring of healthcare informatics poses certain constraints like low-latency, high accuracy, and diverse analysis of medical data. The overall embedded framework of enabling technologies is shown in Figure 1.6.

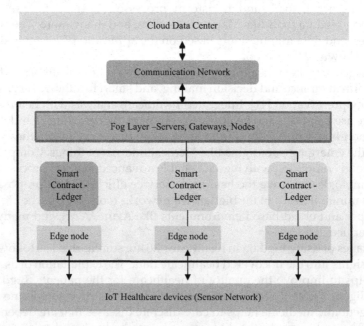

FIGURE 1.6
Healthcare infrastructure with IoT, Blockchain, and fog computing.

1.3 Federated Learning

FL [16] provides promising application in the learning of distributed sensitive data and enhances healthcare analysis on large scale. It provides high-quality global model from the distributed diverse healthcare information. Assume the patient information is distributed among n learning nodes. Each node has its own data distribution D_i for each processing node with the x_i samples available for each instance. It can be formulated as a computation minimization problem and described in Equation 1.9. Assume the model m to be trained with the function F.

$$F(m) = \sum_{k=1}^{n} \frac{x_k}{n} F_k(m) \tag{1.9}$$

The learning model can be simple linear regression to deep neural networks and classification algorithms. Based on the data distribution on the participating nodes, FL can be horizontal or vertical. The efficiency of the global model is dependent on the non-independent and identically distributed (non-IID) data. To cope with these data distributions, FedAvg algorithm is used by the global model in the training phase. With the heterogeneity of data distribution among the local models, these models will converge to varying models based on the initial parameters.

1.3.1 Massive Non-identically Independent Distribution

Each client in the FL system contributes to the training data. The characteristics of the training data are dependent on the source of the data like medical devices, smartphones, and other embedded devices. The data distribution varies from local device to another, and this results in a phenomenon called non-identically independent distribution (non-IID). The adverse effect of non-IID is the divergence of the learning model and minimal performance. Assume the medical image classification task on local node k, with the data sample represented as (f_1, f_2), where f_1 is the feature or attribute of the data and f_2 is the classification label that follows the data distribution of $D_k(f_1, f_2)$. The inference here is D_k varies from the local device to another when it is non-IID. The categories of non-IID based on features and label are described in Figure 1.7.

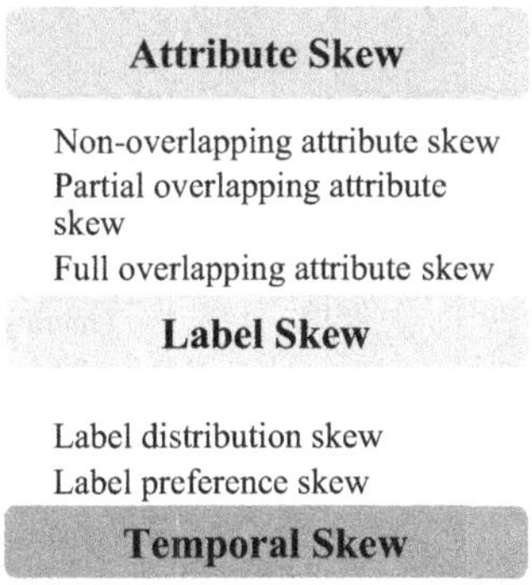

Attribute Skew

Non-overlapping attribute skew
Partial overlapping attribute skew
Full overlapping attribute skew

Label Skew

Label distribution skew
Label preference skew

Temporal Skew

FIGURE 1.7
Non-IID categories in healthcare data distribution.

When the attributes of the healthcare data differ in the distribution $D_k(x)$ across the devices or the local models, it results in the attribute or feature skew. The attribute skew can be mutually exclusive among the devices or clients resulting in the non-overlapping skew of attributes. In the case where some of the features are shared among the participating clients, it is called partially overlapped attribute skew. An inconsistent distribution of shared attributes causes non-IID divergence resulting in degradation of the performance of the system. Label skew occurs when the classification or supervised label distribution differs from client to client. In label distribution skew, the distribution of labels $D_k(f_2)$ and $D_k(f_2)$ is the conditional attribute distribution that differs among the clients. This type of non-IID distribution is caused by an imbalance distribution of class labels and label size. The case where the $D_k(x)$ is the same but the conditional feature distribution differs among the client's results in label preference skew. Mostly in crowd-sourcing data, label preference skew occurs due to noise in label data. Many real-time applications have a skew in the distribution of attributes based on time. The conditional data (feature, label) distribution over time $D_k(t)$ varies among the client in the time series data results in temporal skew. All these feature and label distribution imbalance results in non-IID.

1.3.2 Horizontal Federated Learning

Horizontal Federated Learning is a homogeneous FL with common features but differs in the sample space among the participating entities. Many algorithms like FedAvg performs horizontal FL with the global model aggregates the local model parameters. There are no data leakage but the model parameters or gradients can be phished for security attacks. To secure the gradient leakage, differential privacy or homomorphic encryption can be embedded in the horizontal FL environment. The diagrammatic view of horizontal FL and vertical FL is shown in Figure 1.8. Consider the participating healthcare entities, $N \in (1, 2, 3, \ldots n)$ with their data represented as X_i consists of (f_1, f_2) with the sample space denoted as I. Then horizontal FL can be expressed as shown in Equation 1.10.

$$f_{1i} = f_{1j}, \ f_{2i} = f_{2j}, \ I_i \neq I_j, \ \forall X_i, X_j, i \neq j \tag{1.10}$$

The sample-based learning is incorporated in horizontal FL and finds its application in many products like the Gboard Android phone model and Google products. Homomorphic encryption allows the encryption of gradients and parameters while the exchange between the local models and global model during the learning process. Further, it can be strengthened by approximation of polynomials using non-linear

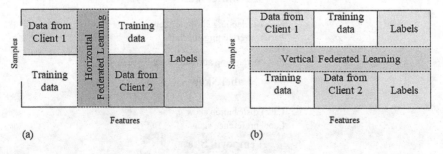

(a)   (b)

FIGURE 1.8
Horizontal federated learning and vertical federated learning: (a) horizontal federated learning; (b) vertical federated learning.

functions that complement security and accuracy of the learning models. The learning gradient algorithms such as Stochastic Gradient Descent (SGD) lag in leakage of the differentiable gradients indirectly leads to information leakage. To avoid these issues, blockchain is considered in the FL model to validate the participating transaction entities among the local and global models. The complexity of the deep learning network can be minimized using optimal block generation techniques [17]. Electroencephalography (EEG) classification [18] leverages horizontal FL for the analysis of brain signals in the healthcare domain to identify the emotion types. It uses the privacy-preserving classifiers using horizontal FL on the high-dimensional brain signal data set. The decentralized approach has been proven to be more efficient with less domain loss. To handle the cross-domain data, symmetric transformation can be applied to transform the medical feature space into domain-independent medical feature space.

1.3.3 Vertical Federated Learning

Attribute or feature-based aggregated learning is the vertical FL model in which the participating healthcare domain entities share the medical sample space but differ in their feature space as shown in Figure 1.8. It is proposed to aggregate the varied features from the local models and train the global model with minimal loss and gradient for privacy preservation of healthcare data. It can be expressed as denoted in Equation 1.11. Based on the association rule, cooperative statistical analysis, and secure linear regression, security can be preserved in the vertical FL. The most efficient learning model can be built by approximation of gradient and loss function using Taylor's approximation. Homomorphic encryption can be used for privacy-preserving transfer of gradient and parameter exchange between the global and local models. This provides the entity resolution for the difference in the feature space.

$$f_{1i} \neq f_{1j}, \ f_{2i} \neq f_{2j}, \ I_i = I_j, \ \forall X_i, X_j, i \neq j \tag{1.11}$$

In the case of multi-class classification of healthcare images, multi-view learning [19] is proposed to resolve the feature extraction among the participating entities. The performance of the global model can be improved using feature selection techniques that can be applied to capture the contributing features. And also, for the primary requirement in vertical FL, there should be synchronous updates among the participating entities. This can be leveraged by asynchronous vertical FL [20] using asynchronous optimization methods with the embedding of vectors and querying on them. This local embedding enforces differential privacy and smoothness using non-linear functions. Gaussian differential privacy is proven to be more efficient during the exchange of parameters and gradients. Many security attacks like model extraction attacks and further model reverse attacks can happen in the vertical FL environment. To address these issues, blockchain-enabled vertical FL is applied for global model aggregation.

1.3.4 Federated Transfer Learning in Healthcare Informatics

In the scenario when the overlapping features and participating entities are unavailable, federated transfer learning can be applied. It fully exploits the gap between differential privacy and deep learning. Further transfer learning allows different deep learning tasks among the healthcare domains like disease prediction, image classification, pandemic

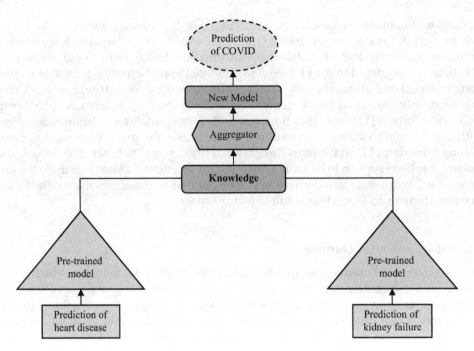

FIGURE 1.9
Federated transfer learning in healthcare domain.

forecast, and so on. Many use cases like wearable healthcare provide distinct features like remote healthcare monitoring, lifestyle monitoring, chronic condition, etc. In a real-time scenario like EEG signal classification, when the training data is meager, aggregation of brain signal data from multiple sources results in diverse features and sample space.

The similarity of the patients [21] among the multiple locations or participating entities can be learned using the privacy-preserving transfer FL. This finds its application in many areas like surveillance of diseases, cross-domain analysis to construct cohort, and placement of clinical trials. Here, the data are transformed into low-dimensional representation like hashes which is a sequence of bits. Based on the hash values, the similarity of the patients can be interpreted using hashing mechanism. In federated transfer learning, the pre-trained model is used to extract the knowledge which can be used to accomplish some other tasks. The pictorial representation of federated transfer learning is shown in Figure 1.9.

The predictive modeling of the particular problem can be done with diverse domain data (EHRs, medical images) using FL which helps the clinical partners to derive insight into the hidden patterns of the observed data. This modeling helps to find the patient's disease condition earlier and provides the required treatment in handy. In the drug industry, FL can be used to predict the resistance of patients to certain drugs and treatments. The continuous validation of the healthcare software and hardware requirements can be improved with FL. FL provides collaborative learning among the vendors and manufacturers to facilitate continuous improvement. Precision medicine needs FL as an enabling technology to provide quality service in the healthcare domain. FL also assures the patients to promote as data donors, the raw data are unexchanged, and hence, the privacy of the patients is maintained. A massive collaborative training model is proposed to infer the binding of chemical compounds to the proteins that enhance the exploration of adverse effects of drugs during the process of drug discovery [22]. Here, the multiple pharmaceutical companies without revealing their private data coordinate in the production of an effective drug for a particular disease.

1.3.5 Privacy Preservation in Federated Learning

The decentralized collaborative learning, FL allows the exchange of the parameters from the local models to the global models and hence assures the privacy of the data belonging to the local model. The parameter exchanges can have security threats that can be overcome by mechanisms like differential privacy preservation and cryptographic algorithms. In distributed environments like FL frameworks, gradient descent works as batches to achieve parallelism among the compute nodes. The various privacy preservation mechanisms [23] that can be adopted in FL environments are as follows:

- Data anonymization
- Differential privacy
- Secure multi-party computation
- Homomorphic encryption

In the data anonymization mechanism, the private information of the healthcare records is hidden with hashing or some other encoding techniques. This de-identification of the information preserves the privacy of the user but the decoding of the information may lead to security flaws like linkage attacks. To prevent this type of attack, the distribution of private information of healthcare informatics is preserved using methods like k-anonymity or l-diversity methods. However, further decoding of sensitive information can be explored during the linkage attack and need more diverse security methods like differential privacy. To hide the sensitive information in healthcare domain, some random noise can be added to the sensitive data to perturbate the sensitive information. There is a tradeoff between reliability and security in the domain of interest when adding random noise.

Secure multi-party computation allows collaborative computation on the healthcare bigdata by using their input which is a subset of the original input. Each participating entity can learn from its own data and prevents data leakage. Consider there are N computation parties $\{C_1, C_2, C_3, \ldots C_N\}$, each has its own data, $\{D_1, D_2, D_3, \ldots D_N\}$ collectively constitute the original domain information. They are mapped by the public function f, denoted as shown in Equation 1.12. The computation entities can have access to their own data D_i and the encoded output data $(O_1, O_2, O_3, \ldots O_N)$. Though this mechanism provides data privacy, it suffers from computational overheads and needs further improvement for highly efficient systems.

$$f\left(D_1, D_2, D_3, \ldots D_N\right) = \left(O_1, O_2, O_3, \ldots O_N\right) \tag{1.12}$$

The most common method to preserve data privacy in centralized systems like cloud, homomorphic encryption is employed. The basic rule is to encrypt private data and decrypt it without using the secret key. It ensures that the decrypted output is similar to the original data but it can be interfered with by the intermediate users. It allows the user to perform the computation on the decrypted data without decoding the data. Hence, the data are secured in the cloud environment being not exposed to security attacks. For the encryption of the data, it uses the public key of the cryptographic systems. It enables data analysis in regulated industries like the healthcare industry, where domain analysis of data can be done safely without being exposed to security risks. There are various types of homomorphic encryption namely partially, somewhat, and fully based on the subset of the function being encrypted and the decryption to the maximal level.

1.3.6 Statistical Challenges of Federated Learning

The federated global model works by aggregation of the local model, and the most widely used algorithm is FedAvg. This algorithm can address certain issues related to non-IID data among the local model but cannot handle the highly skewed data distribution. There will be more divergence of weight with FedAvg when the skew data distribution is observed in the local model data. These statistical challenges in the FL models can be overcome by many techniques as summarized below:

- Consensus solution provides the transformation of uniform data distribution among the local models. Sharing the small subset of the uniformly distributed data among the clients and over the classes of the clients.
- The data can also be drawn from multiple distributions providing multi-task learning. It explores the correlation and insights among the non-IID data and the unbalanced data. This can be achieved by sharing the sparsity of the distribution or structure of it in terms of low rank or relation between them using graphs.

1.4 Blockchain in Healthcare Informatics

The distributed ledger, Blockchain, provides transparency, user tracing, and immutability in a decentralized manner. Blockchain and FL complement each other. The injection of blockchain into FL allows the inspection of the local model updates and by default ensures privacy preservation. The more efficient framework can be a smart FL-Chain can coordinate all the local clients and can use homomorphic encryption to provide more privacy preservation. Some privacy leakage in the framework can also be minimized by the addition of a cryptosystem based on variations of Paillier. Another advantage of blockchain-based FL framework enables us to track the contributing local model to optimize the performance of the global model, hence the scope for incentive mechanism. The performance of the global model can be further enhanced by considering the accuracy and frequency of participation as the training weight to select the clients of high contribution in nature. Since the blockchain is decentralized, it removes the limitation of global model prediction in FL which suffers from bandwidth constraints.

1.4.1 Blockchain Distributed Ledger for Healthcare Informatics

The main advantage of blockchain in the healthcare domain compared to distributed database management systems are decentralization of data and peer-to-peer networks with each node operating its protocol independent of other nodes. This is suitable for the independent units of healthcare domains like hospitals, care providers, pharmaceutical companies, and related entities. Blockchain provides immutable records and the maintenance of critical healthcare records without security flaws. The data provenance of the blockchain enables the ownership of the data being used in the transaction. This enables the traceability of the records over their flow in the network for the management of the critical asset of the healthcare information. The user identity in the distributed blockchain network is provided through the hash code which is irreversible. With these benefits of blockchain in the healthcare informatics, it provides way for enhanced health record management, smart healthcare interoperability with insurance companies, and accelerate biomedical research activities with an advanced healthcare ledger.

1.4.2 Healthcare Framework with Blockchain

The personalized secure healthcare records can be implemented using distributed ledger of the blockchain. As shown in Figure 1.10, patient information takes different forms like images, numeric data, and signals. This information has to be encoded using hashing or cryptographic algorithms for secure exchange among the multiple domains of healthcare informatics. Mostly for reliable and minimal delay of the healthcare data exchange, the centralized medical server is used for private data security. The needed information can be hosted in the cloud platform and enabling technologies like fog and edge computing can be leveraged for minimal latency. During the transfer of information from the medical server to other domains of the healthcare industry, blockchain is embedded for the reliable and trusted exchange of data. The distributed ledger can be a public or private blockchain based on the requirements. For a situation, within the hospital, private blockchain infrastructure can be maintained for the trusted update of records and management of healthcare data. Between the domains of the healthcare industry, public blockchain can be adopted for the multiple participating external entities.

Mostly the blockchain framework [24] in the healthcare industry is segregated into two layers namely blockchain layer and the data storage layer. The blockchain layer contains the core modules for the distributed transaction ledgers and their relationship entities. It is also possible to query the historical transaction that occurred in the chain to understand the interaction between the patients and healthcare information search. The metadata about the storage aspects and non-data aspects like the history of the patient interaction can also be queried from the blockchain module. With this reference architecture of blockchain in the healthcare industry, it is possible to provide record accessibility, preventive healthcare maintenance, transactional services with bilateral communication, self-documentation of

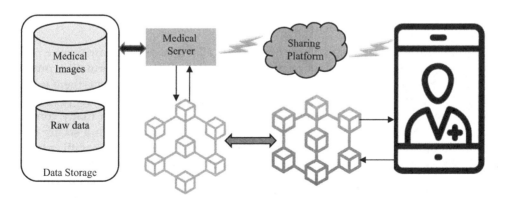

FIGURE 1.10
Healthcare data and blockchain in medical application.

patient data, personalized disease and treatment management, and finally the self-realization of healthcare education. Internet of medical things is the recent trend in the healthcare industry 4.0, and blockchain is an enabling technology for the secure exchange of information. Mostly, Hyperledger platform is used for the management of healthcare records in the blockchain framework. Supply chain management in the healthcare domain enhances the quick and reliable provision of services to the user. In this case, the authenticity of the data has to be verified, since its passage into different domain mainly exposes security risks and those can be leveraged by blockchain frameworks.

1.4.3 Key Challenges of Blockchain in Healthcare Systems

Since the blockchain is a distributed system, there are certain upsides in the implementation of the technology in the healthcare domain. Even the maintenance of electronic healthcare records among the patients is a twisted task and needs more cultural shifts. The blockchain with a distribution mechanism finds it difficult to coordinate the different entities to work on a common solution of different forms. There is a resistance toward sharing of data by the patients as well as by the healthcare service providers. To have an implemented version of the blockchain, there is a need for a central entity to work on the blockchain and its core entities. The various challenges of blockchain in the healthcare industry are summarized as follows:

- Lack of standardization norms for implementation in the healthcare systems.
- The application of cryptographic mechanisms in blockchain requires different levels of access control.
- Scalability is another issue in the implementation of blockchain in large-scale systems.
- Difficult to embed in handheld devices which have limited computational power and energy systems. But blockchain model requires high computation and infrastructure.
- The identity of the user may be revealed at some point of time in the blockchain since the ownership of the block can be claimed.
- The enhancement of security measures results in partial loss of redundancy of data in the blockchain and its transaction systems.

1.4.4 Future Healthcare with Security

In the healthcare industry, a big volume of data is available and healthcare service providers are positioned to derive insight from healthcare data. This transformation promotes customer participation and operational efficiency. With this improvement, there is a need for securing the privacy of the data within the standards rolled out for data protection as shown in Figure 1.11. Cybersecurity attacks [25] are most common in many connected healthcare networks and need preventive and disruptive technology for a secure healthcare ecosystem. The design of a zero trust model in the healthcare domain with automated multi-factor authorization on the identity of the individuals is the need of the hour. Many security attacks like Ransomware attack contribute to 55 % of security breaches in 2020 in the healthcare domain with phishing of 22%, internal threats of 8%, and unsecured back-end databases of 5%. To overcome these security breaches, security intelligence should be in place for the healthcare industry 4.0.

FIGURE 1.11
Security intelligence for healthcare industry 4.0.

1.5 Differential Privacy Preservation in Healthcare Data

The security requirements in healthcare data are described based on the availability of data in the public or private domain. Data privacy can be preserved by certain control of access mechanisms like attribute, role, and identity-based access control techniques.

1.5.1 Deep Learning Models for Privacy Preservation

Many training models provoke false identity during the learning process resulting in performance degradation. Many attacks like model poisoning attack result in the infusion of unrelated data among the distributed systems in the participating entities of the FL. To protect the user (aggregated model) from privacy leakage, many implicit attacks on the intruders will be envisaged. Evasion attacks [26] can be performed to preserve the privacy of the global model of the healthcare domain. Adversarial information is provided as patches to mitigate the intrusion in the deep learning models. Other techniques like clean label attacks can inject correctly labeled intruder data into the training data to misclassify the specific data of interest. The disruption of feature space of the data can be provided by cloaking that protects the privacy of the patient information.

Differential privacy preservation [27] provides the perturbation of the healthcare data by hiding the patient identity but still provides the provision for performing the statistical analysis on the domain data. This technique enables the minimal revealing of personal information with the preservation of the global model statistical distribution. The deep learning models has privacy preservation based on the following classification as shown in Figure 1.12. The generative sequence model can learn the rare information in the training data and provides the preservation of the privacy of the model. Even though the hidden information is enclosed for privacy preservation, there may be information leakage and

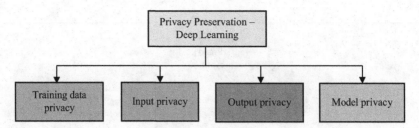

FIGURE 1.12
Mode of privacy preservation in deep learning.

exposure of secret information. The generalization of the learning models is mostly improved with privacy preservation using stochastic gradient descent which is differentially private entities. Mostly on input and output data, techniques like homomorphic encryption, secure multiparty computation, and FL are employed. The model privacy can be achieved using the differential privacy technique with the query being passed in the healthcare domain. Consider a query, q being done in the healthcare domain, D with the randomized function f on the distributed databases D_1 and D_2, and the differential privacy denoted with probability within the range $r \in Range(f)$ can be denoted as shown in Equation 1.13. Here, ε denotes the noise level in the data or model being used for privacy preservation. Mostly, Laplace distribution–based noise is perturbated in the original data for the random data in the training of the model and efficiency of the healthcare system. It can be bounded with ε and based on partial information of the domain with their probability distribution. This leads to approximate differential privacy with the rules for setting the boundary for ignoring partial information. The statistical queries are normalized based on certain predicates to match the information in the sampled data.

$$Pr\, Pr\big(f(D_1)\big) \le \varepsilon Pr\, Pr\big(f(D_2)\big), \quad (D_1, D_2) \in r \tag{1.13}$$

1.5.2 Adaptive Laplace Mechanism

The differential privacy with injecting more noise on less contributing features is on the gradient with the training of the model. Consider the loss function based on model parameter θ, $L(\theta)$ and the deep neural network is trained for optimizing the loss function $L(\theta)$ on the data D using stochastic gradient descent algorithm on the random batches of data for training in parallel. The learning algorithm tries to explore the differentially private parameters as described in the following steps. In each step, layer-wise relevance propagation [28] is used instead of backpropagation algorithm.

Step 1: Find the average relevance of all the input features on the data D using layer-wise relevance propagation in the deep neural network. It is denoted as $A_j(D)$ and represented in Equation 1.14.

$$A_j(D) = \frac{1}{|D|} \sum_{x \in D} A_x(D) \tag{1.14}$$

Step 2: The private differentially affine transformation is provided by each neuron in the hidden layer. Thus, this neuron will be perturbated by injecting the Laplace noise with its affine transformation on the constraint of less relevant features, more noise injection, $\underline{A_j}(D)$.

Step 3: The differentially private hidden layers $\{h_0, h_1, h_2, \ldots h_n\}$ perform computations on the output provided by the affine transformation layer, and hence, the original information will not be disclosed. These layers are stacked to form a deep neural network with non-linear functions like ReLU in normalization layers sandwiched between them.

Step 4: The output layer will be protected with the polynomial approximation loss function, L by injection of Laplace noise to secure the data privacy and denoted by $\underline{L}(\theta)$.

Step 5: The parameters of the differential privacy θ can be derived with the minimization of the loss function, $\underline{L}(\theta)$ with the random batch training on the training samples of D.

1.5.3 Local Differential Privacy Preservation

The biggest challenge in smart healthcare provision is data analysis and data utilization in the healthcare domain. Rather than differential privacy, the privacy of patient information can be preserved during the data collection process. The basic idea behind Local Differential Privacy (LDP) [29] is the data provider itself, adding some noise to the raw data to send to the data aggregator or collector. This guarantees that data will not be exposed to the data aggregator or without the data provider by LDP. The randomized algorithm provides ε- differential privacy based on certain constraints defined by the data contributors, (U_i, U_j) on the overall data D. It can be represented as shown in Equation 1.15.

$$\frac{Pr\left[A\left(U_i\right) == Output\right]}{Pr\left[A\left(U_j\right) == Output\right]} \leq e^{\varepsilon} \tag{1.15}$$

The level of privacy is defined by ε defined as budget in LDP with the implication of lower the value of ε, higher the privacy preservation with less noise. The three main properties of LDP are as follows:

Sequential composition: To satisfy the LDP of $\sum_{i=1}^{n} \varepsilon_i$ on n entities of the healthcare contributors $\{N_1, N_2, N_3, \ldots N_n\}$ and each will satisfy ε_i-LDP is sequential on the private data to derive the output data.

Parallel composition: When the healthcare data contribution forms the disjoint subsets of their private information, each entity of $\{N_1, N_2, N_3, \ldots N_n\}$ must satisfy the constraint ε_i-LDP to form a transformation, $\{M(N_1), M(N_2), M(N_3), \ldots M(N_n)\}$ of output data to satisfy the constraint of $(max(\varepsilon_i))$-LDP.

Postprocessing property: In any set of entities, $\{N_1, N_2, N_3, \ldots N_n\}$, when N_1 satisfies ε_i-LDP and N_2 may not satisfy ε_i-LDP, then there is a possibility of $N_2(N_1(.))$ may satisfy ε_i-LDP.

1.5.4 Differential Privacy in Blockchain

In the healthcare domain, blockchain with differential privacy [5] allows preservation of privacy in each layer of blockchain application on the data stored in it. The main characteristic of differential privacy are dynamic in nature. This property allows data perturbation on an entity based in the distributed healthcare network. Thus, the amount of noise added in I point-wise manner enables the improved level of accuracy of the system. Though the

TABLE 1.2

Differential Privacy in Blockchain

Layers	Technique of Differential Privacy preservation
Data Layer	Random storage in the blocks with randomized hashing
Network Layer	Anonymous communication with privacy-enabled communication protocol
Consensus Layer	Minner selection based on differential privacy technique
Incentive Layer	LDP-based incentive technique for privacy preservation
Contract Layer	Private privacy-enabled smart contracts
Application Layer	Anonymized users with distributed differential privacy

identity of the entity is broadcasted in each transaction of the blockchain, the privacy of the entity is compensated but the information needed to complete the transaction will be available. Hence differential privacy is the essential entity in the healthcare blockchain. During statistical analysis of the blockchain database, the availability of the specific blockchain node can be preserved from the analyst with a differential privacy mechanism. Table 1.2 provides the blockchain layered architecture with differential privacy. Here the optimal noise values are added optimally in each layer of the blockchain to preserve the identity of the entity.

1.6 Improved Federated Leaning–fusion Learning

The one-shot FL [30] is fusion learning, which reduces the communication overhead between the participating entities and the global aggregators. The generative information like the distribution data among the healthcare domain is provided as input to the central global model, and the original data privacy is preserved. The synthetic generated information allows the learning of the global model in the FL environment. Mostly statistical methods are used to estimate the distribution of data among the clients or the participating healthcare service providers. The generalized fusion learning architecture is shown in Figure 1.13. The local model parameters and data distribution of medical clients are

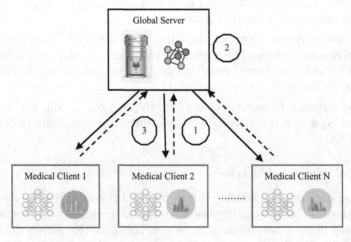

FIGURE 1.13

Architecture of fusion learning.

TABLE 1.3

Performance Improvement in Healthcare Analysis Using FL

Medical domain	Technique	Data set	Performance improvement	Security consideration	Ref
Detection of COVID-19 infection	Dynamic diffusion-based FL	Image data set of COVID-19	Provides improved accuracy than with FL	Dynamic fusion enables the client participation and selection in a secure manner	[32]
COVID-19 screening using chest X-rays	Aggregated FL	COVID-19 chest X-rays	Non-IID and unbalanced data in the data set – high performance	Collaborative learning without revealing the patient's identity	[33]
All domains of industry 4.0	Adaptive privacy-preserving FL	MNIST data set	Minimal convergence time with improved accuracy of the model	Layer-wise relevance propagation with injected noise to preserve privacy	[34]
Medical diagnosis	Homomorphic re-encryption	Clinical data set	Less computational and storage cost	Cryptographic primitives – secure data analysis	[35]

passed to the global aggregation server. The global server generates the synthetic data from the distribution provided by the medical clients and updates the clients with the model parameters. Thus, the clients and server are synchronized with the parameters of the model. Table 1.3 provides the comparative analysis of performance improvement using FL in healthcare analytics.

1.7 Visualizing Knowledge Structure in Healthcare Informatics

In knowledge mapping of healthcare informatics, domain analysis attempt to explore the intellectual structure of a particular healthcare domain by synthesis of discrete information like citation and working model using a coherent model. The semantic analysis provides textual mining of healthcare data based on lexical analysis and linguistic relations. Content map analysis provides the self-organizing map for mapping contents in the healthcare domain. It works based on the similarities of the attributes and map of entities in large-scale healthcare environments. Word co-occurrence analysis identifies the relationship between the matter of interest and the emerging trends in the healthcare domain like COVID vaccines. Burst analysis help to identify the random burstiness in the healthcare system like pandemic diseases (COVID) and the related modeling of information. Health knowledge graph [31] can be extracted from EHRs and provides conceptual extraction of information based on the idea of the Google knowledge graph. The relation between the symptoms and diseases can be exploited in the health knowledge graph. In order to extract the information, enabling technologies like artificial learning, Internet of Things, Web engineering and associated methods has to be embedded for the exploration of knowledge.

1.8 Conclusion

Healthcare informatics is an important area in industry 4.0 with its wide application in the healthcare domain. The bigdata of the healthcare industry provides more insight into knowledge extraction and service provision. Though with these merits and applications, the privacy of the user information in the healthcare framework poses an unidentifiable question for the end users. To secure the private information of the patients, differential privacy with an injection of noise provides a great solution in the distributed environment. Both local privacy preservation and global privacy preservation seem to have more application scenarios and use cases. FL, a distributed learning model, is itself capable of providing privacy preservation and its improvement fusion learning enhances the security of the healthcare system to the core level. Blockchain embedded with the FL model scores on authentication of the user information without providing a way for intermediate tampering of information. Thus, the future of the healthcare system is dependent on important entities like distributed learning models with blockchain embedded with privacy preservation.

References

1. R. Ranchal, P. Bastide, X. Wang, A. Gkoulalas-Divanis, M. Mehra, S. Bakthavachalam, *et al.*, "Disrupting healthcare silos: Addressing data volume, velocity and variety with a cloud-native healthcare data ingestion service," *IEEE Journal of Biomedical and Health Informatics*, vol. 24, pp. 3182–3188, 2020.
2. I. G. Cohen and M. M. Mello, "HIPAA and protecting health information in the 21st century," *Jama*, vol. 320, pp. 231–232, 2018.
3. M. Shuaib, S. Alam, M. S. Alam, and M. S. Nasir, "Compliance with HIPAA and GDPR in blockchain-based electronic health record," *Materials Today: Proceedings*, 2021.
4. O. Choudhury, A. Gkoulalas-Divanis, T. Salonidis, I. Sylla, Y. Park, G. Hsu, *et al.*, "Differential privacy-enabled federated learning for sensitive health data," *arXiv preprint arXiv:1910.02578*, 2019.
5. M. U. Hassan, M. H. Rehmani, and J. Chen, "Differential privacy in blockchain technology: A futuristic approach," *Journal of Parallel and Distributed Computing*, vol. 145, pp. 50–74, 2020.
6. H. Kasyap and S. Tripathy, "Privacy-preserving decentralized learning framework for healthcare system," *ACM Transactions on Multimedia Computing, Communications, and Applications (TOMM)*, vol. 17, pp. 1–24, 2021.
7. R. Richesson, M. Horvath, and S. Rusincovitch, "Clinical research informatics and electronic health record data," *Yearbook of Medical Informatics*, vol. 23, pp. 215–223, 2014.
8. A. R. Rivas, E. L. Iglesias, and L. Borrajo, "Study of query expansion techniques and their application in the biomedical information retrieval," *The Scientific World Journal*, vol. 2014, pp. 1–10, 2014.
9. S. Chenthara, K. Ahmed, H. Wang, and F. Whittaker, "Security and privacy-preserving challenges of e-health solutions in cloud computing," *IEEE Access*, vol. 7, pp. 74361–74382, 2019.
10. A. Rehman, S. Naz, and I. Razzak, "Leveraging big data analytics in healthcare enhancement: Trends, challenges and opportunities," *Multimedia Systems*, vol. 28, pp. 1–33, 2021.
11. Dhanaraj, R. K., Ramakrishnan, V., Poongodi, M., Krishnasamy, L., Hamdi, M., Kotecha, K., and Vijayakumar, V. (2021). Random forest bagging and X-means clustered antipattern detection from SQL query log for accessing secure mobile data. In D. K. Jain (Ed.), *Wireless Communications and Mobile Computing* (Vol. 2021, pp. 1–9).

12. D. Gu, J. Li, X. Li, and C. Liang, "Visualizing the knowledge structure and evolution of big data research in healthcare informatics," *International Journal of Medical Informatics*, vol. 98, pp. 22–32, 2017.

13. A. A. Mutlag, M. K. Abd Ghani, N. A. Arunkumar, M. A. Mohammed, and O. Mohd, "Enabling technologies for fog computing in healthcare IoT systems," *Future Generation Computer Systems*, vol. 90, pp. 62–78, 2019.

14. M. M. Dhanvijay and S. C. Patil, "Internet of things: A survey of enabling technologies in healthcare and its applications," *Computer Networks*, vol. 153, pp. 113–131, 2019.

15. M. U. Hassan, M. H. Rehmani, and J. Chen, "Privacy preservation in blockchain based IoT systems: Integration issues, prospects, challenges, and future research directions," *Future Generation Computer Systems*, vol. 97, pp. 512–529, 2019.

16. J. Kang, Z. Xiong, D. Niyato, Y. Zou, Y. Zhang, and M. Guizani, "Reliable federated learning for mobile networks," *IEEE Wireless Communications*, vol. 27, pp. 72–80, 2020.

17. Q. Yang, Y. Liu, T. Chen, and Y. Tong, "Federated machine learning: Concept and applications," *ACM Transactions on Intelligent Systems and Technology (TIST)*, vol. 10, pp. 1–19, 2019.

18. R. K. Dhanaraj, R. H. Jhaveri, L. Krishnasamy, G. Srivastava, and P. K. R. Maddikunta. "Black-hole attack mitigation in medical sensor networks using the enhanced gravitational search algorithm," *International Journal of Uncertainty, Fuzziness and Knowledge-Based Systems*, vol. 29, pp. 297–315, 2021.

19. S. Feng and H. Yu, "Multi-participant multi-class vertical federated learning," *arXiv preprint arXiv:2001.11154*, 2020.

20. T. Chen, X. Jin, Y. Sun, and W. Yin, "Vafl: A method of vertical asynchronous federated learning," *arXiv preprint arXiv:2007.06081*, 2020.

21. J. Lee, J. Sun, F. Wang, S. Wang, C.-H. Jun, and X. Jiang, "Privacy-preserving patient similarity learning in a federated environment: Development and analysis," *JMIR Medical Informatics*, vol. 6, p. e7744, 2018.

22. E. Cordis, "Machine learning ledger orchestration for drug discovery," ed, 2019.

23. N. Truong, K. Sun, S. Wang, F. Guitton, and Y. Guo, "Privacy preservation in federated learning: An insightful survey from the GDPR perspective," *Computers & Security*, vol. 110, p. 102402, 2021.

24. C. C. Agbo, Q. H. Mahmoud, and J. M. Eklund, "Blockchain technology in healthcare: A systematic review," *Healthcare*, vol. 7, p. 56, 2019.

25. L. Mucchi, S. Jayousi, A. Martinelli, S. Caputo, and P. Marcocci, "An overview of security threats, solutions and challenges in wbans for healthcare," in *2019 13th International Symposium on Medical Information and Communication Technology (ISMICT)*, 2019, pp. 1–6.

26. S. Shan, E. Wenger, J. Zhang, H. Li, H. Zheng, and B. Y. Zhao, "Fawkes: Protecting privacy against unauthorized deep learning models," in *29th {USENIX} Security Symposium ({USENIX} Security 20)*, 2020, pp. 1589–1604.

27. J. Zhao, Y. Chen, and W. Zhang, "Differential privacy preservation in deep learning: Challenges, opportunities and solutions," *IEEE Access*, vol. 7, pp. 48901–48911, 2019.

28. N. Phan, X. Wu, H. Hu, and D. Dou, "Adaptive laplace mechanism: Differential privacy preservation in deep learning," in *2017 IEEE International Conference on Data Mining (ICDM)*, 2017, pp. 385–394.

29. X. Xiong, S. Liu, D. Li, Z. Cai, and X. Niu, "A comprehensive survey on local differential privacy," *Security and Communication Networks*, vol. 2020, pp. 1–2, 2020.

30. A. Kasturi, A. R. Ellore, and C. Hota, "Fusion learning: A one shot federated learning," in *International Conference on Computational Science*, pp. 424–436, 2020.

31. J. Obolewicz, "Knowledge map as a tool for work safety and health protection in engineering construction project," *Science Education Practice*, p. 171, 2020.

32. W. Zhang, T. Zhou, Q. Lu, X. Wang, C. Zhu, H. Sun, *et al.*, "Dynamic fusion-based federated learning for COVID-19 detection," *IEEE Internet of Things Journal*, vol. 8, pp. 15884–15891, 2021.

33. I. Feki, S. Ammar, Y. Kessentini, and K. Muhammad, "Federated learning for COVID-19 screening from chest X-ray images," *Applied Soft Computing*, vol. 106, p. 107330, 2021.

34. X. Liu, H. Li, G. Xu, R. Lu, and M. He, "Adaptive privacy-preserving federated learning," *Peer-to-Peer Networking and Applications*, vol. 13, pp. 2356–2366, 2020.
35. H. Ku, W. Susilo, Y. Zhang, W. Liu, and M. Zhang, "Privacy-Preserving federated learning in medical diagnosis with homomorphic re-Encryption," *Computer Standards & Interfaces*, vol. 80, p. 103583, 2022.

2

Applications, Opportunities, and Current Challenges in the Healthcare Industry

A. Veena and S. Gowrishankar

Dr. Ambedkar Institute of Technology, Bengaluru, India

CONTENTS

2.1 Healthcare Introduction

Healthcare is the maintenance or betterment of a person's well-being through the inhibition, analysis, medication, healing, or prevention of illness, sickness, trauma, and other physical and psychological disabilities. Wellness and health are important aspects of our lives that influence our quality of life. Given increasingly limited economic resources, efficient delivery of quality healthcare is a critical societal goal [1]. In the medical field, we collect large amounts of data on individuals and their medical problems through medical registries and many other medical procedures [2]. Healthcare organizations are transitioning from paper-based records to electronic records. Using electronic health records and other forms of automation has transformed the healthcare industry [3]. Instant access to genuine patient information from anywhere in the globe has brought prospective benefits that cannot be accessed by the widespread usage of digital data in healthcare. Traditional paper-based records have been superseded with electronic healthcare records (EHR). With the rapid growth of electronic gadgets and greater Internet access, more devices

DOI: 10.1201/9781003217435-2

are now linked to the Internet than individuals. The healthcare industry, which has been sluggish to accept new technology, is predicted to have over 80 million linked devices by 2022, despite its slow adoption rate. In addition, different health application areas represent different opportunities for IoT adoption, and according to current trends, application areas of smart health products (e.g., smart drugs, smart dispensers and needles, ingenious device observation, lockers, smart RFID technology, and Digital Medical Records) are the newest [4].

Data sources in the healthcare industry include the human-created information, biometric information, machine-produced information, behavioral information, epidemiological information, transactional information, and publication information [5]. Health monitoring in non-hospital settings, particularly at home, has long piqued the interest of healthcare researchers and developers. Continued observation of physiological data in daily life, such as ECG signals or heart rate, is critical for controlling chronic conditions, such as cardiovascular disease [6]. Big data are a next-generation technology and architecture planned to sparingly derive information from vast amounts of types of data by enabling fast collection, detection, and analysis [7]. In the healthcare context, big data denote a huge and composite gathering of electronic healthcare information that is hard to process, allocate, and analyze using standard methods and methods.

We expect health information investigation to have a noteworthy impression on existing treatments as life expectancy increases with the global population. Health analysis can reduce predict epidemics and treatment costs, prevent preventable ailments, and enhance the standard of care and the lives of patients. Data analytics in healthcare can make it simpler to collect medical data and turn it into meaningful insights that can then be utilized to improve care. For healthcare applications, enormous patient data contain valuable and significant insights that can be exposed through data analysis employing modern artificial intelligence and data mining techniques [8].

In a cloud computing environment, we may examine healthcare data to solve a diversity of challenges in the healthcare industry [9]. Cloud computing inherits the capabilities of high-speed parallel computing, grid computing, and distributed computing, and evolves these methods to achieve location transparency and improve the user experience on the Internet [10]. The use of cloud computing technologies is excellent for healthcare facilities because of its as and when required services, high scalability, and virtualization capabilities. Many articles now report on the amalgamation of cloud and health, and nearly articles call it the e-health cloud [11].

For medical data management, we can use cloud computing in the healthcare domain. Each health professional has accessibility to or sponsors a cloud infrastructure that can collect, interpret, and share information among consumers, physician assistants, and other stakeholders if an outbreak is anticipated. An infrastructure of this type can also house amenities for dealing with the characteristics of all patient consent, recorded consumers, and patient health data and reports. The cloud infrastructure may also help the health professionals with organizational activities, such as updating and generating billing reports and expending payments. Public and private cloud infrastructure used by multiple healthcare providers can integrate by means of a cross-cloud architecture to communicate patient data, create billing profiles, and more to meet patient mobility needs [12].

Because the cloud cannot address all the class of service needs of IoT and the technological revolution it brings, introducing fog computing is a win–win opportunity for a variety of sectors like body area networks (BANs), healthcare, vehicle systems, and smart grids [13]. The goal of fog-based construction is to handle the processing and streaming of information from a variety of healthcare devices and equipment. Moving the dispensation of

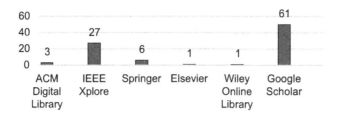

FIGURE 2.1
Database sources for healthcare domain research articles.

healthcare information streams closer to the data sources at the edge can minimize the system stream of traffic and progress the latency of time-critical healthcare applications. Typical fog data stream processing components include a information stream processing apparatus, distributed messaging system, and information storing. The architecture's fog computer layer is based on the popular Apache Kafka's sophisticated message system and the influential Apache Storm workflow appliance that handles large amounts of data [14].

As shown in Figure 2.1, we performed the search across different online databases identifying sample papers between 2010 and 2021.

We organized the rest of the article as trails. Section 2.2 highlights the different types of healthcare information produced from numerous devices. We discussed many research problems and issues in healthcare that originate from various entities Section 2.3. Section 2.4 covers the usage of blockchain knowledge in the healthcare business. A thorough examination of the major contributions of IoT and cloud-based mechanisms in medical applications is covered in Section 2.6. Sections 2.7 and 2.8 cover the security and privacy, and conclusion respectively.

2.2 Healthcare Data

Healthcare is considered a data-intensive sector [15]. The traditional process for capturing critical patient data is labor-intensive for collecting, entering, and analyzing data. These processes are often slow and prone to errors, causing delays in the accessibility of the real-time data [12]. With so many patients and little time, there is a crucial necessity to develop a novel and scalable big data structure and logical approaches that allow healthcare practitioners to entree facts for each particular person. This requires a framework that uses patient EHRs and genetics data to facilitate predictive, personalized, preventative, and participative healthcare decision-making.

Advances in information technology have made it easier to access large amounts of health data, such as Electronic Health Records (EHR), case history, Demographics, prescription, lab test outcomes, and billing information that are all included in EHR data [16]. Operational databases, Transactional databases, domain-specific databases, knowledge bases, temporary caches, memory grids, big data stores, and other data stores are all examples of data storage. Financial and operational databases and Electronic Health Records (EHR) of hospitals and clinics, Genome database, database of insurance pharmaceutical firms, knowledge bases, drug research data, ontologies unique to healthcare, and other important data are available in the healthcare domain. Data can be extracted and analyzed from any of these data storage, depending on the analytical requirements [17].

Most health and medical research rely on clinical data. Clinical data are collected either as part of an ongoing or as part of the formal clinical study program. We can divide clinical data into six prime categories: administrative data, claims data, electronic health records, patient, illness, disease enrolment, clinical trials data, and health surveys. The registry is patient-centered, goal-based, and designed to extract information about identified health and exposure outcomes [18].

Access to high-quality health data is an important requirement for healthcare professionals and pharmaceutical researchers to make informed decisions. According to Ref. [19], health information can be separated into four groups: data from medical insurance (data acquired and held by several health insurance organizations for several years), clinical data (records for patient health, operational and laboratory reports, and medical images etc.), patient behavior data (data collected via wearable devices and monitors), data from drug research (reports on clinical studies, high-performance results screening). The various types of healthcare data that contribute to big healthcare data are depicted in Figure 2.2.

Benefits of electronic health records include higher quality care, more precise patient data, interoperability, improved competence, improved profits, scalability, accessibility, personalization, security, and support. Privacy and confidentiality issues are drawbacks of using EHR. Another difficulty is how subjects use and comprehend the data on patient gateways. It is critical that patients do not misinterpret file entries. Furthermore, staff workers may not use the EHR platform effectively. An EHR system's appropriate implementation could take months or even years. Smaller health centers and more skilled specialists may prefer to do everything on paper, but others do not, which can lead to misunderstanding. At first, implementing EHR may seem to slow down, but once the learning curve is overcome, the benefits far outweigh.

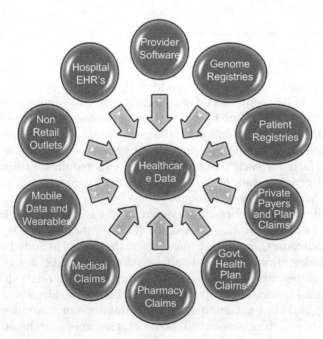

FIGURE 2.2
Different types of healthcare data.

2.3 Healthcare Research Issues

Many issues in healthcare stem from the complicated network of middlemen and the failure to trace transactions. Healthcare data are broken down into multiple silos which have detrimental impacts on research and services [20].

1. In the healthcare system, there are several technical challenges in research and clinical procedures [21].

   - **Policy-Making**: The healthcare system requires interoperability between private and public stakeholders. This emphasizes the need for nationally/internationally coordinated standards and agreements that span boundaries and authorities.

   - **Lack of Regulation**: The development of relevant rules for the governance of proprietary rights of ownership-related clinical transactions for the envisaged healthcare system is proving problematic across the world. Because there are so many parties, data ownership and current health law in the traditional healthcare system are critical concerns that must be addressed. It will be difficult to change the present regulatory structure to meet new administration policy objectives controlling digitally defined, computerized, and ubiquitous nature. The ownership of healthcare data, permitted access privileges, and distributed storage structure should all be well defined.

   - **Confidentiality and Transparency**: in certain situations, technology emphasizes transparency, which may be undesirable in the healthcare realm. Although it provides security through encryption, healthcare stakeholders consider the accessibility of a record, even in encoded form, to be a significant concern. As a result, adequate access control should be addressed in healthcare informatics [22].

   - **Sustainability**: In healthcare informatics systems, the Encryption key is very essential. The private encryption key cannot be recovered. Because of its long-term nature, this increases the difficulty of healthcare data. The trustworthiness and utility of a patient's health record are reduced when parts are missing. In addition, hacking or robbing the private key of a user gives access to all user-specified information.

   - **Manageability of data**: Healthcare system expands when a user adds data. Because of the increased computational power and storage needs, the network may have less edge nodes with sufficient processing capacity to analyze and evaluate data in the Healthcare systems. When healthcare practitioners cannot fulfill the needs of storage and computing capacity, the possibility for more centralization and delayed validation and confirmation of data increases.

   - **Adoption of new technologies**: In the health industry, new methodologies like blockchain and Artificial Intelligence are gaining popularity. Blockchain and cloud computing of both technologies rely on a network of interconnected computers to provide computational power. We must reward contributors for donating computer power through incentive mechanisms. Health organizations may require encouragement to embrace new technologies.

   - **Operating Cost**: The cost of setting up and running the Healthcare system, and the cost of migrating from the existing health informatics system, is unknown, open-source technology and the intermittent nature of the technology can assist operating costs. The ongoing operation and maintenance of the Health Informatics System demands continuous availability of troublesolving, updating, backup, and reporting resources.

2. Several approaches to fall detection have been presented during the last two decades. Because of the speedy growth of novel methodologies, this problem is quite full of life in the scientific community. Even though significant development has been achieved, there are still several difficulties to overcome [23].

- **The scarcity of real-world data**: There is no standard public data set available. There are many replicated information sets by individual sensors accessible, but it is questionable whether representations based on information gathered by new and strong individuals can apply to older persons in realistic settings. There is a necessity to develop a standard information set consisting of information from many sensors.

- **Real-time Detection**: Researchers need to focus more on present arrangements that can be used in the actual biosphere. Safety and confidentiality must be addressed in tandem with fall detection systems.

- **Platform of sensor fusion**: Comprehensive research is required to build entire information systems capable of dealing with data management and transmission in an efficient, effective, and secure manner in a direction to fetch solutions nearer to the marketplace.

- **Locational Constraint**: Sensors remain permanent and static, such as visual ones. Fall detection systems that can be used in both regulated and uncontrolled situations are required.

- **Scalability and elasticity**: with the rising quantity of inexpensive devices, the scalability of fall detection systems must be investigated, when considering heterogeneous sensors [24].

3. Despite AI's claimed accomplishments in cancer imaging, there are several limitations and roadblocks to overcome before widespread clinical usage [25].

- Medical imaging data are seldom curated for labeling, quality assurance, annotations, segmentation, or suitability for the task at hand. Medical data interpretation is a key roadblock in the development of automated healthcare solutions since it causes the employment of trained experts, making the process time and expense intensive. In the medical field, standardized benchmarking is especially important, given the wide range of imaging techniques and anatomic locations, as well as gathering standards and hardware.

- Interpretability and integrity of AI: The value of trust and openness in AI systems is differentiated according to their performance, which makes it possible to identify defects once AI is subhuman and therefore transform phenomenal AI hooked on a future educator. Complex evaluations of biological networks may have a significant influence on response and prognosis assessment, as well as therapy planning, with the integration of AI.

- Imaging is not a stand-alone indicator of illness. It is becoming abundantly clear that cancer genetic fingerprints, such as non-invasive blood biomarkers of tumor, socio-economic position, and even social networks, have an influence on the fate of malignancy individuals.

2.4 Healthcare Blockchain Systems

Because of its advanced characteristics such as traceability, safety, and transparency, Blockchain (BC) has become one of the greatest popular technologies in the internet age [26]. Blockchain technology allows for the storage of data in such a way that it is nearly difficult to improve, eliminate, or alter the data without being discovered by further operatives [27]. As one of the most fascinating technical breakthroughs, blockchain expertise is fast gaining popularity in the healthcare industry [28]. The instances of effective blockchain medicare applications include the Gem Health Network [29], Patientory Inc. (patientory.com/), SimplyVital fitness, and MedRec [30].

Blockchain may be divided into the following categories [31]: Public Blockchain, Federated Blockchain, and Private Blockchain. Public blockchain is a permissionless blockchain, so anybody may conduct transactions namelessly or pseudo-namelessly. Furthermore, it is an open network with the highest level of decentralized trust. This includes cryptocurrencies such as Bitcoin, Ethereum, Waves [32], Dash [33], and Bitshares [34]. Federated Blockchain is a licensed blockchain and works on the initiative of a group called Consortium. The transactions might be open to the public or kept hidden. This category includes EWF (Energy), R3 Corda, and B3i (Insurance). A private blockchain is a permissioned blockchain designed to supervise and validate internal organization transactions. It could be accessible to the general public or not. Blocks are generated more quickly and with better throughput. The private blockchain is used to assess trustworthiness, which depends on the algorithm used, not on authority. This includes Monax and Hyper Ledger with Saw tooth.

The healthcare sector can benefit from a variety of blockchain systems. Figure 2.3 illustrates the combination of blockchain and IoT technologies that allows healthcare organizations to efficiently and accurately manage records, which is critical. We outline the complete process, beginning with the collection of real-time information from patients via IoT and ending with the provision of a suitable drug that ensures the patient's happiness [35]. The blockchain technology comprises several interconnected components. Blockchain technology can make certain guarantees to its users by combining these components.

- **Blockchain**: Blockchain, like a traditional ledger, is a digital ledger or an immutable record at its utmost fundamental level. At the heart of the blockchain is the ledger. This is a recording infrastructure that allows Ledger owners to tell a story about the transactions. Although ledgers can store almost any type of data imaginable, this topic usually centers on asset ownership and history [36].
- **Cryptography**: Cryptography, or the study of how to convey data in a secure or genuine manner, is another vital component of blockchain technology. Utilization of encryption in blockchain technology to preserve anonymity, offer ledger immutability, and authenticate claims made against assets recorded and controlled on the blockchain. Today to connect a block, the information in the block is sent to a process called a "cryptographic hash." A cryptographic hash function that produces a separate output or ID for a particular input. Depending on inputs, each block's hash will always be unique. When the data in a block change, the hash or ID generated on the next chunk in the shackle no longer matches the unique cost. The current block's header carries the hash of the preceding block to connect or chain data blocks together. Changing the contents of any block in a blockchain results in an entirely non-identical hash, and a novel hash does not match the hash

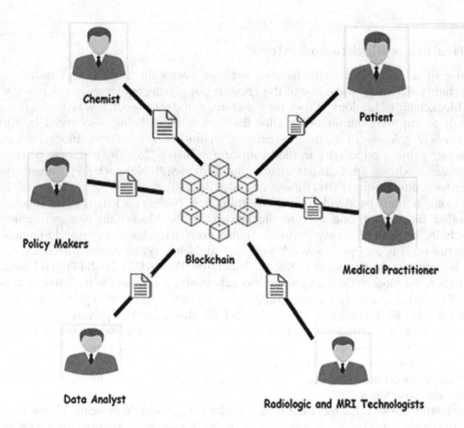

FIGURE 2.3
Blockchain as a Platform for Healthcare. (Adapted from Ahmed Farouk 2020.)

in the following block header, causing the blockchain to break and invalidate all blocks related to the location of the changes. As a result, blockchain technology is highly censorship-resistant and tamper-resistant [37].

- **Peer-to-Peer Network**: Blockchain heavily relies on current computer networking technologies, particularly peer-to-peer network topologies. Blockchain is built on the same technology that underpins our modern internet's backbone. By means of peer-to-peer network, design promotes redundancy and fault tolerance by eliminating single points of catastrophe that are frequent in traditional client/server system topologies [38]. Any transaction initiated by any node in the network will be validated by peer nodes. The block will be expanded to include the validated transaction.

- **Assets**: Eventually, any blockchain system must include assets. Assets are items that we keep track of, the assets that "matter" with a specific outcome or use case scenarios. An asset is something that requires proof of ownership. Healthcare data, event tickets, an auto title, or a patent are samples of monetary, non-monetary, or informational resources. Blockchain started as a registry system for recording the digital data transmission of numerical "coins" or "tokens," like Bitcoin and further cryptocurrencies.

- **Consensus Algorithm**: Consensus is a method of ensuring that all connected devices validate transactions and approve their directive and presence on the register.

There are several options that fit different situations when there is agreement. Opportunity cost (security, speed, etc.) is considered when deciding whether or not to utilize a particular consensus mechanism. The major distinction between them is how consensus systems delegate and reward transaction verification. Proof-of-work and proof-of-stake are the greatest used consensus systems.

- **Smart Contract**: the software or business logic that runs on the ledger.
- **Affiliation/Certificate Authority**: to join the network, the user must be granted authorization. The users' identity is verified by the Certificate Authority and ensures that they have appropriate access to the ledger for the transaction they are executing.

By making substantial improvements, blockchain technology can help streamline data management in healthcare such as improved drug traceability, patient record management, clinical trials, and accuracy medicine, preserving consistent authorizations, protecting healthcare systems, improving health insurance coverage, and healthcare billing systems. The open research challenges in blockchain in healthcare include scalability, interoperability, navigating regulation uncertainty, tokenization of data, irreversibility, and quantum computing, incorporating blockchain technology into established healthcare organizations, ensuring healthcare data accuracy, and blockchain developers' culture adoption [39]. Table 2.1 compares and contrasts the various Blockchain techniques for the healthcare trade, as well as their benefits and drawbacks.

TABLE 2.1

Blockchain Techniques Used in the Healthcare Application

Blockchain Methods Used	Healthcare Examples	Advantages	Disadvantages
Blockchain private Hyperledger fabric [40]	Behavioral Health data collected using a mobile phone	Tamper-resistant healthcare platform for behavioral therapy	Obsolete codes and consensus algorithm
The Ethereum platform and a consortium-managed blockchain [41]	Remote patient monitoring	Real-time health information is gained by sensors is managed, monitored, and securely analyzed	Data transfer is not secure since it uses public networks from body sensors to blockchain nodes. As the number of sensors increases, key management will become an issue, and verification of the healthcare data is delayed
Consortium PoW [42]	Pharmaceutical data	Prevents counterfeit drugs and tracks the flow of drugs	Cost is high, and investigation of policies and regulations
Proof of Concept with timestamp [43]	Clinical trials, Electronic Health Records (EHR)	Consent in clinical trials and HER	Concern over safety of the information, and whether or not the subject has signed the consent
Smart contract with permissioned blockchain [44]	Patient and drug dose information	Delivery of drugs in the secure way with prescription and patient information	The quantity of the users increases the response time and system latency

2.5 Healthcare Analytics

Healthcare Analytics is well-defined as the "methodical application of information and connected clinical and business (C & B) visions established through practical logical disciplines such as numerical, circumstantial, quantifiable, prognostic, and reasoning spectrums to drive decision making based on facts for preparation, administration, dimension, and education" [45, 46]. Healthcare Data analytics is being used not just for the study of clinical data and Electronic Health Records (EHR), but also for getting insights into related businesses such as pharmaceuticals, healthcare insurance firms, and so on [47]. Figure 2.4 shows the three steps of Healthcare Analytics [48]. The first step is data collection. Healthcare comprises different data such as Electronic Health Records (EHR), medical claims, wearable devices and so on. There are several tools for processing, visualizing, and analyzing data after obtaining the data. Finally, it is time to take a decision. A good understanding of the patient's illness is aided by an analytics report. Big data helps healthcare practitioners to negotiate more efficient operations and information on patients and their health. Big data have several applications in the healthcare sector.

2.5.1 Types of Analytics

Healthcare analytics may be divided into three main types: descriptive, predictive, and prescriptive analytics. Figure 2.5 depicts the Analytics employed in the Literature Review.

1. **Descriptive Analytics**: Descriptive analytics is about investigating the information in the data set. As the name suggests, it is used to characterize large data sets,

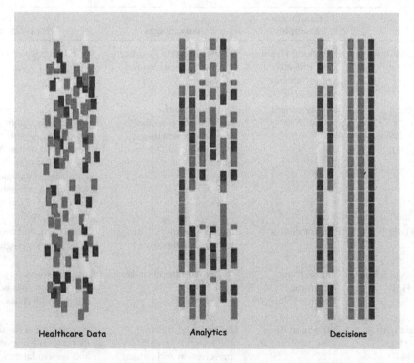

FIGURE 2.4
Healthcare Data, Analytics, and Decisions. (Adapted from Chen, G 2019.)

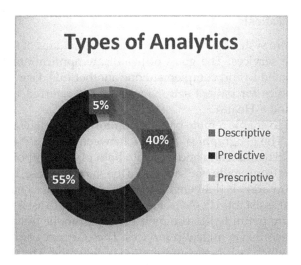

FIGURE 2.5
Types of Analytics Used in Healthcare.

compressing them into manageable data sets, charts, or statistics that physicians can use. To quantify raw data, descriptive analytics employs both historical and present data. Hospitals, for example, may examine readmissions to get insight into trends that might minimize and boost patient care.

2. **Predictive Analytics**: Predictive Analytics are used to forecast outcomes, such as patient outcomes, depending on the quantity and severity of risk symptoms exhibited. This makes use of the same historical data, but differently: as a foundation for projecting future events or outcomes. In healthcare, such as population health, this has obvious benefits. Physicians, for example, might anticipate chronic disease patterns in rural communities and activities.

3. **Prescriptive Analytics**: Stakeholders can predict more futures based on the precautions taken and analyze how useful each tactic is for other options. Prescriptive analytics can help practitioners in defining which sequence of deeds is applied and gives the extremely probable advantage, such as when emerging department-wide performance enhancement goals as decision-making.

Descriptive analytics go back in the period to elucidate what happened and why. Predictive and prescriptive analytics make use of earlier information to anticipate what will happen in the near future and what procedures to take to inspire those consequences.

2.6 Healthcare Applications

All people in today's society are battling in their busy lives to prioritize their health. The extraordinary success of health applications shows that increasing numbers of individuals rely on technology to care for themselves and fulfill their health goals. Cloud computing is being used by healthcare application providers to handle massive processing loads and lower service delivery costs [49]. Personal well-being management necessitates the provision of individualized services via dynamically generated ecosystems [50].

2.6.1 Applications for Patients

For successful healthcare systems, it is crucial to raise the standard of living and experience of patient's healthcare services. The goals of healthcare applications that serve patients differ; yet, they are related to and complement one another [51]. Using different electronic gadgets and technologies for patient self-management is referred to as telehealth, tele-medicine, m-Health, and e-Health.

Telehealth emerged to enable remote patient monitoring and deliver healthcare services across long distances. The geographical distance between the healthcare practitioner and the patient is bridged [52]. m-Health and e-Health both play an important role in support-ing healthcare with electronic gadgets. They serve the same purpose, but the major distinc-tion is in how the information is delivered. Mobile devices, such as handheld devices, cell phone, personal digital assistants (PDAs), or a tablet, are used to assist healthcare practices in mHealth. Patients are permitted to use their personal mobile devices to log, save, and monitor their health records via mHealth services. These services aid in the improvement of the efficiency with which healthcare information is delivered. The m-Health application can be very beneficial for professionals and patients to study and use. The term e-Health encompasses a much larger knowledge of healthcare procedures that are assisted by inte-grating technologies.

Telehealth is the transmission of information and healthcare services between health-care practitioners and patients via telecommunication technologies for patient care and monitoring. To meet the needs of developing countries, telecommunication services neces-sitate significant infrastructure investment [53]. Primary healthcare professionals in rural areas are frequently separated from secluded from experts, such as behavioral healthcare practitioners [54].

Reference [55] presents a list of difficulties in rural areas where telehealth can help in the following ways:

1. The discrepancy in the provision of healthcare between rural and urban areas is "mainly because of the difficulty of creating, maintaining and keeping adequately and properly trained rural health workers." Telehealth has the potential to narrow this gap by giving remote individuals access to additional healthcare services.

2. Healthcare policymakers who wish to improve the rural population's access to care must find measures to increase the number and circulation of healthcare workers enthusiastic to work in remote areas.

3. Countryside residents are often aged, sicker, and less sophisticated than city dwellers. Patients and professionals in rural areas can receive geriatric care and education through telehealth.

4. Despite considerable efforts by government and academic organizations to alle-viate rural provider shortfalls over the last three decades, both the scarcity and misallocation of providers persist. Telehealth can help with distribution issues.

5. Health experts say "the more specialized you are, the more likely you are to settle in the city." Only family physicians are more likely to practice in rural communi-ties that are smaller and more secluded. Telehealth has the potential to deliver specialist treatment to remote areas.

Telehealth has several advantages which include [52] a reduction in the cost of fre-quent doctor visits. It includes telecommunications, information technology, and mobile technologies to provide medical care services that allow patients and medical practitioners to consult across geographic boundaries. These might be innovations that are utilized by users or physicians to improve or support telehealth services. Telehealth is being used in a variety of ways nowadays consultations between physicians and patients are made easier, [54] including the transmission of data or images for analysis, remote monitoring, tele-pharmacy, and enhanced provider communication. Obstruction of Telehealth is as follows [56, 57]:

1. Healthcare practitioners must get a license where they plan to administer medications and visit patients.
2. In rural regions, there is a scarcity of high-speed data transfer capability.
3. Telecommunications administrations face substantial hardware and recurring expenditures.
4. Evidence-based barriers such as financial barriers – telehealth affordability to elderly individuals because of the cost of creating the infrastructure and lack of incentives to healthcare professionals.

m-Health has risen because of the increased adoption and use of innovative, wireless, and mobile technology to improve healthcare research, outcomes, and services [58]. Table 2.2 shows a variety of m-Health applications that are related to healthcare [59].

Voice over internet protocol (VOIP), Internet access, voice calling, multimedia message service (MMS), manuscript messaging, and short message service (SMS) are all examples of m-Health capabilities [60]. The most common m-Health applications are sensors and point of care devices, client teaching and behavior change, data collection and reporting, registries and vital event following, electronic decision-making assistance, electronic health records, communication between providers, work planning and development for providers and provider education and training, management of the supply chain, human resource administration, and financial transactions and incentives [61]. m-Health adoption is hampered by several obstacles. The most significant stumbling block is the cost. Implementing such a technology-based system is expensive, and m-Health systems can only become mainstream if the government and health insurance companies allocate cash for this investment. According to the WHO report, privacy and security are additional challenges

TABLE 2.2

Healthcare Application Categories on mHealth

Categories	Applications
Depending on medical speciality	Family practice, forensic medicine, emergency medicine, immunology, allergy, infectious diseases, disability, pharmacology, internal medicine, palliative care, traumatology, intensive care, physical medicine and rehabilitation, public health, and fitness
Depending on the area of studies	Doctoral associations, education, medical scientific literature, financial resources, biotech, emergency action systems, residential care organizations, policies governing public health, visualizing centers, GSM Operators, hospitals, medical consultancy, association of patients, long-term assistance, data aggregation, health information system
Depending on Operation System	Android, iOS, BlackBerry, Windows

for m-Health systems. Another hurdle is logistics, as some rural areas still lack Internet connectivity due to logistical issues.

Electronic healthcare (e-healthcare) has grown as a radical new approach because of rapid developments in information and communication technologies [62]. E-Healthcare is increasingly displacing traditional healthcare and promoting the creation of innovative healthcare applications because of technological advancements [63]. IoT is becoming increasingly important in the ever-changing healthcare landscape [64]. The Internet-of Things (IoT) is a novel paradigm that allows them to integrate and communicate with objects or objects like RFID sensors, cell phones, tags, and actuators. Devices and people connect, communicate, gather, and share data through integrating physical things, hardware, software, and computational devices in e-Healthcare, which is designated as the Internet of Healthcare Things (IoHT) [65]. Connecting the digital and physical worlds [66], IoT uses ubiquitous and pervasive computing, as well as e-healthcare platforms, to enable healthcare devices (e.g., Mobile devices, Fitbits, Bluetooth, and sensors) to accumulate fitness-connected data (e.g., glucose level, blood pressure, blood oxygen capacity, mass, respiratory and heart rate, and so on) [67, 68] over a long period and store it. There are several areas of healthcare where the IoT plays an important role [69]:

- Elderly care including housing/patient monitoring of elderly people in nursing homes and hospitals.
- It includes several equipments which is seen at the bedside in hospitals such as the monitoring of the electrocardiogram, the data collection which is the most matured filed for healthcare and an area that continues to increase with new advancements in IoT.
- At a reduced cost, real-time location is used to track people and assets.

Hadoop clusters may be used to process healthcare data in the cloud. Applications running on scalable servers can accommodate a significant number of participants [70]. The result data can be transported to the cloud and the information can be integrated by Hadoop MapReduce in many servers on the cloud and managed to produce the results rapidly as shown in Figure 2.6. Deep learning breakthroughs based on convolutional neural networks have empowered significant gains in a variety of activities such as identification of images [71], interpretation of speech [72], discovery of drugs [73], and cancer research using gene analysis [74, 75]. Table 2.3 shows some of the applications of the healthcare domain, as well as their pros and cons.

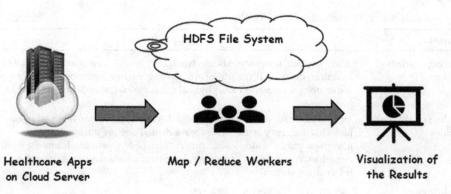

FIGURE 2.6
Healthcare Data Processing on Cloud Server. (Adapted from Kaur, M. J., 2018.)

TABLE 2.3

Machine/Deep Learning Mechanisms Used in Healthcare Domain

Algorithms Used	Healthcare Examples	Pros/Performance Metrics Used	Cons
Fully Convolutional Residual Network [76]	Dermoscopic images	To classify melanoma, a very deep residual network of about 16 blocks is used, Accuracy	Multiscale contextual information integration, to integrate probabilistic graphical models in the network
Deep Learning [77]	Electronic health records	Predicting readmission for heart failure by finding critical factors. Precision, F-1 Score, Accuracy, Recall	Labeling of the admission as positive and negative
U-Net Deep Learning [78]	Electron and optical microscopy images	Segmentation on neuronal structures in EM stacks and cell tracking, very good segmentation performance even with limited data, Rand – error	Data size is small of 30 images, training time of model is high
C5.0 Decision Tree [79]	Pathological, demographic characteristics, physiological fertility, genetic and disease history, and behavioral habits	The cost matrix in the C5.0 model has been substantially improved, The performance metrics used are accuracy, specificity, and sensitivity	The dataset used is small, cancer is highly concealed and unclear, and the data set contains a enormous number of samples with minor illness characteristics.
Ensemble and transfer learning [80]	X-Ray images	On two big data sets, cancer prediction was tested against human readers, AUC–ROC	Use of simulation tool in AI
Two stage FCN [81]	MRI Images	Detects candidate microbleeds before reducing false positives, can be easily applied to another biomarker detection task	Excludes the phase information which includes the possible mimics of calcifications
CNN with fully connected CRF [82]	MRI images	TBI, brain tumors, and ischemic stroke are all segmented on a multi-scale basis, Haussdorf, Precision, and Sensitivity	Dense inference on entire volume requires a forward-pass, Tiling the volume into multiple segments

Fog computing collects and processes massive quantities of raw data produced by IoT/end devices, allowing for real-time investigation and choice creation in the present circumstances. End devices continue to collect information to monitor the situation. As a result, the fog nodes must import data from the end node in real time. In a few applications, like body area networks, body sensors would generate massive amounts of information on a regular basis. Data processing, such as data filtering, data accumulation, and so on, needs to be performed by fog nodes. For instance, the ECG sensors will handle the emergency data quickly, in accordance with local policy, in the fog node. The steps are depicted in a straightforward manner in Figure 2.7 [83]. Since fog can provide on-site data storage, it can perform intelligent computations and investigation of these data, as well as disseminate some policy-based choices to the respective industry to give a better performance.

It is possible that if the end device is hooked up to the internet and generates data, it will not be essential to transmit or sync the information to the cloud due to redundant data [84].

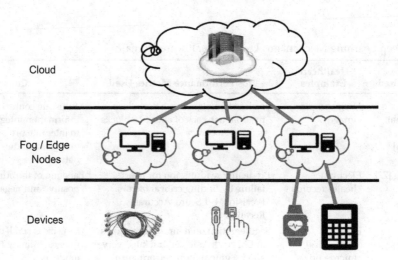

FIGURE 2.7
Fog Computing Architecture. (Adapted from Shi, Y, 2015.)

The cloud keeps its primary "brain-trust" role in the fog model (evaluating information and making all of the major choices). The cloud, on the other hand, can delegate some duties to fog nodes, making it ideal for edge analysis and decision-making. Additionally, if the fog does not require in-depth analytics, they can simply sieve local data and preferentially send it to the cloud [85]. As a result, the transmission efficiency of widely spread sensor networks may be significantly improved.

2.6.2 Applications for Healthcare Professionals

These applications can assist healthcare professionals to improve their working environment, automate tedious chores, and provide increasingly sophisticated services to help them do their jobs even better. Because healthcare applications collect, store, and analyze massive quantities of data, they will also gather information on employees and how they execute their jobs. In a variety of ways, this information may be used to power programs that optimize and improve people management.

1. *Scheduling*: Several factors make scheduling professional healthcare staff such as doctors, surgeons, nurses, and therapists making it extremely difficult to achieve an ideal timetable. In addition to the factors such as start and end time, location, and vacations, specialty, experience level, the condition of the patient, shifts, demand fluctuations, and needed resource availability must all be into consideration. Healthcare applications can be intended to extract information from the faculty, assets, request stages and chronicled information and utilize progressed algorithms to make enhanced timetables, make alternate courses of action, furthermore, represent potential crises. This method will assist with giving the experts better timetables, more unsurprising prerequisites, and a further developed workplace.

2. *Access to Resources*: A lot of resources are needed to accomplish tasks by healthcare workers. Doctors and nurses, among many other resources, are essential. They need counseling rooms, diagnostic devices, operation rooms, and a variety of

TABLE 2.4

Different Types of IoT Devices Used in Healthcare Applications

Healthcare Applications	Type of sensor used	Functioning of sensor
Monitoring of patient [86]	Temperature sensor, respiration rate sensor, pulse rate sensor	Sensors used in this application measure a person's body temperature, pulse rate, and breath rate
Stress Detection [87]	ECG Monitoring sensors, Accelerometer	Collects the ECG signals and measures the angle between user and object
Position Altering [88]	Accelerometer, pulse sensor and ultrasonic sensor	Used to measure the heart rate, and angle between the objects and determines the tilt angle between the person and the entity
Paralyzed [89]	Infrared sensor	Acts as a comparator
Visually Challenged [90]	Ultrasonic sensor	It is used to figure out how far apart two items are
Home Monitoring [91]	CO2 Sensor	Measures CO2 content levels
Elderly Monitoring [92]	Light sensor, airflow sensor, oximeter sensor	Detects light, monitors the quantity of oxygen in the blood and detects hemoglobin
Military [93]	Sensor to detect the explosives	Detects explosives
Alcohol detection [94]	PID Sensor	Detects the chemical content
Diabetes Monitoring [95]	Weight and pressure sensors	Detects the body weight

other resources. Certain approvals may be required for conveying and providing access to certain of these resources, or there may be a restricted amount of specific resources that may need scheduling.

3. *Alliance*: Different areas of the medical system require collaboration between staff within the same organization, between facilities in the same organization, or with other systems and units. Based on the situation of the patient, Medical practitioners need to discuss among peers some cases and from different organizations as well. Managers need to share the data or work-related information to accomplish the overall work of the organization. The administrators also need to collaborate with the health equipment manufacturers, transportation companies, insurance corporations, drug manufacturers, and providers of consumables and healthcare services.

4. *Remote Access*: Most organizations are small and cannot afford sophisticated and expensive equipment. Specialized facilities have their own expertise and equipment. Having a simple and secure means to access and utilize such equipment will be a huge assistance to the requester, allowing them to reap even more advantages from it. Some applications may be to request to use the radiology reports to analyze their results. Table 2.4 shows the different IoT's devices such as sensors used healthcare systems.

2.6.3 Applications for Resource Management

The healthcare systems as a whole are huge and contain thousands of assets. These include furniture and other fixtures, as well as physical infrastructure and related service units such as heating, ventilation, and Air Conditioning (HVAC) such as water, oxygen, electrical and fire alarm systems. Healthcare organizations also have components such as laboratory and diagnostic equipment, sanitizing material, medication treatment tools, security instruments and material, surgical materials and equipment, and food.

1. *Accessibility*: When resources are required, they must be available. Hospital beds, life support equipment, pharmaceuticals, and even employees will be in limited supply during emergencies such as terrorism, pandemic, or natural disasters. And in some situations, resources may not be available due to expiry date, due to failures, maintenance, reallocation, and misuse.

2. *Sharing*: To carry out the processes that need resources, particularly essential and shared resources must be assigned to their appropriate healthcare professionals. The organization shares operation theaters, MRI scanners, X-Ray machines, and ICU equipment across various departments such as OPD, Cardiology, Anaesthesiology, Orthopaedics, and Paediatrics.

3. *Connectivity*: All the devices in the healthcare applications must be linked using some technologies such as wired, wireless, Bluetooth, and NFC. The provision of connectivity-based resources will make better use and details on the resources, their capacities, status, and usage history more easily accessible.

4. *Maintenance of Equipment*: Maintenance management's specific goals are as follows: [96] to boost the dependability of infrastructure and equipment, to keep apparatus and organization in good working order at all times, to make emergency repairs to equipment and infrastructure as soon as feasible to ensure the highest possible accessibility for medical usage, to enhance working security, and to educate medical professionals on precise control techniques, to provide guidance on the purchase, setting up and process of healthcare devices and to provide therapeutic insurance and environmental protection.

2.7 Security and Privacy

On the basis of data, communication, and device anonymity properties, the privacy goals are considered [97–99].

1. **Anonymity of the Device**: The identification of medical equipment must be hidden to the system, such that unauthorized entities ought not to be able to identify the precise device identifier, device type, and conventional identifiers such as MAC address and IP address.

2. **Data Cloaking**: The purpose of information anonymization is to stop intruders from being able to identify a user and their sensitive data. Medical professionals should use pseudonyms or other temporary Identifier rather than their actual identity.

3. **Anonymity of the communication**: An unauthorized entity cannot determine the connection between the end-user and the healthcare system. To ensure anonymous communication, effective techniques such as collision-resistant aliases should be employed.

4. **Link ability**: An intruder who records information exchange between transmission and reception should not be in a position to establish a connection between the sender and the information.

2.8 Conclusion

Healthcare is a major problem for any country's or individual's overall economic and development progress. Analytics is deepening into the medical fabric and will shape the future of medicine and care delivery. Various types of data are needed in the healthcare system to allow seamless communication between doctors and patients, improve patient engagement in the treatment process, offer evidence-based care, and detect security risks and fraud early. The emergence of digital platforms such as mobile devices, cloud computing, analysis of data, and wireless networks has contributed to the effective delivery of medical services, analyze trends and disease, and make better policy decisions. The blockchain ledger allows the safe transfer of patient information, the management of the medication supply chain, and the assistance of healthcare researchers in solving problems. In this paper, we have outlined the architecture of cloud and fog architectures of healthcare applications and various types of data and summarized the various applications in healthcare industry, the use of blockchain knowledge in healthcare domain, the research gap and challenges in cancer imaging, fall detection and research, and clinical procedures. Once new solutions for research gaps and challenges are applied in clinical practice, healthcare informatics is expected to raise the quality of care levels, possibly revolutionizing precision medicine.

References

[1] Pavel, M., Jimison, H. B., Wactlar, H. D., Hayes, T. L., Barkis, W., Skapik, J., & Kaye, J. (2013). "the role of technology and engineering models in transforming healthcare," *IEEE Reviews in Biomedical Engineering*, 6, 156–177.

[2] Tahar Kechadi, M., "Healthcare big data: Challenges and opportunities," BDAW'16, November 10–11, 2016, Blagoevgrad, Bulgaria, ACM. ISBN 978-1-4503-4779-2/16/11.

[3] Nallusamy, Rajarathnam, & Asija, Ruchika, "A Survey on Security and Privacy of Healthcare Data," Conference paper, 2015. doi:10.5176/2251-3833_GHC14.29.

[4] Asif-Ur-Rahman, M., Afsana, F., Mahmud, M., Kaiser, M. S., Ahmed, M. R., Kaiwartya, O., & James-Taylor, A. (2018). "Towards a heterogeneous mist, fog, and cloud based framework for the internet of healthcare things," *IEEE Internet of Things Journal*, 1–1. doi:10.1109/jiot.2018.2876088.

[5] Olaronke, I., & Oluwaseun, O. (2016). Big data in healthcare: Prospects, challenges and resolutions. *2016 Future Technologies Conference (FTC)*. doi:10.1109/ftc.2016.7821747.

[6] Jeong, Sangjin, Youn, Chan-Hyun, Shim, Eun Bo, Kim, Moonjung, Cho, Young Min, & Peng, Limei. (2012). "An integrated healthcare system for personalized chronic disease care in home–hospital environments," *IEEE Transactions on Information Technology in Biomedicine*, 16(4), 572–585. doi:10.1109/titb.2012.2190989.

[7] Burghard, C., "Big data and analytics key to accountable care success," IDC Health Insights, 2012.

[8] Qureshi, B. (2014). Towards a Digital Ecosystem for Predictive Healthcare Analytics. Proceedings of the 6th International Conference on Management of Emergent Digital EcoSystems - MEDES'14. doi:10.1145/2668260.2668286.

[9] Dhanaraj, R. K., Lalitha, K., Anitha, S., Khaitan, S., Gupta, P., & Goyal, M. K. (2021). "Hybrid and dynamic clustering based data aggregation and routing for wireless sensor networks," *Journal of Intelligent & Fuzzy Systems*, 40(6), 10751–10765. IOS Press. doi:10.3233/jifs-201756.

[10] He, C., Fan, X., & Li, Y. (2013). "Toward ubiquitous healthcare services with a novel efficient cloud platform," *IEEE Transactions on Biomedical Engineering*, 60(1), 230–234. doi:10.1109/tbme.2012.2222404.

[11] Liu, Ying, Zhang, Lin, Yang, Yuan, Zhou, Longfei, Ren, Lei, Wang, Fei, Liu, Rong, Pang, Zhibo, Jamal Deen, M., (2019). "A novel cloud-based framework for the elderly healthcare services using digital twin," Healthcare Information Technology for the Extreme and Remote Environments, *IEEE Access*, 35, 49088–49101, ISSN 2169-3536.

[12] Rolim, C. O., Koch, F. L., Westphall, C. B., Werner, J., Fracalossi, A., & Salvador, G. S. (2010). A cloud computing solution for patient's data collection in health care institutions. *2010 Second International Conference on eHealth, Telemedicine, and Social Medicine*. doi:10.1109/etelemed.2010.19.

[13] Shi, Y., Ding, G., Wang, H., Roman, H. E., & Lu, S. (2015). The fog computing service for healthcare. *2015 2nd International Symposium on Future Information and Communication Technologies for Ubiquitous HealthCare (Ubi-HealthTech)*. doi:10.1109/ubi-healthtech.2015.7203325.

[14] Badidi, E., & Moumane, K. (2019). Enhancing the Processing of Healthcare Data Streams using Fog Computing. *2019 IEEE Symposium on Computers and Communications (ISCC)*. doi:10.1109/iscc47284.2019.896973.

[15] Kuo, M. H., Sahama, T., Kushniruk, A. W., Borycki, E. M., & Grunwell, D. K. (2014). "Health big data analytics: Current perspectives, challenges and potential solutions," *International Journal of Big Data Intelligence*, 1(1/2), 114. doi:10.1504/ijbdi.2014.063835.

[16] Xu, E., Mei, J., Li, J., Yu, Y., Huang, S., & Qin, Y. (2019). From EHR data to medication adherence assessment: A case study on type 2 diabetes. *2019 IEEE International Conference on Healthcare Informatics (ICHI)*. doi:10.1109/ichi.2019.8904786.

[17] Sheriff, C. I., Naqishbandi, T., & Geetha, A., Healthcare informatics and analytics framework. *2015 International Conference on Computer Communication and Informatics (ICCCI)*. doi:10.1109/iccci.2015.7218108.

[18] Evans, R. S. (2016). "Electronic health records: Then, now, and in the future," NCBI, PMC, US National Library of Medicine, National Institute of Health.

[19] Chandola, V., Sukumar, S. R., & Schryver, J. C. (2013). Knowledge discovery from massive healthcare claims data. Proceedings of the 19th ACM SIGKDD International Conference on Knowledge Discovery and Data Mining. doi:10.1145/2487575.2488205.

[20] Katuwal, Gajendra J., Pandey, Sandip, Hennessey, Mark, & Lamichhane, Bishal (2018). "Applications of blockchain in healthcare: Current landscape & challenges".

[21] Nagori, M., Patil, A., Deshmukh, S., Vaidya, G., Rahangdale, M., Kulkarni, C., & Kshirsagar, V. (2020). Mutichain enabled EHR management system and predictive analytics. *Smart Trends in Computing and Communications*. Singapore: Springer, pp. 179–187.

[22] Gökalp, Ebru, Gökalp, Mert Onuralp, Çoban, Selin, & Erhan Eren, P. (2018). Analysing opportunities and challenges of integrated blockchain technologies in healthcare. *SIGSAND/PLAIS 2018, LNBIP 333*, pp. 174–183, Springer Nature Switzerland AG.

[23] Wang, Xueyi, Ellul, Joshua, & Azzopardi, George, "Elderly fall detection systems: A literature survey," Frontiers, Robotics and AI (frontiersin.org).

[24] Islam, S. R., Kwak, D., Kabir, M. H., Hossain, M., & Kwak, K.-S. (2015). "The internet of things for health care: A comprehensive survey," *IEEE Access*, 3, 678–708. doi:10.1109/ACCESS.2015.2437951.

[25] Bi, W. L., Hosny, A., Schabath, M.B., Giger, M. L., Birkbak, N. J., Mehrtash, A., Allison, T., Arnaout, O., Abbosh, C., Dunn, I. F., & Mak, R. H. (2019). "Artificial intelligence in cancer imaging: Clinical challenges and applications," *CA: A Cancer Journal for Clinicians*, 69(2), 127–157, March/April, ACS Journals.

[26] Ferdous, M. S., Biswas, K., Chowdhury, M. J. M., Chowdhury, N., & Muthukkumarasamy, V. (2019). "Integrated platforms for blockchain enablement," *Advanced Computing*, 7, 167930–167943, March.

[27] Goel, Uttkarsh, Ruhl, Ron, & Zavarsky, Pavol (2019). Using healthcare authority and patient blockchains to develop a tamper-proof record tracking system. *2019 IEEE 5th Intl Conference on Big Data Security on Cloud (BigDataSecurity), IEEE Intl Conference on High Performance and Smart Computing (HPSC), and IEEE Intl Conference on Intelligent Data and Security (IDS)*.

[28] Dasaklis, T. K., Casino, F., & Patsakis, C. (2018). Blockchain meets smart health: Towards next generation healthcare services. *2018 9th International Conference on Information, Intelligence, Systems and Applications (IISA)*. doi:10.1109/iisa.2018.8633601.

[29] Mettler, M. 2016. Blockchain technology in healthcare: The revolution starts here. *2016 IEEE 18th International Conference on e-Health Networking, Applications and Services, Healthcom 2016*, pp. 16–18.

[30] Azaria, A., Ekblaw, A., Vieira, T., & Lippman, A., (2016). MedRec: Using blockchain for medical data access and permission management. *2016 2nd International Conference on Open and Big Data (OBD)*, Vienna, pp. 25–30, 2016.

[31] Parameswari, C. D., & Mandadi, V. (2020). Healthcare data protection based on blockchain using solidity. *2020 Fourth World Conference on Smart Trends in Systems, Security and Sustainability (WorldS4)*. doi:10.1109/worlds450073.2020.921.

[32] Waves Whitepaper (2018). https://blog:wavesplatform:com/waves-whitepaper-164dd6ca6a23.

[33] Diaz Duffield. Dash. (2018). "A payments-focused cryptocurrency," https://github:com/dashpay/dash/wiki/Whitepaper.

[34] The BitShares Blockchain, 2018. https://github:com/dashpay/dash/wiki/Whitepaper.

[35] Farouk, Ahmed, Alahmadi, Amal, Ghose, Shohini, & Mashatan, Atefeh. (2020). Blockchain platform for industrial healthcare: Vision and future opportunities. *Computer Communications*, Elsevier, pp. 223–235.

[36] Pilkington, M. (2016). Blockchain technology: Principles and applications, in: *Research Handbook on Digital Transformations*, Cheltenham, UK: Edward Elgar Publishing.

[37] Zheng, Z., Xie, S., Dai, H., Chen, X., & Wang, H. (2017). An overview of blockchain technology: Architecture, consensus, and future trends. *2017 IEEE International Congress on Big Data, Big Data Congress, IEEE*, pp. 557–564.

[38] Nakamoto, S. (2019). Bitcoin: A peer-to-peer electronic cash system, Manubot.

[39] Salah, Khaled, Jayaraman, Raja, & Al-Hammadi, Yousof, (2021). Blockchain for healthcare data management: Opportunities, challenges, and future recommendations. *Neural Computing and Applications*, doi:10.1007/s00521-020-05519-w

[40] Ichikawa, D., Kashiyama, M., & Ueno, T. (2017). "Tamper-resistant mobile health using blockchain technology," *JMIR mHealth uHealth*, 5(7, 111–127.

[41] Griggs, K. N., Ossipova, O., Kohlios, C. P., Baccarini, A. N., Howson, E. A., & Hayajneh, T. (2018). "Healthcare blockchain system using smart contracts for secure automated remote patient monitoring," *Journal of Medical Systems*, 42(7), 130.

[42] Tseng, J. H., Liao, Y. C., Chong, B., & Liao, S. W. (2018). "Governance on the drug supply chain via gcoin blockchain," *International Journal of Environmental Research and Public Health*, 15(6), 1055–1071.

[43] Benchoufi, M., Porcher, R., & Ravaud, P. (2017). "Blockchain protocols in clinical trials: Transparency and traceability of consent," *F1000Research*, 6, 66–82.

[44] Shae, Z., & Tsai, J. J. (2017). On the design of a blockchain platform for clinical trial and precision medicine. *2017 IEEE 37th International Conference on Distributed Computing Systems, ICDCS, IEEE*, pp. 1972–1980.

[45] HIMSS. (2013). "Clinical & business intelligence: An analytics executive review," (updated 2013; cited 2013-06-17). Available from: http://himss.files.cmsplus.com/HIMSSorg/Content/files/HIMSS%2CBI%20Analytics%20Exec%20Review_Industry%20Capabilities%20module_2013-02-19_FINAL.pd

[46] Sulkers P. (2011). "Healthcare analytics: A game-changer for North York General Hospital," *Canadian Healthcare Technology*. (updated June/July 2011; 43 cited 2013-06-17) Available from: http://www-03.ibm.com/industries/ca/en/healthcare/documents/NYGH_article_reprint_Cdn_Healthcare_Technology_July%202011.pdf

[47] Sheriff, C. I., Naqishbandi, T., & Geetha, A. (2015). Healthcare informatics and analytics framework. 2015 International Conference on Computer Communication and Informatics (ICCCI). doi:10.1109/iccci.2015.7218108.

[48] Chen, G., & Islam, M. (2019). Big Data Analytics in Healthcare. *2019 2nd International Conference on Safety Produce Informatization (IICSPI)*. doi:10.1109/iicspi48186.2019.9095872.

[49] Kim, I. K., Pervez, Z., Khattak, A. M., & Lee, S. (2010). Chord Based Identity Management for e-Healthcare Cloud Applications. *2010 10th IEEE/IPSJ International Symposium on Applications and the Internet*. doi:10.1109/saint.2010.68.

[50] Hsueh, P.-Y. S., Lin, R. J. R., Hsiao, M. J. H., Zeng, L., Ramakrishnan, S., & Chang, H. (2010). Cloud-based platform for personalization in a wellness management ecosystem: Why, what, and how. *Proceedings of the 6th International ICST Conference on Collaborative Computing: Networking, Applications, Worksharing*. doi:10.4108/icst.collaboratecom.

[51] Al-Jaroodi, Jameela, Mohamed, Nader, & Abukhousa, Eman (2020). "Health 4.0: On the way to realizing the healthcare of the future," *IEEE Access*, 8, 211189–211210.

[52] Yassein, Muneer Bani, Hmeidi, Ismail, Al-Harbi, Marwa, Mrayan, Lina, & Mardini, Wail (2019). IoT based healthcare systems: A Survey. *DATA '19: Proceedings of the Second International Conference on Data Science, E-Learning and Information Systems*, December, Article No.: 30, pp. 1–9. doi:10.1145/3368691.3368721.

[53] Al-Majeed, S. S., Al-Mejibli, I. S., & Karam, J. (2015). Home telehealth by Internet of Things (IoT). *2015 IEEE 28th Canadian Conference on Electrical and Computer Engineering (CCECE)*. doi:10.1109/ccece.2015.7129344.

[54] Ramasamy, M. D., Periasamy, K., Krishnasamy, L., Dhanaraj, R. K., Kadry, S., & Nam, Y. (2021). Multi-disease classification model using strassen's half of threshold (SHoT) training algorithm in healthcare sector. *IEEE Access*, doi:10.1109/ACCESS.2021.3103746.

[55] Larson, E. H., Johnson, K. E., Norris, T. E., Lishner, D. M., Rosenblatt, R. A., & Hart, L. G. (2003). *State of the Health Workforce in Rural America: Profiles and Comparisons*. Seattle: WWAMI Rural Health Research Center, University of Washington.

[56] Mohamed, Walaa, & Abdellatif, Mohammad M. (2019). Telemedicine: An IoT application for healthcare systems. *ICSIE '19: Proceedings of the 2019 8th International Conference on Software and Information Engineering*, April, pp. 173–177, doi:10.1145/3328833.3328881.

[57] Merkel, S., & Enste, P. (2015). Barriers to the diffusion of telecare and telehealth in the EU: A literature review. *IET International Conference on Technologies for Active and Assisted Living (TechAAL)*. doi:10.1049/ic.2015.0128.

[58] mHealth: New horizons for health through mobile technologies: Second global survey on eHealth. Global observatory for eHealth series, 3. WHO Press, Geneva.

[59] Sariyer, Görkem, & Ataman, Mustafa Gokalp (2018). "Utilizing mHealth Applications in Emergency Medical Services of Turkey". 2018, Current and Emerging mHealth Technologies, Springer, Current and Emerging mHealth Technologies:Adoption, Implementation, and Use, Book Chapter.

[60] Nurmatov, U. B., Lee, S. H., Nwaru, B. I., Mukherjee, M., Grant, L., & Pagliari, C. (2014). "The effectiveness of mHealth interventions for maternal, newborn and child health in low- and middle-income countries: Protocol for a systematic review and meta-analysis," *Journal of Global Health*, 4(1), 010407.

[61] Labrique A. (2013). "12 common applications and a visual framework," *Global Health: Science and Practice*, 1, 1–12.

[62] Chehri, A., Mouftah, H., & Jeon, G. (2010). A smart network architecture for e-health applications. *Intelligent Interactive Multimedia Systems and Services*. Berlin, Germany: Springer, pp. 157–166.

[63] Wamba, S. F., Anand, A., & Carter, L. (2013). "A literature review of RFIDenabled healthcare applications and issues," *International Journal of Information Management*, 33(5), 875–891.

[64] Islam, S. M. R., Kwak, D., Kabir, M. H., Hossain, M., & Kwak, K.-S. (2015). "The Internet of Things for health care: A comprehensive survey," *IEEE Access*, 3, 678–708.

[65] Verma, P. K., Verma, R., Prakash, A., Agrawal, A., Naik, K., Tripathi, R., Alsabaan, M., Khalifa, T., Abdelkader, T., & Abogharaf, A., (2016). "Machine-to-machine (M2M) communications: A survey," *The Journal of Network and Computer Applications*, 66, 83–105.

[66] Sethi, P., & Sarangi, S. R. (2017). Internet of Things: Architectures, protocols, and applications. *Journal of Electrical and Computer Engineering*, pp. 1–25, Jan. 2017.

[67] Acampora, G., Cook, D. J., Rashidi, P., & Vasilakos, A. V. (2013). "A survey on ambient intelligence in healthcare," *Proceedings of the IEEE*, 101(12), 2470–2494.

[68] Spanakis, E., Sakkalis, V., Marias, K., & Tsiknakis, M. "Connection between biomedical telemetry and telemedicine," in *Handbook of Biomedical Telemetry*. Hoboken, NJ, USA: Wiley, 2014, pp. 419–444.

[69] Chacko, Anil, & Hayajneh, Thaier, "Security and Privacy Issues with IoT in Healthcare," 2018, EAI Endorsed Transactions on Pervasive Health and Technology.

[70] Kaur, M. J., & Mishra, V. P. (2018). Analysis of big data cloud computing environment on healthcare organizations by implementing hadoop clusters. *2018 Fifth HCT Information Technology Trends (ITT)*. doi:10.1109/ctit.2018.8649546.

[71] Elola, A., Aramendi, E., Irusta, U., Picón, A., Alonso, E., Owens, P., & Idris, A. (2019). "Deep neural networks for ECG-based pulse detection during out-of-hospital cardiac arrest," *Entropy*, 21(3), 305.

[72] Miikkulainen, R., Liang, J., Meyerson, E., Rawal, A., Fink, D., Francon, O., & Hodjat, B. (2019). Evolving deep neural networks, in: *Artificial Intelligence in the Age of Neural Networks and Brain Computing*, Cambridge, Massachusetts: Academic Press, pp. 293–312.

[73] Stephenson, N., Shane, E., Chase, J., Rowland, J., Ries, D., Justice, N., & Cao, R. (2019). "Survey of machine learning techniques in drug discovery," *Current Drug Metabolism*, 20(3), 185–193.

[74] Wong, K. K., Rostomily, R., & Wong, S. T. (2019). "Prognostic gene discovery in glioblastoma patients using deep learning," *Cancers*, 11(1), 53.

[75] Klein, O., Kanter, F., Kulbe, H., Jank, P., Denkert, C., Nebrich, G., & Darb-Esfahani, S. (2019). "MALDI-imaging for classification of epithelial ovarian cancer histotypes from a tissue microarray using machine learning methods," *PROTEOMICS – Clinical Applications*, 13(1), 170018.

[76] Yu, L., Chen, H., Qin, J., & Heng, P.-A. (2017). "Automated melanoma recognition in dermoscopy images via very deep residual networks," *IEEE Transactions on Medical Imaging*, 36(4), 994–1004.

[77] Liu, X., Chen, Y., Bae, J., Li, H., Johnston, J., & Sanger, T. (2019). Predicting heart failure readmission from clinical notes using deep learning. *2019 IEEE International Conference on Bioinformatics and Biomedicine (BIBM)*. doi:10.1109/bibm47256.2019.8983095.

[78] Ronneberger, O., Fischer, P., & Brox, T. (2015). U-net: Convolutional networks for biomedical image segmentation. Proc. Medical Image Comput. Comp.-Assis. Interv. – MICCAI, Navab, N., Hornegger, J., Wells, W., Frangi, A. eds. *Lecture Notes in Computer Science, vol. 9351*, Cham: Springer.

[79] Zhang, Xia, & Sun, Yingming (2018). Breast cancer risk prediction model based on C5.0 algorithm for postmenopausal women. *International Conference on Security, Pattern Analysis, and Cybernetics (SPAC)*, Jinana, China: IEEE.

[80] McKinney, S. M., Sieniek, M., Godbole, V., Godwin, J., Antropova, N., Ashrafian, H., Back, T., Chesus, M., Corrado, G. S., Darzi, A., & Etemadi, M. (2020). "International evaluation of an AI system for breast cancer screening," *Nature*, 577, 89–94.

[81] Dou, Q., Chen, H., Yu, L., Zhao, L., Qin, J., Wang, D., Mok, V. C., Shi, L., & Heng, P. A. (2016). "Automatic detection of cerebral microbleeds from MR images via 3D convolutional neural networks," *IEEE Transactions on Medical Imaging.*, 35(5), 1182–1195.

[82] Kamnitsas, K., Ledig, C., Newcombe, V. F., Simpson, J. P., Kane, A. D., Menon, D. K., Rueckert, D., & Glocker, B. (2017). "Efficient multi-scale 3D CNN with fully connected CRF for accurate brain lesion segmentation," *Medical Image Analysis*, 36, 61–78.

[83] Shi, Y., Ding, G., Wang, H., Roman, H. E., & Lu, S. (2015). The fog computing service for healthcare. *2015 2nd International Symposium on Future Information and Communication Technologies for Ubiquitous HealthCare (Ubi-HealthTech)*. doi:10.1109/ubi-healthtech.2015.7203325.

[84] Aazam, M., Hung, P., & Huh, E. (2014). Smart gateway based communication for cloud ofthings [C]. IEEE, 1–6.

[85] Fog Computing—clearly the way forward for IoT [Online]. Available: http://blog.opengear.com/fog-computing-clearly-the-way-forward-for-iot.

[86] Biswas, S., & Misra, S., "Designing of a prototype of e-health monitoring system," pp. 267–272.

[87] Rodrigues, J. G. P., Kaiseler, M., Aguiar, A., Cunha, J. P. S., & Barros, J. (2015). "A mobile sensing approach to stress detection and memory activation for public bus drivers," *IEEE Transactions on Intelligent Transportation Systems*,6, 3294–3303.

[88] Nowshin, N., Rashid, M., & Akhtar, T. (2019). "Infrared sensor controlled wheel chair for physically disabled people," pp. 847–855.

[89] Mulfari, D., Celesti, A., Fazio, M., & Villari, M. (2015). "Human-computer interface based on IoT embedded systems for users with disabilities," pp. 376–383.

[90] Bhatnagar, V., Chandra, R., & Jain, V. (2019). *IoT Based Alert System for Visually Impaired*, Vol. 1, Springer Singapore, pp. 216–223.

[91] Pitarma, R. (2018). "IAQ evaluation using an IoT CO 2 monitoring system for enhanced living environment," pp. 1169–1177.

[92] Abdelgawad, A., Yelamarthi, K., & Khattab, A. (2016). "IoT-based health monitoring system for active and assisted living," *Goodtechs*, 1, 1–22.

[93] Gondalia, A., Dixit, D., Parashar, S., & Raghava, V. (2018). "Science direct science direct IoT-based healthcare monitoring system for war soldiers using machine learning," *Procedia Computer Science*, 133, 1005–1013.

[94] Umasankar, Y., Jalal, A. H., Gonzalez, P. J., Chowdhury, M., Bhansali, S., & States, U. (2016). "Wearable alcohol monitoring device with auto-calibration ability for high chemical specificity", *2016 IEEE 13th International Conference on Wearable and Implantable Body Sensor Networks (BSN)*, pp. 353–358.

[95] Saravanan, M., & Shubha, R. (2018). "Non-invasive analytics based smart system for diabetes monitoring," *Internet of Things (IoT) Technologies for HealthCare Lecture Notes of the Institute for Computer Sciences, Social Informatics and Telecommunications Engineering*, 1, 88–98, doi: 10.1007/978-3-319-76213-5_13.

[96] Duffuaa, S., Al Ghamdi, A., & Amer, A. (2002). Quality function deployment in maintenance work planning process. In: *6th Saudi Conference*. Vol. 4. Dhahran, Kindom of Saudi Arabia: KFUPM, pp. 503–5012.

[97] Avancha, S., Baxi, A., & Kotz, D. (2012). "Privacy in mobile technology for personal healthcare," *ACM Computing Surveys (CSUR)*, 45(1), 3.

[98] Shahid, A. R., Jeukeng, L., Zeng, W., Pissinou, N., Iyengar, S., Sahni, S., & Varela-Conover, M., (2017). Ppvc: Privacy preserving voronoi cell for location-based services. *2017 International Conference on Computing, Networking and Communications (ICNC)*. IEEE, pp. 351–355.

[99] Yüksel, B., Küpçü, A., & Özkasap, Ö. (2017). "Research issues for privacy and security of electronic health services," *Future Generation Computer Systems*, 68, 1–13.

3

Harnessing Big Data and Artificial Intelligence for Data Acquisition, Storage, and Retrieval of Healthcare Informatics in Precision Medicine

S. Mohana Saranya
Kongu Engineering College, Erode, India

K. Tamilselvi
Chennai Institute of Technology, Chennai, India

S. Mohanapriya
Kongu Engineering College, Erode, India

CONTENTS

DOI: 10.1201/9781003217435-3

3.1 Introduction

The key to greater organization and new advances is the useful information extracted from the bulk of data. We can better organize ourselves to offer the greatest results if we have more information. As a result, data collecting is an essential component of any company. We may also utilize this information to forecast present trends in specific metrics as well as future events. As we become more conscious of this, we have begun to produce and collect more data on nearly everything by using technological advancements. Technological advancements have aided us in generating an increasing amount of data to the point where it is now unmanageable with currently available technology. Big Data is the term used to represent data that is huge, enormous, and not able to process with a single machine. It has gained much importance because of the great potential that is hidden inside it. Many companies are generating, storing, and analyzing big data in order to identify the hidden value present in the data. Many innovative techniques are needed to structure these data so that information needed can be easily fetched.

One such unique societal requirement is healthcare. Hospital records, patient medical records, medical examination results, and internet of things devices are all examples of big data sources in the healthcare industry. Biomedical research also produces a large amount of big data that are relevant to public health. To get useful information from these data, it must be properly managed and analyzed. Each phase of processing large data comes with its own set of obstacles that can only be overcome by adopting high-end computing solutions for big data analysis. As a result, healthcare providers must be fully equipped with sufficient infrastructure to systematically create and analyze big data in order to deliver relevant solutions for improving public health. Big data that is managed, analyzed, and interpreted effectively can change the game by opening new doors for modern healthcare. That is why a variety of companies, including the healthcare industry, are working hard to turn this potential into better services and financial benefits. Modern healthcare organizations may be able to transform medical therapies and personalized medicine with strong integration of biological and healthcare data [1].

Biomedical informatics is a branch of study that involves the use of mathematics, computer-assisted methods, technologies, algorithms, and software tools to record, store, analyze, compile, simulate, and model data from life sciences and biology. Advances in bioinformatics allow us to have supercomputers with a reduced cost which can be used to improve efficiency and novel discovery. Bioinformatics can be viewed as the combination

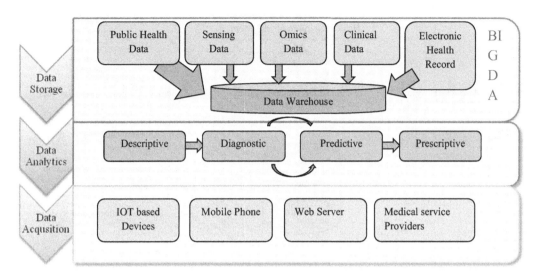

FIGURE 3.1
Healthcare architecture.

of biology and computers. One of the problems faced by humans nowadays is the lack of a personalized health system because every human possesses a unique genome and proteome. Therefore, Bioinformatics is needed in order to know the complexity of the disease and its mechanism. Figure 3.1 shows the different underlying processes in acquiring, storing, and information retrieval process of health care big data.

3.2 Biomedical Informatics and Precision Medicine: Healthcare 4.0

More amount of data are kept on accumulated in the health sector from various sources like patients information, financial details, data from medical devices, administration side data, finance-related data, and any other health data. So there is a big need in creating a holistic way to analyze and store those data in real time as well as in prior. Converting the above-mentioned data to a form such as those suitable for data analytics should be addressed. Since we get data from different devices and in different forms as given in Figure 3.2, more specialized solutions with nominal cost factors should be developed. Currently, there is no centered electronic health record system.

Existing data integration mechanisms include modifications of typical data warehouse solutions from healthcare solution providers like Oracle, Teradata, i2b2, and IBM. The i2b2 develops a data warehouse that allows the integration of data from varied clinical departments to assist the process of identifying patient details.

Structured data from disease diagnosis and lab results are transferred to standardized coding systems in this way. Unstructured data, on the other hand, are not further annotated with semantic information. The i2b2 hive has various other modules in addition to its basic capability of identifying patient cohorts. Modules to generate and use extra meanings are provided in addition to particular modules for data input, export, and visualization operations. The natural language processing (NLP) technology allows you to extort conception from non-understandable format and link them to organized information. Data

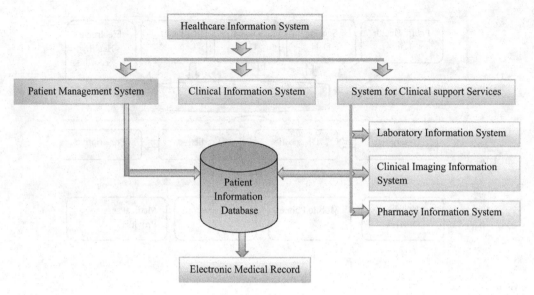

FIGURE 3.2
Clinical information system.

can now be shared via HL7-compliant exchange formats. However, due to security reasons, health data are frequently not shared openly. Diagnoses, treatments, lab reports, prescription, and other information are generally presented in an organized style, although it is not received uniformly.

Furthermore, various medical departments frequently employ customized report formats without providing common meanings. Both circumstances cause problems with data collection and subsequent integration. Protocols for defining advanced meta-information in unstructured material such as words and photos are only partially collected. The Digital Imaging and Communications in Medicine standard for extracting data from the image is available. However, there is no universal standard for extracting meta-information from other clinical data. Initiatives like the RSNA's structured reporting program or semantic annotations utilizing standardized vocabularies are the first steps toward changing this scenario.

Each one provides the data in its own format. This makes it difficult to collect and integrate longitudinal health data. Easy-to-use structured reporting tools are needed that do not add to physicians' workloads. Above all, physicians should be aided by relevant context information.

Because structured reporting tools are designed to be simple to use, physicians may accept them, resulting in the majority of clinical documentation being done in a semi-structured format and an increase in the quality and quantity of semantic annotations. Big data storage, processing, access, and protection must be governed on various levels from an organizational standpoint: institutional, regional, national, and international. Who authorizes which processes, who adjusts processes, and who implements process changes must all be defined.

Integrating the healthcare business offers secure, plug-and-play access to health data whenever and wherever it is required. Clinical trials, clinical studies, population and illness data, and other pharmaceutical and R&D data are often controlled by pharmaceutical corporations, research centers, or the government. Currently, a significant amount of human labor is required to collect all of the data sets needed to undertake medical research and associated examination. The labor-intensive effort required to collect the information is considerable.

3.3 Data Acquisition system

In recent times, the amount of data that are being produced in the real world goes on increasing exponentially, the aforementioned data should be obtained and processed for valuable applications. Measuring the physical activities and altering them into numbers for calculations is termed data acquisition [2]. When it comes to industry, more data means more opportunities, but industries that want to make use of data first need to get a hold of it through proper data acquisition framework.

The Acquisition of Data in the big data value chain process is shown in Figure 3.3. The following DA process steps convert the data into a meaningful one.

The main aspect of information gathering lies in the process of its acquisition from various information sources and storing in data warehouses that are scalable and that can handle extremely huge volumes of multifaceted data.

Newer improvements in technology created cost low, energy–rich, and feature improved devices. All of these may now detect and process data more precisely and pass it to the neighbor node. Sensors are also crucial in electronic healthcare systems that perform constant patient monitoring. Because data are created by sensor nodes, an effective Electronic Healthcare system requires dependable, secure, and attack-resistant data collecting and transmission [2].

The foundation of data acquisition across the various architectures for big data processing pays a way to store the multinomial data. Three essential components are required to attain this goal:

1. Protocols to collect data from disseminated data sources like unstructured, semi-structured, and structured.

2. Frameworks for collecting data from a variety of dispersed sources via various methods.

3. Technologies that enable the frameworks to save the data they retrieve in a persistent format.

Figure 3.4 depicts the aforementioned issues in a presentable manner [3].

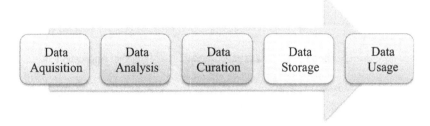

FIGURE 3.3
Data acquisition in the bigdata value chain.

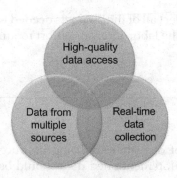

FIGURE 3.4
Data acquisition challenges.

3.3.1 Protocols of Data Acquisition System

The majorly used open data acquisition protocols are shown here.

3.3.1.1 Advanced Message Queuing Protocol

Advanced Message Queuing Protocol (AMQP) that allows compliant clients and message middleware servers to communicate in a fully functional manner. AMQP is a binary wire protocol that was created to allow vendors and platforms to communicate with one another. No matter whatever AMQP client you use to send or receive messages, AMQP provides a uniform messaging protocol that works across all platforms. The architecture of AMQP is shown in Figure 3.5.

AMQP is a well-known protocol for message processing in businesses that cannot own their own protocols due to its widespread adoption and high flexibility. It also helps in creating services around data streams with the impending data-as-a-service industry. RabbitMQ is one of the most widely used AMQP brokers, because of the fact that it supports a variety of messaging protocols, including JMS.

In the discipline of bioinformatics, the database must be obtained from the server using the patient's name. There is a need for information. The interaction between the client and the server necessitates the establishment of a communication link between the two ends. The message must be established according to a set of rules. Message-oriented middleware (MOM) solutions like publishing or subscribing queues are not put into practice as fundamental components. Users themselves are given the opportunity to build these entities by delivering simplified AMQ entities. This architecture combines message patterns like

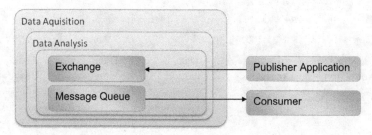

FIGURE 3.5
AMQP architecture.

publish, subscriptions, queues, transactions, and streaming data, as well as adding capabilities like content-based routing that is easy to grow.

The AMQP community is made out of nodes linked through hyperlinks known as entity objects, which might be responsible for securely storing messages dispatched through nodes, termination nodes, or ahead nodes. The AMQP delivery specification specifies a peer-to-peer protocol for speaking with different AMQP community nodes. This segment of the specification is simply worried about how messages are explicitly dispatched from one node to a different, now no longer with the underlying operations of any shape of node [4].

3.3.1.2 Java Message Service

Java Message Service (JMS) is a Java-based API for Message Oriented Middleware that is used to transmit information for asynchronous communication among two programs or in a disseminated system. Most MOM vendors support JMS, which is independent of the platform. JMS can transmit information from a JMS consumer to others with the assistance of messaging services. Messages have two parts such as a header and message content. The header has the message's routing and metadata information. The application's data or payload is carried in the message body [5].

3.3.2 Open Source Data Acquisition Frameworks

Data collection frameworks and technologies have highly specialized features and perfect applications, and it is critical to clarify your overall goals before committing to any of them. Some of the most extensively used frameworks and technologies for data collection are as follows:

3.3.2.1 Storm

Storm is an open-source framework for performing reliable, disseminated, and real-time processing on data streams. It may be used in a variety of information collecting situation like stream processing and distributed RPC for solving heavy functions on the go, and also, it supports a variety of programming languages and storage services. It is used by a variety of large systems including Yahoo, Spotify, Wego, and Twitter.

3.3.2.2 Simply Scalable Streaming System (S4)

S4, a popular platform for designing framework, analyzes data streams launched by Yahoo. It is made to run on low-cost hardware and avoid input–output bottlenecks by using an efficient memory strategy. S4 is a decentralized, symmetric, and pluggable architecture with a simple interface for processing data streams. Table 3.1 shows the Comparison on Different Data Acquisition Frameworks.

3.3.2.3 Kafka

Kafka enables high-throughput persistent messaging. Its capacity to partition real-time use by a group of workstations attempts to combine offline and online processing, and it is developed in such a way that network overhead and sequential disc operations are minimized. It was created on LinkedIn to keep track of the massive amount of activity events generated by the site.

TABLE 3.1

Comparison on Different Data Acquisition Frameworks

Framework	Type	Stream Source	Owner	Delay	Stream Primitive
Storm	Streaming	Spouts	Twitter	Sub-seconds	Tuples
S4	Streaming	Networks	Yahoo	Few seconds	Events
Hadoop	Batch	HDFS	Yahoo	Minutes or more	Key value
Spark	Batch/Streaming	HDFS	Berkley AMPLay	Few seconds	DStream
Flink	Batch/Streaming	KAFKA	Apache	Few seconds	Key value

3.3.2.4 Flume

Flume is a service that collects, aggregates, and moves massive amounts of log data from a variety of sources to centralized data storage in a distributed, reliable, and available manner. Its architecture is based on streaming data flows, making it simple and adaptable while also being resilient and fault-tolerant, thanks to adjustable reliability methods and numerous failover and recovery techniques. Reliability, scalability, management, and extensibility were all significant considerations in the development of Flume. Figure 3.6 shows the key goals of this framework.

3.3.2.5 Hadoop

Hadoop is an open-source project with the goal of developing a framework for scalable, distributed computing on large data sets using commodity hardware clusters. It is used and promoted by a number of well-known organizations, including Facebook, AOL, Baidu, IBM, Imageshack, and Yahoo.

3.3.2.6 Flink

Flink uses both batch and steam processing techniques with a delay of only a few seconds. It streams data in a key-value pair fashion. The famous organizations which use Flink are Walmart, Dell, and GameStop.

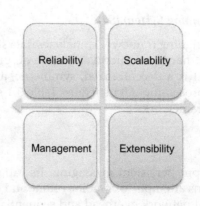

FIGURE 3.6
Key goals of Flume.

3.4 Storage of Data

3.4.1 Bigdata in Biomedical Informatics

Biomedical informatics is a scientific discipline involving mathematics, computer-aided methods, technologies, algorithms, and software tools used to capture, store, analyze, compile, simulate, and model information from life science and biological data. In order to analyze patient data, various data manipulation tools have been provided by big data. Big data in biomedical informatics is used for giving systematic tools for manipulating data and analyzing it. Bioinformatics currently makes use Hadoop and MapReduce for Big Data Analytics. Figure 3.7 shows the various steps in Bigdata Analytics from data collection to output.

3.4.2 Intelligent Medical Big Data System with Hadoop and Blockchain

Medical data service advancement is a necessary part of medical field. With the rapid growth of computer-based technologies, information-based platforms are needed by many medical institutes. Information-based platform helps to improve the service level of hospitals and also workload of hospitals gets reduced. The medical information framework plays a critical part and provides a good solution for the treatment of critical diseases, leveraging medical resources and improving awareness among people on health care. Information technology greatly reduces doctor work, thereby allowing doctors to spend more time seeing patients.

In order to provide a very good intelligent medical system, this paper [6] proposed a secure medical big data ecosystem. The proposed medical ecosystem has been built on top of the Hadoop platform. The flexibility provided by the Hadoop platform like very large data storage and scalability with an increase in data is used in this work which greatly reduces the cost of the system. By utilizing the flexibility given by the Hadoop platform, an efficient medical information system has been constructed. Storage using this Hadoop platform greatly reduces the inconvenience in storage and system upgrades. Mobile applications enable patients and doctors to be connected at any time from anywhere, thereby increasing medical digitalization. Even though the health data tend to increase, the problem of processing a large amount of data and concurrent access is solved using Hadoop, thereby ensuring robustness. Blockchain is used to ensure the security of the backup information.

3.4.2.1 Hadoop Architecture

A distributed system framework called Hadoop was developed by Apache Foundation. Users can create distributed programs using this Hadoop without worrying about the background architecture. Master–slave architecture is followed in Hadoop.

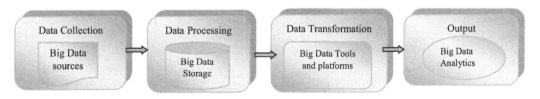

FIGURE 3.7
Big data analytics.

3.4.2.2 Hadoop Distributed File System

A distributed file system followed in Hadoop is called Hadoop Distributed File System (HDFS). HDFS has salient features like fault tolerance. HDFS is the storage part of Hadoop. The massive amount of data to be accessed by the application are stored in this HDFS part of Hadoop.

Namenode and Datanode are the two daemons used in HDFS. Namenode is the master node and Datanodes are the slave nodes. The data are stored only in the Datanodes and Namenode acts as controlling all the Datanodes. The file gets split into blocks and gets accommodated in the slave nodes. The data stored in the Data nodes are replicated so that when one machine goes down it can be fetched from other machines also. Namenode maintains the information of the HDFS filesystem in an FSimage file. There is another node in the Hadoop cluster called Secondary Namenode which acts as a helper to the Primary Namenode by merging FSimage and editing log files periodically. The architecture of HDFS is shown in Figure 3.8.

3.4.2.3 Apache HBase

Apache Hbase is the database management system that is present above HDFS [7]. Hbase uses the key/value data for performing read/write operations on HDFS. Hbase comprises three components: HBase Region Server, HMaster Server, and Zookeeper. HMaster Server is present in the Master node and is responsible for managing and monitoring HBase Region Server. It also performs operations that are related to table schema. HBase region servers are present in the slave nodes and are responsible for managing and executing

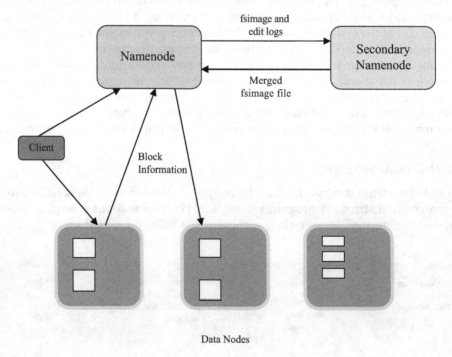

Data Nodes

FIGURE 3.8
Architecture of HDFS.

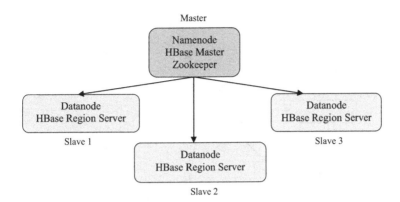

FIGURE 3.9
Components of Apache Hbase.

operations on HBase tables. The final component Zookeeper is responsible for coordinating the Hbase. The components of Apache Hbase are shown in Figure 3.9.

3.4.3 Cloud Computing in Healthcare

According to research, lack of communication and limited access to patient data leads to many medical errors. Cloud computing [8] can be viewed as improving the performance of healthcare industry and reducing medical errors. Cloud computing also provides benefits like increased service delivery, return on investment, and medical research. Using cloud computing data can be transferred across systems. It allows doctors' references, electronic health records, and prescriptions to be shared across multiple systems. With the help of cloud computing, patient data have been shared which allow doctors, hospitals, and pharmaceutical businesses to provide an efficient and quality service. Cloud computing is a cost-effective solution for storing data in the Healthcare industry. Since cloud computing takes care of responsibilities like security, replication, and maintenance, there is no need to invest in expensive hardware and software for digitizing the medical field. Various cloud platforms like "Google Cloud," "Amazon Web Service," "Microsoft Azure," "Oracle cloud," and "vmware" are used nowadays for efficient storage of data. The various cloud platforms used for data storage are shown in Figure 3.10.

Generally, the responsibility of the healthcare provider is to maintain the medical data of patients in the form of Electronic Medical Records (EMRs). Electronic Health Records (EHRs) are developed in such a way that allows the patient's data to be available to multiple healthcare providers. Technology has led to the development of Personal Health Records (PHRs) which is created with the help of sensors such as bracelets to measure heartbeat during workouts, or self-testing device for glucose. In Personal Health Records (PHRs), patients are responsible for data collection and monitoring of their health using smartphones or wearable devices. Figure 3.11 shows how the cloud is useful for managing and sharing healthcare data among providers.

3.4.4 IoT Applications for Healthcare

Remote monitoring in the healthcare industry has been made possible with the help of Internet of Things (IoT) enabled devices. With the help of IoT devices, interactions with

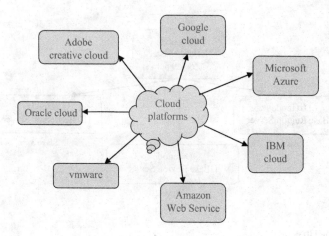

FIGURE 3.10
Various cloud platforms.

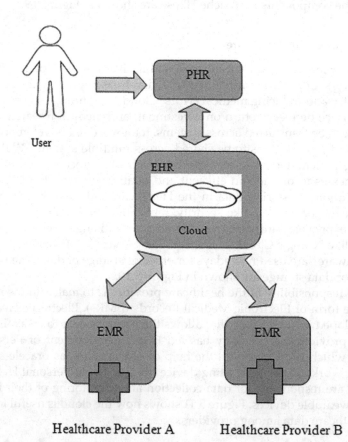

FIGURE 3.11
Cloud-based EMR/EHR/PHR ecosystem.

doctors have been made easier and efficient, and it also improves patient satisfaction. It also increases the monitoring of patients from their place itself, thereby reducing hospital visits. Healthcare costs have been reduced drastically with the help of IoT devices, thereby improving treatment outcomes.

IoT devices have been revolutionizing the healthcare society by reducing the space between patients and doctors and providing a good healthcare solution. With the help of IoT devices, doctors, patients, hospitals, families, and insurance companies get benefited.

The major advantages of IoT in healthcare include the following:

a. cost reduction;
b. improvement in treatment;
c. faster disease diagnosing;
d. earlier treatment of disease;
e. management of drugs and equipment; and
f. error reduction.

3.4.5 Integration of Cloud and IoT

Cloud computing along with IoT [9] provides huge benefits to the healthcare industry. Sensor devices and RFID generate a large amount of data. Processing and storing that large amount of data becomes difficult at sensor nodes. To handle this problem, cloud and IoT has been combined called cloud IoT to handle and store the ever-increasing data. Cloud processing involves three elements: Data storage, Processing on data, and Data analysis. Cloud computing provides a good platform for storing medical data which will be used by doctors for diagnosis.

Figure 3.12 shows the steps from data acquisition using IoT devices to the storage of data using cloud platforms.

3.4.6 Enabling Security for Cloud data

3.4.6.1 Blockchain

Blockchain is a very useful one for creating a reliable platform. Blockchain provides a greater degree of security for the data stored in the database. Using this Blockchain damage to the database from attackers can be prevented. Due to its strengths, it is been adapted in many areas like Finance, Healthcare, and Smart cities.

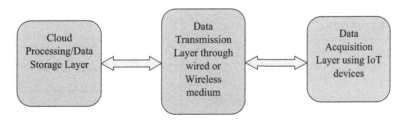

FIGURE 3.12
Integration of IoT and cloud for smart healthcare.

3.4.6.2 Integration of Cloud and Blockchain

Cloud computing has been used in many fields because of its efficiency and availability. Still, cloud computing faces some security issues like confidentiality, authentication, integrity, and access control. To address these security issues in cloud, Blockchain technology is used along with the cloud. Blockchain technology combined with the cloud is used to improve security, service availability, and management of cloud data. Figure 3.13 shows the benefits of having Blockchain in Cloud.

3.4.6.3 Integration of Cloud and Blockchain in Healthcare

Cloud computing used for the storage of data focuses on parallel processing and is distributed in nature. Though some sort of security measures is provided by the cloud architecture, still there are some pitfalls that need to be addressed. These kinds of security measures have been needed for the healthcare data that are stored in the cloud. To address this, Blockchain has been introduced into cloud for applications like healthcare since they are highly subject to security violations. In this paper [10], a survey on the use of Blockchain technology in cloud storage for the security of medical data has been proposed. In recent years, use of Blockchain technology for medical data has been increasing. Blockchain is used to ensure that the data should be reliable, must be verifiable, and must not tampered. This work uses Blockchain technology for creating EMR/EHR/PHR system. In this work, whenever new data are created for a patient, a new block is created and given to all in the network. After approval, the new block will be inserted into the chain. Figure 3.14 shows the EMR/EHR/PHR ecosystem based on Blockchain.

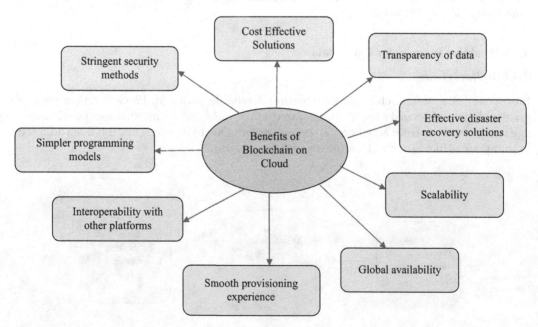

FIGURE 3.13
Benefits of Blockchain in Cloud.

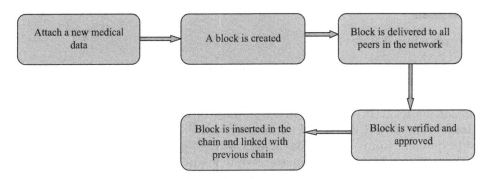

FIGURE 3.14
Blockchain-based EMR/EHR/PHR ecosystem.

3.4.6.4 Fog Computing in Health Sector

Fog computing is used for the efficient storage of data, computation, and networking services between IoT devices and cloud data centers. Figure 3.15 shows the architecture of fog computing where Fog is used between cloud and IoT devices.

Advantages of Fog Computing are as follows:

1. In Fog Computing, all the functionalities are kept nearer to end devices. This makes processing faster because it is done at the place where data are created.
2. Fog improves the efficiency of the system and is used to increase the security of the system.
3. Fog computing plays a major role where a fast and large amount of processing is required.

IoT devices can be used in the health sector for collecting patient data. Periodically IoT devices collect patients' health information and it gets stored in the cloud. Storing medical data in a cloud environment is prone to various types of attacks. Existing systems used RSA and BLS signatures to provide security to the data. However, size of RSA and BLS signatures is very large which increases computation overhead. To overcome this issue, in this work [11], a fog-centric auditing scheme is proposed. Fog nodes are used for performing integrity verification with minimum overhead.

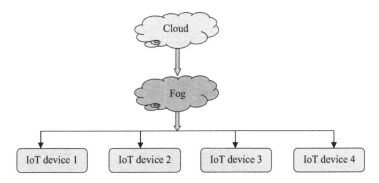

FIGURE 3.15
Fog computing architecture.

3.5 Information Retrieval

Healthcare data analytics mainly focuses on information mining and analysis from patient health reports [12]. To accompany data analytics, information should be retrieved efficiently from diverse resources in different patterns. The most common technique used is Information Retrieval (IR) or search. IR concentrates on many aspects like data acquisition, organization, and knowledge-based information search. The retrieval of information may consist of different forms of data like images, videos, genomic structures, raw text, and so on. The overview of the IR system is shown in Figure 3.16 which consists of the search engine with indexing and retrieval. The brain of the IR process is indexing by contents and retrieval by queries. The sequence consists of posing a query to the IR system to find the contents to meet the query requests. The process of assigning metadata for the contents is given by indexing and retrieval of the user's expected contents [13].

IR is mostly focused on knowledge-based information based on primary sources like books, journals, and other resources. The secondary resources are based on a synthesis of primary resources like opinion mining. Indexing can be manual or automated with annotated contents and bibliographic databases are manually indexed. Automated indexing is done by word mining with expert systems. Word indexing is the common method for automated indexing by defining all the sequences of alphanumeric characters as words. The stop words are removed as they occur with high frequency and low value in searching. Stemming is done for the conflation of words to the common form to index the word by stem form. The query processing will be efficient with stop word removal and stemming with reduced indexing file size. The Inverse Document Frequency (IDF) algorithm used with weighting term frequency (TF) and IDF. The IDF algorithm is defined once for each term by the ratio of a total number of documents in the database to the number of documents with the given term. It is inversely proportional to the frequency of terms in the entire database. The IDF is defined as shown in Equation (3.1).

$$\text{IDF}(\text{term}) = log \frac{\text{number of documents in database}}{\text{number of documents with term}} + 1 \tag{3.1}$$

The term frequency TF provides the measure of frequency of the term in the given document and it is assigned to each term in the document as represented in Equation (3.2).

$$\text{TF}(\text{term}, \text{document}) = \text{frequency of term in the document} \tag{3.2}$$

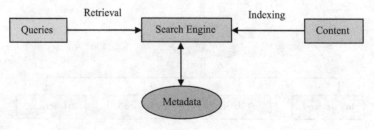

FIGURE 3.16
Overview of IR system.

The weight of the indexing term in the given document is given by Equation (3.3) with a combination of terms TF and IDF.

$$\text{Weight}(\text{term}, \text{document}) = \text{TF}(\text{term}, \text{document}) * \text{IDF}(\text{term}) \tag{3.3}$$

Another statistical method based on the Poisson distribution for weighting approach is BM25 weighting. The mean average precision based on BM25TF is given by Equation (3.4). The frequency of the term is f_{td} with variables k_1 and b that are parameters based on the collection of document features. The typical value of the parameters is in the range of [1, 2] for k_1 and [0.6, 0.75] for b. The notation of BM25TF is given by equation (4) and BM25IDF by equation (3.5) with a total number of documents given by t_d.

$$\text{BM25TF} = \frac{(f_{td})(k_1 + 1)}{k_1(1 - b) + k_1 b \dfrac{\text{length of document}}{\text{average document length}} + f_{td}} \tag{3.4}$$

$$\text{BM25IDF} = \log \frac{t_d - \text{number of document with terms} + 0.5}{\text{number of documents with term} + 0.5} \tag{3.5}$$

Another technique is link-based for precomputing metadata that provides the weight of the page based on its usage on other pages. It is a Page Ranking algorithm that gives more weightage to the relevant pages with a high density of contents. The retrieval process is also dependent on how the contents are being matched and it is segregated into two types: Exact-Match retrieval and Partial-Match retrieval. The precise control over the retrieval of the relevant contents and implemented using Boolean logics. The partial-matching technique involves page ranking or document ranking with TF and IDF of terms in the document. Based on the correlation with the query request, documents with high query terms are ranked higher and can be concluded that the document with more query terms is the most relevant. This relevance ranking is based on words, and its statistical properties provide a more efficient retrieval of information. Based on above-mentioned discussion, the term will be given a weight based on the query and also based on documents. Consider the weight of the term with respect to query W_q and weight related to document as W_d and the document weight is given as shown in Equation (3.6).

$$\text{Document weight} = \sum_{query\,terms} W_q{}^* W_d \tag{3.6}$$

The main drawback of the TF-IDF method is that when the number of words in the documents increases, the weight accumulation will be more rather than its relevance. To overcome this, weights can be normalized. Another approach in partial matching retrieval is relevance feedback that permits the addition of new documents to the previous output with reweighting of the documents retrieved earlier. The advanced approach is query expansion which uses the relevance feedback mechanism without using the relevance information. Query expansion is shown the most promising approach for relevant document retrieval.

3.5.1 Query Expansion

Many times, user-supplied query information is not sufficient for retrieval of the intended information. In this case, Query Expansion (QE) [14] plays a crucial role in enhancing the performance of the information retrieval system by reformulating the original user query. Consider the user query consists of n terms represented as $Q = \{T_1, T_2, \ldots T_n\}$. The enhanced query can be obtained by the addition of new terms and the removal of stop words. The key aspect of new term addition $T' = \{T'_1, T'_2, \ldots, T'_m\}$ is the addition of relevant information to reduce ambiguity for efficient information retrieval on user queries. The stop words are defined as $T'' = \{T''_{i+1}, T''_{i+2}, \ldots, T''_{i+n}\}$. The new terms T' are computed based on estimated parameters like similarity of terms and recall rate in the user query. The reformulated query is defined as shown in Equation (3.7).

$$Q_{exp} = (Q - T'')U T' = \{T_1, T_2, \ldots T_i, T'_1, T'_2, \ldots, T'_m\} \tag{3.7}$$

The QE process can be manual, automated using the intelligence of the system and interactive with a human-in-loop approach. The generalized query expansion process is shown in Figure 3.17. The QE process consists of four steps as follows:

(1) data preprocessing and term extraction;
(2) term weights and ranking;
(3) term selection; and
(4) query reformulation.

Data preprocessing depends on the data source used for information retrieval and not on the user query. In order to augment the new related terms, a set of terms should be extracted from the data sources relevant to the user query. To perform the above-said task, the first whole text should be extracted from the data sources and tokenized into words. Then stop words are removed, and further stemming is done to remove the infected words. After data are preprocessed, weights, and ranks are assigned to the terms in the query. The user query and set of terms obtained during data preprocessing are used to assign the weights based on relevancy, and further ranks are allocated based on the document retrieval process. The relation between the terms of the query and expansion of the query can be obtained using many techniques like one-to-one association, one-to-many association, distribution of features based on top-ranked documents, and query modeling language.

Based on the initial query, top-rated documents are extracted and more detailed information is obtained for the QE process. The relevance feedback mechanism is the most effective mechanism in the expansion of the query. Query language modeling is based on the probability distribution of collected terms. Consider a query q_i and top-rated documents for relevant terms as set d obtained from the relevance model M_{rel}.

FIGURE 3.17
Query expansion process.

The co-occurrence of the term with the terms of the query is provided by the probability of the obtained collection of terms. To approximate the relevance model, the term probability t is computed using conditional probability with initial query terms $q_i (i \in 1,\dots n)$. Then, the probability of the term with respect to the relevance document is given by Equation (3.8) with unigram distribution, θ_d.

$$p(t \mid M_{rel}) = \sum_{\theta_d \in R} p(\theta_d) p(t \mid \theta_d) \prod_{i=1}^{n} p(q_i \mid \theta_d) \tag{3.8}$$

After ranking, terms with top ranks are selected for query expansion. With the obtained terms, the user query is reformulated for relevance. Query reweighting is done with the weights assigned to terms of the reformulated query. This query expansion is used in healthcare for information filtering, personalized content retrieval, and cross-language information retrieval.

3.5.2 Content-Based Medical Visual Information Retrieval

The process that provides image search and low-level visual feature extraction framework from the medical image database is termed Content Based Image Retrieval (CBIR) [15]. The low-level features of the images are color, shape, texture, and so on. The basic goal of CBIR is to sort the image based on visual similarity measures. The images are processed based on the image, and image processing techniques are based on powerful feature extraction techniques. In the CBIR system, the input is the query in the form of an image and the expected output is the set of related images retrieved based on the distance metrics. The general architecture of the CBIR system is shown in Figure 3.18. The CBIR system extracts the low-level features using feature extraction techniques, and these features are stored in the feature database. Based on the similarity measures of the extracted features, the visuals

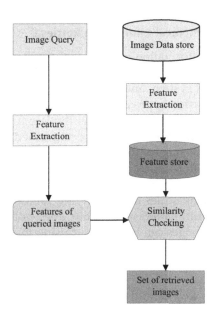

FIGURE 3.18
CBIR framework.

are extracted from the image database. Feature fusion can also be applied to enhance the performance of CBIR systems. Mostly color and salient points in the images are the most contributing features during the feature extraction. And also, image translation and rotation can be included with image color space for modeling the content-based image retrievals in the medical images. The shape features are represented by gradient vector flow, and textures are examined with the two-level grid systems.

The most commonly used visual similarity measures for medical images are Correlation, Euclidean distance, Cosine, City block, and Chebyshev [16]. Consider two images I_i and I_j with their corresponding features F_i and F_j. The visual similarity is given by S_{ij}^v for the k-th element in F_i is shown in Equation (3.9). Machine learning techniques like support vector machine and deep learning classifiers can be used to obtain the images based on features like color and texture. Convolution Neural Network (CNN) with TF-IDF is used for content-based image querying [17]. The main challenge in the CBIR system is the semantic gap between the low-level features extracted by the medical imaging systems and high-level features perceived by the physicians. This is ruled out using deep learning techniques that encode/decode the high- and low-level features [18]. Distance metric learning plays an important role in CBIR systems. Euclidean distance is limited to minimal feature representation and the inability to fill the semantic gaps. To determine the intraclass similarity, Mahalanobis distance is the optimal metric with less interclass similarity. It is given in Equation (3.10) with the transformation matrix, M.

$$S_{ij}^v = \sqrt{\sum_{k=1}^{n}\left(F_{i,k} - F_{j,k}\right)^2} \tag{3.9}$$

$$d_M\left(F_i, F_j\right) = \left(F_i - F_j\right)^T M \left(F_i - F_j\right) \tag{3.10}$$

3.5.3 Fusion Technique in Biomedical Information Retrieval

The central idea of fusion in information retrieval is the merging of information from different sources for the efficient processing of the requested user query. Information fusion can be embedded in the CBIR system, and it is of two types: early fusion and late fusion approaches [19]. In the early fusion approach, features of the medical images are combined before the computation of visual similarity. But in the late fusion approach, the features are combined after visual similarity computation, and based on ranking, information is retrieved. Early fusion is implemented by feature weighting and late fusion by multi-feature space representation. Fusion descriptors like Scalable Invariant Feature transform (SIFT) and Local Intensity Order Pattern (LIOP) are used based on the quality of the image [20]. SIFT suits well for varying scales but unvarying rotation and low contrast images. LIOP works well for low illumination images but does not accommodate the varying scales. Multimodal medical images can be obtained using the fusion technique. Based on rank aggregation, three different effects are exploited by the image fusion technique. They are listed as below:

- skimming effect – list of diverse and relevant images;
- chorus effect – list of relevant and similar images; and
- dark horse effect – list of images from one accurate source.

Recent literature studies reveal an effective image retrieval text technique, Scalable Vocabulary Tree (SVT)[21]. A robust image distance metric, Hausdorff distance is computed between the images with the diminished background to obtain the visual words. Then, image matching is performed by the fusion of three different signatures of the images. Machine learning approaches can be applied for the pre-filtering of images and similarity checks using statistical methods for matching multi-features query images and the datastore image collections. The more reliable features of the medical images are extracted using various mechanisms like wavelet decomposition, bag-of-words feature extraction [22], local binary patterns, texture extraction, and many more. Then, these features are combined and visual similarity is computed to obtain a set of relevant images for the given query. The metrics used in the fusion of image retrieval systems are sum fusion, maximum fusion, and multiplication fusion. Consider K features are fused for the image query q with the target class images in datastore $d_k \in \{d_1,...d_n\}$. The maximum fusion is given by Equation (3.11) with the weight of the feature, w_q^i. The similarity between queried image and the datastore image is given by $D_i(q)$.

$$sim\,(q) = \operatorname{argmax}\left\{w_q^i \mid i = 1, 2, ... K\right\} \tag{3.11}$$

During feature fusion of images, the adaptive weight updation mechanism gains more performance on image retrieval systems. Furthermore, graph-based fusion technique allows multiple levels of feature extraction and multiple fusion of information.

3.5.4 Tag-Based Information Retrieval

Tag is a small-sized word set [23] and acts as an interface between the user query and the image stores. Tag-based image and document retrieval are based on low-level feature representation. Tag-based document retrieval aims to retrieve a set of documents based on a set of given tags. Latent Dirichlet Allocation (LDA) is a generative process and modeled as a generative model with a generator and discriminator. The words are generated based on the hidden topics in the documents. The documents are represented by randomly chosen hidden topics by the generator while the discriminator provides the sample words based on a given condition. The general form of LDA is shown in Figure 3.19. In the generative process, w is the observable variable from document d consist of N words. The topic

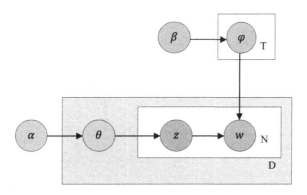

FIGURE 3.19
LDA tag-based process flow.

is z with word distribution φ, and T is the total number of topics. φ is obtained from α, Dirichlet prior based on the topic distribution for the given document count D and θ is the topic distribution for the documents.

Many variants of LDA are labeled LDA, partially labeled LDA, Tag-Weighted topic model, and Dirichlet multinominal regression. Tag-based image retrieval provides the interface between user and the query. Low-level features of images suffer from the big data of images, whereas high-level features suffer from a lack of semantic mapping of the images with the concepts. Tag refinement and tag recommendation are the two methods in tag-based image retrieval. The quality of the tag associated with the resources can be improved by redefining the original tag is called tag refinement. The original tag may be noisy and sparse and can be overcome by methods like Random Walk with Restarts-based method, Content-based image annotation, Ranking-based Multi-correlation Tensor Factorization, and many more. The most relevant image or document can be obtained by identifying the suitable tag using a strategy known as tag recommendation. The recent advancement in tag recommendation is collaborative tagging with the set of tags for the given images and also collaborating with other factors like popularity of tags, user activities, etc.

3.5.5 Biomedical Word Embedding

The representation of a word in the form of real-valued vector based on the content is the word embedding. Biomedical data are available in large volumes in domains like medical subject headings (MeSH) and Unified Medical Language System (UMLS). Most of the public domain word embedding models like word2vec, GloVe, FastText, ELMo, BERT, and recent BioWordVec. The BioWordVec [24] provides word embedding from two different data sources which are biomedical literature and MeSH for domain knowledge. The schematic flow is shown in Figure 3.20. The MeSH graph is constructed from the bio-medical data and by random sampling sequence of terms is obtained. In a unified n-gram embedding space, the subword embedding model is built to learn the text sequence from MeSH.

To improve embedding further, clinical concepts like UMLS or ICD-10 codes can be augmented with word embedding. The clinical knowledge representation can be injected during the training phase for embedded training. The co-occurrence matrix about the clinical notes is given by the UMLS identifier using the relationship between them. With the

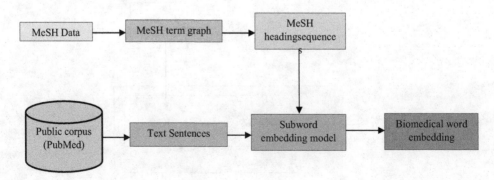

FIGURE 3.20
Schematic model of BioWordVec.

training data, the target data can be converted into a word embedding format. The out-of-vocabulary words are replaced with zeros with the target data mapped to the word vector with the trained model. The low dimensional features are embedded into biomedical words using distributed stochastic embedding with neighboring data. Even though word embedding is powerful in biomedical information retrieval, it has certain limitations. The evaluation of biomedical word embedding is given by benchmark, Biomedical Language Understanding Evaluation (BLUE) with associated five tasks. The aim is to provide the benchmark for the comparison of the models. The inconclusive evaluation leads to poor performance of the model. The interpretability of the word embedding varies and word intrusion test can be used for correct interpretation. Other issues are the privacy of clinical data, lack of more public word embedding models, and so on.

3.6 Discussion and Future Directions

Big data acquisition software must deal with huge volume, diverse, and real-time data. As a result, data acquisition tooling must assure high efficiency. Data can originate from a variety of sources like social networks, sensors, web mining, logs, and have various forms or unstructured ones like text, video, photos, and media files and arrive at a rapid rate. As a result, providing advanced platforms that provide the appropriate solution for the situation at hand without any data loss is the primary challenge in acquiring big data. The following are some of the developing issues for large data collecting in this context:

- Few tools provide the needed input data for processing like sensor data, web mining data, and logs, and help us with easy data acquisition. Since there are multiple application program interfaces present, any scientific solution that attempts to collect data from several sources must be capable of dealing with such a diverse set of implementations.
- In both the historical and real-time levels, the data collection process should be in parallel with data preprocessing and storage. To accomplish so, the data capture tools should be able to access groups of data and send those to real-time data processing tools. Many tools are available for these purposes like Flume, Spark, and Hadoop.
- The gathering, processing, and preservation of multimedia data like audio, image, and video are more difficult.
- For a proper data analysis, the data insights should be obtained clearly from unstructured and semi-structured models. Pre-processing step normally contains the combination of data acquisition and analysis steps as shown in Figure 3.21.
- The complexity of the process goes on increasing when we move from acquisition to storage of multimedia applications.
- Open-sources, commercial tools, and frameworks assisting with data preprocessing are emerging at a higher speed. When developing a proper data acquisition plan, the key goal is to understand the system's requirements in terms of data size, diversity, and velocity, and then to choose the optimal instrument to assure the acquisition and necessary throughput.

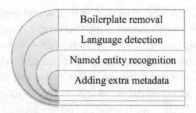

FIGURE 3.21
Data cleaning in clinical information system.

3.7 Conclusion

Exabyte of healthcare data is generated by the healthcare business, mostly in the form of electronic health records (EHRs). However, the majority of the possible data usage levels do not reach their full potential. Because predictive modeling and simulation tools for assessing healthcare data as a whole have not yet matured, this process is still in its infancy. Big data is a launch that will transform Universal Health Care on a variety of levels, propelling the organization forward. Data analytics in health offers shifts in medicine, infrastructure, and support, resulting in solutions that maximize clinical treatment and boost the value of medical personnel. In medicine and healthcare, big data analytics has a lot of promise for the development of decision support systems and knowledge-based healthcare information systems that combine, investigate, and analyze huge amounts of data. Patient-, clinical-, and population-centric decision-making systems should work in tandem with these integrated information systems. The properties of big data give a very adequate foundation for using potential software platforms for the development of applications that can deal with healthcare and medical big data, according to further research. Furthermore, the development of healthcare information systems must take into account all parties' security and privacy concerns, particularly the sensitive data of patients, and these software solutions must enable patient-centric, population-centric, epidemic-centric, clinical-centric, and country-centric data analysis to improve decision-making.

References

1. Dash S, Shakyawar SK, Sharma M, Kaushik S: Big data in healthcare: Management, analysis and future prospects. *Journal of Big Data* 2019, 6(1):1–25.
2. Yaseen M, Saleem K, Orgun MA, Derhab A, Abbas H, Al-Muhtadi J, Iqbal W, Rashid I: Secure sensors data acquisition and communication protection in eHealthcare: Review on the state of the art. *Telematics and Informatics* 2018, 35(4):702–726.
3. Zou N, Liang S, He D: Issues and challenges of user and data interaction in healthcare-related IoT: A systematic review. *Library Hi Tech* 2020, 38, 769–782.
4. Liang Y, Chen Z: Intelligent and real-time data acquisition for medical monitoring in smart campus. *IEEE Access* 2018, 6:74836–74846.
5. Cai Y, Xiao X, Tian H, Fu Y, Wu P, He H: A multi-source data collection and information fusion method for distribution network based on IOT protocol. In: *IOP Conference Series: Earth and Environmental Science*: 2021. IOP Publishing: 022076.

6. Zhang X, Wang Y: Research on intelligent medical big data system based on Hadoop and block-chain. *EURASIP Journal on Wireless Communications and Networking* 2021, 2021(1):1–21.

7. Rehman A, Naz S, Razzak I: Leveraging big data analytics in healthcare enhancement: Trends, challenges and opportunities. *Multimedia Systems* 2021, 1:1–33.

8. Atianashie Miracle A, Adaobi CC: Cloud computing in health care: Opportunities, issues, and applications: A systematic evaluation.

9. Shah JL, Bhat HF, Khan AI: Integration of Cloud and IoT for smart e-healthcare. In: *Healthcare Paradigms in the Internet of Things Ecosystem*. Elsevier; 2021: 101–136.

10. Kumar DR, Krishna TA, Wahi A: Health monitoring framework for in time recognition of pulmonary embolism using Internet of Things. *Journal of Computational and Theoretical Nanoscience*, 2018, 15(5):1598–1602.

11. Yoosuf MS: Lightweight fog-centric auditing scheme to verify integrity of IoT healthcare data in the cloud environment. Concurrency and Computation: Practice and Experience:e6450.

12. Gupta R, Tanwar S, Tyagi S, Kumar N: Tactile-internet-based telesurgery system for healthcare 4.0: An architecture, research challenges, and future directions. *IEEE Network* 2019, 33(6):22–29.

13. Hollis KF, Roberts K, Bedrick S, Hersh WR: Addressing the search challenges of precision medicine with information retrieval systems and physician readers. In: *Digital Personalized Health and Medicine*. IOS Press; 2020:813–817.

14. Azad HK, Deepak A: Query expansion techniques for information retrieval: A survey. *Information Processing & Management* 2019, 56(5):1698–1735.

15. Ashraf R, Ahmed M, Jabbar S, Khalid S, Ahmad A, Din S, Jeon G: Content based image retrieval by using color descriptor and discrete wavelet transform. *Journal of Medical Systems* 2018, 42(3):1–12.

16. Ma L, Liu X, Gao Y, Zhao Y, Zhao X, Zhou C: A new method of content based medical image retrieval and its applications to CT imaging sign retrieval. *Journal of Biomedical Informatics* 2017, 66:148–158.

17. Latif A, Rasheed A, Sajid U, Ahmed J, Ali N, Ratyal NI, Zafar B, Dar SH, Sajid M, Khalil T: Content-based image retrieval and feature extraction: A comprehensive review. *Mathematical Problems in Engineering* 2019, 2019:62–81.

18. Swati ZNK, Zhao Q, Kabir M, Ali F, Ali Z, Ahmed S, Lu J: Content-based brain tumor retrieval for MR images using transfer learning. *IEEE Access* 2019, 7:17809–17822.

19. Piras L, Giacinto G: Information fusion in content based image retrieval: A comprehensive overview. *Information Fusion* 2017, 37:50–60.

20. Yousuf M, Mehmood Z, Habib HA, Mahmood T, Saba T, Rehman A, Rashid M: A novel technique based on visual words fusion analysis of sparse features for effective content-based image retrieval. *Mathematical Problems in Engineering* 2018, 2018, 1–23.

21. Che C, Yu X, Sun X, Yu B: Image retrieval by information fusion based on scalable vocabulary tree and robust Hausdorff distance. *Eurasip Journal on Advances in Signal Processing* 2017, 2017(1):1–13.

22. Krishnasamy L, Dhanaraj RK, Ganesh Gopal D, Reddy Gadekallu T, Aboudaif MK, Abouel Nasr E: A heuristic angular clustering framework for secured statistical data aggregation in sensor networks. *Sensors* 2020, 20(17):4937.

23. Lee S, Masoud M, Balaji J, Belkasim S, Sunderraman R, Moon S-J: A survey of tag-based information retrieval. *International Journal of Multimedia Information Retrieval* 2017, 6(2):99–113.

24. Zhang Y, Chen Q, Yang Z, Lin H, Lu Z: BioWordVec, improving biomedical word embeddings with subword information and MeSH. *Scientific Data* 2019, 6(1):1–9.

4

Analogous Healthcare Product Identification in Online Shopping

N. Archana, R. Menaka, S. M. J. Blessy Regina, and P. M. Lakshmi Prabha
Chennai Institute of Technology, Chennai, India

CONTENTS

4.1 Introduction

Make no mistake, online shopping has grown in popularity in recent years, owing to widespread Internet access. This has resulted in online shopping being a frequent new medium for consumers. Modern technology has grown dramatically with the usage of cameras and mobile phone cameras, making them cheaper, more lightweight, and more practical than ever before. Because of advancements in Internet and interactive media technology, a wide range of fields, including clinical consideration, satellite information, video and still picture stores, advanced legal sciences, and reconnaissance advances, are now being utilised in as much sight and sound as sound, video, and photos as well as video and still pictures. As a result, programmes that can preserve and recover multimedia data are in high demand all of the time. There have been several visual and audible data storage and recovery frameworks developed to date in order to meet these requirements, among them: Image recovery is the term used to describe the process of extracting semantically important photographs from a collection of images [1]. Image retrieval is the process of extracting semantically significant pictures from a large collection of photographs, which is also known as image search. In object database analysis, the bulk of the work is devoted to the automated extraction of semantically meaningful information from the object text. When searching for images, consumers have just a vague idea of what they are looking for and how to find it. Even while current image recovery frameworks have made significant progress in addressing this problem, they are still unable to grasp the semantic meaning of images that are susceptible to human perception [2]. The semantic gap issue is the term given to this particular situation.

We did extensive research to get a better understanding of the expectations of and behaviours of a diverse variety of users since the major goal of the application is to be easy to use while still providing an engaging interface. As a consequence of the application's design, the end user will find the application's functioning to be easy and straightforward.

It is possible to classify users into two groups based on their comprehension of the goods that best satisfy their needs. These individuals fall into two categories: those who are already acquainted with the product that will fulfil their needs and those who are still in the process of determining which product will suit their needs. With the push of a button, users who are already acquainted with the product should be able to find it quickly and easily with a single click. Users who fall into this group may seek a product by searching for it using the product name as the search query in their browser. Searching for products using a keyword and then filtering the results based on various factors such as product type, manufacturer, price range, platform supported, and so on should be feasible for users who are seeking to identify which product will fulfil their needs.

While using the product, buyers should be able to see the whole product specification as well as many images taken at different zoom levels. In order for the user to see product reviews and ratings that have been provided by previous customers, the following information should be provided: They should be able to write their own reviews if they so want. Among other things, the specifications of a product should be printed, and the product page should be able to be shared with friends.

If at all feasible, the option to add a product to the shopping cart by dragging and dropping it into the shopping cart should be provided to improve the user's experience. The ability for a user to make adjustments to the goods in their shopping cart should be provided. Those who use the cart should be able to make any necessary adjustments to the quantities of products that have been added to it, as well as remove things from the cart. A product should be able to be removed from a user's shopping cart by pulling the product out of the cart and dropping it outside of the shopping cart's confines.

Pop-up messages may be used to make the software more interactive by showing them when a product is added to or deleted from the shopping cart. Upon reaching a drop location and detecting the item that is likely to be dropped, the user might be informed 4. Furthermore, people are impatient, which makes it vital for websites to load fast for them to be successful.

Additionally, I undertook substantial research into other methodologies for constructing this application and was able to include a few more powerful features into the final product as a result of this.

Although it is not needed, it is recommended that you use the ASP.NET controls and the AJAX Toolkit controls in your application since they improve navigation, usability, and interaction with the application.

Generally speaking, the system's viability may be divided into the following categories, which are listed alphabetically:

Considering that the sole investment necessary is the acquisition of a computer that fits the aforementioned fundamental parameters, this project is both feasible and affordable. Only the costs of gaining Internet access will be incurred by users in order to benefit from the software.

In addition, it provides final assurances that software meets all functional, behavioural, and performance standards that have been established. The employment of techniques such as black box testing is common.

Generally speaking, there are three primary components to consider.

As part of the validation test criteria, an examination of the software configuration is carried out in order to ensure that it is fully functional (no. in place of no. & char in place of char).

The following are the differences between Alpha and Beta testing: Alpha testing is performed at the developer's location, i.e. at home, while Beta testing is performed after the programme has been deployed. I was unable to join in the Beta testing since my application had not yet been released to the public.

Exemplifications of Test Cases – When it came to putting the device through its paces, I used a range of test scenarios. In order to assess whether or not the appropriate output was generated, a variety of inputs were used in a variety of situations and for a variety of inputs.

Adding a new product to the shopping cart should not need the creation of a new row inside the cart. It is necessary to adjust the amount of a product in your basket when you add it to your cart from another location. The summary must be updated as soon as any alterations to the goods are made to the cart's contents.

Because the same page is entering data into more than one table in the database at the same time, it is required to confirm the atomicity of the transaction before continuing. A product should be able to be dragged into a cart and then added to a cart by clicking on a button on the system, and vice versa.

It is possible to run tests to ensure that internal operations are carried out in accordance with the specification and that all internal components have been properly tested when performing white box testing because the tester is aware of the product's internal workings when performing white box testing. In white box testing, logic pathways across software are validated by providing test cases that exercise specific sets of conditions and loops, which are then run by the programmed logic path verification system.

White-box testing allows software engineers to design test cases that guarantee that all independent paths inside a module have been attempted at least once.

- Put all logical alternatives through their paces on both the true and false sides of the spectrum.
- Inspect all loops to ensure that they are exercised both at their maximum capacity and within their operating boundaries.
- Verify that the internal data structure is correct and up to date by performing a validation test.

In order to ensure that the logic of the programme was tested at every step of its development, I fed erroneous inputs into it and observed the resulting error messages at each stage of its development. Each one of the loops and conditional statements is submitted to boundary condition testing and validation in order to guarantee that they work appropriately.

Jakarta To analyse the system's performance, it was required to create virtual consumers (clients) and evaluate the system's performance using JMeter, which is an application testing tool. Also possible is the use of the tool to evaluate the performance of static and dynamic resources (files, Servlets, Perl scripts, Java Objects, Data Bases, and Queries), in addition to additional services such as FTP servers. It is possible to simulate a significant amount of demand on a server, network, or object in order to analyse their overall performance. It may also be used to assess their overall performance under a variety of different load conditions. When a significant number of concurrent users are present, it may be used to do a graphical examination of performance as well as to analyse the behaviour of the server, script, and object.

It has been my responsibility to conduct performance testing in order to offer an estimate of the peak and sustained load that the application can bear, as well as the time it will take to do so. Several pages, such as the Shop Products page (which has extensive database access, business logic, and extra photos), and the Cart Details page, have been created to do this (simple page). A few samples of test results that have been captured on a screenshot are provided in the next section. Both the application (server) and JMeter were running simultaneously on the same machine throughout the testing. This test does not take into account issues such as network speed since the server and JMeter are both running on the same computer system.

4.2 Content-Based Image Recovery

CBIR has a wide range of applications and is important in a wide range of fields, including military relations, medical research, education, architectural architecture, the justice department, and agriculture, because photographs contain a wealth of information and have no language restrictions, which encourages international trade, among other things. A number of CBIR systems have evolved throughout the years. The following are some examples of CBIR retrieval schemes: QBIC, Virage, picture book, visual search, netra, and simplicity, to name a few.

Content-Based Image recovery (CBIR) is an acronym that refers to image data that has been particularly obtained by looking at images that have specified qualities or that include unique information from an object archive [3]. The core premise of CBIR is the study and use of feature vectors as picture indexes to understand image information utilising low-level properties such as colour, texture, shape, and spatial reference objects, among other things. Retrieval approaches, which are generally focused on an image's multi-dimensional features, are concerned with retrieving images that are similar to each other. The phrase "stuff" in this context refers to the colours, forms, surfaces, or other materials that might arise from the real thing. CBIR is beneficial since most picture search engines on the Internet concentrate primarily on metadata, resulting in a large amount of trash [4].

Humans may also be inefficient, expensive, and incapable of manually collecting all keywords characterising the topic for items in a large database when working with large datasets. A more reliable indexing and returning result to a device that can sort objects according to their content [5] will be part of this. In the image retrieval based on content, just the texture, colour, and shape of the objects are employed to identify them.

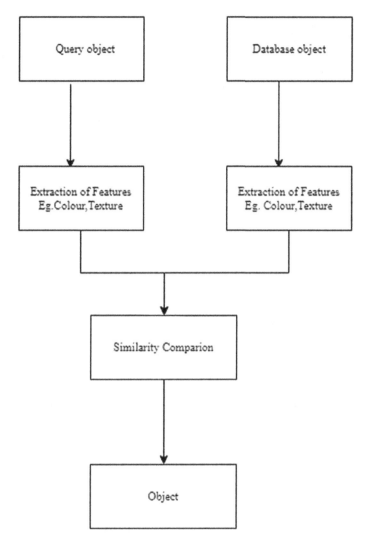

FIGURE 4.1
Content-based image recovery represented as a Block Diagram.

4.3 Text-Based Image Recovery

It is possible to recover content-based images using the process of embedding information, such as watchwords, endorsements, or image representations, inside the image content. Due to the recovery employed over the annotation words, the annotation process is tough and time-consuming, and it requires a significant amount of work to manually annotate the photographs. In the case of TBIR, the semantically zed text is not present [6]. Using an immersive image recovery technique combined with user term input, we may gather words from all sectors, increasing ambiguity while also increasing the likelihood of generating unrelated concepts [2].

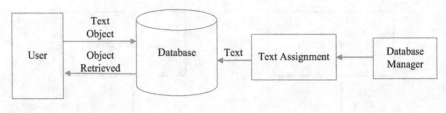

FIGURE 4.2
Text-based image retrieval.

4.4 Retrieval by Colour

The colour-based object retrieval strategy is the most straightforward and fundamental approach for CBIR. The colour properties of a material are the most visually appealing and intuitive to the human eye. It is also an important component of interpretation. The colour qualities of things are very robust and durable when compared to other features of objects such as texture and form [7]. It is impervious to changes in rotation, translation, or size of the object. Furthermore, the colour function [8] may be calculated with a reasonable amount of ease. A colour histogram is the most often used technique for extracting colours from images.

The geometric shape, the colours, and the texture of the material are the most distinguishing aspects of CBIR. The colour element is one of the most widely used picture recovery functions, and it is one of the most versatile. Colours are recognised based on the colour space that has been selected. There are a variety of colour spaces available, most of which are intended for different purposes. They are there to help. Using colour to create spaces that are akin to human experience.

4.5 Existing Method

In their present approaches, the writers have used a variety of various methodologies. They have coupled the processed form and item data with shading highlights extracted from the spatially organised L2 standardised coefficients in order to create a more realistic appearance. A fraction of the current techniques use the SIFT (scale invariant component change) process, which is a computation that is used to locate and depict close highlights in computer-generated images [9]. Finding specific core concerns and then providing them with quantitative data (referred to as descriptors) that may be used for object recognition are among the applications for which it is suitable.

When dealing with vast volumes of data, a brute force search is not feasible; thus, more effective search strategies must be used. The bag of features is a straightforward encoding system that uses a small number of visual word histograms to represent a big number of pictures in a little amount of space. This approach, which makes use of an Inverted index data structure, enables small storage while yet providing for excellent search [10]. When it comes to retrieval functions, the kind of items in the database has a lot to do with what is utilised.

FIGURE 4.3
Query object.

A function bag is a technique for extracting the characteristics of an object from its surroundings. According to the classification theory (Word Bag), once numerous representative keywords have been excluded from the object, a dictionary is generated, and an object is calculated based on the number of events that occur in order to get the attribute vector [11]. When it comes to developing a robust vocabulary, a large quantity of data is necessary, which means a large data set. The most linked cluster centres in the dictionary may be found for each characteristic of the item, and a vector representation of the item called a Bag can be found for each feature of the item by searching for the most connected cluster centres in the dictionary. It should be possible to discern between photos belonging to separate categories in this situation as a consequence of the use of this vector. In order to categorise items, we may utilise this information to train classification models, which we can then use to categorise objects [3].

Afterwards, the features and descriptors for each object are collected, often via SIFT, and mapped into the descriptor space, which varies depending on the descriptor representation used to represent the features in the first place. The image database can be searched to find the most similar visual word in the lexicon for each SIFT function in the picture [12], which we can then use to find the most related visual word. Making a k-dimensional histogram of the SIFT function of each individual item in the dictionary may be used to count the items in the dictionary as one method of counting the objects. The Retrieve objects are responsible for returning the IDs of the photos as well as the scores for each result. The outcomes are arranged in decreasing order from the greatest to the most disappointing [13].

When it comes to accurately identifying locations, we must effectively reflect the features of an item, which can then be grouped together and scanned after they are found to be comparable to one another. Objective recovery may be used to discover objects in things when objects close to the specified object can be readily identified, as well as for other purposes such as object recovery [14].

FIGURE 4.4
Output for the given query object.

4.5.1 Drawback

However, the present approach is primarily focused on the flowers and fails to accomplish accuracy in the colour moment, chi-square test, HSV, Specificity and Sensitivity tests, Gabor wavelet, Edge gradient, and retrieval score tests. We were able to accomplish the aforementioned restrictions using the suggested approach.

4.6 The Proposed Method

The Covid-19 outbreak has caused a significant increase in online buying activity in recent months. Covid-19 has a moderating influence on the consumer's awareness of services, allowing shoppers to purchase goods and services on the internet. For the purpose of extracting identical photographs utilising the Bag of Features approach, we recommend that you use Analogous Product Identification in Online Shopping service. Training a sequence of random items from the data set results in the generation of Bag of Features. Afterwards, we index the object that needs to be retrieved, and then, we retrieve objects that are identical to the query object that was obtained.

As previously stated, the prior approaches based on picture retrieval had certain limits in terms of accuracy, as well as concerns with the data sets used in their development. As a result, we chose to improve the quality of the datasets while simultaneously making improvements to the data sets themselves in order to overcome the constraints of the prior articles.

The following are the steps to obtain comparable items for shopping:

A). select the item to be retrieved;

B). create a bag of characteristics for the object to be retrieved;

C). catalogue the item; and

D). look for comparable objects in the index.

(A) Select the item that will be retrieved:

The type of function used to find the objects in the array depends upon the type of objects.

A global object characteristic, such as a colour histogram that captures the colour contents of the whole scene, is better when searching for an image collection that consists of sceneries (beaches, towns, and roads), for example. However, if the goal is to find certain things in a collection of photographs, it is more convenient to employ local image characteristics extracted around the key objects.

(B) Construct a bag of features:

The bag of features is built by selecting a random collection of items from the data set and then training them on those objects. Bag of Feature does not need associated labels to learn while extracting features; hence, it is a weekly supervised learning approach that does not require a large number of labels. This method, on the other hand, does not take into account the spatial connection between characteristics in any way. In particular, it is regrettable when there are multiple prospective matches that are appropriate, but only one of them is picked because it scores a little higher [15]. In such a situation, it is important to devise a legitimate strategy for differentiating between various solutions in order to identify the most appropriate one. We can get around this problem if we provide geometric information as well.

(C) Create an index of the photographs:

A big enough data set and a large enough amount of data are required to develop a suitable vocabulary. In subsequent steps, for each item, the features and descriptors are retrieved. Typically, this is done by mapping into the descriptor space, which is dependent on how the descriptor is represented. In order to search for visual words in a query object, we must first determine which visual words are included inside the query object. For each of the occurring words, we check to see whether any additional objects contain the same phrase. The voting array [4, 16] is increased by one for each of the items in question. An item in the voting array is a list with one entry for each object that has a counter variable, as seen below. At the conclusion of the process, we choose the item in the voting array that has the greatest counter value as the match for the query object. Every characteristic in the query object, on the other hand, must still be compared to all visual terms in the vocabulary.

(D) Look for things that are comparable to yours:

The next step is to utilise the fetch objects method to look for items that are comparable to the ones you have already found.

When it comes to image retrieval, we have found that there are certain restrictions in terms of accuracy and that only a few data sets are employed in the current literature. We have overcome these limitations by increasing the accuracy of retrieving objects that are similar to the query object, as well as by adding datasets that will assist customers in purchasing the items that they require, increasing the purchase rate, and encouraging customers to search for additional products in order to achieve an online shopping application.

Step 1: Select the picture query that will be returned (i.e. input object). It is necessary for him to utilise the query picture as a user image in order to get photographs from the data set as a sample. There are no restrictions on the picture query's source, and it does not have to be from our dataset. The computer takes a picture of the query image that was provided as input.

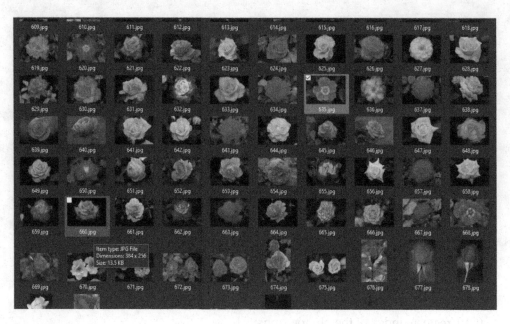

FIGURE 4.5
Flower data set.

Step 2: With the feature type defined, the next step is to learn the visual vocabulary within the bag of Features using a set of training products. The bag of features is created by picking some random set of products from the data set and by training them using 'Custom Extractor' option which is used to take out features from each product. Now that the bag of Features is created, the entire flower image set can be Indexed for search.

Step 3: The entire flower picture collection can now be indexed for searching until the feature bag is generated. The indexing process extracts features from each product using the step 1 personalised extractor function. The features extracted are encoded and added to the product index in a graphic word histogram.

FIGURE 4.6
Index object.

Step 4: The final step is to use the retrieve images function to search for similar images. Thus the accuracy of objects was met by output 1.

Output 1:

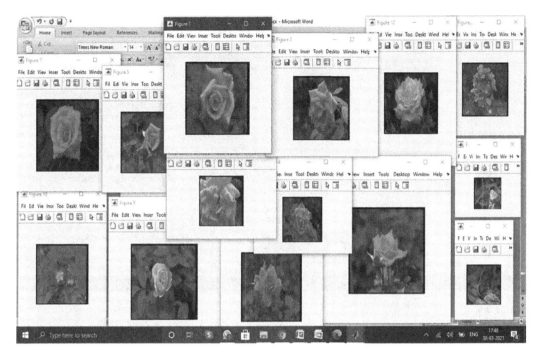

FIGURE 4.7
Output flower objects.

Figure 4.8 shows another index object. The output of this object is shown in Figure 4.9.

FIGURE 4.8
Index object.

Output 2:

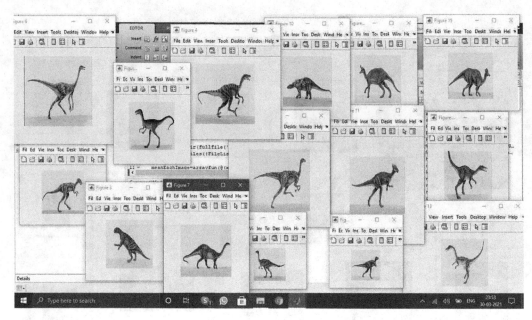

FIGURE 4.9
Similar objects.

Thus, we added other objects like toys, sceneries, and buses in the data set other than flowers as in output.

Results:

(a) **Results for Examination of Different Techniques**

Name of the object	HSV Method		Moment of the colour method		Gabor Wavelet Method		Edge Gradient Method		Chi- Square Method	
	Exis.	Pro.	Exis.	Pro.	Exis.	Pro.	Exis.	Pro.	Exis.	Pro.
Roses	0.49	0.52	0.65	0.72	0.7	0.79	0.65	0.72	0.68	0.73
Dinosaur	0.45	0.5	0.8	0.84	0.8	0.85	0.70	0.78	0.75	0.82
Buses	0.4	0.49	0.68	0.75	0.8	0.87	0.75	0.8	0.8	0.9
Cars	0.55	0.6	0.68	0.74	0.68	0.75	0.69	0.74	0.68	0.71
Sunflower	0.5	0.58	0.75	0.81	0.7	0.77	0.65	0.71	0.65	0.7
Scenery	0.48	0.55	0.68	0.73	0.68	0.73	0.7	0.77	0.75	0.81
Spectacles	0.5	0.59	0.7	0.79	0.78	0.84	0.7	0.78	0.88	0.94
Avg. accuracy	0.47	0.547	0.68	0.768	0.75	0.8	0.7	0.757	0.76	0.801

The above-mentioned values are plotted, and the proposed method values are compared with the existing methods.

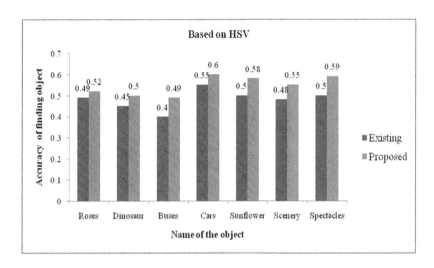

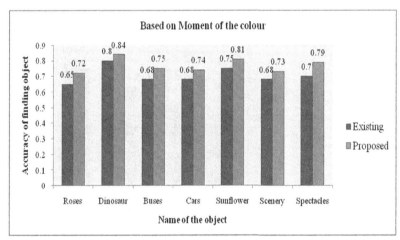

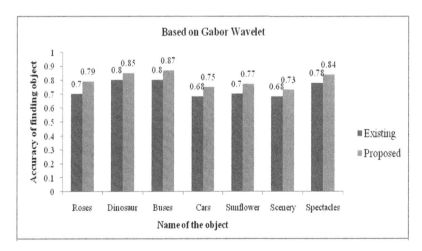

FIGURE 4.10
Comparison of different techniques.

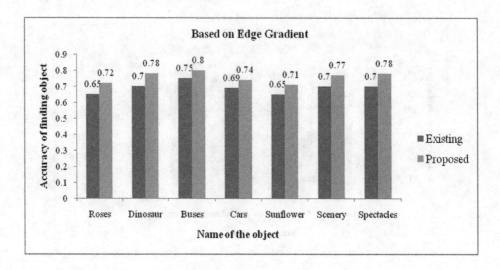

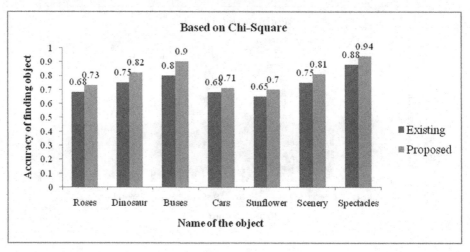

FIGURE 4.10 Continued
Comparison of different techniques.

According to the previous graph, the object detection accuracy increased by 7 percent in the proposed method when compared to the HSV method, 6 percent when compared to the Color moment method, 7 percent when compared to the Gobor wavelet method, 6 percent when compared to the Edge Gradient method, and 6 percent when compared to the chi-square method, respectively.

Methods that are currently in use include I HSV (Hue Saturation Value)

In the HSV, we utilised hue to differentiate between the colours, saturation to add white lights to pure colour, and value to detect the strength of light in the image. A colour histogram depicts the distribution of colours in a particular object. According to the findings of this research, the colour properties of an image were used to construct a vector for the categorisation of photographs. It performs well in certain data formats while performing poorly in others. HSV, or Hue Saturation Value, is a technique for distinguishing between image brightness and shading data. The use of this method is more convenient when dealing with or requiring brightness of the things.

(i) The Color of the Moment:

Based on the colour features that have been proved to define the colour distribution of an item, we used the colour moment to distinguish between photographs from the data set that were similar in colour.

A colour moment was used on colour photos in the existing project, and the Local Binary Pattern was used to create a textural element, but the shape features were not taken into consideration [17]. Color moments are computed by taking the mean, the standard deviation, and the skewness of an item and multiplying them together.

(1) Gabor Wavelet: This is a wavelet that was developed by Gabor himself.

This parameter was used to extract texture from an item in order to retrieve it, and it was shown to be incredibly effective. Essentially, a wavelet caught energy at a certain frequency and orientation, and it was found to be extremely efficient. The colour-based CBIR technology incorporates two extra features that are computed using the Gabor wavelet to apply the texture feature, despite the fact that retrieval time is becoming more and more inefficient with each passing generation [4] [18]. It is used to extract texture from objects so that it may be retrieved later.

(ii) Edge Gradient: We utilised this option to ensure that our feature and texture matching was as robust as possible. In this case, it informs us about the abrupt variations in picture brightness that have occurred. Because of the rise in noise, the gradient magnitude of the edges worsens as well, leading to imprecise results in the current research, which employs sobel operators for edge detection [19]. The edge detection block locates edges by searching for the local maximum of the gradient of the input object in the surrounding area.

(iii) The Value of the Chi-Square Test

Using the chi-square approach, we have been comparing observed data with projected outcomes. They are designed to determine if a disparity is the result of an accident or a relationship between the elements that affect the actual data and what is anticipated by computer models. In the current study, they used a chi-square analysis to match photos [20], although this method does not work for all of the photographs in the collection, which is problematic. When comparing predicted and actual outcomes, it is utilised to determine the difference in size between the two [21].

The attributes that are observed are those that we have accumulated ourselves. The predicted values are calculated based on our null hypothesis, which describes how the anticipated frequencies should be distributed.

(b) Experimental Results for Parameters of Proposed System

Name of the object	Sensitivity		Specificity		Accuracy		Retrieval score	
	Exis.	Pro.	Exis.	Pro.	Exis.	Pro.	Exis.	Pro.
Roses	0.85	0.9	0.75	0.8	0.75	0.8	0.86	0.9
Dinosaur	0.88	0.93	0.8	0.85	0.85	0.9	0.9	0.95
Buses	0.9	0.98	0.85	0.9	0.9	0.95	0.95	0.99
Cars	0.75	0.8	0.7	0.75	0.68	0.75	0.75	0.8
Sunflower	0.75	0.8	0.65	0.7	0.65	0.76	0.7	0.77
Scenery	0.87	0.9	0.8	0.85	0.8	0.88	0.85	0.9
Spectacles	0.86	0.9	0.78	0.85	0.85	0.92	0.93	0.97
Average	0.85	0.882	0.78	0.814	0.83	0.851	0.86	0.897

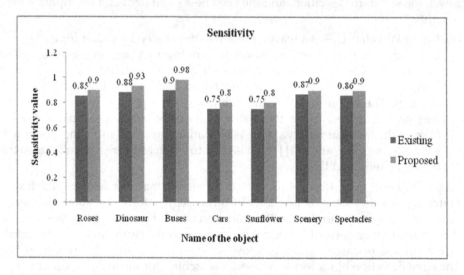

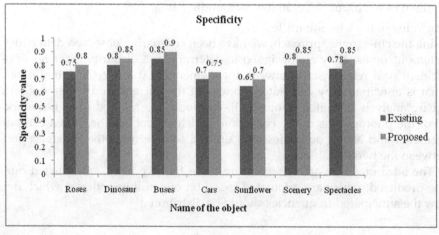

FIGURE 4.11
Comparison of different parameters.

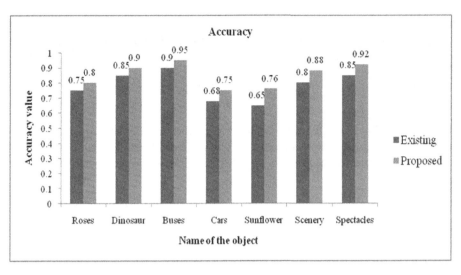

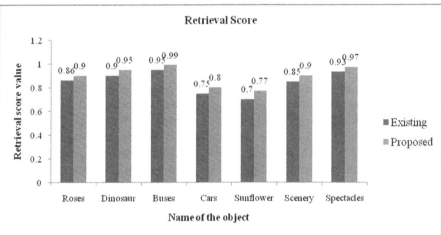

FIGURE 4.11 Continued
Comparison of different parameters.

Parameters:

(a) Sensitivity:

This parameter is used to find the value of number of objects that are correctly matched. It is calculated as follows:

$$\text{Sensitivity} = \text{TP} / (\text{TP} + \text{FN}) \tag{4.1}$$

where TP is the True Positive which means the number of matched products which are correctly identified; FN is the False Negative which means the number of matched products which are not correctly identified.

(b) Specificity:

This parameter is used to find the value of the number of products which are not matched. It is calculated by

$$\text{Specificity} = TN / (TN + FP) \tag{4.2}$$

Where TN is the True Negative which means the number of products which are not matched and those that are correctly identified; FP is the False Positive which means the number of not matched products which are not correctly identified.

(c) Accuracy:

It gives us the average of sensitivity and specificity and is calculated as follows:

$$AC = (\text{Sensitivity} + \text{Specificity}) / 2 \tag{4.3}$$

(d) Retrieval Score:

It is computed for each query product. Its formula is given by

$$\text{Retrieval Score} = 100^* \left[1 - (\text{mismatches} / n) \right] \% \tag{4.4}$$

where n is the number of closest products to the query product.

Tables (a) and (b) provide experimental results obtained using traditional methodologies and the suggested technology, respectively. This employment contributes to the reduction of a person's burden. With the use of an algorithm, a computer may be taught to recognise different types of photographs. When a computer extracts features from an image, just the collection of features is saved, and only that feature set is sufficient when the picture satisfies the criteria. When you extract characteristics, they are no longer required. Table 1 shows the exact parallel of the proposed process to the existing procedure (a). It demonstrates that the precision of the technology being offered has increased. Table b shows the values of the various parameters that may be derived from the outcome of the experiment.

4.7 Conclusion

Using this gadget, you may connect a purchasing portal to a knowledge platform. Through this machine, the client will automatically scan for comparable photographs from the information portal in accordance with his favourite images that he has saved. Last but not least, the purchasing ratio of consumers would improve. In addition, the gadget will automatically acquire information from the other online shopping site, give customers the same image recovery straight from the device, and display the search results in a personalised way. Consequently, by adopting the above-mentioned approach, the HSV, Color Moment, Gabor wavelet, Edge Gradient, Chi-Square, Sensitivity, Specificity, Accuracy, and Retrieval scores will be raised by 7%, 6%, 7%, 6%, 6%, 4%, 5%, 7 %, and 4%, respectively.

References

1. Athanasios Kallipolitis and Ilias Maglogiannis, Senior Member IEEE, "Creating Visual Vocabularies for the Retrieval and Classification of HistopathologyImages", *2019 41st Annual International Conference of the IEEE Engineering in Medicine and Biology Society (EMBC)*, 2019, pp. 7036–7039.
2. M. Sathyamoorthy, S. Kuppusamy, R.K. Dhanaraj et al. "Improved K-Means Based Q Learning Algorithm for Optimal Clustering and Node Balancing in WSN", *Wireless Pers Commun* 122, 2745–2766 (2022).
3. Javed M. Aman, "Content-based Image Retrieval on CT Colonography using Rotation and Scale Invariant Features and Bag-of-Words Model", IEEE, 2007.
4. Pradeep Kumar Jena, B. Khuntia, C. Palai, S. R. Pattanaik, "Content Based Image Retrievalusing Adaptive Semantic Signature", *2019 IEEE 5th International Conference for Convergence in Technology (I2CT)*, 2019, pp. 1–4, doi: 10.1109/I2CT45611.2019.9033541.
5. Meenaakshi N. Munjal, Shaveta Bhatia, "A Novel Technique for Effective Image Gallery Searchusing Content Based Image Retrieval".
6. Manpreet Kaur, Neelofar Sohi, "A Novel Technique for Content Based Image Retrieval Using Color,Texture and Edge Features", IEEE.
7. Gustaro Carneiro, "Supervised Learning of Semantic Classes for Image Annotation and Retrieval", IEEE, 2007.
8. En Cheng, Feng Jing, Chao Zhang, Lei Zhang, "Search Result Clustering based Relevance feedback for Web Image Retrieval", *2007 IEEE International Conference on Acoustics, Speech and Signal Processing - ICASSP '07*, 2007, pp. I-961–I-964, doi: 10.1109/ICASSP.2007.366069.
9. Jimman Kim, "A New Way for Multi dimensional Medical DataManagement", IEEE, 2006.
10. Hayit Greenspan, "Medical Image Categorization and Retrieval for PACS using the GMM-KL Framework", IEEE, 2007.
11. Hua Wang, "An AES-Based Secure Image Retrieval Scheme Using Random Mapping and BOW in Cloud Computing", IEEE Publications, 2020.
12. Kai Kunze, Hitoshi Kawaichi, Kazuyo Yoshimura, Koichi Kise, "TheWordometer– Estimating the Number of Words Read Using Document Image Retrieval and Mobile Eye Tracking", *2013 12th International Conference on Document Analysis and Recognition*, 2013, pp. 25–29, doi: 10.1109/ICDAR.2013.14.
13. Khawaja Tehseen Ahmed, Humaira Afzal, Muhammad Rafiq, Arif Mehmood, Gyu Sang Choi, "Deep Image Sensing & Retrieval using Suppression, Scale Spacing & Division, Interpolation and Spatial Color Coordinates with Bag of Words for Large and Complex Datasets", IEEE Access, 2020, pp. 1–1. doi:10.1109/ACCESS.2020.2993721.
14. Jingdam Zhang, "Detection and Retrieval of CYSTS in Joint Ultrasound B-Mode and Elasticity Breast Images", IEEE, 2010.
15. Mohan Muppidi, Paul Rad, Sos S. Agaian, Mo Jamshidi,"Container Based Parallelization for Faster and Reliable Image Segmentation", *2015 IEEE International Conference on Imaging Systems and Techniques (IST)*, 2015, pp. 1–6.
16. S. Mohanapriya, M. Vadivel, "Automatic Retrieval of MRI Brain Image using Multi Queries System", *2013 International Conference on Information Communication and Embedded Systems (ICICES)*, 2013, pp. 1099–1103.
17. Roufei Zhang, Z. Zhang "Effective Image Retrieval Based on Hidden Concept Discovery in Image Database", *IEEE Transactions on Image Processing*, 16(2), pp. 562–572, Feb. (2007), doi: 10.1109/TIP.2006.888350.
18. Sobhan Naderi Parizi, Ivan Laptev, Alireza Tavakolitarghi, "Modeling Image Context Using Object Centered Grid", *2009 Digital Image Computing: Techniques and Applications*, 2009, pp. 476–483.

19. T.N. Sadan Kumar, A. Sreenivasa Murthy, N. Rajani. "HPCIR: Histogram Positional Centroid for Image Retrieval." *2016 IEEE Industrial Electronics and Applications Conference (IEACon)*, 2016, pp. 256–260.
20. S. Dhiviya, S. Malathy, D. R. Kumar. "Internet of Things (IoT) Elements, Trends and Applications", *Journal of Computational and Theoretical Nanoscience* 15(5), 1639–1643 (2018).
21. Zhongwei Li, Chiahung Wei, Yue Li, Tsaiyang Sun, "Research of Shoeprint Image Stream Retrieval Algorithm with Scale Invariance FeatureTransform", IEEE, doi: 10.1109/ICMT. 2011.6002147.

5

Segmentation-based Comparative Analysis for Detection of Bone Tumour Using Healthcare Data

J. Eric Clapten, A. Tamilselvi, K. Oviya, and M. Swetha
Chennai Institute of Technology, Chennai, India

CONTENTS

5.1 Introduction

He who is referred to regarded as the "Father of Medicine," [1] the Greek physician Hippocrates, is credited with coining the term cancer (460–370 BC). Cancer, on the other hand, has its origins as far back as 3000 BC, when osteosarcoma (bone tumours) were discovered in petrified human dead bodies in Ancient Egypt. According to the most recent statistical data, cancer is one of the leading causes of death all over the world, and it is a frightening syndrome. Cancer in humans occurs when the chromosome, which is the source of the cell's hereditary code, becomes contaminated as a result of interaction with chemicals, radiation, an inheritance, or pathogens that cause mutations in the genetic code [2].

The human body is divided into four types of tissue: connective tissue, sensory tissue, epithelial tissue, and muscular tissue. Connective tissue is the most abundant kind of tissue in the body. It is possible to split connective tissues into two independent tissue

DOI: 10.1201/9781003217435-5

sections, such as fitting connective tissues and specialized connective tissues, inside the connective tissues. Specifically, the connective tissues are vascularized by blood vessels and have a stiff consistency due to their inflexible nature.

They are referred to as bone tissues in medical terminology. The high concentration of mineral salts and collagen strands in bone tissue's extracellular network accounts for the hardness of bone tissue. Three layers make up bone tissue: osteoblasts, osteoclasts, and osteocytes. Osteoblasts are the cells that build bone tissue. The skeleton is made up of 206 bones in total; cortical bone accounts for about 80 per cent of all bone mass, with trabecular bone accounting for the remaining 20 per cent. Mineralization in each bone tissue is reliant on its biological arrangement, which is connected with the presence of a Haversian tube, which is generally surrounded by concentric deposits of bone cells, and the amount of mineralization in each bone tissue [3]. Any fracture or abnormality (such as cancer) in the bone must be anticipated to be cured at the earliest possible stage. Feature segmentation is a method used in medical image processing that splits a picture into its constituent parts. Segmentation may be utilized as a first stage in the process of visualization and compression. The process of segmenting an item is achieved by designating all of the pixels or voxels that are associated with that entity. Diagnostic imaging relies on segmentation for a variety of reasons, including feature extraction, picture measurements, and image presentation. When compared to other methods of diagnosis, magnetic resonance imaging (MRI) is unique in that it may be utilized to examine the volumetric pattern of bone tissues. Optimization of the skeletal structure has become critical in the treatment of disorders such as multiple sclerosis, schizophrenia, epilepsy, and Parkinson's disease, among others.

On a global scale, the highest degree of cancer prognosis before the metastatic phase is the most important factor in determining cancer mortality. Abrasions are known to develop in a variety of organs, including the breast, lung, prostate, and kidney, and they are responsible for 80 per cent of all bone metastases in the human body.

Approximately 1.04 million novel kinds of lung cancers were found and authorized based on survey data collected [3]. In some cases of bronchogenic carcinoma, a bone scan can reveal the possibility of bone metastasis, and it has been suggested that scanning of the affected bone regions with 99m monophosphate detected premature bone metastasis in a few cases before the lesions were recognized clinically or radiographically [4].

Tomographic imaging, which is associated with nuclear medicine, is dependent on the metabolic activity of tissue cells and could be useful in recognizing anatomical variations before their identification by radiological assessments such as CT scans, and it presents the anatomical organization and SPECT and PET scans, among other things. PET imaging provides information on the functional content of organs and tissues, and it is the most accurate imaging approach available for predicting the stage of bone cancer [5]. Furthermore, procedures were carried out after the administration of radiation therapy (RT), which was followed by the processes of observation, treatment, and assessment. It was discovered that the outcomes of CT and MRI scans were reliant on the mechanisms described earlier [5]. Although these techniques are referred to as anatomical imaging, the primary advantage they provide is the ability to analyse the structure on a large scale and with great force, which allows them to be involved in highly complicated RT techniques such as three-dimensional, conformal RT, stereotactic RT and radiosurgery, concentration and altered radiotherapy, and radiotherapy with heavy particles.

A CT scan provides information about the anatomical organization, whereas SPECT and PET scans provide information about the practical information held in organs and tissues. Positron Emission Tomography (PET) scans with 18FFDG (18F-fluorodeoxyglucose) have the advantages of higher sensitivity and specificity when compared to chest CT scans and are widely considered to be the most precise imaging method for identifying abnormalities in patients with bone cancer, according to the American Society of Nuclear Medicine. On the other hand, there are constraints associated with the constructive prognostic evaluation of this system since there may be 5'FDG curious in provoking units, which is a constraint in this scheme [6]. It is also possible to minimize the amount of time spent thinking when lymph node metastases are insignificant or below the spatial resolution threshold of current, state-of-the-art scanners. Because of the high cost of equipment, PET is only available at a limited number of locations. Instead, Single-Photon Emission Computed Tomography (SPECT) is widely available, costs less than PET, and does not need the presence of a cyclotron next to the sickbay, as is the case with PET. Bone characteristic drawing out system is, on the other hand, a standard procedure [7].

It is used in radiography to analyse problem areas such as cancer and multiple sclerosis indications, as well as to partition an overall scene into sub-parts such as the WM, GM, and CSF spaces of the body, using an automatic drawing of distinct feature components.

Graph-cuts are one of the most recent picture segmentation algorithms for bone identification. Since 2001, it has been employed for image analysis via the application of global energy reduction. Several algorithms are employed in conjunction with it for quantitative analysis and picture search based on content. The most powerful graph cuts algorithm produces the best and most accurate segmentation with the smallest amount of cut and maximum flow.

5.2 Literature Survey

It is common to practise using a wavelet thresholding de-noise system that takes into consideration the Discrete Wavelet Transform (DWT) introduced by Donoho and Johnstone in 1994 as a component of the denoising process for ECG data. To remove the additional ingredient commotions, Wavelet provides a representation of photographs that is both poor and unproductive. Recently, several wavelet-based strategies for bone tumour study have been given to the scientific community. In this part, we discussed the various wavelet-based image processing solutions that are currently available. In the case of images, Wavelet provides an unusually poor and effective depiction. There has been a proposal made on the latest approaches for mammography assessment that make use of wavelet transforms. As part of their mammography analysis, they conducted a study on the organization of measurable components using a doubletree classifier, which resulted in a novel analytical framework for the inspection process. Using wavelet coefficients with high values in the low recurrence (close estimation) of wavelets modification [8] demonstrated that a mark vector for the process of comparing abnormalities in a mammogram could be created. When performing multilevel disintegration, Ref. [9] used a multi-determination mammography examination in which the estimate was concentrated on a fraction of the largest coefficients of the estimate.

This segmentation technique makes use of maintaining filtering and mean shift clustering [10]. The mean shift technique for a data point in space begins by identifying the area of interest in the data point in space. It is a non-parametric approach for evaluating and categorizing feature clusters in a complicated multi-modal feature space that is not dependent on the number of features in the cluster. The only variables that can be changed in this strategy are the size and shape of the targeted area. To calculate the density gradient, mean shift segmentation governs density estimation, which is accomplished using mean shift segmentation. A two-step discontinuity series produced in the manner of a spherical window is shown herein.

Because it is both quick and cost-effective to calculate, histogram thresholding is the most basic picture segmentation approach. To distinguish between context and artefacts, a threshold known as the brightness constant is employed. The modifications to this approach include band, local, and multi. Thresholds are also used to refer to single thresholds that may change in different picture components [11]. Global thresholds are a single criterion that may be applied to the whole image by combining many criteria. Several approaches that are based on threshold identification are utilized to automatically calculate the threshold. The optimum, p-tile, and histogram modelling techniques are used to recognize pictures with many bands in this study. The use of multi-spectral thresholding is allowed in certain circumstances. It is determined by using this approach that the threshold is established to correspond to the lowest probability between the maxima of two or more normal distributions as a minimum between the two or more normal distributions, In the normal distribution of maxima, the threshold is defined as the closest grey-level corresponding to the minimal probability. This generates the best threshold, which results in fewer erroneous sectionalization. In bi-modal histograms, the threshold is chosen based on the colour of the histogram or the location of the two largest local maxima [12].

When using the region rising/region merging segmentation procedure, pixels with equal intensities are grouped. When this approach is used, the first phase starts with a seed, which is a pixel or set of pixels that belong to the system under consideration. In the next stage, pixels in the tiny neighbourhood zone are evaluated and centred on the homogeneity criteria used for the growing area, which is then applied to the whole growing region. This method will be continued until there are no more pixels that can be added to the growing regions that can be added to the growing areas can be added. Finally, all of the pixels that have been added to the expanding areas are utilized to show the object's appearance.

A survey of existing methods in image processing for bone cancer was conducted. The current approaches for the detection of bone cancer via the use of digital image processing techniques are explained in depth in this part, taking into account the most recent articles published in peer-reviewed journals [13].

5.2.1 Image Capture and Display

This is the first phase in the prediction of bone cancer, and it occurs at the very beginning. When using the electron microscope to examine bone, the cross-section of microscopic pictures generated with the microscope was utilized to forecast malignancies [14].

5.2.2 The Biological Significance of Bone

To distinguish between different age groups of samples, the key features in the bone cross-section were collected for the following: Haversian canals, osteon fragments, lamellar bone, bony trabeculae, and myxoid matrix.

5.2.3 Conversion of a Picture into a Greyscale Level

To make it easier for subsequent procedures, the RGB (Red, Green, and Blue) digital input picture must be transformed into binary data [15].

An application called MATLAB is used to carry out this conversion procedure. The final product will be a grayscale picture.

5.2.4 Preparation of the Material

The preprocessing activities are contracted out to get the information contained in the picture and to disclose the features that are necessary for an image to be revealed. The cross-section microscopic pictures of bone cancer were collected using an electronic microscope and analysed.

5.3 Main Contributions

Area-rising methods are often employed in the field of medical picture segmentation for a variety of applications, including kidney segmentation, cardiac imaging, and bone surface extraction, among others. The benefits of this segmentation approach include the capacity to construct linked areas as well as the ability to appropriately segment regions with matching attributes [16]. An inherent drawback of this strategy is that various beginning locations may not always result in similar areas rising in size. As a consequence, since the homogeneity criteria determine the outcome of region development, failing to choose the proper criterion may result in the adjustment of areas that do not belong to the object of their type.

5.3.1 Outline of the Paper

Section II contains building blocks. In section III, the proposed methodology is developed, and section IV has the data requirement and results in analysis.

5.4 Segmentation

In computer-aided diagnosis, image extraction of features and graph theory are ineluctably related. Graph detaching in this follows the Gibbs exemplary with cost or power function C and picture clustering since the conclusion is globally optimal for an objective function. Edge-based techniques are computationally efficient, and they typically do not require prior knowledge of image content [17]. The most common flaw with this method is that the edges do not always fully enclose the target. The path and magnitude can be viewed as images using this segmentation technique. A post-processing phase of uniting or grouping edges is obliged to outline the data.

Hard thresholding is a way of determining whether to retain or kill a signal during the denoising process. It goes above and beyond to minimize the amount of noise present in the picture while still preserving the relevant information, without taking into account the frequency components of the signal. It is entirely composed of variable content and includes parameters with very low frequency, resulting in the recovery of meaningful information as a consequence of the procedure [18].

Following the application of the soft and hard thresholds, scientifically sound and traceable calculations were carried out to determine the threshold wavelet transform and acquire the denoising picture as the final output result. Nevertheless, the hard threshold does not implicate when doing fewer computations, such as the GCV technique, although noise coefficients may overcome the hard threshold and continue to show up as annoying "blips" in the yield in certain cases [19].

5.5 Classification

The hanging-togetherness method is used in this method to recognize image essentials from the same object. The fuzzy logic is used to describe the hanging-togetherness. Fuzzy affinity is used to explain the nearby fuzzy relationships. One global fuzzy relationship in this segmentation technique is fuzzy connectedness, in which each pair of picture is assigned a value in all possible paths between the two pictures.

5.5.1 Min/Max Algorithm For Graph Cuts

Boykov and Kolmogorov look at energy-saving techniques for computer vision and autonomous information extraction. Two reusable and non-overlapping search trees based on imbuing paths are given for the min-cut/max-flow algorithm: S stands for sources, and T stands for sink t. Non-saturation emerges from the source node to the destination in tree S, but not from the children to the parent node in tree That. There may be active or passive nodes, focusing on the outer and inner bounds.

5.6 Existing System

A typical primary bone tumour with a high risk of recurrence is referred to as a GIANT cell tumour of bone (GCTB). This osteolytic tumour can be malignant or is in the middle between becoming benign and malignant. GCTB is made up of multinucleated giant cells in a sea of fusiform to oval mononuclear cells histologically. The GCTB recurrence rate has been stated to be as high as 18–50 per cent. A prompt and accurate diagnosis is needed. The MMPM imaging method is used to acquire the GCTB's muller matrix. The imaging system's microscope is a polarization transmission microscope. The polarization state generator (PSG) and polarization state analyzer are the key components of the imaging system (PSA). The PSG is made up of the quarter-wave plate R1 and the linear polarizer P1 (GCL-060703, Daheng Optics). Weighted graph $G=V, E$ for a set of source nodes P can be used to present the image in 3D format. Both voxels and terminals are included in the set of nodes V; $V = P\ U\ T$, where T indicates the terminal point. All n-links and t-links are included in the set of edges E; E=ENUET, where t- links nodes are included. ET is a set of voxel and n-links nodes (Figure 5.1).

We evaluated by comparing MPFN to state-of-the-art classifiers such as confirmatory factor forests (CCF) random forest (RF), and SVM using the element pictures collection of GCTB tissue. The performance of MPFN trained with pertinent spatial information is aligned to other prediction models trained with a single image input and four metrics.

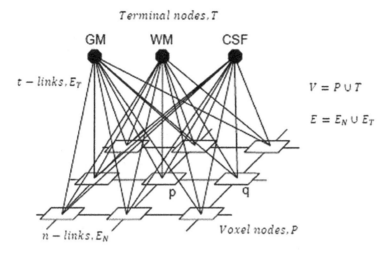

FIGURE 5.1
GM, WM, and CSF segmentation.

5.7 Proposed System

The suggested scheme is as follows: An MRI bone picture is chosen from the data of one picture to be pre-trained. Soft bone tissues including white matter, grey matter, and cerebrospinal fluid are surrounded by outer bone structure. To choose a slice from a bone image with bones, MRIcroN software is used. The sectionalization accuracy is driven by slice sorting; a manual method is used to sort a slice of the presented bone image. Finally, Matlab software is used to transition the extracted slice to a two-dimensional image format.

The FSL isolated bone image is sliced using the MRIcroN application. Slice selection specifies segmentation accuracy; a procedure is used to pick a slice of the rendered bone picture. Finally, using MATLAB code, the picked slice is changed to a two-dimensional picture format (Figure 5.2).

In LNIP (Local Neighborhood Intensity Pattern) algorithm, for calculating the binary pattern, two neighbouring pixels are considered. In this method, only the closest pixels are considered because of the texture information given by the neighbouring pixels. This 3x3 window method is used to get the information by predicting the binary pattern. This information is predicted following the neighbouring pixels (Figure 5.3).

During the spotting edges, a median filter is used to eliminate noise and maintain edges while maintaining the image data's cost function low. The following equation from the three-by-three community surrounding the corresponding pixel in the source bone image is used in any pixel. The 'canny' detection study aims to create a graph to assess the unique edges.

FIGURE 5.2
Preprocessing approach A.

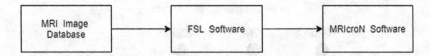

FIGURE 5.3
Preprocessing approach B.

Light and dark edges, and perhaps even the inclusion of low points when they are coupled to the high rim, would be used in this model. The edge analysed representation for both associated and – anti characteristics must be much softer and sensitivity directed. As a result, we smoothed the edge detected image using absolute two-dimensional convolution for both connected and non-connected components.

Hexagonal histogram of the thresholding step is required when using graph cuts to create. Thresholding is chosen by hand for each picture. The calculation of the histogram following pixel density and grey levels is critical for identifying the image's objects and context. The active node aids in the growth of the tree by looking for nearby non-saturated nodes and obtaining new children from them, while the passive node is unable to expand because it is clogged by other edges in the same tree. During this juncture of growth, the newly seized node joins the corresponding search tree as an active member (Figure 5.4).

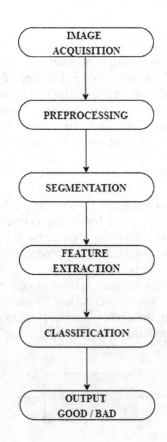

FIGURE 5.4
Block diagram of image processing.

5.8 Result and Observations

A bone image is created from the input, which is then converted into a near estimation coefficient (low-pass filter) and subtle element coefficient (high-pass filter) using a 5-level wavelet decomposition algorithm. The close estimate coefficient may be adjusted to zero at that time; the key design feature is that it eliminates low frequencies from the image. The image has been rebuilt using just the surviving wavelet coefficients, and a new close estimation coefficient has been calculated. New estimate coefficients are then added along with the subtle element coefficient to produce a new coefficient. Using wavelet reproduction, it is possible to convert this new coefficient into a preprocessed image.

The mother wavelet is used to produce several wavelets using different window function combinations. These functions are often localized in two fundamental parameters, namely time and frequency, which serve as the basis for their operation. An input picture is represented as the sum of a large number of wavelet functions with varying spatial and temporal resolutions and scales.

According to the detailed contents of the picture, the decomposed wavelet image is formed of a pair of input waveforms that represent the high-frequency components of the detailed contents of the image. The wavelet function is what is used to describe this. As the name implies, the scaling function is composed of low-frequency components or portions of a picture including smooth areas. The wavelet transform's essential qualities of regularity, orthogonality, and space- or time-set-out are all zero-valued functions, and it is because of these properties that the wavelet transform plays an unavoidable role in image processing techniques. The Haar Wavelet is the easiest wavelet to understand.

Haar wavelet is a bipolar step function that may be represented as a wavelet. The most significant benefit of employing the Haar wavelet is that it is a discontinuous function of time and that it has superior localization properties in terms of both time and frequency when compared to other wavelets. Multi-focus picture fusion is accomplished by the use of a pixel-level fusion rule known as the maximal technique. The low-frequency sub-band coefficients are fused by picking the coefficient with the highest spatial frequency from among those with lower frequencies. It displays the overall degree of activity in a photograph. The high-frequency sub-band coefficients are fused by picking coefficients with the highest LDP code value and fusing them (Figure 5.5).

An anaplastic growth of tissue in the bone has been classified into three types: primary tumours that began in the bone or from bone-derived cells and tissues, secondary tumours that began in other locations and spread to the skeleton, and metastatic tumours that began in other locations and spread to the skeleton.

Because of this well-known characteristic, it is even more critical for therapists to forecast and identify the tumour stage to treat it properly. To detect and identify bone tumours, the normalized 99' image was conducted to get a predetermined standard picture, after which improvements were applied to the image during the preprocessing step. The K-means clustering method was used to identify the picture regions and forecast the likelihood of a tumour forming in those locations. In the last step, the genetic algorithm is applied to the population set that has been created. As a result of this specification, genetics is triggered, and the algorithm then proceeds to carry out the genetics via its continuous stages of selection, crossover, mutation, and so on. Following the completion of the genetic process, the correct threshold values were applied to the bone picture to identify the tumour region.

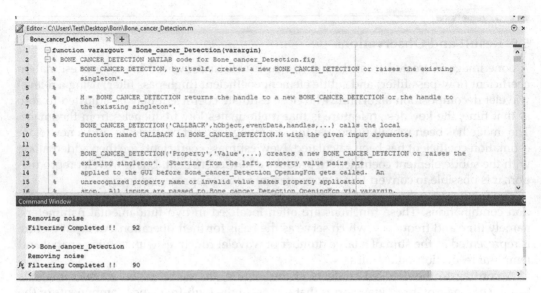

FIGURE 5.5
Code used to obtain an output with an accuracy of 90%.

To conduct the study, a sample database of MRI scan images was diagnosed utilizing image preprocessing activity as the first step, followed by denoising the picture after that. However, data should not be wasted during the process of removing noise, since these data are eventually required for the detection of the tumour. It was discovered that the hard thresholding method, which is dependent on the wavelet thresholding process, did not always provide recoverable denoising results. After doing a hard and soft analysis on noisy forms of the conventional one-dimensional signals, we were able to determine a threshold value by using Visu shrink software. However, to get an augmented image as an output, the added surface photos must first be denoised.

When it comes to signal to a process, the wavelet method is a valuable tool. Therefore, in this context, To identify the malignancy, researchers employed the Haar capacity. This portion of the effort will, in turn, improve the visual character of the bone image via image processing, which will, in turn, aid in the identification of bone tumours at an early stage. The MRI picture was used in conjunction with image processing to provide a more improved result. It was carried out by the two components, which included crude guesses and nuanced elements as well. According to our findings, in the context of rough guesses (low recurrence), points of interest outperform points of interest when it comes to execution. As a result, we focus our attention on the denoised portion of the image. As a result of our results, it is evident that pre-processing of the picture is required to get an adequate image (Figure 5.6).

To evaluate the results, it is not enough to simply look at the separated picture produced by different algorithms. It is critical to assess the picture segmentation accuracy using the flow algorithm as well as the current cut algorithm's various graph cuts approach. In the experimental MRIs, the GM and WM were considered, as well as other bone tissues.

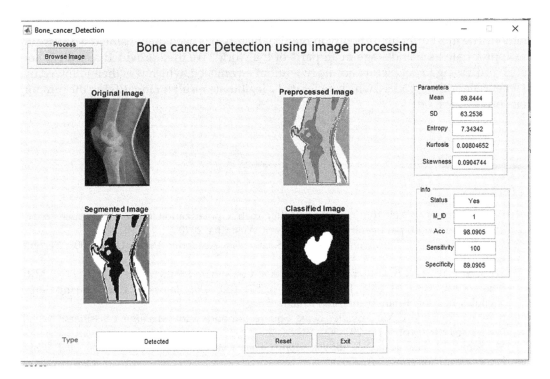

FIGURE 5.6
Processed output.

5.9 Conclusion

For project simplicity and time constraints, 10 separate slivers of two bone pictures were examined in our research for bone MR image segmentation. The cut algorithm flow algorithm was used in the MR image segmentation experiments. The preliminary test suggests that the min-cut/max-flow algorithm takes far less time and is more complex than the normalized cut algorithm to section the bone MRI picture into WM, GM, and CSF.

Image pre-processing methods were used to lessen the influence of noise on the photos while still achieving a smooth appearance. As a result, picture segmentation was carried out in conjunction with the K-means method to improve the quality of the segmentation. Using an average filter and a bilateral filter, the photos that did not include a tumour or any other associated image were deleted. Furthermore, a mix of threshold segmentation and edge detection was employed to provide a more exact segmentation of the data. The margin region, on the other hand, was deleted without interfering with the object concentration section. Finally, the picture was captured to detect a bone tumour; nevertheless, the stage of the tumour must be determined to provide suitable therapy. To maintain the current condition, a method known as a genetic algorithm was used.

The genetic algorithm is primarily based on the optimization approach and works with the concepts of genetics and natural selection to achieve its results. We were able to estimate the kind of tumour in 122 out of 122 samples of afflicted patients by using the GA method. The most difficult difficulty in medical history has been diagnosing the disease at the appropriate time and stage in all parts of the world. We then provided a strategy for image processing to get picture accuracy without any misled, which was then followed by a Genetic algorithm process, which generated a legitimate result for identifying the tumour in its proper location.

References

1. Detection of giant cell tumour using muller matrix polarization microscopic microscopic imaging, and multi parameters fusion network, Australia, 2020.
2. Issac N. Bankman, *Framework of Medical Sonography*, Academic Press, USA, 2008, Second Edition.
3. MICCAI 2006, LNCS 4191, pp. 831–838, 2006. Coordinated Pattern Slashes for Bone MRI Binarization, MICCAI 2006, LNCS 4191, pp. 831–838, 2006. James C. Gee, Zhuang Song, Nicholas Tustison, Brian Avants, and Zhuang Song.
4. J. A. K. Suykens, J. Vandewalle. Least Square Supportvector Machine Classifiers. *Neural Processing Letters*, vol. 9, pp. 293–300, 1999.
5. M. Sonka, V. Hlavacand, R. Boyle, *Apportionment Mechanism, Argumentation, and Image Recognition*, Thomson, USA, 2008.
6. D. Rajesh Kumar, A. Shanmugam. A Hyper Heuristic Localization Based Cloned Node Detection Technique Using GSA Based Simulated Annealing in Sensor Networks. In *Cognitive Computing for Big Data Systems Over IoT* (pp. 307–335). Springer International Publishing, 2017.
7. J. Shi, J. Malik N Cut and Image Segmentation, IEEE Trans, August 2000.
8. Amit Verma, Gayatri Khanna. A Survey on Digital Image Processing Techniques for Tumor Detection, *Indian Journal of Science and Technology*, vol. 9, no. 14, pp. 1–14, 2016.
9. Anand Jatti. Segmentation of Microscopic Bone Images, *International Journal of Electronics Engineering*, vol. 2, no. 1, pp. 11–15, 2010.
10. Anam Mustaqeem, Ali Javed, Tehseen Fatima. An Efficient Brain Tumor Detection Algorithm Using Watershed & Thresholding Based Segmentation, *International Journal of Image, Graphics and Signal Processing*, vol. 10, no. 1, pp. 34–39, 2012.
11. Anita Chaudhary, Sonit Sukhraj Singh. *Proceedings of the International Conference on Computing Sciences*, September 14–15, Lung cancer detection on CT images by using image processing, Punjab, 2012.
12. S. Arora, P. Raghavan, S. Rao. *Proceedings of 30th Annual ACM Symposium on Theory of Computing*, May 24–26, Approximation Schemes for Euclidean k-median and Related Problems, Dallas, 1998.
13. S. Irfan, R. K. Dhanaraj. BeeRank: A Heuristic Ranking Model to Optimize the Retrieval Process. *International Journal of Swarm Intelligence Research (IJSIR)*, 12(2), 39–56, 2021.
14. Ashwini Zade, Mangesh Wanjari. Detection of Cancer Cells in Mammogram Using Seeded Region Growing Method and Genetic Algorithm, *Journal of Science and Technology*, vol. 2, no. 3, pp. 15–20, 2014.
15. Madhuri Avula, Narasimha Prasad Lakkakula, Murali Prasad Raja. *Proceedings of the 8th Asia Modelling Symposium*, September 23–25, Bone Cancer Detection from MRI Scan Imagery Using Mean Pixel Intensity, Washington, DC, 2014.
16. Azian Azamimi Abdullah, Bu Sze Chize, Yoshifumi Nishio *Proceedings of the International Conference on Biomedical Engineering*, February 27–28, Implementation of an Improved Cellular Neural Network Algorithm For Brain Tumor Detection, Macao, Malaysia, 2012.

17. Bart Goossens, Aleksandra Pižurica, Wilfried Philips. ImageDenoising Using Mixtures of Projected Gaussian Scale Mixtures. *IEEE Transactions On Image Processing*, vol. 18, no. 8, pp. 1689–1702, 2009.
18. E. Behnamghader, R. D. Ardekani, M. Torabi, E. Fatemizadeh. *Proceedings of 5th International Symposium on Image and Signal Processing and Analysis*, September 27–29, Another Approach to Detection of Abnormalities in MR-Images Using Support Vector Machines, Turkey, 2007.
19. Avik Bhattacharya, K. S. Patnaik. *Proceedings of International Conference on Machine Intelligence and Research Advancement*, December 21–23, Modified Rough Fuzzy C Means Algorithm for MR Image Segmentation, Katra, India, 2013.

6

Challenges, Progress and Opportunities of Blockchain in Healthcare Data

Dinesh Komarasamy, M. K. Dharani, and R. Thamilselvan
Kongu Engineering College, Perundurai, India

J. Jenita Hermina
Er. Perumal Manimekalai College of Engineering, Hosur, India

CONTENTS

DOI: 10.1201/9781003217435-6

6.1 Different Ways of Managing Healthcare Data

Nowadays, the patient's history is maintained in different forms throughout the world. The maintenance of patient's information in hospitals varies based on the policy of the country. The different ways are

- Patient maintains their records.
- Hospitals maintain patient records on local servers.
- Hospitals maintain patient records on centralized servers.
- Hospitals maintain patient records in the cloud.

6.1.1 Patient Maintains Their Records

In some developing and underdeveloped countries, the patient's information is maintained only by the patients, and the hospital does not maintain the history of the patients. In this case, the patient's history will be handed over to the patient itself, and the patients will be responsible to maintain the data.

Figure 6.1 shows the patient maintaining their own records. In this diagram, the patients initially meet the doctors for consultation. After consultation, the doctor may give a prescription or recommend a lab test. After that, the specimens of the patients are collected in the lab, and reports are given back to the doctor or patients. But the patients maintain all the records on file as a hard copy. This way has some drawbacks, such as information loss, repetition of lab tests, and physical recordings deterioration [1]. Moreover, some of the patients sometimes do not have much knowledge about the importance of maintaining their health records. The information loss in patient health data may cause wrong treatment without knowing the past records, which sometimes puts the patients at risk. Furthermore, some of the patients do not have knowledge about the lab test. So, there is a possibility of retaking the same test. Sometimes, the repetition of the lab test is unnecessary

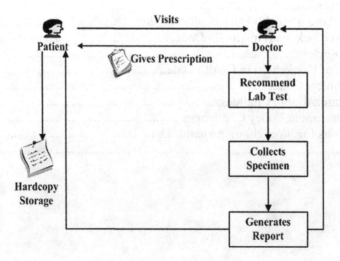

FIGURE 6.1
Patient maintains their records.

and is a waste of time and money. Moreover, if the patients maintain data in physical form, there is a possibility of missing and deteriorating physical records [2].

6.1.2 Hospitals Maintain Patient Records on Local Servers

In order to avoid such a situation, the patient's details are maintained in the hospital. Since some of the patients rarely visit the hospital, only once every 5–10 years, it is unnecessary to maintain their details. Initially, the hospital keeps physical copies of records on-site. But hospitals find it difficult to maintain all of their patients' records. Figure 6.2 represents the hospitals' maintenance of patient records on a local server. Here, medicines are provided in the hospital itself, and patient records are also maintained in the hospital. This strategy also has some drawbacks in the real environment. In this scenario, the patient's information can be lost in many cases, like when the patients shift from one location to another location, the patients visit other hospital, and the patient's history is unknown at the time of emergency. Even though hospitals maintain physical records of patients, the details will deteriorate over time [3].

6.1.3 Hospitals Maintain Patient Records on Centralized Servers

Instead of maintaining physical records, hospitals may plan to maintain their patients' history in the form of softcopy. Therefore, hospitals will maintain the patient history in the form of electronic health record (EHR). An EHR is a digital copy of a patient's medical records. Moreover, EHR can be developed, maintained, and accessed by authorized physicians, personnel from several healthcare institutions, and patients. The EHR data will be

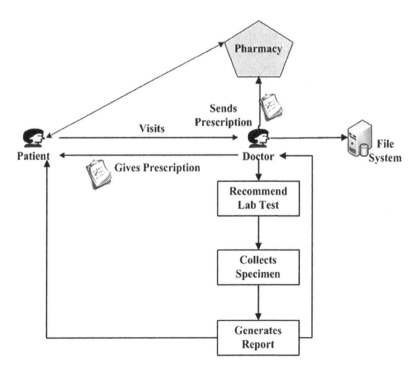

FIGURE 6.2
Hospitals maintain patient history.

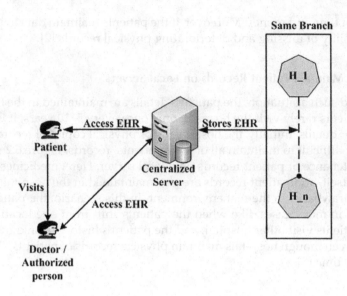

FIGURE 6.3
Hospitals maintain patient records on a centralized server.

maintained on the centralized server. Each and every time, the patients are examined by different doctors. With the aid of a centralized server, the doctor will know the patient's history at that time. In some cases, the hospital has branches that are located in different locations [4]. In this circumstance, the patients visit any one of the branches for their treatment. At that time, the doctor can access the patient's data from the centralized server. Figure 6.3 depicts a centralized server that stores patient history. It made a platform for a doctor to discuss the patient and take some decisions at the time of risk by maintaining the data on a centralized server. Still, there are difficulties in this scenario. Moreover, the hospital under the same group is able to access the server. Since the patient's data is maintained on a centralized server, the patient's history will be lost when there is a failure on a centralized server. Therefore, doctors or specialists in different hospitals cannot interact and make decisions. Moreover, the hospital has full authority to maintain the database, whereas the patients do not have the right to access their records.

6.1.4 Hospitals Maintain Patient Records in the Cloud

In some cases, patients may visit different hospitals for their treatment. In this case, doctors from different hospitals do not have access to the patient's past history. Therefore, doctors do not have access to a patient's medical history when the patient visits the doctor for the first time in another hospital. The only possible ways are to get access from the hospital in which the patient has already taken medication to know the patient's history or the patient needs to give his whole report. The corresponding hospital should provide the full details of the particular patient. But in the real environment, it is very difficult to get the complete details of a patient from a hospital. Figure 6.4 depicts the storing of EHR in a cloud database.

Therefore, the patients' records are stored and maintained in the cloud instead of maintaining their history on a local server. Even though the patients' data are stored in the

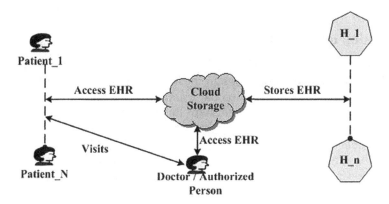

FIGURE 6.4
Storing of EHR in a cloud database.

cloud database, the doctors do not have direct access to their patients' records. The patients want to store their data securely. Therefore, storing this crucial EHR in the cloud requires security protocols. From the state of the art, security approaches may be cryptographic or non-cryptographic. Some of the cryptographic approaches are Public Key Encryption (PKE), Symmetric Key Encryption (SKE), searchable encryption, (Hierarchical) Identity-Based Encryption (HIBE), Proxy Re-encryption (PRE), Predicate/Hierarchical Predicate Encryption (HPE), and (Fully) holomorphic encryption. Similarly, some of the non-crypto-graphic approaches are hash functions and digital signature verification. Therefore, the doctor can also view the patient's history only with the aid of their key. Even though there are several security approaches to secure the patients' data, some of the sensitive health data are being shared with unauthorized outsiders. Therefore, data confidentiality is less in the cloud-based system [5]. Despite the fact that medical data are stored on the cloud, there remains a security vulnerability that could result in a security breach. As cloud computing faces security issues when storing healthcare data, blockchain technology has evolved to securely store healthcare data.

6.1.5 Drawbacks in Current Technology

The health industry requires security, interoperability, data sharing, and data access to the health data of the patient. The health data contains some private data like addresses, payment data, and health data, which need to be secured before being stored in the cloud. Current systems, like smart devices that store medical data, lack security concerns. Access to health data like access control and proper authentication to the system are the major security threats in the current system. Even though some systems have access security, many systems do not have the feature of interoperability. Interoperability means the ability to exchange information among systems. The use of centralized data storage in medical facilities is the biggest barrier to interoperability. The centralized database may cause issues like slow retrieval of data, insecurity of data, and loss of data. Data sharing between the systems or organizations becomes difficult as the data are stored in different locations. Because blockchain provides decentralized storage and security authentication, it can be preferred to store healthcare records in a distributed network [6].

6.2 Introduction of Blockchain

Blockchain is the collection of individual blocks in which all the information are stored as individual blocks. Individual blocks contain the following information: current hash value, timestamp of the transaction, transaction data, and previous hash value. Initially, the hash value of the previous hash is considered zero. Blockchain maintains a ledger in a decentralized manner, which contains complete information about a successful transaction. The ledger is immutable and distributed across the network. Similarly, the ledger is maintained in each node. The available information can be accessed by all the nodes in the chain. Thus, all the transactions in the blockchain are more transparent than the centralized transactions, which do not include any third-party organization. Blockchain is a technique that ensures safe data transfer without the use of a third-party system. Moreover, it stores and transfers the data in a secure way such that the data cannot be hacked or modified by eyedroppers [7].

Figure 6.5 indicates the block representation. The individual blocks are connected to form the blockchain. The blocks are arranged in a specific order by following any given node structure. The individual blocks are linked with each other by using list concepts. The size of the lists will grow continuously with the confirmation and collection of nodes. The information in the blockchain is stored in the network and the information is replicated in a distributed environment. Even if the data are replicated across all nodes, blockchain can ensure data security in a distributed environment. Each node has a copy of the chained block, which can also be updated when a new block is added [8].

Figure 6.6 represents the structure of a blockchain. The blockchain has a current hash and a previous hash. The previous hash is used to link the current hash with the existing hash. The current hash value is a unique one.

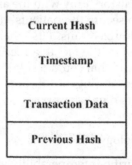

FIGURE 6.5
Denotes the block representation.

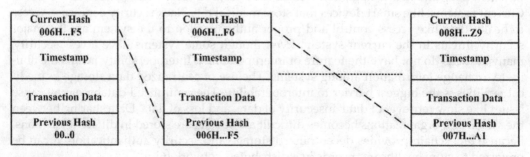

FIGURE 6.6
Structure of blockchain.

Table 6.1 shows the information about the transactions of the patient that are to be stored in the block. It gives the timestamp of the block when the particular block is connected to the other block.

Figure 6.7 represents the blockchain representation of an individual transaction T1. As shown in Table 6.1, T1 appears thrice in the database. Figures 6.7, 6.8, and 6.9 depict the collection of blocks that represent the particular transaction T1, T2, and T3, respectively. Each block in the blockchain contains a timestamp, which is the time the block connects to another block. And the data of the patient occurs in transaction T1. Moreover, a hash value is used to connect the newly created block with the other block. The previous hash has the

TABLE 6.1

Information about the Transactions

Transaction	Timestamp	Transaction Data
T1	2021-17-10 06:54:15	X-ray report
T2	2021-17-10 08:34:10	Prescription
T3	2021-17-10 11:03:11	MRI report
T1	2021-17-10 09:04:11	Scan report
T1	2021-17-10 09:15:19	Medical bill
T3	2021-17-10 15:32:15	Prescription

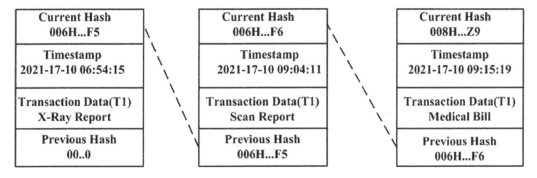

FIGURE 6.7
Blockchain representation of an individual transaction T1.

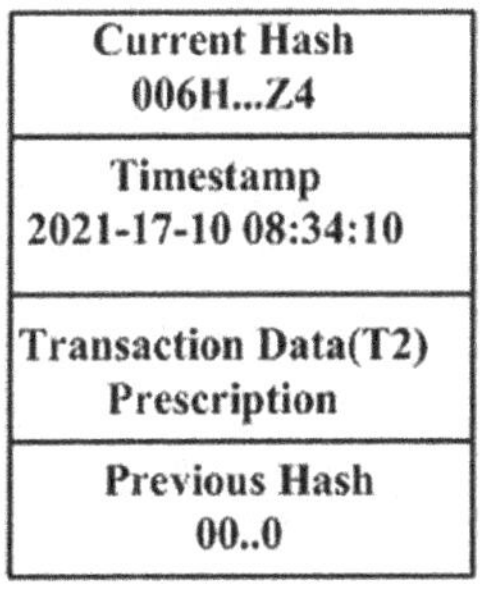

FIGURE 6.8
Blockchain representation of an individual transaction T2.

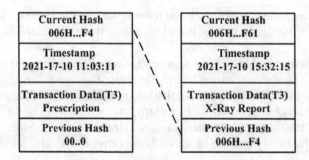

FIGURE 6.9
Blockchain representation of an individual transaction T3.

hash value of the previous block's current hash value. The current hash value is generated by the cryptographic hash function called Secure Hash Algorithm 256-bit (SHA-256), which gives 256 bits of the value. The SHA algorithm will be discussed in Section 6.2.1.

6.2.1 Secure Hash Algorithm in Blockchain

Hashing plays a major role in providing the network modules that are more important in the blockchain. Therefore, Secured Hashing Algorithm 256 is used to provide highly secured hashing. It is one of the most widely used security-based algorithms used for real-world applications. Thus, the hash key value is generated using the Secure Hash Algorithm in the blockchain. SHA-256 uses plain text with variants of size, which provides a hash key value of 256 bits. Hashing provides a password to validate the integrity of the user. Specific standalone features of the SHA algorithm are as follows:

- Message Length: The size of the plain/clear text should be less than 264 bits. It should be compared to keep the digest as random as possible.
- Digest Length: In SHA-256, the length of the hash digest is 256 bits. It can be varied with the version of an algorithm like SHA-512, which will have a digest length of 512 bits since the rate of increase in digest slightly increases the cost and speed.
- Irreversible: It is designed in such a way that SHA-256 is irreversible. When the digest is provided early, it should not return the original value or plain text when it is passed through the hash function for the second time.

Steps involved in SHA:

Step-1: Preprocessing – Convert the given text/hexa values into binary.

Step-2: Padding – Do the process of padding with 0's until it reaches a multiple of 512, where L is the length of the initial message.

Step-3: Appending – If L $<2^{64}$, then append the 64 bits to its end.

Step-4: Initialize hash values – Create eight constant hash values using the factional square root of the first eight prime numbers, which are hard-coded constants.

Step-5: Initialize the Round Constants (k) using the fractional cube root part of the first 64 prime numbers between 2 and 311.

Step-6: Repeat the preceding steps for each 512-bit chunk of input data where the eight hash values (h0–h7) are used.

Step-7: Message Schedule(S) – Create a copy of input data from Step-1 where each entry will have 32 bits.

Modify the zero indices using the following steps:
For I 16–63 from values of S

- w0 = (S[i-15] RR 7) XOR (S[i-15] RR 18) XOR (S[i-15] RS 3)
- w1 = (S[i- 2] RR 17) XOR (S[i- 2] RR 19) XOR (S[i- 2] RS 10)
- S[i] = S[i-16] + w0 + S[i-7] + w1

Where RR – Rightrotate, RS – Rightshift

Step-8: Compression – Initialize the values from a to h and equalize them with respective hash values h0–h7.

Run the c the values v0–v7
For i from 0 to 63

w1 = (v4 RR 6) XOR (v4 RT 11) XOR (v4 RT 25)
ex= (v4 AND v5) XOR ((NOT v4) and v6)
temp1 = v7 + w1 + ex + k[i] + S[i]
w0 = (v0 RR 2) XOR (v0 RR 13) XOR (v0 RR 22)
major = (v0 AND v1) XOR (v0 AND v2) xor (v1 AND v2)
T1 := w0 + major
v7 = v6
v6 = v5
v5 = v4
v4 = v3 + T0
v3 = v2
v2 = v1
v1 = v0
v0= T0 + T1

Step-9: Modify the final value – Modify the hash value by adding the variables a–h along with modulo 23

Step-10: Concatenate all the calculated chunk values into a single string.

Thus, blockchain is preferred to store healthcare data in a distributed environment. The following section describes the various applications of blockchain in different domains.

6.3 Application of Blockchain

Nowadays, blockchain is applicable in various fields such as business, industry, banking, climate, transactions, healthcare, and so on. Among these, the business sectors maintain Business Process Management (BPM). BPM generally means the combination of methods like analysis, improvement, optimization, and automation of the business process to achieve the business goals. Among these, the automation system is the most difficult because of security protocols. With the help of blockchain technology, automation can be achieved without breaking tradition and security. Nowadays, blockchain is applicable in all fields. Therefore, the few lists of blockchains are

1. Bank application
2. Healthcare application
3. Bitcoin
4. Secure Internet of Things networks
5. Data storage

Moreover, in the banking sector, there are lots of issues in traditional banking applications like double spending, more transfer fees, hacking, and so on. Blockchain technology maintains a distributed ledger of all the transaction details as a block. The blockchain only maintains successful transactions. Therefore, blockchain allows users to do only simultaneous transactions, thereby saving bank applications from double spending, transfer fees, and so on. In addition to that, blockchain is a more secure way to store healthcare data, and it is very difficult for hackers to fetch the information. In healthcare data, patients' data is maintained over the internet, which is more sensitive. But the traditional algorithm is not suitable for storing the health record in a distributed environment.

In addition to that, large amounts of data are generated from different sources, such as the Internet of Things (IoT), smart devices, sensors, social media, and so on. The generated data cannot be stored in a unified location, and it is also very difficult to store a large volume of data in any individual system. Instead of storing in an individual system, the generated data is collected and stored in a distributed environment [9]. However, the users panic about storing their data in a distributed environment since a large amount of data is maintained in a decentralized network. The existing techniques cannot assure security for storing the data over the internet. Therefore, blockchain technology has evolved to secure the data stored in the distributed environment. Therefore, the medical data are stored on blockchain networks to avoid security breaches. The need for blockchain in healthcare is described in Section 6.4 [10].

6.4 Need for Blockchain in Healthcare

From the state of the art, several researchers introduced different approaches to blockchain to address different problems in society. Since most hospitals find it difficult to maintain their data manually, hospitals are willing to record patients' history electronically. Therefore, EMR plays a major role in healthcare. EMR is the digitized version of graphs and charts of the patients' reports that are managed in hospitals. Nowadays, in healthcare, it is very difficult to maintain the patient's history on a centralized server because the patient's history may be lost when there is any failure in the centralized server. Hence, the patient's history has been maintained on the distributed server. But the patient's history is more sensitive, and the distributed environment is not very secure to store the patients' data. Thus, hospitals maintain the EMR data on a centralized server. But the patients are struggling to consult doctors in different hospitals. Therefore, patients are interested in maintaining their data on a distributed server. Thus, hospitals are willing to maintain the data in a distributed environment due to the evolution of blockchain. In the healthcare sector, blockchain is used in several cases, like managing electronic medical records (EMR), remote patient monitoring, and health insurance claims. Among these, EMR is widely used for storing healthcare data [11].

Figure 6.10 represents the storage of medical data on a blockchain. The blockchain concept is used to track the address of a block that contains the EMR data. Similarly, different department data like remote patient monitoring, health insurance, and EMR are stored in the blocks. Each patient profile is linked to the corresponding blocks in the group of blocks [12]. Moreover, Remote Patient Monitoring becomes more extensible for monitoring patients with the use of IoT devices. In order to manage the huge volume of data, blockchain is used to maintian the patient records acquired by the IoT devices in a secure manner. The blockchain use the Ethereum protocol in which the device invokes the smart contract and all the patient records are stored in the individual blocks. With the help of a smart contract, notifications are sent to both the doctors and patients who are associated with the network [13]. As the expense of healthcare rises, health insurance becomes the only option to ensure the safety of the people. Quality care is provided in the event of an accident or significant sickness through insurance. A major task in health insurance is managing the records in a secure way. Many fraud activities happen by giving false details to insurance providers. Therefore, blockchain is preferred to maintain insurance records in order to combat fraud activities and secure data [14].

Moreover, blockchain stores healthcare information. It also interconnects insurance with the customers. Therefore, blockchain technology acts as an intermediary between the customer and the insurance company. In developed countries, hospital bills are provided only

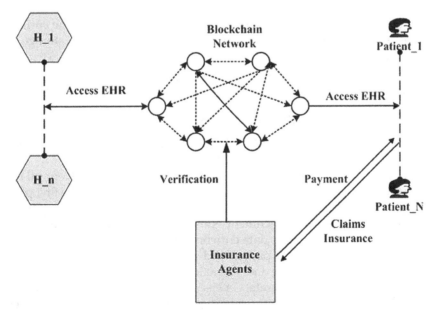

FIGURE 6.10
Storing medical data in blockchain.

through insurance. Therefore, the wrong details and fraud can be prevented since blockchain interconnects the EHR and insurance companies. Therefore, the patient can easily claim insurance. The payment is initiated once the patient's records are verified in the blockchain network [15]. In some developed countries, people can consult with a doctor only after making a prior appointment. Moreover, the patient cannot directly purchase any medicine. In some developed countries, medicalcoding techniques are used for the treatment of patients.

In this diagram, hospitals have details of an 'n' number of patients. The details are stored in the blockchain. Afterwards, the insurance agents can access the details of the customers from the blockchain network. After verifying the patient's medical history, the insurance will be handed over to them, and all medical records, along with the insurance, will be recorded in the blockchain [16].

6.4.1 Advantages of Distributed Storage in Blockchain

From the state of the art, healthcare data is stored in cloud storage. But security is a major concern in cloud storage. Along with that, it needs permission from the government and most of the cloud storage is centralized. But, the issue with centralized storage is the occurrence of bottlenecks, the risk of hacking the data, and the loss of information when the server fails. In order to sort out the issues, healthcare data are stored in blockchain data storage. Blockchain data storage combines two technologies, such as decentralized storage and the concept of blockchain. The main advantages of distributed storage are

- The authorized user can access healthcare data anywhere at any time since the data is available on a decentralized server.
- Unauthorized users or hackers cannot access the data because it is available on an encrypted distributed network.

Moreover, nodes in the distributed network maintain a detailed log for the entire transaction of the patient's record. Therefore, security is achieved in distributed storage.

6.5 Managing Patient Health Data in Blockchain

Managing patients' health data on blockchain comprises four major steps: data collection, data enrichment, storing health data, and the role of smart contracts.

Figure 6.11 represents the EHR details in a distributed environment. Here, all the hospitals and the patients are connected in a distributed environment. Here, the first phase is the data collection about the patients in a hospital through different sources in a different format. After data collection, data enrichment is used to convert the standardized way of storing and retrieving the data. After data enrichment, the data will be stored in the blockchain, which can be accessed by a patient and also by a doctor, but only with patient knowledge. Section 6.6 describes the data collection.

Patient information must be accurate, concise, and well-structured. Patients' data like X-rays, MRI scans, and ultrasound reports are generated through various devices. These data are in different formats like text, numeric, pictures, videos, and so on, which are collected and stored in different formats in the cloud. Once the data are collected, they have

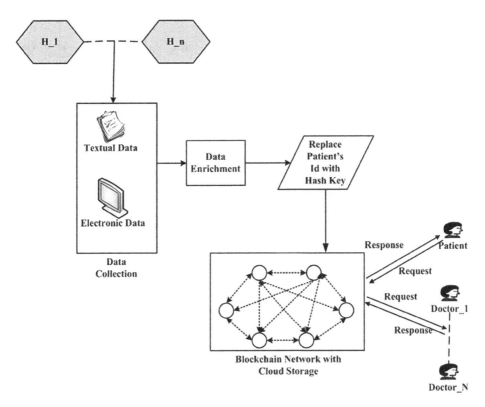

FIGURE 6.11
Represents the EHR details in a distributed environment.

to be refined to use it further. The process of data enrichment is used to add value and improve data quality. The data enrichment phase has the following properties: compliance, computation, and identity. In the compliance phase, the data connected to different sources are in different formats that are reorganized and available to retrieve at any time. Afterwards, the meta data needs to be created for the data for linking and retrieving the data in the future in the computation phase. Later, the identities of the patients are removed before storing the data in a distributed environment. In order to remove the patients' personal details, each patient's data contains the patient's ID which is replaced with the hash key to make it secure and difficult to decode. Moreover, medical data is categorized in multiple formats like administrative claim records, clinical registries, biometric data, and patient-reported data. All these data are well structured and stored to access the data in a more efficient manner. After data enrichment, the data will be stored in the blockchain. Therefore, blockchain is preferred to store a huge amount of healthcare data in a distributed network. As a result, patients have complete access to data at any time.

Because centralised data storage is insecure, blockchain has the potential to alleviate this key issue. In blockchain, the patient's data are stored among the different nodes within a network rather than centralized. The data to be stored is provided by the healthcare provider, which has a patient's ID in the form of a hash key. The hash key acts as a unique value, hence it is used while data retrieval also. Smart contract gets activated when the medical data provider tries to store data or retrieve the data in the blockchain [17]. Smart contracts are maintained on a blockchain and are essentially programmers that run when

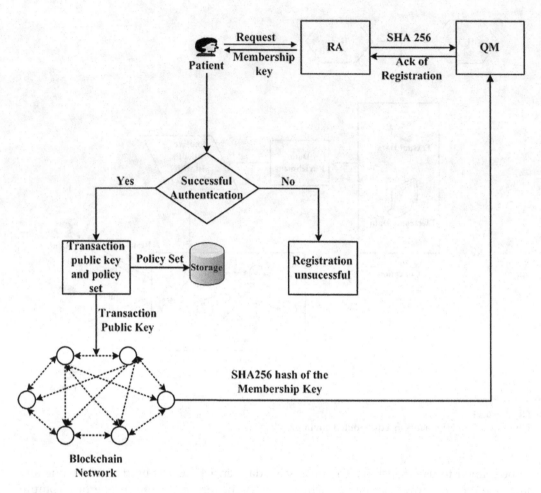

FIGURE 6.12
Patient registration modules in the blockchain.

certain criteria are satisfied. It is activated whenever the data is saved in the blocks. And the information is retrieved by the healthcare provider by giving the hash key, which is generally a patient's ID, whenever required. The logic is built on the basis that the data access is restricted according to the departments. For example, only invoices and diagnostic records are accessible to insurance providers and no other information, such as prescriptions given by doctors, are available. Similarly, patients also have the privilege of sharing the data. Patients can share the data that they want [18]. The following section describes the working on blockchain in health data.

6.6 Working on Blockchain in Health Data

Initially, patients are asked to join the group in order to access or share their health data. Since the blockchain network is permissioned, the user must be authorized to access the data.

Therefore, the patients send a request to the Registration Authority (RA). RA provides the right for patients to manage their data. RA generates an SHA-256 hash key and sends it to the Query Manager (QM), who converts the requests into a standardized manner. QM sends acknowledgement for the registration. SHA-256 is a cryptographic security algorithm that generates the hash key. The generated hash keys are unique and immutable. Along with the SHA-256 hash key, RA also generates a Membership Key and sends it to the patient. The Membership Key signifies that the patient is the authorized user in the network and is used to request data. The patient can sign in to the blockchain network using a Membership Key. Once the patient successfully signs in with the Membership Key given by RA, the patient generates a Transaction Public Key and policy set to share the data during the first-time registration [19].

A public key is used in the transaction of sharing health data. The data can be shared or viewed by the patient with the help of a Transaction Public Key. There are two types of transaction keys in general, such as Transaction Public Key and Transaction Private Key. The Transaction Public Key is similar to our email address; if someone knows our email address, they can write us an email. As a result, the Transaction Public Key can be shared with others, while the Transaction Private Key is protected and cannot be shared. The policy set contains the access that is given to the records. The access can be read, write, or delete. Moreover, the policy set is stored in the storage layer rather than the blockchain network. A private key, like email, cannot be shared with anyone, whereas the public key is shared and stored in the network. The generated Transaction Public Key is transmitted to the blockchain network. The user can store the data and access the data on a blockchain. While storing the data, the patients also generate an SHA-256 hash with the Membership Key that is submitted to the QM. The QM checks the hash key generated by the user along with the Membership Key, which is received from RA. The information is stored in the blockchain only when the user has registered in a group. After verification, an acknowledgement is sent to RA about the status of the verification. Similarly, the user can request data from QM along with the patient's Transaction Public Key and Membership Key in a blockchain network.

Once QM receives the request from a patient, it starts two-step verification to secure data sharing. Initially, it generates the SHA-256 hash of the Membership Key, which the user sends along with the data request, and checks it with the hash received from RA. After the successful verification, QM retrieves the Transaction Public Key from the blockchain network and verifies it with the data request from the user. Once the two-step verification is successful, QM retrieves the policy set generated by the user initially from the storage layer, reads the policy set, recognizes which operation on the data can be carried out, and forwards the information to the processing nodes. Processing nodes are the chain of nodes that receive and handle data requests. The processing nodes retrieve data and its associated policy and send it to Smart Contract Center.

Smart Contract Center generates a smart contract ad appended with the request and sends it to the processing node. The processing node creates a block with the details sent from the Smart Contact Center and transmits them to the blockchain network. The smart contract contains a predefined set of instructions that monitor the use of data received. It also employs a set of timing and connectivity functions. The connectivity function checks the connectivity between the storage layer and the user node. If the connection is lost then the system assumes that the connection is lost because of the unauthorized operation of the data. When the connection is lost, the timer is reset to 0, and data get destroyed with the help of instructions in the smart contract. The report is transmitted to the processing nodes to create blocks in the blockchain network [20].

6.7 Literature Review

In healthcare, various forms of data such as patient history, electronic medical information, and pharmaceutical details are to be maintained in large quantities and also in a secured manner. Nowadays, blockchain is used as an efficient medium for maintaining EMR [21]. Blockchain has the properties of distributed service, immutable, reliable, data origin, privacy, and security, which stand as a benchmark feature to store the EMR effectively. The European General Data Protection regulation works with blockchain technology to provide patient-centric data to a few specific stakeholders [22, 23]. This medium provides a platform to analyze the patient's history to give better suggestions on medication and also restrict sensitive information. In the United States, Gem Health Network uses the Ethereum platform, which allows different healthcare sectors to access the shared data. As far as the law of the world, human beings were considered as products of commodities, so few countries started the initiative of health coin, which paves the way for universal collection and sharing of EMR. Even though the blockchain offers a way for the secured transaction of EMR, it still has some practical difficulties with its huge volume of data, lack of standards in EMR data, lack of patient willingness to share the data, and lack of incentives towards it [24]. A private blockchain network was created using IBM's Blockchain Hyper ledger fabric and it was deployed on Bluemix. The main goals of this modular architecture are to maintain health data confidentiality, scalability, and security. It provides the chain code to maintain the controlled authorization and privileges on the IBM blockchain network [25].

To strengthen the security and privacy of EMR in blockchain cryptographic algorithm along with discrete transform and the genetic algorithm which enhance the security and also optimizes the performance of the system [26]. The attribute-based signature with multiple authorities' algorithm works on the basis of sharing the specific attribute information alone to specific registered authorities, where in this technique, the user itself limits the level of sharing. To protect the values in blockchain with respect to attributes or specific instances, some encryption techniques are used, namely: Attribute-based encryption, identity-based signature, and identity-based encryption [27, 28]. The other security service related to the blockchain was Granular Access Authorization Supporting Flexible Queries, which provides secured access to the different levels of data without the public key. In order to preserve privacy, blockchain favorably relies on asymmetric encryption, which makes sure of the system availability and patient identification in EMR systems [29, 30].

Another confirmed model for blockchain is supply chain management in the pharmaceutical/pharmaceutical industry and its allied healthcare. Shipping forged or poor-quality drugs will have a serious risk for patients. However, in the field of medicine, adulteration is prevalent. It turns out that blockchain technology can solve this problem. According to Engelhardt, few companies use the blockchain network to secure pharmaceutical drugs transactions. The common idea is to register all transactions related to drug prescriptions on a blockchain network where all the stakeholders are connected. So, any changes to the receipt or malicious changes can be detected either way. In order to verify the quality control of pharmacy products during the transportation startup, Modum.io AG uses blockchain to achieve data immutability [31–33].

In the research space of biomedical science, blockchain plays an important role. In research, blockchain helps to retain the original interpretation by avoiding unwanted risks in case studies, avoidance of misinterpretation of information. Blockchain makes it less difficult for sufferers to provide permission for his/her information for use in scientific trials due to the anonymous data which is naturally encoded inside the information [34].

The default feature of immutability of blockchain guarantees the integrity of the information available for scientific study. The obvious and open environment of blockchain additionally makes it less difficult to duplicate studies from blockchain-primarily relying on total information. All those are a number of the reasons why blockchain is anticipated to modernize biomedical studies and the peer-evaluation manner for scientific studies. This is mainly based on its basic properties, such as immutability and decentralization. Another capability utility of blockchain to fitness professions education (HPE) which offers the total competency based on the credit offerings without the count of a third party. Evidence of the initiative of consent traceability in scientific trial through the use of blockchain protocol is given to show how clever contracts on the Ethereum blockchain platform may be used to enhance information clarity in scientific trials [35, 36].

6.8 Challenges of Blockchain in Health Data

Blockchain provides a platform for storing and retrieving healthcare data. There are numerous impediments to blockchain technology's widespread adoption in the healthcare industry. The challenges are categorized as technical challenges, organizational challenges, and government policy challenges. But, blockchain faces several challenges in effectively storing and retrieving data in a distributed environment. Researchers introduced various algorithms for storing and retrieving patients' health data in the blockchain. Huge data is stored in the cloud for accessing data anywhere [37].

6.8.1 Technical Challenges

Let us discuss some of the technical challenges, like storage and data modifications.

Storage: A huge amount of data is generated from the patients daily. Due to the evolution of technology, the patient's history is maintained in the IoT devices in the hospital. The data generated may be in the form of the EMR, signals, or sensor data. These data require more space, but blockchain has limited storage of data. Furthermore, as the bulk of the data rises, the cost of data access and manipulation will increase. This causes the storage issue.

Data Modification: One of the main characteristics of blockchain is data immutability. Hence blockchain does not allow modification of the data in the existing block. Rather a new block has to be created and linked to the chain. This shows that the data stored are secured.

6.8.2 Organizational Challenges

The execution necessitates in blockchain like the most advanced infrastructure and interconnectedness which cannot be readily obtained by the startups. The cost of implementing blockchain technology in the healthcare industry is a major aspect that influences the entire choice of choosing blockchain.

6.8.3 Government Policy Challenges

Some of the health data from the government will not have authentication. There are many rules in different nations that govern the use of protected health data [38].

6.9 Opportunities for Blockchain in Health Data

The medical industry is projected to require more protection in the future than it does now. Therefore, blockchain technology exploded onto the scene. Health insurance, biomedical research, electronic health records (EHR), drug supply and procurement systems, and medical education are all possible applications in the field of medicine that could use blockchain technology in the future. Nowadays, blockchain technology is used in some applications, but it is still in its infancy, with little public or expert knowledge, making a strategic vision of its full future potential difficult [39]. Similarly, some other opportunities like patient record management, improved drug traceability, and medical billing systems exist. There are several experiments the researchers did on the blockchain in patient record management in health data. Medicine is one of the blockchain methods to store health data. MedRec is the decentralized system to store ERM. The ERM contains the medical history of the patient, including chart-like data. MedRec is made up of blocks that indicate data permissions like view and edit that are shared among members of a private P2P network. The change in the permissions is tracked on the blockchain with the help of smart contracts. MedRec consists of three contracts, namely, the registrar contract, summary contract, and patient–provider relationship contract. The registrar contract is used to identify the user; the summary contract is used to identify the patient information; and the patient–provider relationship is used to identify the relationship that the patient has between the hospitals. There are two nodes, namely provider nodes and patient nodes. Both nodes are created by the Ethereum Blockchain technology and are authenticated. With the decentralized database, the providers and the patient can share the data between them [40]. Improved drug traceability reduces drug fraud, which has become a prevalent concern in the healthcare industry. After the medicines are manufactured, they need to be supplied to the wholesaler. Nowadays, fake medicines are being replaced while being supplied to the wholesaler. The use of blockchain technology can aid in the tracking of the drug's production process. Medical billing systems have become easier with blockchain technology. Traditional patient billing systems have been vulnerable to numerous sorts of fraud in the past. Furthermore, the existing billing procedure requires more resources and time to generate billing data. In most cases, blockchain technology has the potential to make the payment process considerably easier and more secure than standard billing methods, which in most cases require an unusual amount of time to claim invoices. In particular, in the case of insurance claims, where traditional payment procedures are used to cause even more delays in bill payment [41].

References

1. Schabetsberger, T., Ammenwerth, E., Andreatta, S., Gratl, G., Haux, R., Lechleitner, G., Schindelwig, K., Stark, C., Vogl, R., Wilhelmy, I., Wozak, F., 2006. From a paper-based transmission of discharge summaries to electronic communication in health care regions. *Int. J. Med. Inform.*, 75(3–4), 209–215.
2. Gururaj, H.L., Goutham, B., Janhavi, V., Suhas, K.C., Manu, M.N. 2021. Medchain: Securing electronic medical records with a peer to peer networks and distributed file system. In: Singh, P.K., Veselov, G., Vyatkin, V., Pljonkin, A., Dodero, J.M., Kumar, Y. (eds) *Futuristic Trends in Network and Communication Technologies. FTNCT 2020. Communications in Computer and Information Science, Vol 1395.* Springer, Singapore. https://doi.org/10.1007/978-981-16-1480-4_1

3. Quantin, C., Jaquet-Chiffelle, D.O., Coatrieux, G. Benzenine, E., Auverlot, B., Allaert, F.A. 2011. Medical record: Systematic centralization versus secure on demand aggregation. *BMC Med. Inform. Decis. Mak.*, 11, 18. https://doi.org/10.1186/1472-6947-11-18

4. He, X., Cai, L., Huang, S., Ma, X., Zhou, X. 2019. The design of electronic medical records for patients of continuous care. *J. Infect. Public Health* 17, Aug.

5. Abbas, A., Khan, S.U. 2014. A review on the state-of-the-art privacy-preserving approaches in the e-health clouds. *IEEE J. Biomed. Health Inform.*, 18(4), 1431–1441, July. https://doi.org/10.1109/JBHI.2014.2300846

6. Jaiman, V., Urovi, V. 2020. A consent model for blockchain-based health data sharing platforms. *IEEE Access*, 8, 143734–143745. https://doi.org/10.1109/ACCESS.2020.3014565

7. Singhal, B., Dhameja, G., Panda, P.S. 2018. Introduction to blockchain. In: *Beginning Blockchain*. Apress, Berkeley, CA. https://doi.org/10.1007/978-1-4842-3444-0_1

8. Niranjanamurthy, M., Nithya, B.N., Jagannatha, S. 2019. Analysis of blockchain technology: Pros, cons and SWOT. *Cluster Comput.*, 22, 14743–14757. https://doi.org/10.1007/s10586-018-2387-5

9. Martino, Raffaele, Alessandro Cilardo. 2020. SHA-2 acceleration meeting the needs of emerging applications: A comparative survey. *IEEE Access*, 8, 28415–28436.

10. Ali Syed, T., Alzahrani, A., Jan, S., Siddiqui, M.S., Nadeem, A., Alghamdi, T.. 2019. A comparative analysis of blockchain architecture and its applications: Problems and recommendations. *IEEE Access*, 7, 176838–176869.

11. Prasanth, T., Gunasekaran, M., Kumar, D.R. 2018. Big data applications on health care. 2018 4th International Conference on Computing Communication and Automation (ICCCA). *2018 4th International Conference on Computing Communication and Automation (ICCCA)*. December.

12. Ben Fekih, R., Lahami, M. (2020) Application of blockchain technology in healthcare: A comprehensive study. In: Jmaiel, M., Mokhtari, M., Abdulrazak, B., Aloulou, H., Kallel, S. (eds) *The Impact of Digital Technologies on Public Health in Developed and Developing Countries. ICOST 2020.* Lecture Notes in Computer Science, vol. 12157. Springer, Cham.

13. Griggs, K.N., Ossipova, O., Kohlios, C.P. Baccarini, A.N., Howson, E.A., Hayajneh, T. 2018. Healthcare blockchain system using smart contracts for secure automated remote patient monitoring. *J. Med. Syst.*, 42, 130.

14. Saldamli, G., Reddy, V., Bojja, K.S., Gururaja, M.K., Doddaveerappa, Y., Tawalbeh, L. 2020. Health care insurance fraud detection using blockchain. *Seventh International Conference on Software Defined Systems (SDS)*, 2020, 145–152.

15. Chen, Y., Ding, S., Xu, Z., Zheng, H., Yang, S. 2019. Blockchain-based medical records secure storage and medical service framework. *J. Med. Syst.*, 43, 5. https://doi.org/10.1007/s10916-018-1121-4

16. Liu, X., Wang, Z., Jin, C., Li, F., Li, G. 2019. A blockchain-based medical data sharing and protection scheme. *IEEE Access*, 7, 118943–118953. https://doi.org/10.1109/ACCESS.2019.2937685

17. Zghaibeh, M., Farooq, U., Hasan, N.U., Baig, I.. 2020. SHealth: A blockchain-based health system with smart contracts capabilities. *IEEE Access*, 8, 70030–70043. https://doi.org/10.1109/ACCESS.2020.2986789

18. Pirtle, C., Ehrenfeld, J. 2018. Blockchain for healthcare: The next generation of medical records? *J. Med. Syst.* 42, 172.

19. Zhuang, Y., Sheets, L.R., Chen, Y.-W., Shae, Z.-Y., Tsai, J.J.P., Shyu, C.-R.. 2020. A patient-centric health information exchange framework using blockchain technology. *IEEE J. Biomed. Health Inform.*, 24(8), 2169–2176, August. https://doi.org/10.1109/JBHI.2020.2993072

20. Amofa, S., Sifah, E.B., Kwame, O.B., Abla, S., Xia, Q., Gee, J.C., Gao, J., 2018. A blockchain-based architecture framework for secure sharing of personal health data. *2018 IEEE 20th International Conference on e-Health Networking, Applications and Services (Healthcom)* (pp. 1–6).

21. Angraal, S., Krumholz, H.M., Schulz, W.L. 2017. Blockchain technology applications in health care. *Circ. Cardiovasc. Qual. Outcomes*, 10, e003800.

22. Engelhardt, M.A. 2017. Hitching healthcare to the chain: An introduction to blockchain technology in the healthcare sector. *Technol. Innov. Manag. Rev.* 7, 22–34.

23. Alhadhrami, Z., Alghfeli, S., Alghfeli, M., Abedlla, J.A., Shuaib, K. 2017. Introducing block-chains for healthcare. In *Proceedings of the 2017 International Conference on Electrical and Computing Technologies and Applications (ICECTA)* (pp. 1–4), Ras Al Khaimah, UAE, 19–21 November 2017.

24. Gordon, W.J., Catalini, C. 2018. Blockchain technology for healthcare: Facilitating the transition to patient-driven interoperability. *Comput. Struct. Biotechnol. J.*, 16, 224–230.

25. Androulaki, E., Barger, A., Bortnikov, V., Cachin, C., Christidis, K., De Caro, A., Enyeart, D., Ferris, C., Laventman, G., Manevich, Y., et al. 2018. Hyperledger fabric: A distributed operating system for permissioned blockchains. In *Proceedings of the Thirteenth EuroSys Conference; EuroSys '18* (pp. 30:1–30:15), Association for Computing Machinery, New York, NY, USA.

26. Hussein, A.F., ArunKumar, N., Ramirez-Gonzalez, G., Abdulhay, E., Manuel, J., Tavares, R.S., Hugo, V., De Albuquerque, C., Tavares, J.M.R.S., de Albuquerque, V.H.C. 2018. A medical records managing and securing blockchain based system supported by a genetic algorithm and discrete wavelet transform. *Cogn. Syst. Res.*, 52, 1–11.

27. Guo, R., Shi, H., Zhao, Q., Zheng, D. 2018. Secure attribute-based signature scheme with multiple authorities for blockchain in electronic health records systems. *IEEE Access*, 6, 11676–11686.

28. Rajesh Kumar D, & ManjupPriya S. 2013. Cloud based M-Healthcare emergency using SPOC. *2013 Fifth International Conference on Advanced Computing (ICoAC)*, December.

29. Al Omar, A., Rahman, M.S., Basu, A., Kiyomoto, S. 2017. MediBchain: A blockchain based privacy preserving platform for healthcare data. In: *Human Centered Computing* (pp. 534–543), Springer Nature, Basingstoke, UK, Vol. 10658.

30. Angeletti, F., Chatzigiannakis, I., Vitaletti, A. 2017. The role of blockchain and IoT in recruiting participants for digital clinical trials. In Proceedings of the 2017 25th International Conference on Software, Telecommunications and Computer Networks (SoftCOM) (pp. 1–5), Split, Croatia, 21–23 September.

31. Angraal, S., Krumholz, H.M., Schulz, W.L. 2017. Blockchain technology applications in health care. *Circ. Cardiovasc. Qual. Outcomes*, 10, e003800.

32. Engelhardt, M.A. 2017. Hitching healthcare to the Chain: An introduction to blockchain technology in the healthcare sector. *Technol. Innov. Manag. Rev.*, 7, 22–34.

33. Mettler, M. 2016. Blockchain Technology in Healthcare the Revolution Starts Here. In *Proceedings of the 2016 IEEE 18th International Conference on E-Health Networking, Applications and Services (Healthcom)* (pp. 520–522), Munich, Germany, 14–17 September.

34. Roman-Belmonte, J.M., De la Corte-Rodriguez, H., Rodriguez-Merchan, E.C.C., la Corte-Rodriguez, H., Carlos Rodriguez-Merchan, E. 2018. How blockchain technology can change medicine. *Postgrad. Med.*, 130, 420–427.

35. Funk, E., Riddell, J., Ankel, F., Cabrera, D. 2018. Blockchain technology: A data framework to improve validity, trust, and accountability of information exchange in health professions education. *Acad. Med.*, 93, 1791–1794.

36. Nugent, T., Upton, D., Cimpoesu, M. 2016. Improving data transparency in clinical trials using blockchain smart contracts. *F1000 Res.*, 5, 2541.

37. Kumar, T., Ramani, V., Ahmad, I., Braeken, A., Harjula, E. and Ylianttila, M., 2018. Blockchain utilization in healthcare: Key requirements and challenges. In *2018 IEEE 20th International Conference on e-Health Networking, Applications and Services (Healthcom)* (pp. 1–7). IEEE, September.

38. Gökalp, E., Gökalp, M.O., Çoban, S. and Eren, P.E. 2018. Analysing opportunities and challenges of integrated blockchain technologies in healthcare. *Eurosymposium on systems analysis and design* (pp. 174–183). Springer, Cham, September.

39. Radanović, I., Likić, R. 2018. Opportunities for Use of Blockchain Technology in Medicine. *Appl. Health Econ. Health Policy*, 16, 583–590. https://doi.org/10.1007/s40258-018-0412-8

40. McGhin, T., Choo, K.K.R., Liu, C.Z., He, D.. 2019. Blockchain in healthcare applications: Research challenges and opportunities. *J. Network Comput. Appl.*, 135, 62–75.

41. Yaqoob, I., Salah, K., Jayaraman, R., Al-Hammadi, Y. 2022. Blockchain for healthcare data management: Opportunities, challenges, and future recommendations. *Neural Comput. Applic.*, 34, 11475–11490.

7

SepSense: A Novel Sepsis Detection System Using Machine Learning Techniques

V. Aruna Devi
Madras Institute of Technology, Anna University, Chennai, India

Sakthi Jaya Sundar Rajasekar
Melmaruvathur Adhiparasakthi Institute of Medical Sciences & Research, Chengalpattu, India

Varalakshmi Perumal
Madras Institute of Technology, Anna University, Chennai, India

CONTENTS

7.1 Introduction

In the field of medicine, there are so many endangering diseases that are growing day-to-day. Some diseases cause death or have a sustainable impact on people. Detection of sepsis has a significant impact on reducing the death rate. It is proven that early detection of sepsis could be curable with the help of antibiotics and thus protect the lives of people. As mentioned earlier, most of the existing works employed one or a few machine learning algorithms that could not yield effective conclusions. The importance of making the dataset balanced has not been considered. However, balancing the dataset would be vital for significant performance improvement. Shahul and Pushpalatha [1] have examined the various machine learning algorithms used for sepsis divination. Based on existing studies, the suggested machine learning algorithms are discussed in the later section.

DOI: 10.1201/9781003217435-7

Neonatal sepsis, a kind of neonatal infection, is a disease that affects infants or newborn babies. There are two categories of neonatal sepsis known as late-onset sepsis (LOS) and early-onset sepsis (EOS). EOS exists in the first 7 days of the infant, whereas the LOS will defect the infant after 7 days. Joshi et al. [2] have concluded that with the help of characteristics such as heart rate variability and respiratory system along with ECG-derived estimates, the prediction of LOS is possible in the early stages of the evaluation on 49 preterm infants. Feature extraction has an impact on the step of preprocessing. All the features in the dataset are not impactful in terms of decision-making.

Pettinati et al. [3] used two different datasets, where each differed in its features. One has 168, and another one has 37 features. The notable point is that they have used the subsampling method. It is a well-known truth that machine learning can generalize the common pattern in the data. In [3], the XGBoost algorithm was used for classification purposes. The models were evaluated using AUROC values. Mohamed et al. [4] have utilized most of the machine learning algorithms for the early prediction of sepsis using electronic medical records (EMR). Notably, they mentioned that the neural network (NN) classifier performed well. And the use of a rule-based classifier that is optimized using the genetic algorithm is also discussed. Compared to the above two algorithms, the Support Vector Machine (SVM) provides better results.

The proposed work considers various Machine Learning and Ensemble models with a balanced dataset to get better performance compared to the existing work. The best models are also statistically selected among various implemented Machine Learning and Ensemble models based on the t-test method.

This article can be organized into four sections as follows. In Section 7.1, the introduction to sepsis, its types, and the need for the early prediction of sepsis are discussed. Section 7.2 explains some of the existing sepsis prediction methodologies that mainly deal with machine learning algorithms. A detailed explanation of our proposed system for the forecasting of sepsis is given in Section 7.3. In Section 7.4, the implementation details and results of our model are examined. Section 7.5 includes the conclusion.

7.2 Related Works

Early prediction of sepsis allows people to survive longer and gradually reduces the death rate. It has a considerable impact on the field of healthcare. The role of the Recurrent Unit-based deep learning algorithm in detecting sepsis was completed within 6 hours [5]. They have presented the bi-directional gated recurrent units (GRU) and compared the architecture against long short-term memory (LSTM). And they got the highest AUROC value for the proposed architecture. The specificity and sensitivity metrics of the model were estimated against baseline classifiers like SVM, random forest, and logistic regression. In data preprocessing, all the unwanted values were removed and the required missing information was replaced through data normalization. In [6], the noise in the data was removed and the data normalization was done using the z-scoring method with the usage of mean and standard deviation. For classification, they have used three models, namely RNN-LSTM architecture, adaptive CNN (ACNN) model, and SVM algorithm. Finally, they obtained the highest accuracy of 93.18% with the ACNN model. From the medical results, heart rate variability (HRV) is the most significant feature of the prognosis of sepsis.

It has been proved that the patient who has sepsis has irregular HRV. In [7], 52 features of HRV were extracted with the utilization of an electrocardiogram (ECG) from 500 patients. In preprocessing, to remove the poor frequency elements, Fast Fourier Transform was employed in MATLAB. For classification, they used the one-dimensional convolutional neural network (1D CNN), and its performance was evaluated using three different optimizers known as Adam, SGDM, and RMSProp. Consequently, they obtained better results with the RMSProp optimizer. Hidden Markov Models (HMMs) were deployed for the identification of sepsis [8] in which a discriminative approach was added to improve the NN-based HMM. In [9], for the forecasting of sepsis, they have used machine learning algorithms, including random under-sampling (RUS) boosting, bagged trees, SVM, logistic regression, and discriminant analysis for the MIMIC-III dataset that contains the continuous EHR records of patients. In preprocessing of the dataset, LASSO method was used for selecting the features. Among all the abovementioned ML algorithms, the LASSO method got better results than the RUS algorithm. The artificial neural network (ANN) model was presented [10] for sepsis prognosis. They have taken 555 images with unequal distribution over sepsis and non-sepsis images. They have evaluated the effect of balancing the dataset using random up sampling and down sampling approaches. Downsampling was not their preferred choice because they thought it would exhaust the existing information. However, up-sampling did not make that much enhancement in classification because of the chi-squared test used for feature selection.

In [11], from the vital and lab sporadic data, the features were extracted in terms of continuous features (34 features were extracted from 336), categorical features (totally 34 out of 136), and demographic (important features like gender, age, and other information regarding ICU). The combo of Random Forest and Logit Boost algorithm was presented for classification and the performance was evaluated using the normalized utility score (NUS). In [12], they have developed an open-source platform called ALDEx to forecast the presence of sepsis in humans. ALDEx took the input from the Fast Healthcare Interoperability Resources (FHIR). The security of the application was insisted on by authentication and authorization steps. The sepsis predictor module works by employing its novel ALSE algorithm. The source and target features were diffused with the help of (the Kolmogorov–Smirnov) KS test. To overcome the imprecise launch of vasopressor, a model was proposed in [13]. Initially, all the information regarding the patient was taken from the clinical documentation with the help of clinical experts. Their model has developed using logistic regression (LR) with L1-regularization employed at the decision time. The AUC, specificity, and sensitivity of the proposed model were taken for evaluation purposes. The novel visualization of HRV using graph analysis was introduced by the authors [14]. Features were extracted from the HRV of the patient and the selection of features was done with the help of principal component analysis (PCA). They have used machine learning techniques for classification purposes. They got better results of 87.7% for AUC while using logistic regression.

If people encounter an unexpected situation like an accident or an undesired event, then there might be a chance of Trauma. In the case of complex trauma, people could not live long. At an extreme level, it will be a leading cause of death. As a result, a complex type of trauma will increase the mortality level in the whole world. According to [15], of the total number of death caused by trauma, a significant percentage was caused by sepsis. So, sepsis will also be a cause of endangering diseases like trauma. They have proposed a novel deep forest algorithm for the timely forecasting of trauma in intensive care unit (ICU) patients. Their proposed algorithm was evaluated using the MIMIC-II I dataset, and they got 80% for the AUROC value and 79 and 64 for sensitivity and specificity. Consequently, they have concluded that using their proposed algorithm, the sepsis patient will get identified within 6–12 h. Considering the quick sequential organ failure assessment (qSOFA), another norm to identify the presence of sepsis, they have found out the essence of the qSOFA parameter and how it related to the presence of sepsis. They took the same dataset as in [15], which is MIMIC-III, and diagnosed the result into three categories, including no sepsis and two- and three-factored sepsis [16].

A novel mathematical theory was developed in [17] to avoid death correlated with sepsis. This system evolved over artificial intelligence. They presented two decision processes that are Boolean switchable and claimed that the process could be done within a specified time with the help of the Pareto Optimality algorithm. The changes occurring in stressed blood volume (SBV) and arterial elastance (Ea) were analyzed using fluid therapy. The state of these two characteristics, SBV and Ea, played a vital role in the time analysis of induced sepsis. They have done this experiment with the help of the cardiovascular system (CVS) model [18]. To enhance the prognostic of sepsis, a two-layer machine learning approach was developed in [19]. A novel hierarchical approach was proposed in that study to improve the diagnosis of sepsis in the affected people. The dataset was taken from 586 patients.

They have compared their model's performance with the existing systemic inflammatory response syndrome (SIRS) norm, which is normally used for the recognition of sepsis. On average, their system was able to recognize the sepsis 3–4 h earlier than the usual SIRS standard. They have concluded this through the enhanced performance improvement in the F2 score. It will not be useful unless sepsis is treated properly, even if it is discovered at an earlier stage. A novel reinforcement learning algorithm was developed to treat sepsis [20]. It will be different from other works since it was intended for the treatment of sepsis. Similarly, a reinforcement algorithm was developed in [21] for the treatment of sepsis. To cure sepsis, the patient might need to take vasopressors at the prescribed dosage. Most of the time, the dosage required for the patient will be decided only by the patient's current status. If the dosage intake of a patient is not suitable for their current situation, it might cause other side effects. Their proposed algorithm was intended to address the aforementioned problem.

Considering developing countries where they may not get proper resources to diagnose the presence of sepsis and also many people may be unaware of the consequences of the disease. In such cases, a simple mobile application might be a solution to the problem [22], in which there is no more equipment needed other than to analyze the factors. Once all the parameters have been derived from the standard procedure, they will be given as input to the application and diagnose the state of the patient. They trained the system over the MIMIC-III dataset [15, 16] and designed the system. The only drawback is that the user has to manually enter the parameters in the application, which might be digitalized in future versions. The dataset should be preprocessed (all values should be present in the dataset, all should have the same data type, and all classes should have an equal number of samples) before being classified as sepsis or non-sepsis. The last observation carried forward (LOCF) is a kind of approach that was used for replacing missing values, and the analysis of variance (ANOVA) test was utilized to select features and was done as data preprocessing in [23]. They used the Random Forest algorithm for classification, followed by data preprocessing. The need for devices to detect sepsis in earlier stages also plays a crucial role. For this purpose, a Point-Of-Care (POC) device was developed in [24], where the device was constructed with the help of sensors and Surface Plasmon Resonance (SPR) technology.

7.3 Proposed System

Some existing works were examined, and the majority of them used an imbalanced dataset, with which they were unable to achieve better results. In [11], over-sampling did not make any recognizable enhancement in their model. One may get better accuracy with the imbalanced dataset, but sensitivity, F1-Score, recall, specificity, and precision values are also essential to evaluate the model. Various machine learning (ML) and deep learning approaches are proposed in this paper with a balanced dataset. The proposed work is organized into three sections as follows: data preprocessing, classification, and model selection. In data preprocessing, the dataset is processed and balanced with the standard algorithm called SMOTE. Various machine learning algorithms and ensemble models deployed in this work were discussed in the classification section. Finally, in model selection, the two best models were selected and compared to choose the best one. For this purpose, the t-test evaluation method has been used.

The proposed architecture of the system is given in Figure 7.1. Initially, the dataset is loaded, which is an imbalanced dataset. Once the dataset was loaded, the significant features were selected and the missing (Not a Number) values in those attributes were replaced with the median values in order to take care of outlier problems. Then, the dataset is balanced using the SMOTE algorithm, which makes the dataset balanced. Then the dataset is split into training and testing sets. After this, the ML and ensemble models were developed using Python. Once the model is trained, the model is evaluated using the testing data. From the results, the top two algorithms that provide better results were chosen for further analysis. Those two selected algorithms were employed in the paired t-test algorithm to decide which one best suits the dedicated problem statistically. This paired t-test algorithm generates two values, t and p values, based on which we can select the best algorithm for the dedicated problem.

7.3.1 Data Preprocessing

The dataset is aggregated from the Kaggle Repository (https://www.kaggle.com/maxskoryk/datasepsis) [25]. The dataset has a total of 36,302 records under 41 attributes, including the label. Most of the values were in the form of NAN in the dataset. So, 17 columns from the dataset were removed, which had more NAN (Not a Number, i.e., does not have a number value) values compared to others. So, 24 attributes out of 41 present in the dataset were taken. To remove the NAN values from the selected 24 attributes, the median value (i.e., the middle element in the list of sorted elements in ascending order) of that attribute has been used instead of the mean value, in order to mitigate the outlier problem. The NaN values were replaced with the median value, which is one of the preferable functions for replacement. Among the 36,302 records, 33,655 are non-sepsis records, and only 2,647 are sepsis records. From this, it is known that the dataset is an imbalanced one. Balancing the dataset plays a vital role because it will avoid the skewness problem. Thus, having an imbalanced dataset, it will always skew towards the majority class. The imbalanced distribution of sepsis and non-sepsis classes is shown in Figure 7.2.

Some of the important features, namely Heart Rate (HR), Mean Arterial Pressure (MAP), Oxygen Saturation (O_2Sat), Spontaneous Bacterial Peritonitis (SBP), and also age and Intensive Care Unit Length of Stay (ICULOS), have been explored to visualize the data distribution and correlation between these important features in our dataset. Figures 7.3 and 7.4 show the correlation of sepsis with the two features of Age and ICULOS. From the

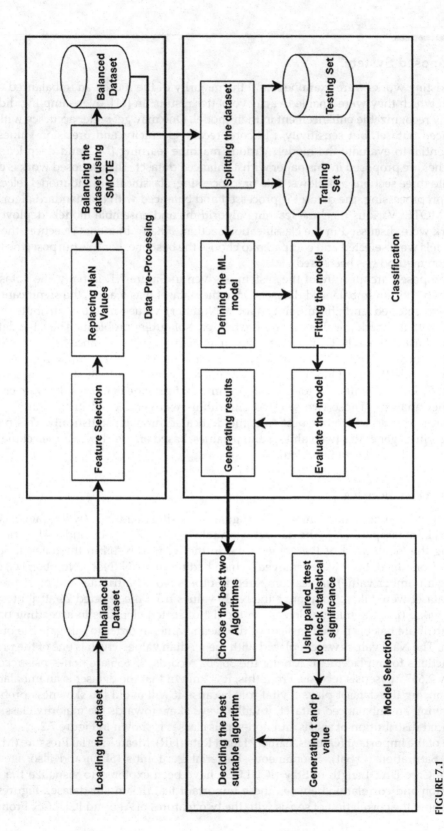

FIGURE 7.1
Architecture of the proposed system.

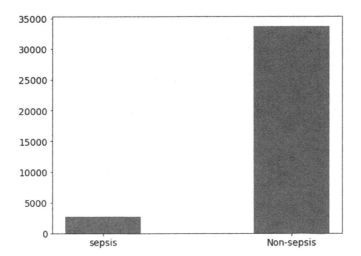

FIGURE 7.2
Class distribution of sepsis dataset.

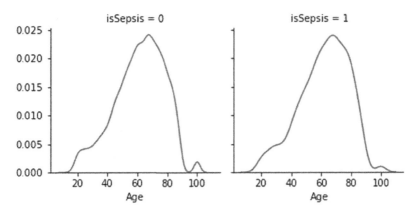

FIGURE 7.3
Correlation between age and sepsis.

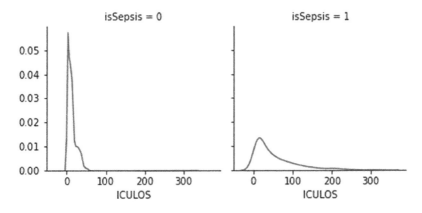

FIGURE 7.4
Correlation between ICULOS and sepsis.

analysis, it could be known that increasing the value of ICULOS also increases the possibility of sepsis (isSepsis = 1), whereas age does not have any significant relation with sepsis identification. Figure 7.5 shows the relationships between features and their frequency of occurrence. Meanwhile, Figure 7.6 shows the correlation between each feature. From Figure 7.6, the correlation between the four notable features (HR, SBP, O$_2$Sat, and MAP) was described. The features were selected based on attributes with a lower number of missing values. To equalize the dataset, the standard data augmentation technique,

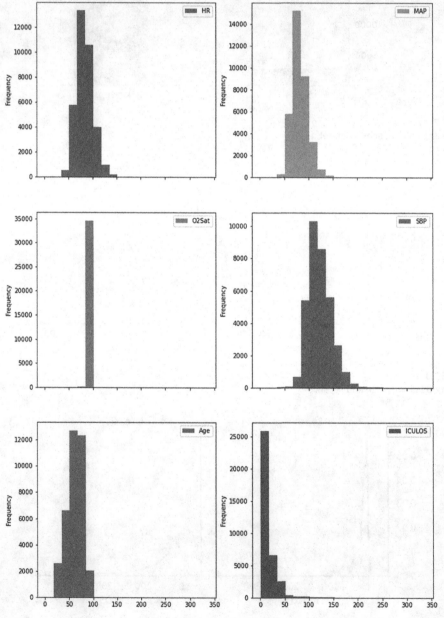

FIGURE 7.5
Frequency of occurrence for HR, MAP, O$_2$Sat, SBP, Age, and ICULOS.

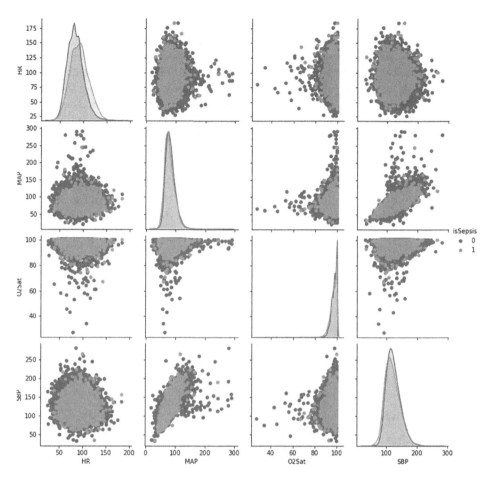

FIGURE 7.6
Interrelation between HR, MAP, O₂Sat, and SBP.

synthetic minority oversampling technique (SMOTE) was used, intended for numerical over-sampling. After using the SMOTE algorithms, both minority (sepsis) and majority (non-sepsis) classes have an equal number of records as in the majority class, which means both have 33,302 and a total of 66,604 are present in the dataset.

7.3.2 Classification

After preprocessing, the next step is to classify the input into sepsis or non-sepsis cases according to the features present in the dataset. For classification, several machine learning algorithms have been implemented. The employed algorithms are eXtreme Gradient Boosting (XGB), Stochastic Gradient Descent (SGD), AdaBoost Classifier, K-Nearest Neighbour (KNN) Classifier, Random Forest Algorithm, Quadratic Discriminant Analysis (QDA) algorithm, SVM using polynomial, RBF and sigmoid kernels, Multi-Layer Perceptron (MLP) classifier Logistic Regression, Gaussian Naïve Bayes (GB) and Decision Tree using Gini index, and Entropy as a criterion for classifying sepsis and non-sepsis cases. All the algorithms were run with their default parameters. The performance of every machine learning model was evaluated using the evaluation parameters like accuracy, sensitivity, specificity, precision, recall, F1-Score. Since this is a binary classification problem (two-class classification), the AUC (Area Under Curve) has been used as another important evaluation metric. All the classification results are discussed in the following section. But, comparatively, the two algorithms, Random Forest Classifier and XGBoost classifier, show better results with an insignificant difference. The XGBoost algorithm is a boosting algorithm that works to attain the maximum result by adding more weight to the data points. The algorithm works by self-analysis until it gets the correct predictions. In the beginning, the boosting algorithm produces fallacious predictions, and those inexact predictions will be self-analyzed by the algorithm. As a result, it will add more weight to the data points and calculate the predictions. This cycle takes place until the algorithm produces accurate predictions. Meanwhile, Random Forest is a boosting algorithm that generally creates a set of decision trees with random initializations. Finally, the result will be calculated by taking the mean of the results obtained from individual decision trees. From the nature of these boosting and bagging algorithms, we could say the XGBoost algorithm performs better since it produces results by its self-examination, whereas the Random Forest algorithm could not promise results by self-learning. Going forward, to conclude the best algorithm, we are using the model selection method. It is known that due to the stochastic nature of the algorithms, the result will vary over the run, so finding the best-suited algorithm for the problem will be another task to do. In most cases, the authors have usually used K-Fold validation to know the cumulative performance of the model. K-Fold cross-validation alone could not decide the best-suited model for the dedicated problem. So, model selection has been used to find the best-suited algorithm for sepsis detection, which will be discussed in the following section.

7.3.3 Model Selection

In machine learning, model selection is used to decide the best-suited machine learning model among the numerous machine learning models for a particular problem. Most probably, it worked as a decision-making scheme for the selection of the best model. This can be done through statistical significance between the models. The hypothesis statistical test was used to decide the final model using the paired t-test. The paired t-test will decide whether the mean difference between the two models is significant or not. As a result of the paired t-test over XGBoost and Random Forest, the XGBoost algorithm will be selected as the best-suited model for this problem. The performance of two models (Random Forest classifier and XGBoost classifier) will be shown in the following sections.

7.4 Implementation and Results

This work has been done in Anaconda's Jupiter notebook with Python 3.8 installed. For data preprocessing, the functions of the NumPy and Pandas modules have been utilized. Along with that, for data augmentation, the SMOTE algorithm was imported from the imblearn module. Classification took advantage of the scikit-learn module, dedicated to machine learning algorithms. The splitting of training and testing data, creating the model, and evaluating the performance of the model were all done with the help of this sklearn module.

In model selection, the module called Machine Learning Extensions (Mlxtend) was utilized to import the paired t-test function for the statistical hypothesis test. Besides these libraries, matplotlib was utilized for data visualization and performance analysis. For training, nearly 80% of the whole dataset was used, and the remaining 20% has been taken for testing data. All the machine learning models were evaluated in terms of accuracy, sensitivity (same as recall), precision, sensitivity, and F1-Score. The above-mentioned metrics for both balanced and imbalanced datasets have been evaluated. Using the scikit-learn library, all the algorithms were implemented and evaluated for the imbalanced and balanced datasets. The results obtained for the imbalanced dataset are shown in Table 7.1. Table 7.2 shows the results obtained for the balanced dataset.

TABLE 7.1

Results Obtained for Imbalanced Dataset

Machine learning algorithms	Accuracy	Specificity	Precision	Recall (sensitivity)	F1-Score
Random Forest Classifier	**98.14**	**98.14**	**98**	**98**	**98**
XGBoost	**98.27**	**97.70**	**98**	**98**	**98**
Decision tree (Entropy)	95.79	96.54	96	96	96
Decision tree (Gini)	95.08	95.79	95	95	95
K-Neighbours classifier	91.83	99.67	93	92	92
Logistic regression	74.59	60.07	75	75	74
SGD Classifier	69.53	41.66	78	69	67
SVM (kernel= poly)	75.73	63.86	77	76	75
SVM (kernel= RBF)	77.50	69.01	78	78	77
SVM (kernel=sigmoid)	56.49	55.91	56	56	56
Gaussian Naïve Bayes	78.33	83.71	79	78	78
MLP classifier	88.59	93.02	89	89	89
AdaBoost classifier	94.16	93.28	94	94	94
Quadratic discriminant analysis	82.95	75.36	84	83	83

TABLE 7.2

Results Obtained for Balanced Dataset

Machine learning algorithms	Accuracy	Specificity	Precision	Recall (sensitivity)	F1-Score
XGBoost	**96.91**	**67.48**	**92**	**83**	**87**
Random Forest Classifier	**97.09**	**64.83**	**95**	**82**	**87**
Decision tree (Entropy)	95.08	65.21	82	81	82
Decision tree (Gini)	94.39	63.51	88	73	78
K-Neighbours classifier	95.22	46.50	93	92	92
Logistic regression	95.11	34.78	95	67	74
SGD classifier	87.78	60.11	64	75	67
SVM (kernel= poly)	94.39	23.44	96	62	67
SVM (kernel= RBF)	94.39	23.44	96	62	67
SVM (kernel=sigmoid)	91.02	24.38	64	60	62
Gaussian Naïve Bayes	92.97	52.36	74	74	74
MLP classifier	95.22	35.91	96	68	75
AdaBoost classifier	96.77	64.46	93	82	86
Quadratic discriminant analysis	91.51	46.12	69	71	70

The XGBoost and Random Forest Classifier algorithms were found to be the better choices for Sepsis Detection System.

Figures 7.7–7.16 show the comparison of the above-tabulated evaluation metrics for the imbalanced and balanced dataset. Figure 7.7 shows the comparison of machine learning algorithms in terms of accuracy for the imbalanced dataset.

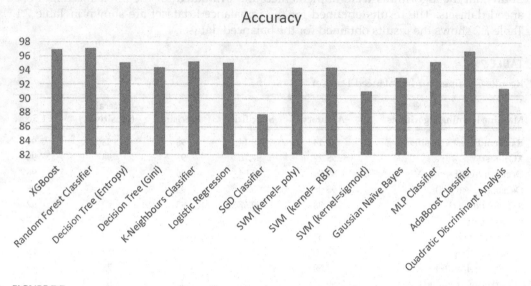

FIGURE 7.7
Accuracy comparison of imbalanced dataset.

Figure 7.8 represents the comparison of accuracy between various machine learning algorithms for the balanced dataset.

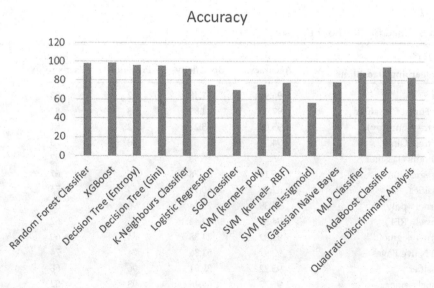

FIGURE 7.8
Accuracy comparison of balanced dataset

In Figure 7.9, the specificity values of all the algorithms were compared for the imbalanced dataset.

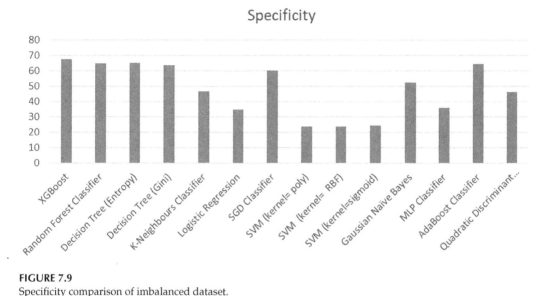

FIGURE 7.9
Specificity comparison of imbalanced dataset.

Figure 7.10 represents the specificity comparison of ML techniques for the balanced dataset.

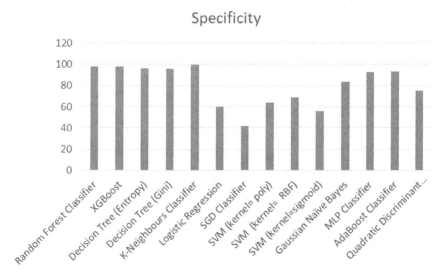

FIGURE 7.10
Specificity comparison of balanced dataset.

The precision values of different machine learning algorithms were compared in Figure 7.11 for the imbalanced dataset.

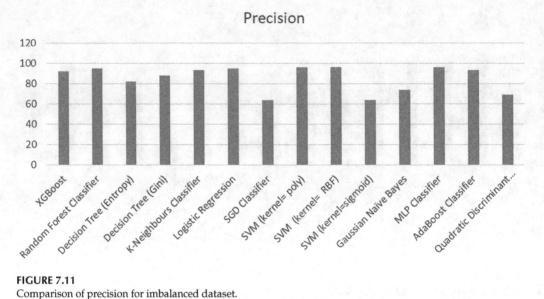

FIGURE 7.11
Comparison of precision for imbalanced dataset.

The precision values of machine learning algorithms were compared for the balanced dataset as shown in Figure 7.12.

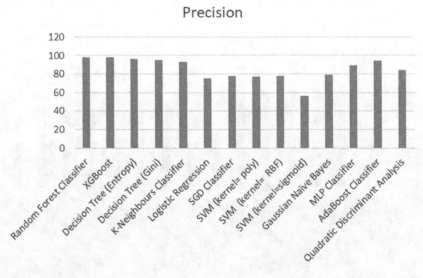

FIGURE 7.12
Comparison of precision for balanced dataset.

Figure 7.13 shows the comparison of recall values for various ML models for an imbalanced dataset.

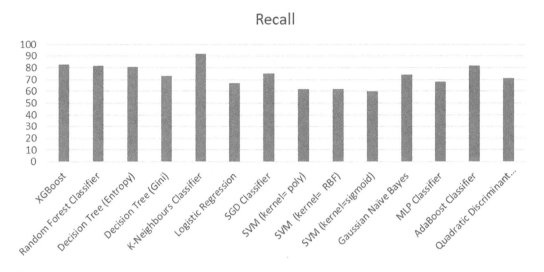

FIGURE 7.13
Comparison of recall for imbalanced dataset.

Figure 7.14 represents the comparison of recall made among the aforementioned models for the balanced dataset.

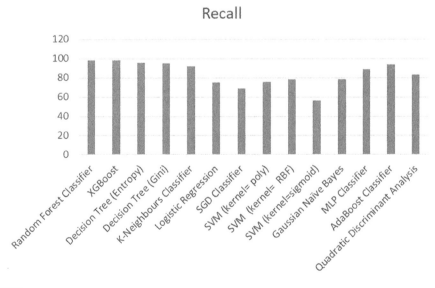

FIGURE 7.14
Comparison of recall for balanced dataset.

Figure 7.15 showcases a comparison of different machine learning algorithms in terms of F1-Score for the imbalanced dataset.

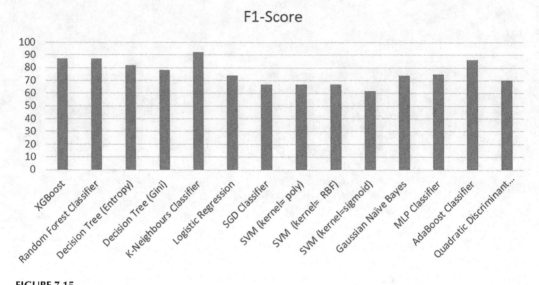

FIGURE 7.15
Comparison of F1-score for imbalanced dataset.

Similarly, F1-Score values of all the mentioned machine learning algorithms are compared for the balanced dataset in Figure 7.16.

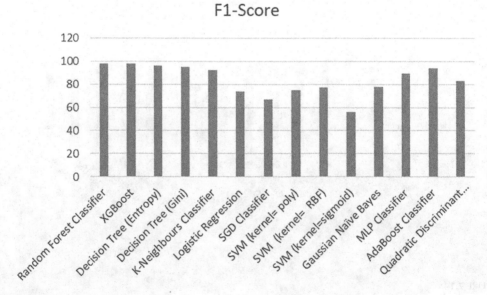

FIGURE 7.16
Comparison of F1-score for balanced dataset.

From the results of Table 7.2, it is known that it produces a better accuracy result compared to the accuracy results in Table 7.1. But other than accuracy, all the other evaluation metrics mean a lot for medical-related problems. The imbalanced dataset may result in very good accuracy, but the sensitivity and specificity values are not so good, since these performance metrics are very important, specifically for medical-related decisions. If examined carefully with the balanced dataset, very good results were achieved for all the evaluation metrics. The following Figure 7.17 shows the result of model selection applied to XGBoost (XGB) and Random Forest (RF) classification algorithms.

Figure 7.18 shows the Area Under Curve result of 99.6% for the best-suited XGBoost model chosen by the paired t-test model selection function.

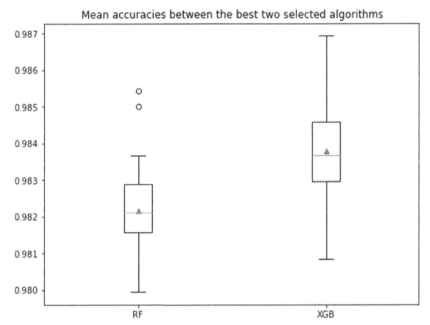

FIGURE 7.17
Mean accuracies between the selected algorithm.

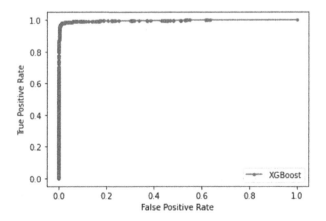

FIGURE 7.18
AUC for XGBoost algorithm.

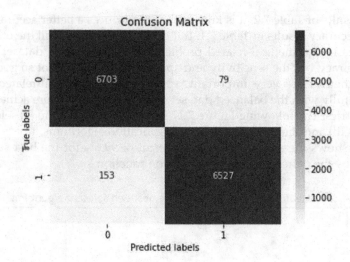

FIGURE 7.19
Confusion matrix for XGBoost algorithm using balanced dataset.

The confusion matrix for the XGBoost algorithm trained using a balanced dataset was shown in Figure 7.19. For the visual representation, the various performance measures given quantitatively in Tables 7.1 and 7.2, are repeated in Figures 7.7–7.16.

7.5 Conclusion

Sepsis is an important medical condition in ICU and needs to be predicted early to save the life of the patient. The sepsis dataset was preprocessed and over-sampled with the numerical data augmentation technique, SMOTE, to bring out a balanced dataset. Various machine learning algorithms were employed to predict the class as sepsis or non-sepsis and estimate the performance level of these models. From the experimental results, the two models, Random Forest and XGBoost, which produce the highest accuracies, were chosen. Consequently, a model selection algorithm is deployed to pick the best model among the two. As a result, the XGBoost algorithm is the best-suited model for the problem, with a mean accuracy of 98.4% and a 99.6% AUC value.

References

[1] M. Shahul and K. P. Pushpalatha, "Machine Learning Based Analysis of Sepsis: Review," *2020 International Conference on Emerging Trends in Information Technology and Engineering (ic-ETITE)*, pp. 1–4, 2020.

[2] R. Joshi, D. Komme, L. Oosterwijk, L. Feijs, C. van Pul and P. Andriessen, "Predicting Neonatal Sepsis Using Features of Heart Rate Variability, Respiratory Characteristics, and ECG-Derived Estimates of Infant Motion," *IEEE Journal of Biomedical and Health Informatics*, vol. 24, no. 3, pp. 681–692, March 2020.

[3] M. J. Pettinati, G. Chen, K. S. Rajput and N. Selvaraj, "Practical Machine Learning-Based Sepsis Prediction," *2020 42nd Annual International Conference of the IEEE Engineering in Medicine & Biology Society (EMBC)*, pp. 4986–4991, 2020.

[4] A. Mohamed, H. Ying and R. Sherwin, "Electronic-Medical-Record-Based Identification of Sepsis Patients in Emergency Department: A Machine Learning Perspective," *2020 International Conference on Contemporary Computing and Applications (IC3A)*, pp. 336–340, 2020.

[5] S. D. Wickramaratne and M. Shaad Mahmud, "Bi-Directional Gated Recurrent Unit Based Ensemble Model for the Early Detection of Sepsis," *2020 42nd Annual International Conference of the IEEE Engineering in Medicine & Biology Society (EMBC)*, pp. 70–73, 2020.

[6] B. Y. Al-Mualemi and L. Lu, "A Deep Learning-Based Sepsis Estimation Scheme," *IEEE Access*, vol. 9, pp. 5442–5452, 2021.

[7] P. Amiri, H. Abbasi, A. Derakhshan, B. Gharib, B. Nooralishahi and M. Mirzaaghayan, "Potential Prognostic Markers in the Heart Rate Variability Features for Early Diagnosis of Sepsis in the Pediatric Intensive Care Unit using Convolutional Neural Network Classifiers," *2020 42nd Annual International Conference of the IEEE Engineering in Medicine & Biology Society (EMBC)*, pp. 5627–5630, 2020.

[8] Antoine Honoré, Dong Liu, David Forsberg and Karen Coste, Eric Herlenius, Saikat Chatterjee and Mikael Skoglund, "Hidden Markov Models for Sepsis Detection in Preterm Infants," *ICASSP 2020 - 2020 IEEE International Conference on Acoustics, Speech and Signal Processing (ICASSP)*, pp. 1130–1134, 2020.

[9] M. Mollura, G. Mantoan, S. Romano, L. -W. Lehman, R. G. Mark and R. Barbieri, "The Role of Waveform Monitoring in Sepsis Identification within the First Hour of Intensive Care Unit Stay," *2020 11th Conference of the European Study Group on Cardiovascular Oscillations (ESGCO)*, pp. 1–2, 2020.

[10] R. H. Alvi, M. Habibur Rahman, A. Al Shaeed Khan and R. M. Rahman, "Predicting Early Neonatal Sepsis using Neural Networks and Other Classifiers," *2020 IEEE 10th International Conference on Intelligent Systems (IS)*, pp. 443–450, 2020.

[11] V. Sharma, C. Bhattacharyya, T. Bhattacharjee, S. Khandelwal, M. Poduval and A. D. Choudhury, "Sepsis Prediction using Continuous and Categorical Features on Sporadic Data," *2020 IEEE International Conference on Pervasive Computing and Communications Workshops (PerCom Workshops)*, pp. 1–6, 2020.

[12] F. Amrollahi, S. P. Shashikumar, P. Kathiravelu, A. Sharma and S. Nemati, "AIDEx - An Open-source Platform for Real-Time Forecasting Sepsis and A Case Study on Taking ML Algorithms to Production," *2020 42nd Annual International Conference of the IEEE Engineering in Medicine & Biology Society (EMBC)*, pp. 5610–5614, 2020.

[13] Baturay Aydemir, Varesh Prasad, James C. Lynch, Brett Biebelberg, Iain Kehoe, Andrew T. Reisner and Thomas Heldt, "Validation of a 'Usual Care' Model for Vasopressor Initiation in a Cohort of Emergency Department Patients with Sepsis," *2020 42nd Annual International Conference of the IEEE Engineering in Medicine & Biology Society (EMBC)*, pp. 2772–2775, 2020.

[14] C. León, G. Carrault, P. Pladys and A. Beuchée, "Early Detection of Late Onset Sepsis in Premature Infants Using Visibility Graph Analysis of Heart Rate Variability," *IEEE Journal of Biomedical and Health Informatics*, vol. 25, no. 4, pp. 1006–1017, April 2021.

[15] M. Fu, J. Yuan and C. Bei, "Early Sepsis Prediction in ICU Trauma Patients with Using An Improved Cascade Deep Forest Model," *2019 IEEE 10th International Conference on Software Engineering and Service Science (ICSESS)*, pp. 634–637, 2019.

[16] N. Sakib, D. Saxena, L. He, P. M. Griffin, S. I. Ahamed and M. Haque, "Unpacking Prevalence and Dichotomy in qSOFA Parameters: A Step towards Multi-parameter Intelligent Sepsis Prediction in ICU," *2019 IEEE EMBS International Conference on Biomedical & Health Informatics (BHI)*, pp. 1–4, 2019.

[17] R. M. Demirer and O. Demirer, "Early Prediction of Sepsis from Clinical Data Using Artificial Intelligence," *2019 Scientific Meeting on Electrical-Electronics & Biomedical Engineering and Computer Science (EBBT)*, pp. 1–4, 2019.

[18] L. Murphy, S. Davidson, J. L. Knopp, J. G. Chase, T. Zhou and T. Desaive, "State Analysis of Total Stressed Blood Volume and Arterial Elastance During Induced Sepsis," *2019 41st Annual International Conference of the IEEE Engineering in Medicine and Biology Society (EMBC)*, pp. 2951–2954, 2019.

[19] F. van Wyk, A. Khojandi and R. Kamaleswaran, "Improving Prediction Performance Using Hierarchical Analysis of Real-Time Data: A Sepsis Case Study," IEEE Journal of Biomedical and Health Informatics, vol. 23, no. 3, pp. 978–986, May 2019.

[20] C. Yu, G. Ren and J. Liu, "Deep Inverse Reinforcement Learning for Sepsis Treatment," *2019 IEEE International Conference on Healthcare Informatics (ICHI)*, pp. 1–3, 2019.

[21] Y. Jia, J. Burden, T. Lawton and I. Habli, "Safe Reinforcement Learning for Sepsis Treatment," *2020 IEEE International Conference on Healthcare Informatics (ICHI)*, pp. 1–7, 2020.

[22] R. Sathish, and D. R. Kumar (2013, March). "Proficient Algorithms for Replication Attack Detection in Wireless Sensor Networks & A Survey," *2013 IEEE International Conference ON Emerging Trends in Computing, Communication and Nanotechnology (ICECCN). 2013 International Conference on Emerging Trends in Computing, Communication and Nanotechnology (ICE-CCN)*.

[23] F. Mahmud, N. S. Pathan and M. Quamruzzaman, "Early detection of Sepsis in critical patients using Random Forest Classifier," *2020 IEEE Region 10 Symposium (TENSYMP)*, pp. 130–133, 2020.

[24] S. Kundu, S. Tabassum and R. Kumar, "Plasmonic Point-of-Care Device for Sepsis Biomarker Detection," *IEEE Sensors Journal*, vol. 21, no. 17, pp. 18837–18846, 2021.

[25] Sepsis Prediction from Clinical Data, Kaggle Repository, https://www.kaggle.com/maxskoryk/datasepsis, Accessed on 14 June 2021.

8

Oral Cancer Detection at Early Stage Using Convolutional Neural Network in Healthcare Informatics

S. Bhuvaneswari, R. Pandimeena, M. Sridhar, and S. Vignesh
Chennai Institute of Technology, Chennai, India

CONTENTS

8.1 Introduction

According to the World Health Organization, this is the most common type of cancer in the world's population. Oral cancer is characterised by high rates of morbidity and mortality, as well as the fact that it is often diagnosed late. It usually starts off as a white spot with

DOI: 10.1201/9781003217435-8

little pain, progresses to red patches and ulcers, and then continues to grow indefinitely beyond that point [3].

According to the World Health Organization, over 6 lakh people are diagnosed with mouth, throat, and pharyngeal cancer every year, and over 3,30,000 people die as a consequence of the condition. The lips, mouth cavity, and throat are the most frequently affected regions by oral cancer, with the vast majority of instances happening in South Central Asia as a consequence of exposure to certain potentially hazardous materials such as asbestos. Most individuals in low- and middle-income countries across the globe suffer from oral cancer, which affects the majority of the population. The use of cigarettes and excessive consumption of alcoholic drinks are the leading causes of mouth cancer in the majority of instances. These are some of the most significant considerations [3]. These oral tumours might be difficult to differentiate from typical mouth sores because of their appearance. A consequence of this is that more than two-thirds of patients are in the last stages of their disease, at which point "the number of patients who survive is reduced." One of the malignancies that is particularly sensitive to early detection and which does not require the use of expensive medical equipment is oral cancer. A precursor lesion accounts for 80% of all occurrences of mouth cancer; as a consequence, the oral cavity is accessible for visual examination, which gives an opportunity to detect lesions and act to prevent the illness from spreading. Early detection of infection is complicated by a number of factors, including a lack of competence to identify lesions, difficulties in diagnosing and treating oral lesions, and geographical barriers that exist in remote places that make it difficult to detect infection. Oral cancer is not categorised as a late diagnosis since it is characterised by visible mouth lesions referred to as oral potentially malignant diseases (OPMDs) that may be found during routine screening by a clinical oral examination done by a regular dentist. If a problematic lesion is identified, the patient is sent to a specialist for additional assessment and confirmation of the diagnosis, which may take several weeks [1]. The findings of previous Indian research indicate early detection of this sickness, which has resulted in the downstaging of the illness and a decrease in mortality among individuals who smoke and drink. Because there are a limited number of specialisations and health resources available, low- and middle-income nations bear the lion's share of the burden of oral cancer (LMICs). Most significantly, screening is a cost-effective and efficient strategy for diagnosing diseases that is beneficial in a variety of circumstances. Telemedicine is used in the development of such approaches [1].

It is also known as "digital image processing" because the technique by which a two-dimensional picture is processed by a digital computer is referred to as "digital imaging." In this graphic, which is symbolised by the word "bit," there is a finite number of bits that represent an array of complicated and real values. These bits are represented by the word "bit." The photos are digitalized and kept in the computer's memory, where they may then be further processed [2]. The image that has been processed is shown on a high-definition television monitor with surround sound.

Oncologists at Amrita Hospital in Bangalore did a retrospective study between January 2004 and December 2006 to assess the risk factor profile for patients with head and neck cancer. Patients who presented with head and neck cancer between January 2004 and December 2006 were included in the study, and data were collected from them. Furthermore, it has been shown that more than half of all oral tongue cancer occurrences occur in individuals who do not have any known risk factors for the illness. Several studies have been undertaken in an attempt to investigate the role of HPV in the development of oral and tongue malignancies. Initially, it was claimed that tobacco intake, whether in the form of chewing or smoking, was a risk factor for oral malignancies [4–6]. Later on, it was determined that alcohol intake was an independent risk factor for oral cancer, even though it has been demonstrated to have additive and synergistic effects with tobacco usage in other studies (Notani 1988; Sankaranarayanan 1989; Franceschi 1990) [7,8]. According to the results of an Indian study, smoking and chewing tobacco were both linked to an increased risk of oral cancer (Jayant 1977) [9]. The finding that diet may have a role in the development of oral cancer was made later in the research process (Winn 1984; Notani 1987; La Vecchia 1997). Researchers established a relationship between the human papillomavirus (HPV) and head and neck cancer as early as 1960, and the virus is still being studied today. Over the past two decades, a substantial body of data has accumulated supporting the idea that HPV is a causative factor in the development and progression of head and neck cancers, particularly those of the oropharynx. Finding out how common HPV DNA is in HNSCC is problematic since the disease is difficult to diagnose. According to some research, the HNSCC test has been reported to be positive in as many as 60% of cases. A large body of research has been conducted on the association between HPV and the oropharynx, with estimates ranging from 45% to 100% of tonsillar malignancies being found to be HPV positive (Mellin 2000; Gillison 2001; Mellin 2002; Dahlgren 2003; Mellin 2003) [10–14]. A viral reservoir is hypothesised to exist in tonsillar crypts, resulting in a higher incidence of tonsillar malignancies and a much reduced or non-existent prevalence of other head and neck cancers, according to this theory. Several studies have shown that periodontal pockets act as reservoirs for the human papillomavirus, and one study discovered a relationship between long-term periodontitis and the chance of developing tongue cancer (Hormia 2005) [15]. The year is 2007 (Tezal 2007). The role of HPV in the development of oral cavity malignancies, notably tongue cancer, has only been investigated in a few studies. We wanted to look at the prevalence of HPV in oral tongue cancers since current research indicates that the incidence of tongue cancers is growing in the United States (Schantz 2002) [16]. For the first time, a variety of detection technologies have been used to determine the existence of HPV, and the virus's integration status, and to further examine the pathway by which the virus enters the body and causes illness. According to prior research, a test was done to assess whether the patients had HPV 16, which has been linked to head and neck cancer in the past. It is important to note that the presence of HPV does not necessarily suggest that it is engaged in the formation of cancer; thus, considerable molecular research is being planned to confirm the virus's etiological role in cancer cases in the near future. It is possible that if the role of HPV in these malignancies is established, the development of vaccines – both preventive and therapeutic – that are specifically targeted at HPV16 will have an impact on the occurrence of oral cancer in the future. According to recent research, poor compliance (25.7%) with attending oral cancer screening after being asked has been linked to a lack of public awareness of mouth cancers (Jullien 1995). In addition to the general public, there has been evidence of a lack of oral cancer knowledge among dental professionals, such as dentists, dental hygienists, nurses, and general practitioners [17]. To the best of our understanding, there is no information available on the level of public awareness of oral cancer and its risk factors in India. It was decided to conduct this research in a semi-urban area of Kerala to find out how much knowledge there was about oral cancer among the residents. Aspects of strategies to raise awareness and encourage early detection will differ from one geographic place to another depending on the lifestyle and habits of the people who live in that region [18]. Raising awareness of the condition among the general population may contribute to the attainment of a significant reduction in the disease's prevalence. The practice of 'oral self-examination' has been promoted as a way to raise awareness and facilitate early detection as a consequence of this. A brochure was prepared in order to give comprehensive information on oral cancer, its risk factors, and premalignant lesions. The pamphlet also featured drawings of the different processes for doing oral self-examination, which was intended to educate the public. Through the distribution of self-examination pamphlets, which were to be distributed by health experts recruited from the local community, it was hoped to educate the general public. Initially, fliers were distributed, and members of the public were advised to do an oral visual check and report any odd lesions to their local screening clinic if they were discovered to prevent further spread.

8.2 Literature Survey

Roshan Alex Welikala et al. [1] described a method for collecting and attenuating images of the mouth cavity and establishing the result for mouth cancer that is detected automatically as soon as possible by taking advantage of deep learning and its potential to aid in the task. This article was written by Hemantha Amarasinghe and Ruwan Duminda, who are both Sri Lankan. The cost analysis of the learning process that passes through the briefly mentioned cross-section of the oral cancer patient was done by Jayasinghe and Dharma Gunawardene utilising action-based spending with cost apportionment and decreased cost, according to the authors [2].

Jeyaraj et al. [3] have contributed to this work. According to Jeyaraj, mouth cancer is a dangerous tumour that has spread across the body's complex systemic network. Deep learning is required to discover and diagnose issues. Following this research endeavour, an algorithm for the automatic identification of oral cancer using hyperspectral images of patients was developed, which was tested on a large number of patients. A three-dimensional CNN-based image processing method for detecting cancer in oral lesions as quickly as possible was created by Shipu et al. [4]. The researchers used a three-dimensional CNN to identify cancer in oral lesions as quickly as possible. During the performance, the corresponding functions and dynamics of a three-dimensional convolutional neural network are extracted and shown (CNN). Nabihah et al. [5] investigated the feasibility of Mobile Mouth Screening Anywhere (MeMoSa) for the diagnosis of oral cancer in the absence of a dental examination.

8.3 Existing System

This study illustrates how oral lesions may be discovered and recognised automatically using deep learning in the earliest stages of the disease, which is important in preventing oral cancer. When it comes to image classification, this kind of system makes use of ResNet-101, but R-CNN is used to recognise objects in the picture, which is quicker than ResNet-101 and is thus more efficient [1]. These are only a handful of the drawbacks associated with the current system. It is conceivable that finishing a run may take longer than expected. Certain specialised hardware requirements must be met in order for it to be processed, which increases the overall cost to the consumer.

Another typical medical picture categorisation approach is used in order to get the final result. Comparing the obtained findings to one another allows one to determine the accuracy of the diagnostic procedure. The suggested regression-based partitioned CNN learning strategy for a challenging medical image of oral lesion identification is used to improve the overall quality of the diagnosis by increasing the accuracy of the diagnosis [3].

For this work, accuracy categorisation is employed to evaluate the performance of the partitioned deep CNN, which has been explained in further detail elsewhere. On a hundred picture data sets that served as training sets, the researchers discovered that the specificity was 0.91%, the classification accuracy was 91.4%, and the sensitivity was 0.94%. Tissue accuracy was used to categorise tumours in a task classification test, and the task categorisation of tumours was 94.5% accurate for 500 training patterns in this task classification.

A statistical software programme that analyses trends by using joinpoint models, in which independent lines are brought together at the joinpoints, rather than regular regression models, is used instead of the more traditional regression models. Joinpoint regression is a method of fitting yearly age-adjusted cancer incidence rates with a sequence of linked straight lines on a log scale, and it is used to estimate the trends in cancer incidence rates. At certain places in the sequence, the straight lines are joined together. Line segments are connected together at joinpoints, which are the points where they are drawn together in line drawing. Trend changes that are statistically significant ($P = .05$) are shown by the presence of a joinpoint at each node. The programme takes trend data and fits it to the simplest joinpoint model that the data enables it to be, which is determined by the data that is currently available. The programme will begin with the smallest number of joinpoints possible (e.g., 0 joinpoints, which is a straight line), and the programme will determine whether or not further joinpoints are statistically significant and should be included in the model as an addition to the initial model (up to that maximum number) [19–22]. We can determine whether or not an apparent shift in trend is statistically significant when we use this approach. $Y = mX + b$ denotes the regression equation when using the Least Squares method, where Y denotes the outcome or dependent variable (the age-adjusted rate), X denotes the independent variable (the year of diagnosis), m denotes the annual percentage change, and b denotes the intercept of the regression line when using the Least Squares method (the age-adjusted rate). When there is a statistically significant difference between two groups, the Monte Carlo permutation approach is used to determine which group is superior. An estimated annual percentage change (EAPC) is produced for each of the trends indicated by the joinpoints in the final model, using generalised linear models to determine how much the trend has changed. In order to offer the most exact calculations possible, a total of three joinpoints were permitted. The projected yearly per cent change is used to detect and analyse the statistical significance of trends in the model as soon as they are created, which allows for faster identification and analysis of trends. As soon as the line segments are formed, this is done using the expected annual per cent change to ensure that the results are accurate. Similarly, testing the hypothesis that the yearly percent change is equal to zero (two-sided P value $= .05$) is equivalent to testing the hypothesis that cancer rates are neither rising nor decreasing (two-sided P value $= .05$). The Annual Percent Change (APC) gauge provides a comprehensive view of the development of the market over the course of a particular year. If a small segment increases at a rapid pace and does not attain statistical significance, the statistical significance of the segment may be lost. Consequently, in order to summarise the trend over a given preset time, the Average Annual Percent Change (AAPC) is used; this measure computes the summary measure over the specified predefined interval during which the trend is being assessed. Furthermore, the data are favourable when it comes from a certain geographic location, such as Barshi, where the data is acquired and stored. Each of these organisations is included in the tables because each has a unique point of view on the subject matter under consideration. This project made use of Joinpoint 3.3.1, which may be downloaded for free from the Joinpoint website. The researchers evaluated the cumulative incidence risk percentage as well as the lifetime risk of getting head and neck cancer and the various subsites within it on the basis of registry data from both urban and rural regions, using data from both urban and rural locales. In the case of a person, the cumulative risk (CuR) is the likelihood that he or she would get specific cancer over the length of a certain age period if no other cause of death happens during that time period. The Cumulative Rate is a percentage that represents an estimate of the total risk over a certain period of time. When calculating the cumulative risk, the annual age-specific incidence rates for each 5-year age interval (for whatever age group is being used to calculate the cumulative risk) are multiplied by 5 (representing the 5-year age interval), and the resulting number is divided by 100,000 CuR = 5 × (ASpR) × 100,000,000 (for whatever age group is being used to calculate the cumulative risk). The cumulative incidence rate may be interpreted in a probabilistic manner, which is advantageous to the researcher. As an added benefit, this technique avoids the arbitrary aspect that might be associated with the process of selecting a representative sample of the general population. The confidence intervals are determined with the use of the CIRP ± formula, which stands for confidence intervals plus or minus one standard deviation (1.96 × S.E.). Particular cancer with an anticipated cumulative incidence rate expressed as a percentage multiplied by the reciprocal of the projected cumulative incidence rate yields the likelihood of developing that cancer in one out of every 'n' people. As a part of the research, I involved looking at tumours of the oral cavity, pharynx, and larynx, which are all classified as head and neck malignancies and are being investigated (ICD-9, 141, 143-146, 148, 149, and 161). The tongue (ICD-9, 141) was segregated from the remainder of the oral cavity (ICD9, 143-5) in our statistical analysis to account for the fact that various studies have demonstrated that the incidence of tongue cancer is growing in young people (Schantz 2002; Stimson and Guo-Pei 2002).

The E1 protein, which is descended from the E4 protein, is used to synthesise the mRNA from which it was produced by splicing together two other mRNAs. As far as transcripts have been found in warts, this is one of the most significant discoveries to date. According to the researchers, when the human keratin–cytoskeleton interacts, it causes collapses in the cytoplasmic network of the cytokeratin protein, which may allow viral particles to escape from the infected cell. It can only be found in the differentiated layer of the epithelium, and it gets its name from the fact that it can only be found in this layer of the epithelium. A notion has been advanced that the protein E4 may interfere with normal differentiation in order to provide favourable conditions for viral particle production. Therefore, E4 seems to be essential for the establishment of productive infection in humans. The E5 protein (4.1.4.5) is a subset of the 4.1.4.5 protein family of proteins, which includes the 4.1.4.5 protein. This membrane protein, which has 83 amino acids in total, is found in significant amounts in the Golgi apparatus and the plasma membrane. It is a membrane protein that is very hydrophobic and is located in the plasma membrane. The HPV-16 strain, for example, has a low ability to convert into another virus (Pim 1992). Cervical tumours are often found to have the E5 gene, which is located inside the ORF, missing. According to Schwartz and Harf, the capacity of a host cell to alter may be necessary for the onset of transformation, but it is not necessarily required for the maintenance of malignant transformation (1996). Furthermore, it has been shown to interact with a variety of extracellular matrix proteins, including the receptors for an epidermal growth factor (EGFR), platelet-derived growth factor (PDGF), colony stimulating factor-1, and other transmembrane proteins (Hwang 1995). On the other hand, it has been shown in vitro that the EGFR is required for the E5 protein of HPV-16 to transform murine cells (3T3) into a transformed state (Syrjänen 1999). Several researchers, including Haraf (1996) and Syrjänen (1999), have demonstrated that the E5 protein of HPV-16 slows the destruction of EGFRs that have been internalised. As previously reported, there is experimental evidence that the E5 protein may cause an increase in the activation of the EGFR in a ligand-dependent way, which is consistent with previous findings (Straight 1995; Crusius 1998). 4.1.5 Oncoproteins E6 and E7 are two of the most important oncoproteins in the body, and they are both found in high concentrations. In the world of oncoproteins, E6 and E7 are two of the most significant. E6 and E7 collaborate to guarantee the success of the process of immortalisation and transformation of cells that carry HPV DNA. This collaboration is essential to the process' success (Bedell 1987; Phelps 1988). Only the enzyme E6 has the capacity to prolong the life of human mammary epithelial cells in the laboratory (Haraf 1996). Researchers have discovered a relationship between the inactivation of the p53 tumour suppressor and the retinoblastoma (pRB) tumour suppressors and the significant transforming effects of high-risk HPV E6 and E7 proteins (Munger 2004). (See Figure 4.2 for an example.) According to the E6 and E7 proteins produced by the "high-risk" virus, HPV type 16 has the potential to immortalise and change human keratinocytes1, indicating that it is capable of doing so.

8.4 Proposed Method

In this study, many computer vision-based majority techniques for the machine-controlled detection of oral lesions at an early stage were investigated. The findings were really encouraging. It is possible to properly complete the process of photo classification by using Convolutional Neural Networks. To detect oral lesions and test for them at an early stage in their development, the researchers set out to do the following research: When cancer is detected in its early stages, it is significantly more straightforward to eradicate or cure it.

8.4.1 Image Processing System

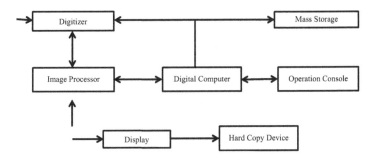

FIGURE 8.1
Block diagram for image processing system.

8.4.1.1 Digitizer

It changes an image into a numerical representation appropriate for the input into a data processor with some common digitizer area unit microdensitometer, image dissector, Videocon camera, and light-sensitive solid date array.

8.4.1.2 Image Processor

It performs the functions of image acquisition, preprocessing, recognition, storage segmentation, illustration, and interpretation and eventually displays or records the ensured image. The basic sequence concerned the image processing system.

8.4.1.3 Image Processing Fundamental

It is the process in which the image is processed in digital form. Nowadays, cameras can have the image directly in digital form, but actually, the images are generated in optical form. The digital images are captured in video cameras in digital form and then they are digitalized.

8.5 Methodology

8.5.1 Input Image and Pre-processing

Using the in read command, the workspace is updated with the contents of the supplied picture. Let us assume that image processing is the activity of getting an image from a hardware-based source in order to do preprocessing, and that preprocessing is performed with the picture that has the lowest degree of deliberation between information and yield of force. In order to prevent undesired upgrading or contortion, it is necessary to enhance the visual information, and this approach makes use of a large number of repeats.

8.5.2 Resizing Images and Changing the Colour Space

If just one input picture is provided, it will resize all of the input images to the same size and resolution. The method of converting colour space into colour information is an attempt to speed up the process of a picture to differentiate between colours from one another. In this case, transforming an RGB picture to a GRAYSCALE format image serves a functional purpose.

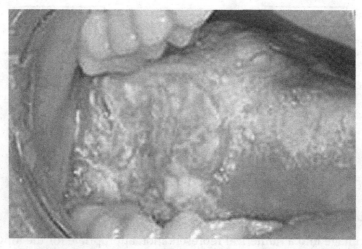

FIGURE 8.2
Example of a greyscale image.

8.5.3 Gaussian Filtering and Gamma Correction

It is a linear filter that is often used to blur a picture while also reducing noise. This filter is used for "unsharp masking," as the name suggests. Gamma correction, also known as image enhancement, is a nonlinear filter that is used to encode and decode luminance values in an imaging system in order to increase the visibility of the imaging system.

8.5.4 Segmentation

It is the process of subdividing a digital picture into several segments, which are referred to as "super pixels." The pixels in this procedure are grouped together because they have the same properties as one another. The division of an image into several areas is the first step in isolating it. As a result, each area has a homogeneous appearance. The segmentation accuracy is calculated by the number of times the analytic technique fails and succeeds in the same time period.

8.5.5 Colour Space Conversions

There is a shift in colour representation from one colour representation to another during this conversion. It occurs during the process of transitioning from one colour image space to another that colour space conversion occurs. Consequently, it will produce a picture that is identical to the original. The GRAYSCALE picture has been replaced with a BLACK AND WHITE one.

8.6 CNN

Applications using deep learning algorithms and image processing are two examples of situations in which this is often done. This is a diagram of a typical CNN architecture, which has three levels, which are as follows:

In computer programming, the Image Input Layer (also known as the Image Input Layer) is a layer that enables you to enter images into a programme. This layer is used to specify the size of the image that will be shown. Due to the grayscale image created by the RGB values, it will measure the height, breadth, and length of the picture, as well as the length of the channel, and it will do it in three dimensions. The data does not need to be jumbled since the data are scrambled by default before the training process starts, and the input image is then transferred to the Convolutional Layer, eliminating the requirement for data jumbles altogether. It contains two arguments, which are also present in the convolutional layer, and they are used to calculate the final result. The first parameter in this layer is the filter size, and the second and third arguments are the width and height of the filter, which are scanned along the image as the first and second arguments, respectively. Secondly, the number of filters is defined as the number of neural networks that are connected to the same input region in a collection of neural networks. The third parameter is the number of filters. This will ensure that the number of feature maps is kept at a constant level. In the case of a convolutional layer with the stride 1 set as the default, the spatial output size is determined by the "same" padding, which is a number that is nearly equal to or less than the size of the input. In the case of a convolutional layer with the stride 1 set as the default. The learning of this layer is performed via the use of the Convolution2dlayer class of functions.

Following the convolution layer, the data will be passed to the Max Pooling Layer, which will further process the information. This layer performs a function known as pooling, which selects the highest number of components feasible from the filter-covered feature map at a given place based on the filtering criteria. One of the most notable features of the map may be seen in the data produced by this layer. Down sampling takes advantage of the greatest amount of pooling available as well. With the help of maxPooling2dlayer, it is feasible to create this effect. This layer yields the maximum value of the input, which is determined mostly by the size of the pool used in the calculation (first argument). The greatest pooling layer has a relationship with the next layer. The Fully Connected Tier is the next layer in the hierarchy. Every other layer is stacked on top of the one-to-many entirely connected layer at the top of the stack, and so on down the stack. A layer in which every neuron interacts with every other neuron in the future layers and is entirely connected to the previous levels. During this layer, students study every facet of the image that will be utilised in spotting large patterns. This is done in combination with the other layers of the picture. The Classification Layer is the final of the layers to be described in this section. It is the last layer of the three-layer structure. To calculate the misfortune, the characterisation layer makes use of the enacting capability of the softmax to generate probabilities in which each piece of information is assigned to a class that is essentially unconnected to the other and to assign probabilities in which each piece of information is assigned to a class that is essentially unconnected to the other.

According to the research, integration seems to be more prevalent in cervical cancers associated with HPV 18 than it is in cervical cancers associated with HPV 16, according to the research. Crusius (1997) defined formalised (Crusius 1997). At some point during the process of HPV DNA integration, the viral genome breaks, most often in the E1/E2 region of the virus. The majority of the time, the E1 and E2 portions are lost as a consequence of the break in the middle. Detection techniques that are often used Each HPV detection method have its own set of benefits and limitations, and each one may be used to identify different types of HPV. Even with the most severe isolation measures, it is impossible to entirely eradicate all traces of contamination. Every strategy has its own set of difficulties. In order to undertake an acceptable analysis, it is thus required to examine both the detection method and the clinical significance of the data collected. This technique, known as polymerase chain reaction (PCR), is the most sensitive HPV detection method available, enabling the detection of even a single gene copy of HPV. Primers may be either consensus/general primers or primers that are specifically designed for a particular kind of DNA. When utilised in screening techniques, the consensus primers are advantageous since they bind to a wide range of HPV strains, making them an excellent choice. In HPV, the consensus primers bind to sequences that are highly conserved across many different HPV types (typically in L1), but the type-specific primers link to a sequence that is unique to a particular HPV type (commonly in E6 or E7) and does not cross over to other HPV types (as is the case with type-specific primers). In addition to type-specific PCR, sequencing of the PCR products obtained using consensus primers may be used to distinguish between the different types of bacteria. The importance of doing negative controls throughout the process cannot be overstated in order to minimise false positives. There have been several efforts to build universal primers for HPV DNA sequences that are conserved across all strains of the virus. However, although the technique's high specificity is a benefit, it also has many downsides, the most prominent of which is that it is time-consuming and requires large amounts of DNA to be used. On a dot blot, hybridisation has occurred. This approach avoids the need for enzyme digestion of the extracted DNA before it is transferred and bonded to a membrane in its single-stranded condition (see figure). Hybridisation with tagged cloned HPV DNA allows for the detection of HPV-specific sequences in a variety of viruses. When using 300-500ng of sample DNA, the sensitivity is around 1 genome copy per cell when using this method (Syrjanen 1987) A major benefit is that it is quite rapid to complete. The drawback is that the specificity is lower, and it is necessary to account for false positive signals as a result. One further HPV typing approach is reverse dot blot, which involves transferring DNA from known HPV types onto a membrane and employing labelled genetic material (genomic DNA or PCR products) as probes to distinguish the different HPV types. Capture via the use of a hybrid approach After the polymerase chain reaction, it is the second most sensitive detection technology available (PCR). According to the manufacturer, the number of HPV DNA copies detected per cell is around 0.05. Specifically, it is based on non-radioactive hybridisation using HPV RNA probes as probes, which has the advantage of creating stronger bonds than DNA-DNA contact and is thus more effective in this scenario. A collection of hybrid RNA-DNA molecules is made up of tubes that have been coated with monoclonal antibodies that are specific to the hybrid molecule. A picnotic nucleus is made of picnotic nuclei that are surrounded by wide transparent halos, the volume of which is higher than the volume of the cytoplasm itself. Koilocytosis was deemed a pathognomonic sign of HPV infection. Their traits include the following, to name just a few: An increase in the size of the nuclear arsenal (two to three times normal size) • Nuclear contour irregularity is a medical disorder that affects the nucleus (occasionally) Hyperchromasia is the medical term for this condition (occasionally) • Decontamination of the internuclear space.

8.6.1 Operation

CNN is used to organise information in instances when the information is displayed visually in a manner that is as tight as a violin's stringing pattern. CNNs are used to perform tasks like characterisation and recognition. In order to describe or grasp a picture, it is feasible to run images that are a 2D framework of pixels via CNN's image processing algorithm. A CNN is used in the differentiating proof cycle to alter the appearance of a picture to that of a bicycle or a human or to change the comparison of two sets of numbers at a location to that of a bicycle. In the same way that neuronal organisations acquire ideas from the mind, CNN gets ideas from the mind. Combining two or more states into a single state is called convolution. Convolution is a numerical activity in which input, a contention, and a kernel k are all dealt with in order to obtain a requisite yield that will describe whether or not it is possible to change the state of each other's state. In regard to a picture, the following is true: It is referred to as an element map. It is known as an element map because the result of this activity is an image "x" with a 2d display and various shading channels (RGB-Red, Green, and Blue) as well as a portion "w." The result of this activity is known as an element map.

Formula for the kernel

$$s[t] = (x * w)[t] = \sum_{a=-\infty}^{a=\infty} x[a]w[a + t] \qquad (8.1)$$

Feature map   *input* *kernel*

Its likeness to two signals is derived using this mathematical equation. A feature detector or filter may help us to identify the image edges, they can be identified using the convolution operation. The implementation is carried out by summation and infinite summation functions derived within a finite array element

TABLE 8.1

Channel Allocation

1	1	0	0	1
0	0	0	0	1
0	1	1	1	1
0	0	1	0	1
1	0	1	1	1

1	0	1
0	1	0
1	1	0

$$S(i,j) = (K*I)(i,j) = \sum_m \sum_n I(i-m, j-n) K(m,n) \qquad (8.2)$$

It can be implemented by a convolutional layer. It is the main block of CNN that helps to detect features. An easy way to understand that convolutional layer is to find the huge image in a lightless location using a torch light. This is the process carried out in the convolutional layer. We are trying to make a map with multiple features and detect features for image classification or identification. These feature detectors can identify shapes, colours, etc.

Let us have a 5 × 5 images that can be carried as default with three channels, as same as a 3 × 3 detectors with three channels over the image the feature detector is scanned (Table 8.1).

8.7 Image Feature Detector

We can perceive that the 5 × 5 info picture is diminished to 3 × 3 component maps. The channels continue as before as 3(RGB). We utilise different component identifiers to discover the edges and to hone the picture or to obscure the picture. In the event that we would prefer not to change the component map measurement, we can utilise zero cushioning of one as demonstrated.

Applying a zero padding,

$$(W - F + 2P)/S + 1 \implies (5 - 3 + 2)/1 + 1 = 5 \qquad (8.3)$$

The output is provided with three colour channels and 5 × 5 dimensions.

If we have only one feature detector. Then a linear transformation is applied,

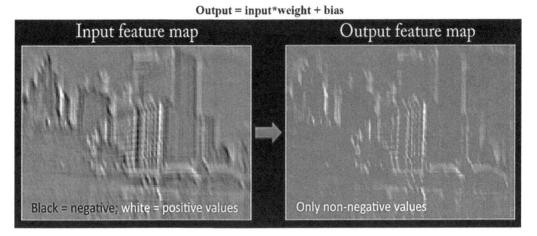

FIGURE 8.3
Greyscale.

Upon reaching this step, all of the image's features have been identified entirely from its local regions, and the image will be joined by the picture's spatial neighbourhood feature detector, which will allow the image to be recognised and scanned comprehensively.

Translational invariance is obtained by the use of a pooling technique. Translational invariance indicates that even if the input is modified by a small amount, the output remains unchanged. It will assist us in identifying common characteristics of a picture, such as colour and edges. A more efficient pooling function is the maximum pooling function.

8.8 Trainee

A tool that may be utilised in an interactive manner. GUIDE is a software tool that is used to construct, develop, and update user interfaces. It is available for free download. Alternatively, we may programmatically construct graphical user interfaces (GUIs) by using MATLAB functions and MATLAB functions. The data collected from different external devices is analysed and changed into presentation-quality data by means of visualisation, preprocessing, and other methods as part of the overall analysis process, which analyses the data obtained from various external devices. Furthermore, it is utilised for data analysis and data visualisation, in addition to numerical analysis, in order to provide exact findings. Charting features include 2D and 3D charting, which enable you to create charts in real-time and then export the results. Compared images that have been modified or not by the trainee programme should be done using this approach. When writing this assignment, the CPU was a Pentium Dual Core 2.00GHz with 4GB of RAM, and the trainee made extensive use of this processor.

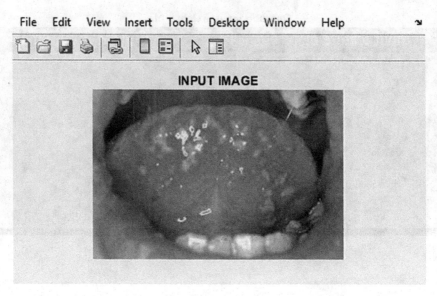

FIGURE 8.4
Input image.

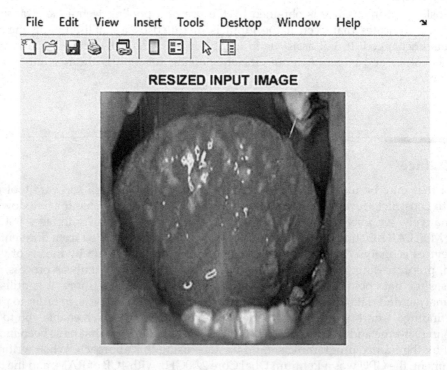

FIGURE 8.5
Resize input image.

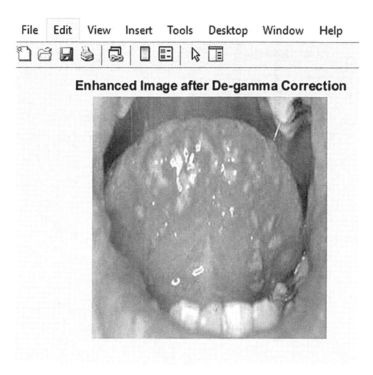

FIGURE 8.6
Enhanced image after De-Gamma correction.

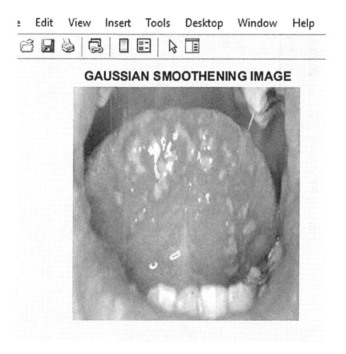

FIGURE 8.7
Gaussian smoothening image.

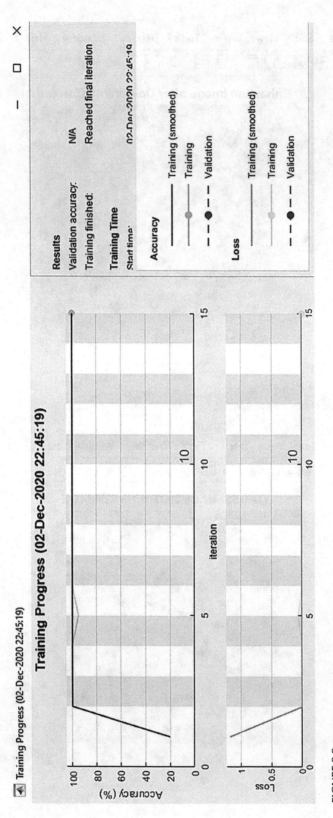

FIGURE 8.8
Trainee progress.

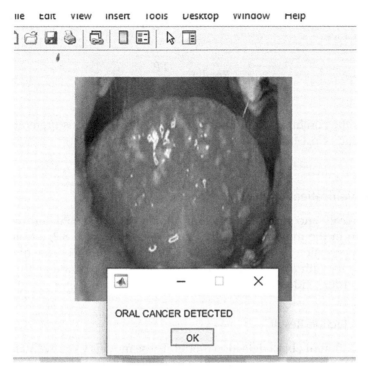

FIGURE 8.9
Final output image.

8.9 Results and Discussion

The output result is detailed by performance measures and the result of image classification and object detection.

8.9.1 Performance Measures

The performance of this method is to classify the image and differentiate it. For those classifications, the predicted data was compared to the expected data, which was acquired from composite annotation. As a result of this classification, the binary image had to overcome true negative (TN), true positive(TP), false positive (FP)and false negative (FN).

Recall precision and then an F1 score (combination of both precision and recall) could then be calculated, which preferred accuracy, specificity, and sensitivity. If those properties could mislead when the data distribution was imbalanced. These outcomes produce the best operating point which was classified by F1.

Precision: when the properties of the cancer are 100% accurate in cancer patients then it is precision.

$$Precision = \frac{TP}{TP + FP} \tag{8.4}$$

Recall: when the properties of cancer with cancer patient was diagnosed by the algorithm for cancer.

$$Recall = \frac{TP}{TP + FN} \tag{8.5}$$

F1 score: It is the combination of both precision and recall. It is preferable to use F1 score instead of precision and recall.

8.9.2 Image Classification Result

The precision, recall, and F1 score were all evaluated in order to determine the presence of an oral lesion in the imaging data. In accordance with Table 8.2, a lesion picture was obtained with a precision of 84.77%, a recall of 89.51%, and an F1 score of 87.07%, respectively. Referral data with a precision of 67.1%, a recall of 93.88%, and an F1 score of 78.30% are required in order to identify the lesion, as shown in Table 8.3.

8.9.3 Object Detection Result

There are three different object detection model. These models were evaluated on the given sample set and the results. The resulted lesion achieved a precision of 46.66%, recall of 38.16% and an F1 score of 42.35% as shown in Table. 8.4. For testing, the resulted lesion that require referral achieved with precision of 32.94%, a recall of 54.90% and a F1 score of 41.18% as shown in Table 8.5. Also Table 8.6 and 8.7 gives the Precision, Recall and F1 score for the image cavity and referral value of object detection.

TABLE 8.2

Component Map

0	0	0	0	0	0	0
0	1	1	0	0	1	0
0	0	0	0	0	1	0
0	0	1	1	1	1	0
0	0	0	1	0	1	0
0	1	0	1	1	1	0
0	0	0	0	0	0	0

TABLE 8.3

Outcome of Binary Image Classification

Outcome	Description
TP (True positive)	When both predicted and actual cases are true
TN (True negative)	When both predicted and actual cases are false
FP (False positive)	When actual data is false and predicted is true
FN (False negative)	When actual data is true and predicted is false

TABLE 8.4

Image Classification Result of Lesion Image of Cavity

Image class	TP	FP	TN	FN	Precision (%)	Recall (%)	F1score (%)
Lesion	128	23	38	15	84.77	89.51	87.07

TABLE 8.5

Image Classification Referral Data

Image class	TP	FP	TN	FN	Precision (%)	Recall (%)	F1score (%)
Referral	92	45	62	6	67.15	93.88	78.30

TABLE 8.6

Object Detection of Lesion Image of Cavity

Object class	TP	FP	FN	Precision (%)	Recall (%)	F1 score (%)
Lesion	56	64	94	46.66	37.31	41.46

TABLE 8.7

Object Detection Referral Value

Object class	TP	FP	FN	Precision (%)	Recall (%)	F1 score (%)
Referral	58	112	44	34.11	56.86	42.64

8.10 Conclusion

As a result of this study, we have developed an automated system for diagnosing oral cancer from mouth images that are based on the use of image processing algorithms. The findings of the trials demonstrate that the background and bone parts may be distinguished exceedingly effectively from one another. Researchers revealed experimental discoveries that will be of considerable assistance to physicians in the creation of an automated oral cancer diagnostic system as result of this study. As accuracy and time duration for collecting the most prominent output from another new algorithm for recognising oral cancer improve in the future, clinical practitioners may recognise minute and profound alterations in a timelier manner.

References

[1] Roshan Alex Welikala, Paolo Remagnino, Jian Han Lim, Chee Seng Chan, Senthilmani Rajendran, Thomas George Kallarakkal. "Automated Detection and Classification of Oral Lesions Using Deep Learning for Early Detection of Oral Cancer", in IEEE Access, vol. 8, pp. 132677–132693, 2020, doi:10.1109/ACCESS.2020.3010180

[2] D. Rajesh Kumar, K. Rajkumar, K. Lalitha, V. Dhanakoti. "Bigdata in the Management of Diabetes Mellitus Treatment", In *Studies in Big Data* (pp. 293–324). Springer, Singapore, 2020.

[3] Edward Rajan Samuel Nadar Jeyaraj, Pandia Rajan Jayaraj. "Computer-assisted Medical Image Classification for Early Diagnosis of Oral Cancer Employing Deep Learning Algorithm", *Journal of Cancer Research and Clinical Oncology* vol. 145,4 (2019): pp. 829–837. doi:10.1007/s00432-018-02834-7

[4] Shipu Xu, Chang Liu, Yongshuo Zong, Longzhi Yang. "An Early Diagnosis of Oral Cancer based on Three-Dimensional Convolutional Neural Networks", vol. 7, pp. 158603–158611, 2019, October.

[5] Nabihah Haron, Rosnahbinti Zain, Anand Ramanathan, "m-Health for Early Detection of Oral Cancer in Low- and Middle-Income Countries", vol. 26, 3: pp. 278–285, 2020, March.

[6] F. Bray, J. Ferlay, I. Soerjomataram. "GLOBOCAN Estimates of Prevalency and Death Worldwide for 36 Cancers in 185 Countries in 2018: GLObocan Estimates of Cancer Prevalence and Mortality in 185 Countries in the World, Global Cancer Statistics 2018", *CA: G Clinicians Cancer Journal, B* 68(6), pp. 209–249, 2018, November.

[7] M.J. Thun, S.J. Henley, W.D. Travis. *Lung cancer. Epidemiology and Prevention of Cancer*, 4th Ed., 519–542, Thun MJ, Linet MS, Cerhan JR, Haiman CA, Karlovy Vary, eds. Oxford University Press, New York; 2018, December, 2017.

[8] World Health Organization. "Global Health Observatory", The World Health Observatory Database of WHO can be obtained from who.int/gho/database/en. Checked back on 21 June 2018.

[9] H. Sung, J. Ferlay, R. L. Siegel, M. Laversanne, I. Soerjomataram, A. Jemal, F. Bray. "Global Cancer Statistics 2020: GLOBOCAN Estimates of Incidence and Mortality Worldwide for 36 Cancers in 185 Countries", *CA: A Cancer Journal for Clinicians* 71(3), 209–249, 2021. https://doi.org/10.3322/caac.21660

[10] G. F. Funk, L. H. Karnell, R. A. Robinson, W. K. Zhen, D. K. Trask, H. T. Hoffman. "Presentation, Treatment, and Outcome of Oral Cavity Cancer: A National Cancer Data Base Report", *Head & Neck* 24(2), 165–180. https://doi.org/10.1002/hed.10004

[11] H. Chen, Q. Dou, L. Yu, L. Zhao, J. Qin, D. Wang, V.C. Mok, L. Shi, Heng, P.A., "Automatic Detection by 3D Convolutionary Neural Networks of Cerebral Microbleed from Images from MR", *IEEE Transactions On Medical Imaging* 35(5), 1182–1195, 2016, December 29. https://doi.org/10.129/TMI.2016.25281

[12] Z. Jie, W. Xizhao, W. Shufang, Y. Guoqing, M. Liyan. "Multi-image Recognition for Objects", *IET Computer Vision* 12(3), 350–356, 2018.

[13] Jun Gao, Qian Jiang, Bo Zhou, Daozheng Chen. "Convolutional Neural Networks for Computer-Aided Detection or Diagnosis in Medical Image Analysis: An Overview[J]", *Mathematical Biosciences and Engineering* 16(6), 6536–6561, 2019.

[14] Y. Wen, Y. Lu, J. Yan, K.M. von Deneen, P. Shi, "The Algorithm for Plaque Licence Recognition Applied to Intelligent Transportation System", *IEEE Transactions on Intelligent Transportation Systems* 12(3), 967–3845, 2011, September.

[15] M. Chandraprabha, R.K. Dhanaraj. "Machine Learning Based Pedantic Analysis of Predictive Algorithms in Crop Yield Management", *2020 4th International Conference on Electronics, Communication and Aerospace Technology (ICECA). 2020 4th International Conference on Electronics, Communication and Aerospace Technology (ICECA)*, 2020, November 5.

[16] Nabihah Haron, Rosnahbinti Zain, Anand Ramanathan, "m-Health for Early Detection of Oral Cancer in Low and Middle-income Countries", 2020, March.

[17] K. Lalitha, R. Thangarajan, S. Ponni, "Radial Shaped Clustering- A Novel Technique for Lifespan Elongation of WSN", *IEEE sponsored Int. Conf. on Science, Technology, Engg. And Management (ICONSTEM 2017)*, 2017, March.

[18] K. Lalitha, R. Thangarajan, C. Poongodi, D. Vijay Anand, "Sink Originated Unique Algorithm for Clustering and Routing to forward Aggregated data in Wireless Sensor Networks", *Int. Conf. on Intelligent Comm. for Smart World (I2C2SW 2018)*, 2018, December.

[19] M.M. Colombet, J. Ferlay, M. Ervik, F. Lam, Mery L. Pin, Ervik M. Lyon, "France: International Agency for Research on Cancer", *Cancer Today*, 2018. Displayed on https://gco.iarc.fr/today (Accessed December 26, 2018).

[20] S. Tantiwipawin, S. Dejsuvan, S. Tomolmalai, S. Chuachamsai, " An Oral Cancer Exam Over the Course of 10 Years, Focusing on Northern Thailand's Young People", *The Journal of Oral Science* 57, 327–334, 2015.

[21] T. Abiramia, K. Lalitha, P. Jayadharshini, T. Madhuvanthi, "Future: HCI in Public Conveyances", *AIP Conference Proceedings* 2387, 140042, 2021. https://doi.org/10.1063/5.0069393

[22] K. Lalitha, V.M. Barkavi, R. Thangarajan, V. Manju Barkavi, K. Sree Preethi, "Program Length Based Estimated Facts Assembly with Minimal Information Loss in Wireless Sensor Networks", *Advanced Computing and Communication Systems (ICACCS), 3rd Int. Conf., IEEE Xplore*, 2016, October.

9

Lung Diseases Identification

A. Sivabalan, Jai Jaganath Babu Jayachandran, D. Sandhiya, and M. B. Sharada
Chennai Institute of Technology, Chennai, India

CONTENTS

9.1 Introduction

Lung diseases are a general term that refers to a variety of illnesses or issues that prevent the lungs from functioning properly. Lung disease may have an impact on respiratory function, which is the ability to take in air, as well as pulmonary function, which is the efficiency with which the lungs operate. In recent studies, it has been shown that lung disorders may affect people in their 20s–45s, despite the fact that it is depicted as a condition that has been around for more than 50 years in the literature. According to estimates, lung infection will be the third leading cause of death across the world by 2030. It is estimated that 300 million people worldwide suffer from the symptoms of asthma and that this ailment claims the lives of around 250,000 people worldwide each year, according to the World Health Organization (WHO). As a result, it is critical to identify and implement practical solutions for reducing air pollution and fossil fuel byproducts. The importance of early detection of lung infections has increased more than in any previous period in history. As a result, artificial intelligence and deep learning may play an increasingly important role. Recent years have seen a substantial increase in the importance of computed tomography scan innovation all over the globe. With the assistance of a comprehensive learning strategy, this examination article may provide doctors and other analysts with a plan for recognising lung illness. The images from computed tomography (CT) and magnetic resonance imaging (MRI) scans of the lungs are used as a dataset. In this paradigm, the secure region-of-interest (S-ROI) is used to divide the lung anatomy into two halves. Furthermore, we offer a unique approach for determining the location of a lung infection that is reliant on the inclusion of S-ROI split photos inside the framework of the co-event measurement. When the gray-level co-occurrence matrix (GLCM) is used, the underlying data of lung image structures are integrated. Finally, we apply a characterisation approach that distinguishes between different types of lung illness and healthy lungs.

The presence of lung cancer on an X-ray is generally obvious after the disease has begun to manifest symptoms. A lung cancer that has not yet shown itself was discovered on a chest X-ray that was obtained for another reason. A CT scan of the chest may be recommended for a more thorough examination.

Lung cancer may arise anywhere in the lungs at any stage. The right lung has three lobes, whereas the left lung has just two lobes. The right lung is larger than the left lung. A breath of air enters via our nose and mouth before travelling down the trachea (the windpipe) and into one of the major stems of the bronchial tube system. It then passes via a bronchus to either the right or left lung, depending on which one it is.

This is due to the quick development rate and proclivity to metastasize of small cell lung cancer. Depending on whether the disease might be curable with a single field of radiation or not, these tumours are categorised into groups [1–3].

9.1.1 Squamous Cell Lung Cancer in the Early Stages

About one-third of people with small cell lung cancer, also known as limited stage lung cancer, had the disease detected in its early stages. Although they may have migrated to nearby lymph nodes, these tumours are limited to a single lung.

9.1.2 Advanced Small Cell Lung Cancer in the Extensive Stage

Small cell lung cancer affects about two-thirds of people who are diagnosed with the illness at an advanced stage. Even at the time of diagnosis, these malignancies may be present in both lungs and have often migrated to other parts of the body. They are often found in the brain. Non-small cell lung malignancies (NSCLC) are the most prevalent malignancy, accounting for 80%–85% of all cancers in the population. Specifically, this is the form of lung cancer that is more typically detected in non-smokers, women, adolescents, and young adults. In contrast to other patterns, NSCLC develops in bigger and more central bronchi; spreads locally; and metastasizes in a greater area than the other patterns. However, the pace of development in the site of origin is generally faster than the rate of growth in the other patterns [1].

9.1.3 Difficulties in Determining the Nature of Lung Cancer Cells

A variety of tests are required when it comes to diagnosing lung cancer. Identify the kind and stage of cancer in more detail, which will aid in determining treatment choices.

Chest X-rays have been demonstrated to be inefficient in the screening for lung cancer, but, for some people, a disease in the lungs may be discovered for the first time by a chest X-ray. A chest X-ray may reveal certain cancers, while others may be too tiny or concealed under bone to be seen by the X-ray machine. An X-ray is often required if anything of concern is seen on the film. A CT scan is then performed. When compared to chest X-rays, CT scans provide a more comprehensive image and may identify very tiny cancers because of the three-dimensional imaging of the tumour. CT scans may also be used to assess whether or not the tumour has migrated to the lymph nodes that surround the lungs. A biopsy must be conducted in order to verify whether or not a problem region is indeed lung cancer, since a biopsy not only verifies the existence of cancer but also generally indicates the kind of lung cancer present. When doing a biopsy, tissue or fluid may be acquired in a variety of different methods. Needle biopsy, also known as needle aspiration, is a procedure in which a hollow biopsy needle is introduced through the skin in order to extract tissue or fluid for examination. The process is carried out with the use of imaging tests such as CT, MRI, fluoroscopy, or ultrasound [2], and several kinds of needles are employed. Lung cancer cells appear as a round item on chest X-rays because they are typically brightly contrasted and have a round shape. A chest X-ray may reveal nodules that are not always indicative of lung cancer; instead, they might be caused by another condition such as pneumonia, TB, or calcified granuloma, among others. As a result, lung cancer detection has been a tepid endeavour.

9.2 Literature Survey

For this purpose, they created an ant colony optimisation approach. The authors in [1] concentrated on lung cancer classification to identify and diagnose the health disorders. Lung cancer is a serious public health problem across the globe, and it is one of the leading causes of early death. As a result of this classification, proper rules were expected to be generated with clear illness categorization, which pilots to a precise low degree of precision. On the other hand, [2] gives a detailed evaluation of the technical advancements made by US researchers in the field of lung disease diagnostics. A convolutional neural network (CNN) framework is used to categorise lung tissue patterns into distinct groups, such as normal, reticulation, ground-glass opacity, honeycombing, and so on. Normal lung tissue patterns are classified as follows: The framework is comprised of five convolutional layers, followed by two fully connected layers, and is based on the LSTM algorithm. The designed technique produced accurate findings with a precision of 0.82. Rodrigues et al. [3] determined the likelihood that a cancerous tumour is present in the lungs of a patient for that particular procedure. A deep neural network is comprised of layers of CNNs that can search for abnormalities in great detail (cancer) [4]. The existing system is based on CT image segmentation of the lungs, which is combined with a region-growing algorithm to create a functional system. The CT input pictures that were taken as input are not very clear, making it very difficult to analyse them properly. In segmentation, the region-expanding technique is applied, which clusters the surrounding pixels together, making it difficult to create an accurate representation of the affected area [5–7].

9.3 Proposed Method

The S-ROI approach for lung structure segmentation is used in conjunction with CT and MRI pictures to increase the quality of the image input. We also utilise fusion methods to improve the input picture quality, such as fusing CT and MRI images. The GLCM is responsible for synthesising the structural information included in lung image structures. In the last step, we conduct a classification experiment on this collection of variables in order to distinguish between different forms of lung illnesses and healthy lungs. The suggested approach has an accuracy of roughly 97% in detecting the presence of illnesses and classifying them accordingly.

It is possible to identify lung characteristics and classify them using one of the various methods that are currently available. Techniques such as deep learning and machine learning may be used. The first approach is one that can be used. When it comes to classification, algorithms from deep learning, such as LNN and Convolutional Neural Networks, are applied. There are four major processes that take place in the identification of illnesses originating in the lungs [8, 9]. They are listed in the next section and shown in Figure 9.1.

- Preprocessing
- Data segmentation
- Feature extraction
- Classification
- Preprocessing
- Data segmentation

The GLCM is responsible for orchestrating the main datasets of lung image structures.

Finally, we conduct an experiment using this combination of features in order to distinguish between different types of lung disorders and solid lungs.

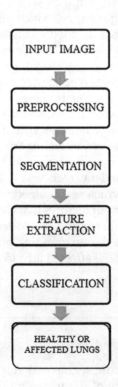

FIGURE 9.1
Block diagram.

9.3.1 Input Image

When a CT scan is performed, X-rays are used to generate images of the inside of the body, but an MRI scan makes use of fantastic attracting fields and radio recurrence heartbeats to provide detailed images of organs and other interior body components. The goal of image fusion is to combine data from many photographs of a comparable subject into a single photograph that has the most important and needed highlights from each of the initial photographs. The most important task of picture fusion is the integration of integral data from several images into a single image. Compared to any of the input pictures, the combined image will be more informative and intelligible. It is also more suited to visual and machine discernment than any of the individual pictures [10, 11].

9.3.2 Preprocessing

The preprocessing step follows after that. It is possible to alter the image at this location. To differentiate the area of interest (ROI), image-enhancing techniques such as lung division and bone disposal might be used. The ROI would then be able to be used for the detection of lung illnesses, which would then be done on the ROI. The end result of this evolution is a collection of photographs in which the quality of the photographs has been enhanced or undesired elements have been removed. Preprocessing is primarily comprised of two processes. They are as follows:

- RGB to Grayscale conversion is shown in Figure 9.2.
- Filter based on the histogram

When we convert an RGB picture to a grey-level image, the overall pixel values are reduced in magnitude.

9.3.3 Segmentation

The segmentation of images is one of the most important procedures in the assessment and treatment of patients. The primary goal of this phase is to extract the most important information from the images. It is a method in which a picture is broken into several essential areas and the needed data is separated by employing appropriate mathematical algorithms. A region of interest (ROI) is a part of an image that you need to channel or act out another operation on in order to complete the task at hand. To describe a return on investment (ROI), you must first create an image of similar size to the image you need to

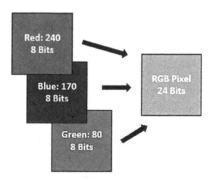

FIGURE 9.2
RGB image pixel.

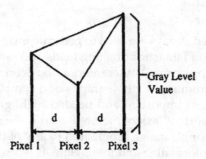

FIGURE 9.3
Pixel value arrangement.

measure, with pixels that describe the ROI invested set to 1 and any leftover pixels set to 0. This image is then used as the basis for a paired mask, with pixels that describe the ROI invested set to 1 and any leftover pixels set to 0.

9.3.4 Feature Extraction

The ability to extract features from an image is a huge step forward in any undertaking. Following the completion of an image division, the extraction process produces a list of capabilities that contains information about the anomalies contained in the outputs. This approach is essential to know to determine if a disease is beneficial or detrimental. The highlights are extricated in accordance with the form, edges, unbending character, and so on of the object. GLCM is an abbreviation for Gray Level Co-Occurrence Matrix. It is a network that emits surface highlights that are dispersed on the exterior of the image or in the area surrounding the picture and that is composed of pixels. This lattice, for the most part, computes the probability that an event with the same measure of image component p(i) will occur at some distance d and in the scenario of picture component p(j) at a certain location. The grey levels at both foci are compared and contrasted.

9.3.5 Classification

The lung neural network (LNN) is one of the most effective classifications of machine learning algorithms. We conduct an experiment based on this set of characteristics in order to distinguish between two types of lung illness and healthy lungs. We evaluate the segregation capacity of the suggested lung image descriptors by planning each aspiratory condition using LNN, including 4–10 neurons in the hidden layer and 3 neurons in the yield layer, then evaluating the results with LNN. The holdout approach was used to develop and approve this organisation, and it was successful [12–15].

9.4 Result and Output

The results are shown in the following MATLAB window. The initial windows are shown in the following image, which may be seen after hitting the refresh button.

In this window, you may look at the MRI and CT pictures that are necessary for the procedure. Following the submission of the photos as input images, the software will execute them according to the provided code as shown in Figures 9.4–9.7.

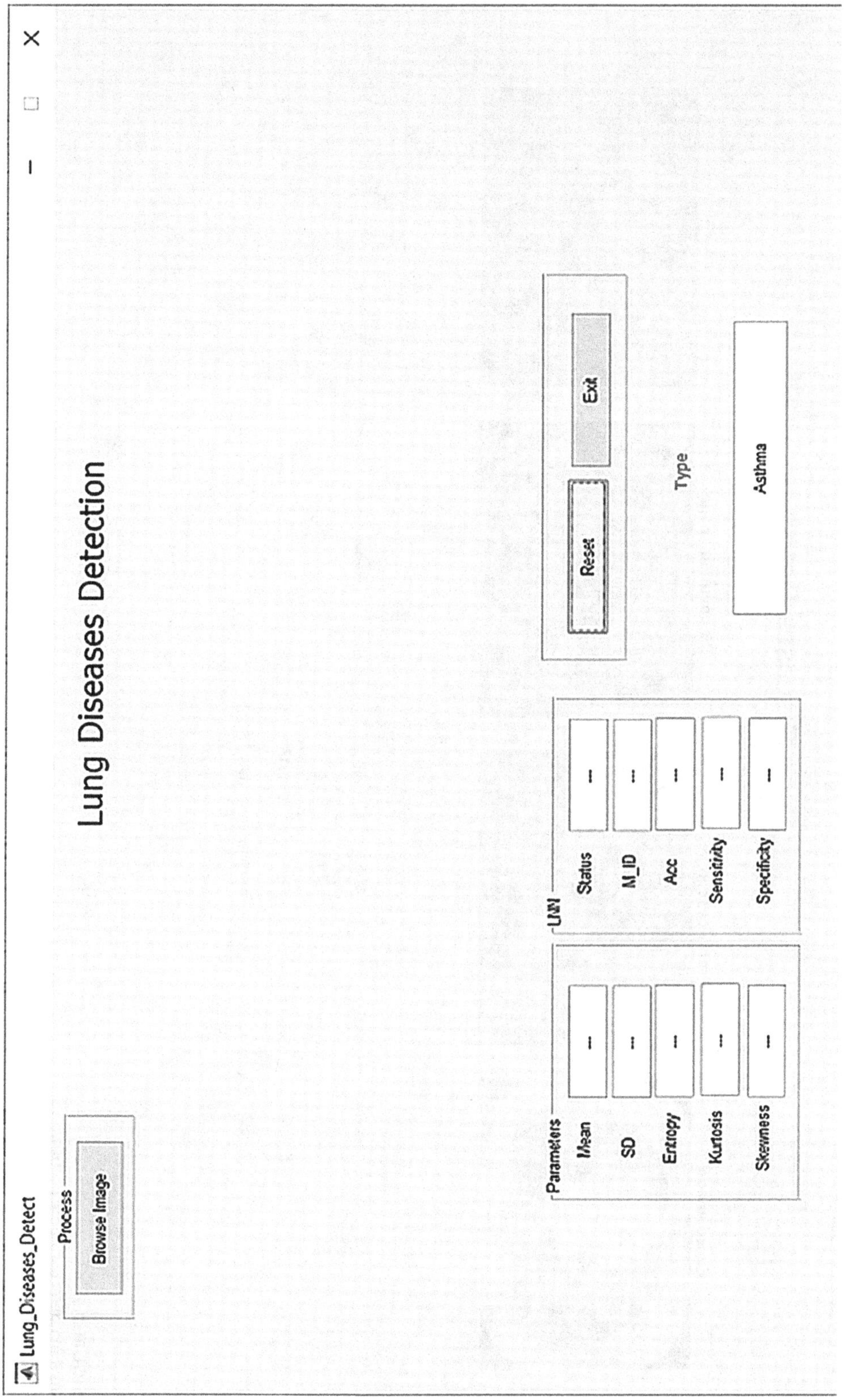

FIGURE 9.4
Output screen.

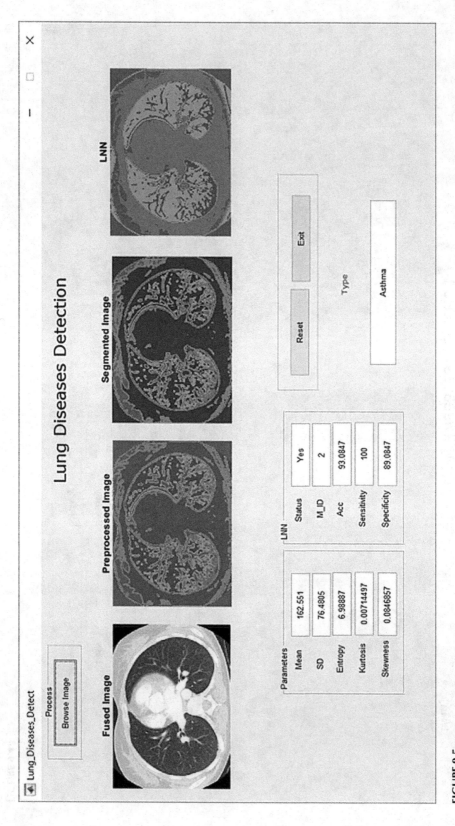

FIGURE 9.5
Asthma detected in the output.

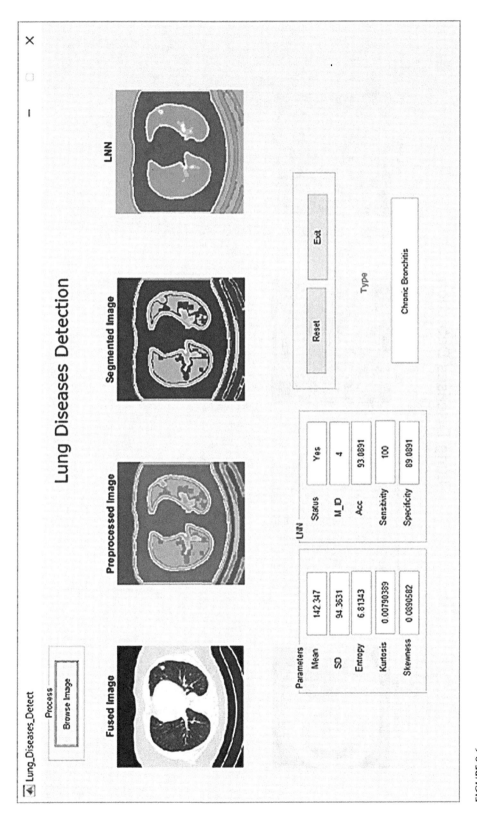

FIGURE 9.6
Chronic bronchitis detected.

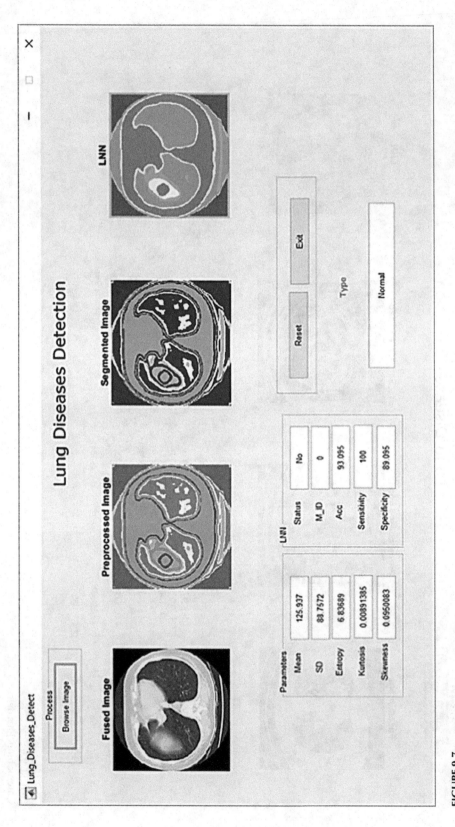

FIGURE 9.7
Healthy lungs.

The programme detects the following diseases.

- **Disease Detected**: Asthma
- **Disease Detected**: Chronic Bronchitis
- **Disease detected**: NIL – since the lung seems unaffected.

9.5 Conclusion

The primary goal of the research is to develop a code that can effectively identify the damaged parts of the lungs, as well as to utilise an LNN that can accurately categorise the illnesses. The first step is to get the dataset, which is a collection of CT scan and MRI scan pictures of the lungs that have been identified as having been impacted. Obtaining the dataset was accomplished over the internet. In the next stage, the segmentation algorithm will be used to separate the damaged area from the rest of the lung. For picture segmentation, we employed the area of interest method (also known as the region of interest algorithm). MATLAB includes a number of different feature extraction algorithms for use in the project's feature extraction phase. These characteristics are exclusively taken from the impacted locations. This research goes one step farther than all of the preceding experiments in that it detects illnesses such as asthma, cancer, pneumonia, emphysema, and chronic bronchitis in addition to other conditions. The results of the tests showed that the suggested technique for identifying illnesses that affect the lungs was successful with 97% accuracy, demonstrating the practicality of the strategy. The findings support the conclusion that the approach is suitable for coordinating clinical decision-making.

References

[1] Lung Cancer, Non-Small Cell Statistics, Cancer.net
[2] Snehal Dabade, Snehajhadav Shubhangic Haudhri, A review paper on computer aided system for lung cancer detection *"2017 International conference on Big Data, IOT and Data science (BID)*, 2017.
[3] Murillo Barata Rodrigues, Raul Medeiros, Shara Alves, Pedro Pedrosa Filho, Joao Duarte, Arun Sangaiah, V.H.C. Albuquerque "Health of things Algorithm for malignancy level classification of lung nodules", *IEEE Access*. vol 6, pp. 1–1, 2018. https://doi.org/10.1109/ACCESS.2018.2817614
[4] https://wiki.cancerimagingarchive.net/display/public/LIDC-IDRI
[5] Ning Guo, Ruoh-Fang Yen, 2015 IEEE nuclear science symposium and medical imaging conference, 2015.
[6] https://www.mathworks.com/help/images/ref/graycomatrix.html
[7] Rajesh, Kumar D., K. Rajkumar, K. Lalitha, V. Dhanakoti Bigdata in the Management of Diabetes Mellitus Treatment. In: Chakraborty, C., Banerjee, A., Kolekar, M., Garg, L., Chakraborty, B. (Eds.). *Internet of Things for Healthcare Technologies. Studies in Big Data*, vol 73, Springer, Singapore, 2021. https://doi.org/10.1007/978-981-15-4112-4_14

 [8] C. Poongodi, K. Lalitha, Rajesh Kumar Dhanaraj, "The Role of Blockchains for Medical Electronics Security". In: Saini, K., Chelliah, P.R., Saini, D.K. (Eds.). *Essential Enterprise Blockchain Concepts and Applications* (1st ed.). Auerbach Publications, 2021. https://doi.org/10.1201/9781003097990

 [9] K. Lalitha, D. Rajesh Kumar, C. Poongodi, Jeevanantham Arumugam, "Healthcare Internet of Things–The Role of Communication Tools and Technologies", In: Chilamkurti, N., Poongodi, T., & Balusamy, B. (Eds.). *Blockchain, Internet of Things, and Artificial Intelligence* (1st ed.). Chapman and Hall/CRC, 2021. https://doi.org/10.1201/9780429352898

[10] S.W.-C. Lam, "Texture feature extraction using gray level gradient based on co-occurrence matrices", *1996 IEEE International symposium in biomedical imaging (ISBI)*, 2012.

[11] M. Sathya, M. Jeyaselvi, Lalitha Krishnasamy, Mohammad Mazyad Hazzazi, Prashant Kumar Shukla, Piyush Kumar Shukla, Stephen Jeswinde Nuagah, "A Novel, Efficient, and Secure Anomaly Detection Technique Using DWU-ODBN for IoT-Enabled Multimedia Communication Systems", *Wireless Communications and Mobile Computing*, vol. 2021, 12 pages, 2021, Article ID 4989410, https://doi.org/10.1155/2021/4989410

[12] Rajesh Kumar Dhanaraj, Rutvij H. Jhaveri, Lalitha Krishnasamy, Gautam Srivastava, Praveen Kumar Reddy Maddikunta, "Black-Hole Attack Mitigation in Medical Sensor Networks Using the Enhanced Gravitational Search Algorithm", *International Journal of Uncertainty, Fuzziness and Knowledge-Based Systems, World Scientific*, vol. 29, Suppl. 2, pp. 297–315, December 2021. https://doi.org/10.1142/S021848852140016X

[13] Rajesh Kumar Dhanaraj, K. Lalitha, S. Anitha, Supriya Khaitan, Punit Gupta, Mayank Kumar Goyal, "Hybrid and Dynamic Clustering Based Data Aggregation and Routing for Wireless Sensor Networks", *Journal of Intelligent & Fuzzy Systems*, vol. 40, no. 6, pp. 10751–10765, 2021.

[14] M. D. Ramasamy, K. Periasamy, L. Krishnasamy, R. K. Dhanaraj, S. Kadry, Y. Nam, "Multi-Disease Classification Model using Strassen's Half of Threshold (SHoT) Training Algorithm in Healthcare Sector," in IEEE Access. https://doi.org/10.1109/ACCESS.2021.3103746

[15] S. Anitha, P. Jayanthi, K. Lalitha, V. Chandrasekaran, "Secured Ant Colony Optimization based on Energy Trust System for Replica Node Attack Detection", *International Journal on Emerging Technologies*, vol. 11, no. 2, pp. 104–109.

10

Brain–Computer Interface-based Real-Time Movement of Upper Limb Prostheses

Kalpana Kasilingam and Hakkem Babu
Hindustan Institute of Technology, Coimbatore, India

Teresa V V and Dhanasekar J
Sri Eshwar College of Engineering, Coimbatore, India

Ramya S
Hindustan Institute of Technology, Coimbatore, India

CONTENTS

DOI: 10.1201/9781003217435-10

10.1 Introduction

The goal of interaction between people and computer systems is to improve non-muscular communication between humans (users) and computers (computers themselves) (or machines). The brain–computer interface (BCI) is the most common kind of human–computer interaction, and it tries to translate thoughts into signals that may be used to operate a computer or move a robot (in brain signals). Researchers are now investigating the potential of BCI technologies for use in industrial and military applications, including repair, gaming, communication, and hands-free robot control. The goal of this study is to offer an overview of the advantages of electroencephalography (EEG) in BCI for rehabilitation purposes. Furthermore, the different types of EEG signals gathered during distinct cognitive processes are addressed in the proposed research. Several extractions, feature selections, and classification procedures that have been developed by researchers all around the world in recent years are highlighted in detail. The primary focus of this study is on various control systems for artificial instruments, such as wheelchairs, upper limb prostheses, and cursor and keyboard controls using BCI technology.

The visually evocative (SDV) potential, the SCP, the P300, the ERD/ERS, and the error-related potential (ErRP) are only a few of the well-known brain signals (depending on the cognitive tasks performed). The EEG–BCI analysis chooses brain signals based on the individual's cognitive task, which is determined by the task (or the modality of signals). When it comes to the detection of visually inspired mistakes—whether it is motor planning, imagination, or performance (also known as motor image signal), the findings of ERD/ERS have been promising. Therefore, these signals are important in our present investigation.

The effectiveness of the hybrid BCI (i.e., the detection of at least two blood states concurrently or sequentially) in control applications has been shown in a recent study. Pfurtscheller et al. [1] used a motor-image-based switch to alter the ON/OFF state of a BCI-based SSVEP, as an example of how this might be accomplished. Long et al. [2] used an engine and P300 signal imaging to operate a continuous 2D cursor as well as the direction and speed of a wheelchair, respectively. Furthermore, the BCI control system, like any other communication modality based on biologically based signals and physical channels, is prone to making errors when recognising an object (e.g., muscle activity, talk, and gesticulation). As a result, in the real world, just using MI signals to control an external device is not sufficient for operating the device. In order to improve the performance of a control system, it is necessary to use a different signal modality in addition to MI signals to detect and correct errors. Furthermore, if the mistake is caused by the individual, the brain creates a distinct kind of EEG. An aspect of the BCI control system that may be compared to this kind of EEG is the ErRP, which is a type of error feedback.

The majority of ErRP research consists of standard tasks for responding to a stimulus when participants respond, and when the subject performs an incorrect action, ErRP occurs. Others include using ErRP as a feedback mechanism that displays erroneous interface responses rather than the subjects themselves. An example of this would be when a human attempts to move a robot arm to a target but the system either fails to reach the target or completely crosses it. In the presence of ErRP, error-related negativity (ERN) and error-related positivity (Pe) are distinguishable from one another, as seen in Figure 1.3. Even when the participant is not aware of the mistake, the ERN component is detected in the moments immediately after the error when making new choices. In contrast to other types of erroneous responses, the ERN is characterised by a strong negative signal that starts in the same manner as any other wrong reaction and often peaks 80–150 ms after the misrepresentation has occurred.

10.1.1 Motor Imagery Signal Decoding

Engine imagery is one of the most often studied brain signals in the field of BCI. Cososchi et al. [3] provided a method for distinguishing between left and right pictures that is based on a self-organising flush neural network time series predictor. For each electrode, a separate fuzzy neural network is used to extract the functions associated with that electrode over time. The average squared error of the predictions is used to construct the features, which are constructed using a sliding window. There are numerous inputs and only one output in the architecture of the two-organised fuzzy neural networks, which have several inputs and only one output. The deployment of an automated, fumigated neural network was justified by the fact that they can acclimatise themselves to the EEG signals of each person with very little information about the subject or the parameter choices. Each person's EEG dynamic is constantly being learned from and adjusted by the system, which is meant to function in real-time and in real-time with the individual. The algorithm was assessed over the course of 300 trials with two people. More than 75 percent accuracy was achieved in 3–4 s, indicating a quick turnaround.

The Approximate Entropy statistic technique was used in another study, which was described in [4], to provide the extraction procedure (ApEn). It is possible to classify intricate situations with ApEn since it measures the predictability of oscillations in a time series. ApEn has the advantage of being both robust and free of artefacts. Initially, ApEn was designed to deal with short and noisy data from series times, and it was capable of detecting changes in the underlying episode that would otherwise not be reflected in peak events or amplitudes of the underlying episode. The ApEn value increases in direct proportion to the complexity of the data sequence. Fang et al. [5] employed two standard data sets as the foundation for feature extraction, with the classification of linear discrimination as the classification method of choice. The accuracy for all participants in both data sets was more than 90 percent in all cases. When compared to rapid Fourier transformations, which were used by another extractor, ApEn produced a better result with 10 percent greater accuracy for all themes when compared to quick Fourier transformations.

10.2 Literature Survey

When Zhou et al. [6] created a wavelet independent packet-based component analysis (WPICA), they utilised it to extract the ERD/ERS patterns from different frequency bands in a complex low-limb motion image. In the case of WPICA processing, no imaginary component that cancels out the effect of frequency permutation appears. In addition, the original signal is transformed into a sparse distribution, which emphasises the non-Gaussian nature of the signal that was discovered. EEG data were collected in this experiment as a result of the three difficult imaging movements, which included standing, right/hand movement, and homolateral motions, all of which were integrated. Then, for each characteristic frequency band, its independent components are extracted from the WPICA, and the primary ones that contain the highest amount of ERD/ERS information are redirected to the electrode time–frequency domain that corresponds to that characteristic frequency band. The technique that was offered was tested with a total of 10 people. In around

80 percent of cases, the accuracy of WPICA was greater than that of the traditional ICA (72.3 percent) and did not need the use of spatial filter conditions (68.34 percent). When it comes to detecting ERD/ERS designs, this technique is a great strategy since it boosts the performance of hard mental tasks such as pattern classification.

Corralejo et al. [7] employed Genetic algorithms (GAs) as a feature selection strategy for categorising motor imaging data into two groups, and they found that it worked well. Spectral features and continuous wavelet transformation are used in the research, as well as discrete wavelet transformation, autoregressive models, and a matching rhythm filter. The Mother Wavelet Morlet and the Mother Wavelet Morlet are used in the study. The GA is used to choose the most suitable collection of qualities from among a large number of available options. A coefficient of 0.613 kappa was obtained using the methods given in this article when they were applied to the BCI competition IV data set IIb. CSP is very well-suited for differentiating between ERD/ERS patterns in the mind. The use of common spatial patterns is quite beneficial. Many different forms of the CSP have been created to help with the elimination of discriminating patterns from EEG. One technique [8] employed time delay to extend the CSP method to state space, and this was applied in another way [9]. According to the researchers, this kind of CSP was shown to outperform regular CSP in terms of classification accuracy and generalisation capability.

The CSP adaptive learning techniques [9] are used in another strategy that extracts the first CSP component and then uses an online deflation process to estimate the minor CSP components. According to the authors, this approach has lower computation costs than retraining all data and is a better match for the development of the BCI online system. For the CSP subband (SBCS P), a fixed filter bank of Chebyshev Type 2 IIR filters is utilised, and a CSP extractor for each frequency band (CSP) is followed by the extraction of CSP functions [10]. In order to discover the best frequency bands, a suggestion was made to the Filter Bank CSP (FBCSP) to compute the reciprocal information with a class label between the CSP features [11]. According to the findings of an investigation into the fisheries connection of an EEG-filtered signal of channels C3 or C4[12], the FCSP (DFBCSP) discriminative was proposed to reach a specific discriminating subject FB. An unattended technique known as Affinity Propagation (AP) is used to select a discriminatory function set from raw EEG data using the CSP (SWDCSP) sliding window.

The raw EEG data is filtered into a series of overlapped frequency bands using a sliding window, and then the discriminatory function set is selected using the CSP (SWDCSP) sliding window [13]. Liyanage et al. [14] constructed an Artificial Neural Evolutionary Network for the classification of motor imagery data, which was published in [14]. In this work, the ANN design was evolved via the use of GAs and Particle Swarm Optimisation (PSO) to fine-tune its parameters. It was decided to use the CSP as a feature vector, and the PSO-based approach demonstrated a 28 percent reduction in execution time when compared to the traditional technique while maintaining an average accuracy of 78 percent, which was comparable to the best result. As discussed in [15], the differential evolution (DE) approach to financial simulation was shown to be superior to the GA and PSO approaches to financial simulation. DEFS has also seen a drop in the amount of memory required as well as the cost of processing. It was discovered in the research of Wang and Makeig [16] that EEG information produced from the parietal cortex was retrieved as subject-specific properties of the time and frequencies. A sliding window was used to enhance the latency and frequency of the signal, and a low-pass filter was used to eliminate the frequency components from the signal.

Following that, the standardised amplitudes for each window were determined. The feature vector is coupled to a support vector machine (SVM) classification using RBF as the kernel, which is performed on the feature vector. The final result was a classification rate of 80.25 percent [17]. Another study found that the accuracy of classifications ranged from 90.5 to 99.7 percent, with an average of 96 percent, when a linear SVM was used as a classification algorithm. In a study done by Pfurtschellers et al. [18], Linear Vector Quantisation (LVQ) was used for online classification, and the results were published. The features used for classification were generated from two channels from a 1-second epoch, four band power estimates, each of 250 ms, per EEG channel and range, and two channels from a 1-second epoch, per EEG channel and range. Through trials, the LVQ classifier provides a classification as well as an accuracy measure based on these 16 characteristics.

The accuracy measure is used to determine the confidence of the classification. The online rating results in terms of inaccuracy ranged between 10 to 38.12 (in percentage), is actually producing incorrect predictions and actually the inaccuracy falls between 6.4 to 21.9. Obermaier and colleagues [19, 20] employed two HMMs, one for left motor imagery and the other for right motor imagery. They were given instructions with the use of trials throughout their individual motor pictures. In this case, Hjorth Parameters were used as a feature-vector set to represent the data. In a separate work [20], Lee et al. investigated the following two classification approaches: (i) PCA + HMM + SVM (HMM1) and (ii) PCA + HMM + SVM (HMM2) (HMM2). According to the results of PCA, the accuracy of HMM1 is assessed at 75.70 percent, while the accuracy of raw data is calculated at 60.63 percent. A similar increase was seen in HMM2, despite the fact that HMM1 was more precise. As a result, hybrid classifiers for the classification of motor pictures are also a possibility.

10.3 Methodology of the Proposed Work

Currently, research in neuroprosthetics is aimed at developing different computational models and approaches to aid in the rehabilitation of people with physical disabilities. In this chapter, we intend to classify finger, elbow, and shoulder movements as well as left and right movements, to steer a simulated robot arm in three dimensions to a certain location. With the classification output for the robot arm, this chapter makes a significant contribution by developing an energy-optimal trajectory planner based on differential developments that can calculate the optimal path towards a target by using the classification data. The categorisation result for each individual movement package triggers the activation of a trajectory planner for that movement package. The distribution of the probability of Hurst coefficients, which is generated after a multi-fractal declining fluctuation analysis of the incoming EEG data, is used as one of the components of the study. In addition to neural-network-based classifiers like the Adaptive Neural Fuzzy Inference System (ANFIS), the type-2 interval fuzzy system has been developed to enhance the handling of distorted EEG data. In addition, a classifier in a real-time situation must be able to distinguish between more than two mental states. So, in this chapter, we will propose a multi-class discriminating algorithm based on the merging of interval type 2 and ANFIS, which will be used to distinguish between classes [21–23].

Two variants of this strategy have been developed, using One-vs-All and One-vs-One procedures, respectively, which are used to build the final hyperplane from each ANFIS contradiction and are described in detail below. In trials to design the trajectory of a simulated robot arm, the control and classification schemes were tested. The accuracy of the classification was more than 88 percent, and the success rate of the robot arm in reaching the target exceeded 85 percent of the classifier. The outcome illustrates the superiority of our classification approach in the area of uncertain and uncertain signal classification over other traditional classification methods in this sector.

10.3.1 Proposed Control Scheme

The essential technique for controlling a limb of a robot using engine execution signals as control instructions is shown in Figure 10.1a and 10.1b, which summarises the approach.

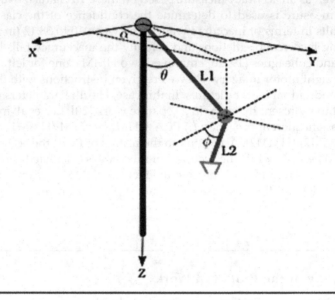

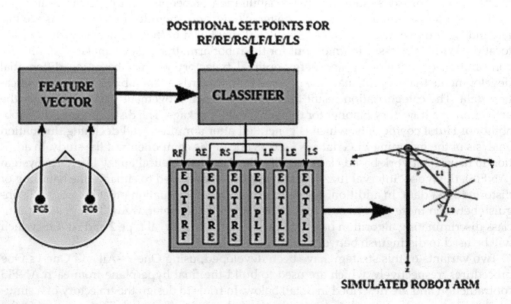

FIGURE 10.1a
The proposed robot arm management approach employing the energy optimised trajectory planner (EOTP).

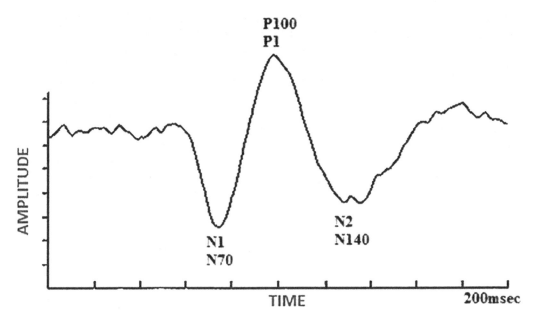

FIGURE 10.1b
Waveform of related potential.

Volunteers for the study project must navigate the virtual robot arm to a predetermined ultimate destination in its starting position from where they started. In order to complete this assignment, the subject must determine the current movement of the robot in relation to the known target (or objective) position based on the current location of the robot. It would be possible to create the controlling signals by executing the following execution instructions. The EEG signs of the subject's left finger (RF), right elbow (RE), and right shoulder (RS) are recorded from the subject's scalp, and the EEG signs of the subject's left elbow (LE) and right shoulder (RS) are also recorded from the subject's scalp. Table 10.1 lists the execution controls for the robot arm subject, as well as the control signals that are associated with them.

TABLE 10.1

Scheme 1 Control Instructions

Motor Execution Commands	Encoding	Motion
Right Shoulder	1-100	$\alpha sp = \alpha sp + 10°$
Right Elbow	1-200	$\alpha sp = \theta sp + 10°$
Right Finger	1-300	Release object α
Left Shoulder	2-100	$sp = \alpha sp - 10circ$
Left Elbow	2-200	θ
Left Finger	3-300	$sp = \theta sp - 10circ$ Grasp object
No motion	1-000/2-000	no motion

A two-channel filter is applied to the recorded EEG before a multi-factor, trend-strength fluctuation analysis is performed to identify features linked to motor execution signals. The attributes should then be submitted to the proposed ANT2FIS multiclass classificatory for use in deciding the engine execution outputs once they have been categorised.

It is then sent into the local trajectory planner as control signals (e.g., there are several trajectory planners for each control signal), which simulates robot-arm movement by using the most energy-efficient approach possible for the trajectory planner. In order to maximise energy efficiency, the trajectory planner creates the most energy-efficient route possible and provides comments on the subject matter. Using the comments received, the subject would choose its next step, and this would continue until the goal was reached. More importantly, the local trajectory planner would interpolate the position of every robot arm link (in relation to the goal location) for each state, therby reducing the amount of energy used.

10.3.2 One Versus All Adaptive Neural Type-2 Fuzzy Inference System (OVA-ANT2FIS)

In order to discriminate between each class and the relevant (N − 1) classes, N binary ANFIS classifiers are needed in line with the OVA approach. The i-th classifier constructs the hyperplane fi, and there are N of them, resulting in the final output combination.

In OVA-ANT2FIS, the distance between each binary classifier output and its associated hyperplane fi is determined for all known classes of a given collection of vectors for each binary classifier output. If the data-point distance x from f1 is positive or zero, then x is classified as class 1 x. Instead, if the distance between x and class 1 is negative, x will not be considered to be a member of class 1. Under ideal circumstances, the classificatory related to that class should provide a positive or zero distance for a particular class, say class 1, depending on the situation. The other classifier must produce a negative distance between the two classes. In actuality, however, it is possible for more than one classifier to attain a positive or zero distance [24, 25]. The distances between each of these classificatory structures are compared, and the classifier for the final output class to which the data point belongs is chosen based on the distance between the data point and its appropriate hyperplane connection.

The rationale behind this step is that, as the distance between two points becomes progressively positive, the likelihood of x belonging to class I rises. This is true regardless of the differences made by earlier classifiers in the process (N-1).

10.3.3 Position Control of Robot Arm Using Hybrid BCI for Rehabilitation Purpose

The trials were conducted on five normal right-handed individuals aged between 22 and 28 years.

The test session is equivalent to a training session with an additional 2-s feedback time after each exam. Again, an additional feedback time of 2 s is provided after a statement in the online test stimulus (b). The test stimuli comprise 20 error-responding studies and 80 correct answers investigations.

The ErRP classification concept and test are similar to those for P300 detection. In Schemes 1 and 2, if the ErRP detector produces y = 1 output, then the system moves the robot's arm farther; and if y =0, then the robot's arm continues to travel. The main difference between Schemes 1 and 2 is observed after error detection. In Scheme 1, the detector registers the preceding system status. After the MI detector is activated prior to ErRP (directional error), the robot arm is stopped and returned to the former location of the

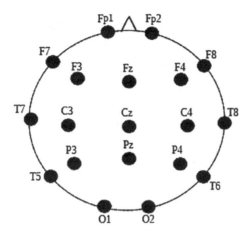

FIGURE 10.2
Channels and electrode sites.

detector. When a P300 detector is enabled before the ErRP detector is active (positional error occurrence), the system re-aligns the robot arm with an offset toward the target position. In System 2, the detector pauses the robot arm movement and offsets the robot arm to the target point as shown in Figure 10.2.

10.3.4 Jaco Robot Arm

Built by Kinova, the Jaco Robot Arm is a six-axis, three-fingered hand robotic manipulator. With a maximum coverage range of 90 cm radius and a rotation range of 30 cm/s, the arm has entire flexibility at 6 degree. It consists of three sensors: strength, location, and speed.

This arm can be fitted to a wheelchair for someone with an upper arm impairment. The robot's top arm consists of three bonds, which resemble the human body's top extremity. The manufacturer provides an API which provides additional user control flexibility.

10.3.5 Scheme 1: Random Order Positional Control

The directional movement of the robot arm is controlled by MI detectors. Once the robot arm is reached, the P300 detector stops moving, as shown in Figure 10.3a and 10.3b.

The robot arm here may spin its Link1 in the direction of the clock and translate its Link2 and Link3 to the direction of the forward one. In order to comprehend the motor, the user intended to move the robot arm, and the obtained C3 and C4 signals are decoded.

If the user intended, for example, to reverse the robot, he thought he would kinestically shift his hand to the left.

The user observes the robot arm's progress and recognises the inaccuracy visually as the robot moves to the target point as shown in Table 10.2. The robot would return to his spot, and if he wanders in a direction not intended by this topic, the subject would have to repeat the instructions again (direction error). When a visually achieved or crossed target is identified, the final robot arm effector is generated by a P300 waveform that stops moving the robot arm. After an ErRP has been identified, it means you have crossed the connection end for your robot arm.

The scheme must show that when you activate the P300 or ErRP detector, no outputs are given.

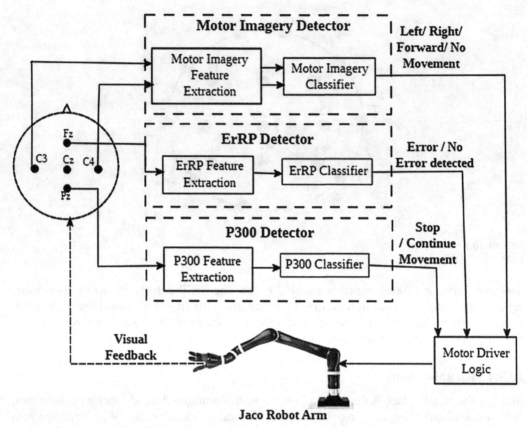

FIGURE 10.3a
The suggested scheme block diagram 1.

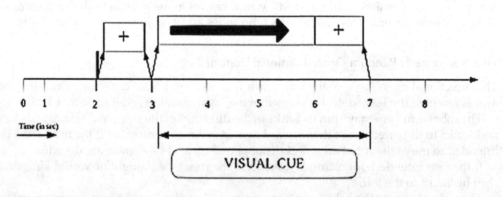

FIGURE 10.3b
Timing diagram of the proposed model.

The topic begins with the imagining of turning link 1 in the first slot; therefore, in this instance, the engine's purpose classification for link1 is active. If the error signal for connection is detected1, all the engine imagining classifiers except for Link2 will be automatically disconnected as given in Figure 10.4. While the actuator for connection1 strives to align Link1 with the target position, the engine imagination classification for connection2

TABLE 10.2

Scheme 1 Mental Tasks and their Respective Control Instructions

Mental Task	Control Commands
Left-hand responsibility metaphors	Interchange Link1 Counter-Circular
Right movement metaphors	Interchange Link1 Circular
Onward movement metaphors	Interchange Link2 and Link3 Onward
No Measure	Break in proceedings at present place and wait for succeeding command
Concentration on mark spot (P300)	Rest Robot Movement
Recognition of ErRP	Make required improvement

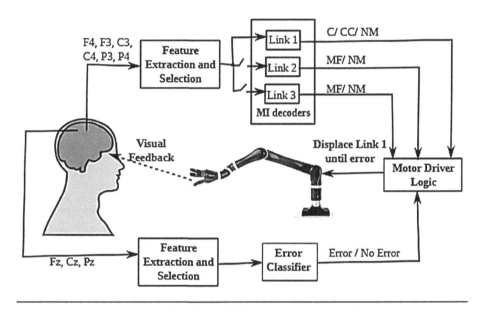

FIGURE 10.4
Schematic diagram of the proposed model.

is ready to accept information from the selection unit. A similar situation happens when the error signal happens for Link2 and Link3. The aforementioned ErRP motor intention classification switch is not included but is added for clarity and simplicity.

The logic on the motor driver in Figure 10.5 is employed when the decoded motor movement command of a particular limb has been received. The motor is also activated to halt and turn in the back direction, attached to a particular connection. The Boolean function that follows motor driver logic is forward (TFi) and stops and reverses ($STBi$).

$$TFi = MICi$$
$$STBi = ErRPi \tag{10.1}$$

where $MICi$ = true indicates that motor intention classifier i has classified the motor imagination.

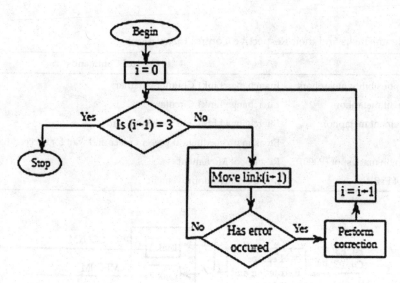

FIGURE 10.5
Logic of motor driver.

The error-related potential for link *I* shows, in favour of linking *I* and *ErRPi* = true, that for link *I* a position mistake has occurred. This scheme uses the same settings as prior robot control methods.

10.4 Experiments and Data Processing

In EEG sensors (electrodes) from the user's scalp, neuronal activity during motor imagery, error detection, or detection tasks of P300 is collected. A noteworthy component of this work is thus the decoding of motor intents and the identification of P300 and ErRP signals by EEG analyses. EEG is a non-Gaussian and non-stationary signal, and it is not easy to recognise mental processes directly from the raw signal. Experimentally, EEG signals produce a special signature in the treatment of the signal for various motor imagery tasks, and these distinct signatures are referred to as "features". Due to the non-linearity and characteristics of the signal, the various mental states of users have to be detected by classifiers. Once the user has recognised his motor intents using the classifiers, the outputs are created as commands for doing the work the subject wants to do. This section describes experiments to activate the subject's motor images, P300, and ErRP signals. It outlines the various strategies used to provide control signals for signal processing and classification in this study. The design of the controller for the real-time application is covered towards the conclusion of this section.

The guidance of a robot arm is controlled by the left, right, and front (or foot) motor signals, as discussed before in the preceding section. reveals that the ERD/ERS occurs in the contralateral area of the brain (respecting the moving hand), as well as in the case of imagined foot movements in the frequency range of 8–12 Hz (mu-rhythm) and 16–24 Hz between the two hemispheric (central). A 4-class classifier is used for generating directional output based on the control mechanisms for Scheme 1: left, right, forward, and no motion. The Link1 decoder, like Scheme 2, is used to decode left- and right-hand motion instances, while binary gradations are used when Link2 and Link3 are activated to decode between foot motor imagery and no movement.

A visual stimulus was first intended to guide users through the stimulation, to carry out the required engine imagining activities. The user is thereby trained to recognise the stimuli's signature. The participant is instructed in seven sessions in this study. The motor imagery stimulus. It can be seen from Figure 10.6 that the stimulus is composed of three

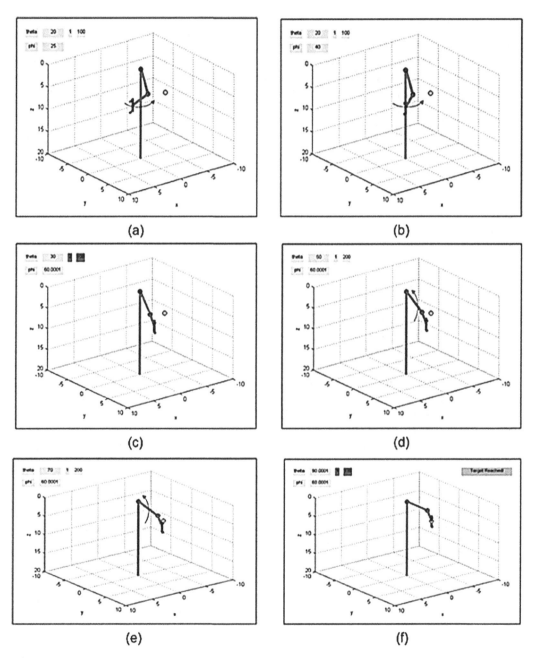

FIGURE 10.6a
Trajectory movement of the proposed work.

components, each in a defined order over a specific period of time: 1 s of fastening cross, 4 s of motor activation, followed by 2 s of a blank line. The fixing cross is meant to warn the individual to prepare for a future engineered imagination. This activity relates to one of the three categories of motor imagination: (i) predefined direction translation, (ii) defined orientation rotation, and (iii) halt movement simply.

10.4.1 Feature Extraction

Incoming EEG signals are first filtered spatially by means of common average references, and an 8–24 Hz elliptical band-pass filter of the sixth order is applied. The advantage of the choice of an elliptical filter is the good features of its frequency domain due to its sharp rolling off and the good attenuating effect of the ribbon and stop-band. Next, the EEG data from sites defined by

$$x(k) = \sum_{i=1}^{p} a_i(k) x(k-i) + \eta(k) \tag{10.2}$$

with

$$\eta(k) = N\left\{0, \sigma_{\eta,i}(k)^2\right\} \tag{10.3}$$

where $x(k)$ is the observation of the k-th sample, $a(k)$ is the zero-mean gay noise, μ, $\eta(k)^2$, and a $i(k)$ are the time coefficients of AR changing. As indicated in (10.3), former samples and the new information supplied in the route prexlect a current sample. So, the innovation process is sometimes referred to as $\beta(k)$.

Details on AAR as an estimator using the Kalman filter are discussed. Experiments conducted here demonstrate that an AAR order 6 model and a coefficient of update = 0.0085 adequately differentiate the MI tasks. The vector range [−1,1] is also available. The AAR coefficient is the ultimate dimension of the data set (for all sessions). An example of the C3 and C4 AAR features. The figure illustrates the coefficients for various engine imaging jobs.

Classification Accuracy (CA): Ratio of the properly recognised number of examples to the total number of occurrences.

True Positive Rate (TPR): Percent of the accurately detected positive cases.

False Positive Rate (FPR): It is the fraction that is wrongly determined to be positive in negative circumstances.

CT: The time the trained classifier takes to achieve the target performance.

Transfer rate of information (ITR): ITR (Bt) [48] is the method bit rate (in bits/min) that is indicated as

$$Bt = \left(\log 2N + P \log 2P + (1-P) \log 2\right) \times 2 \tag{10.4}$$

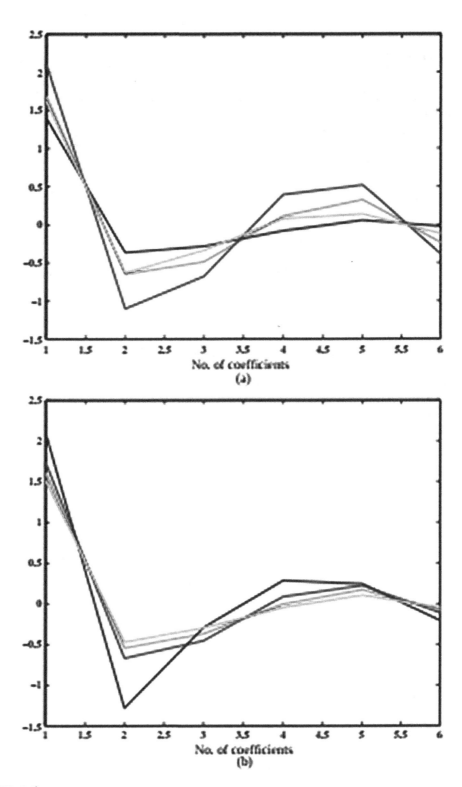

FIGURE 10.6b
ARR coefficient.

10.4.2 Performance Analysis of the Detectors

10.4.2.1 Scheme 1

CA, TPR, FPR, and ITR are summarised in Table 10.3 in the course of training and on-line testing of detectors MI, P300, and ErRP. The best outcome of this training is provided by the motor imagery classifier for subject 3, as stated in Table 4.3. Table 10.3 shows that the P300 subject 2 and 3 classifications produce the highest results in training and their training performance during the test subject 3. The best outcomes for training and testing in the ErRP experiment may be seen in Table 10.3. These findings show that, given the same number of experiments, the performance of each person differs. The rationale is that each participant sees the experiment differently and hence requires a varied period for training. It is also observed that the subject does well in the training phase in the same way.

Table 10.4 for Link1 motor picture classifier, Link2 and Link3 engine image classifier, and ErRP graders is presented similar to Scheme 1 in the CA, TPR, FPR, and ITR grades. It is important to note that since the Link2 and Link3 classifiers provide the same output type, the two links are trained in a single classifier. The switch is dependent on the engine driver's logic outputs.

The results of experiments in Table 10.4 reveal that the training accuracy of all classifiers exceeds 90 percent for all detectors. For Scheme 1, this is also stated in Table 10.4.

A separate training result is produced by each classifier for each subject. As demonstrated in Table 10.4, the strongest qualifying classifiers are the Link1, Class 2 and Link3, Subject 4, and the ErRP, Class 5. The greater accuracy is also apparent in the results of online training for the same categorization group.

TABLE 10.3

Performance Metrics

| Detectors | Subject ID | Training | Online Testing | | | |
		CA	TPR	FPR	CA	ITR
MI	1	96.00	0.96	0.00	75.00	15.88
	2	91.00	0.91	0.06	78.00	11.11
	3	100.00	1.00	0.00	81.00	19.51
	4	96.00	0.91	0.08	80.00	11.75
	5	97.00	1.00	0.05	80.00	11.75
Average	96.20	0.96	0.05	79.10	11.11	
P300	1	88.00	0.85	0.11	80.00	11.57
	2	100.00	1.00	0.00	77.50	11.97
	3	100.00	1.00	0.00	85.00	15.51
	4	96.00	0.91	0.01	85.00	15.18
	5	91.00	0.81	0.06	81.00	11.91
Average	95.20	0.91	0.05	81.50	11.81	

TABLE 10.4

Accuracy of Classification (CA in Percent) and The Information Transfer Rate of Five Individuals Link 1-Engine Imaging, Link 2 and 3-engine Imaging and ErRP-Detectors for Online Education and Testing

		Training	Online Testing			
Detectors	Subject ID	CA	TPR	FPR	CA	ITR
Link1	1	97.33	0.88	0.20	76.00	27.53
cline2-7	2	100.00	1.00	0.00	88.00	15.46
	3	88.67	0.95	0.25	80.00	22.67
	4	95.50	0.98	0.06	78.00	25.35
	5	92.67	0.90	0.11	82.50	17.23
	Average	94.83	0.94	0.12	80.90	21.65
Link2 and 3	1	97.50	0.95	0.00	86.67	16.50
	2	98.67	1.00	0.05	88.50	15.54
	3	95.00	0.92	0.10	87.50	16.00
	4	100.00	1.00	0.00	91.50	11.10
	5	96.33	0.95	0.04	88.50	15.54
Average	97.50	0.96	0.04	88.53	14.94	
ErRP	1	96.67	0.96	0.00	84.50	20.56
	2	97.50	1.00	0.00	82.00	22.37
	3	93.33	0.97	0.09	79.50	25.74
	4	92.67	0.91	0.06	79.50	25.74
	5	98.00	0.95	0.03	85.00	18.83
Average	95.63	0.96	0.04	82.10	22.65	

10.4.3 Performance of the Real-Time Robot Arm Controllers

For five participants across 20 experimental instances, the percentages of SR, ess, Mp, and ts are averaged to achieve the ultimate results for Schemes 1 and 2 controllers in Table 10.5. Furthermore, only the motor-image detector findings of another controller are contained in the comparative table. The addition of ErRP and P300 as control instructions improves the overall performance of the controller by a more than 30 percent improvement in SR, 3.4 percent in ess, and 1 percent in Mp, as shown in Table 4.5. As other detectors are involved in the two systems, they both take a little longer to settle.

When comparing our two proposed systems, Scheme 2 has a higher target success rate than Scheme 1. Both techniques achieve a static error and a maximum overflow with an insignificant variance, which may be attributed to the occurrence of several experimental circumstances. Although Scheme 2 succeeds more than Scheme 1 in achieving the objective, it takes longer to attain its ultimate position. Due to the sequential technique and the delays incorporated into Scheme 2, the robot arm is controlled, whereas Scheme 1 uses a random strategy for similar control.

The classifiers provided by McNemar's test were also statistically similar. In order to accomplish the real-time control, the proportion of successful hits, the percentage departure from the target, and the average calculation time required are defined. For the OVA-ANT2FIS and OVO-ANT2FIS algorithms, the average success rate achieved from the 112 participants is 85 and 90 percent.

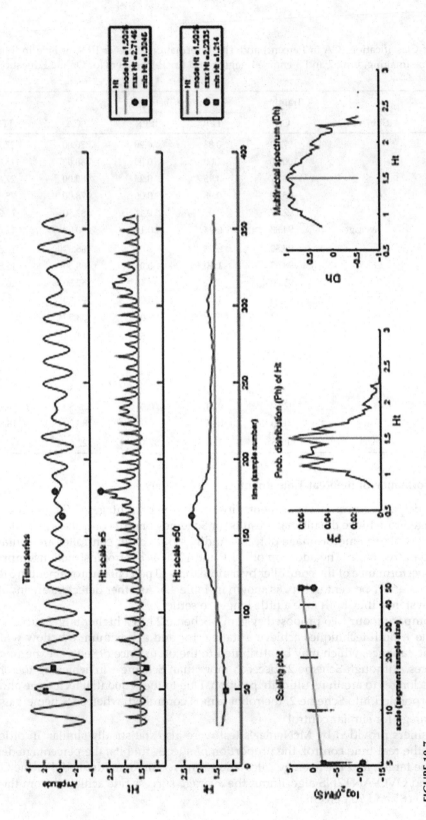

FIGURE 10.7
Results of the proposed work.

For the OVA-ANT2FIS and OVO-ANT2FIS, the standard deviation of more than 20 is 4.75 percent, for 11 subjects 3.75 percent. This finding indicated an effective way to handle non-stationary and unpredictable signal data categorization, such as EEG, under the suggested ANT2FIS methodology to multiclass detection. The OVO strategy has also been more successful in attaining the goal than the OVA technique. The OVA technique would be preferable for online application if the balance between success rate and calculation time was maintained.

10.5 Discussion

The second strategy is significantly simpler than the first scheme, as a fixed-order connection monitoring procedure is followed by a position control of the connections in a (predefined) set order and only needs a MI and ErRP signal. However, between the activation of two linkages, this approach involves a large change effort. Of course, in Scheme 2, the engine imagination should be decoded at a predetermined time interval to make single link motions, where the i-th interval corresponds to the motor imagination decoding for the robot's connection. The other schema relating to control of fixed-order links demands that the (i+1)-th category be automatically selected when the engine imagination has automatically finished its i-th work (for the i-th link). This is achieved by measuring the decoded error signal offset for the third time slot in the proposed system. There are, then, two objectives for the error signal decoded in the i-th-time slot. To accurately modify the link position (by a slight offset angle to turn it back), the error sensor is first used to regulate the position controller.

The results in the preceding section indicate that both methods provide similar outcomes throughout training and online testing. However, it should be noted that the precision of training and online testing varies widely. Such changes in accuracy might be due to the non-static nature of EEG signals and, in this instance, the mental state of the individual. The classifier offline training and online testing are conducted by means of two separate data sets that are obtained throughout several experimental sessions. This raises the chances that our results will show a misclassification.

An ideal feature classifier combination must thus be developed, so that these challenges may be dealt with.

A feature selection or reduction phase can even be included between the extraction of the feature and its categorization in the same way. This component of this study is accessible for researchers to choose from. Both systems also have similar controller performance. The controller of Scheme 1 is more advanced than that of Scheme 2. The success probability of Scheme 2 therefore exceeds that of Scheme 1. However, because of the fixed order, Scheme 2 consumes time over Scheme 1.

Order method and delays between switches followed by the system. The advantages and disadvantages of both schemes are observed, therefore, and the choice of schemes is entirely allowed to be applied. If the robot arm requires an application to move all its associations to complete a job, Scheme 2 is the best solution. If a robot arm is only to be moved regardless of the positioning of the linkages, Scheme 1 is the best solution. Finally, both techniques, indicating the purpose to manage the robotics system position of the subject's own limbs, have direct applications in smart control of prothesis limbs.

10.6 Future Research Directions

While innovative and self-sufficient, the efforts detailed in this thesis offer up new paths in the BCI area. Further research relating to the functioning of the brain is required to enhance the control systems. In future investigations, studies will be conducted in conjunction with the movement of the upper limb. Studies on several movement features, such as speed and location, will be carried out in order to manage the prosthetic device more precisely.

As to the suggested algorithms for selection of features, more work will be carried out in terms of accuracy and calculation time to improve their performance and to allow them to be operational in real time. More studies will also be undertaken in the future to increase the performance of our suggested ANT2FIS classification. In addition, we would employ strategies based on statistical approaches and probabilistic models to satisfy our real-time monitoring requirements. Further efforts will be made to build an optimum mix of extraction selection features for real-time control.

The BCI System based on EEG may also be employed to enhance the functioning of other physiological parameters, such as electromyography (EMG), galvanic skin resistance, and other non-invasive bio-potential signals. Studies based on the connection between the EMG and EEG data might give us additional information to assist us in building better prosthetic limb control strategies. In order to bring it closer to real-time monitoring, initiatives to minimise the computing time of the BCI system must also be taken. Finally, we intend to incorporate the optimum control system into an embedded platform to address rehabilitation challenges with real-world solutions. The control programmes would be further refined on topics with clinical problems.

References

1. G. Dornhege, J. del R. Millan, T. Hinterberger, D. J. McFarland, K.-R. Muller (2007) *Towards Brain-Computer Interfacing*. MIT Press.
2. D. S. Tan, A. Nijholt (2010) *Brain-Computer Interfaces: Applying Our Mind to Human-Computer Interaction*. Springer.
3. J. Wolpaw, E. W. Wolpaw (2012) *Brain-computer Interfaces: Principles and Practice*. Oxford University Press.
4. H-J Hwang, S. Kim, S. Choi, C-H. Im (2013) EEG-based Brain-computer Interfaces: A Thorough Literature Survey. *International Journal of Human-Computer Interaction* 29(12), 814–826.
5. R. P. N. Rao, R. Scherer (2010) Brain-Computer Interfacing [In the Spotlight]. *IEEE Signal Processing Magazine* 27(4), 150–152. doi: 10.1109/MSP.2010.936774.
6. A. Kubler, K. R. Muller (2007) An Introduction to Brain-Computer Interfacing. In *Toward Brain-Computer Interfacing*, G. Dornhege, J. R. Millan, T. Hinterberger, D. J. McFarland, K. R. Muller (eds) MIT Press, 1–25.
7. R. K. Dhanaraj, K. Rajkumar, U. Hariharan (2020) Enterprise IoT Modeling: Supervised, Unsupervised, and Reinforcement Learning. In *Business Intelligence for Enterprise Internet of Things*, Chlamtac, (eds) Springer International Publishing, 55–79.
8. J. Kassubek, A. Unrath, H. J. Huppertz, D. Lule, T. Ethofer, A. D. Sperfeld, A. C. Ludolph (2005) Global Brain Atrophy and Corticospinal Tract Alterations in ALS, as Investigated by Voxel-based Morphometry of 3-D MRI. *Amyotrophic Lateral Sclerosis and other Motor Neuron Disorders* 6(4), 213–220.

9. H. A. Hanagasi, I. H. Gurvit, N. Ermutlu, G. Kaptanoglu, S. Karamursel, H. A. Idrisoglu, M. Emre, T. Demiralp (2002) Cognitive Impairment in Amyotrophic Lateral Sclerosis: Evidence from Neuropsychological Investigation and Event-related Potentials. *Cognitive Brain Research* 14(2), 234–244.

10. M. T. Jurkiewicz, A. P. Crawley, M. C. Verrier, M. G. Fehlings, D. J. Milkulis (2006) Somatosensory Cortical Atrophy after the Spinal Cord Injury: A Voxel-based Morphometry Study. *Neurology* 66(5), 762–764.

11. L. R. Hochberg, M. D. Serruya, G. M. Friehs, J. A. Mukand, M. Saleh, A. H. Caplan, A. Branner, D. Chen, R. D. Penn, J. P. Donoghue (2006) Neuronal Ensemble Control of Prosthetic Devices by a Human with Tetraplegia. *Nature* 442(7099), 164–171.

12. H. Huber (2005) The Use of Virtual Realities in Psychological Treatment. *Psychologie in Osterreich* 25(1), 13–200.

13. K. Oum, H. Ayaz, P. A. Shewokis, P. Diefenbach (2010) MindTactics: A Brain Computer Interface Gaming Platform. In: *2010 International IEEE Consumer Electronics Society's Games Innovations Conference (ICE-GIC)*, 1–5. doi: 10.1109/ICEGIC.2010.5716901.

14. C. Angeloni, D. Salter, V. Corbit, T. Lorence, Y.-C. Yu, L. A. Gabel (2012) P300-based Brain-computer Interface Memory Game to Improve Motivation and Performance. In: *2012 38th Annual Northeast Bioengineering Conference (NEBEC)*, 35–36. doi:10.1109/NEBC.2012.6206949.

15. R. Parafita, G. Pires, U. Nunes, M. Castelo-Branco (2013) A Spacecraft Game Controlled with a Brain-computer Interface Using SSVEP with Phase Tagging. In: *2013 IEEE 2nd International Conference on Serious Games and Applications for Health (SeGAH)*, 1–6. doi: 10.1109/SeGAH.2013.6665309.

16. J. S. Brumberg, S. D. Lorenz, B. V. Galbraith, F. H. Guenther (2012) The Unlock Project: A Python-based Framework for Practical Brain-computer Interface Communication \app" Development. In: *2012 Annual International Conference of the IEEE Engineering in Medicine and Biology Society (EMBC)*, 2505–2508. doi: 10.1109/EMBC.2012.6346473.

17. T. Ebrahimi, J. Vesin, G. Garcia (2003) Brain-computer Interface in Multimedia Communication. *IEEE Signal Processing Magazine* 20(1), 14–24. doi: 10.1109/MSP.2003.1166626.

18. Z. Biao, J. Wang, T. Fuhlbrigge (2010) A Review of the Commercial Brain-computer Interface Technology from Perspective of Industrial Robotics. In: *2010 IEEE International Conference on Automation and Logistics (ICAL)*, 379–384. doi: 10.1109/ICAL.2010.5585311.

19. A. P. Garcia, I. Schjolberg, S. Gale (2013) EEG Control of an Industrial Robot Manipulator. In: *2013 IEEE 4th International Conference on Cognitive Infocommunications (CogInfoCom)*, 39–44. doi: 10.1109/CogInfoCom.2013.6719280.

20. M. Al-Sagban, O. El-Halawani, T. Lulu, H. Al-Nashash, Y. Al-Assaf (2008) Brain Computer Interface as a Forensic Tool. In: *5th International Symposium on Mechatronics and Its Applications (ISMA 2008)*, 1–5. doi: 10.1109/ISMA.2008.4648820.

21. S-M. Zhang, Q-C. Zhan, H-M. Du (2010) Research on the Human Computer Interaction of E-learning. In: *2010 International Conference on Artificial Intelligence and Education (ICAIE)*, 5–8. doi: 10.1109/ICAIE.2010.5641406.

22. K. Lalitha, R. Siba Thangarajan, K. Udgata, D. Poongodi, Ambika Prasad Sahu (2017) GCCR: An Efficient Grid Based Clustering and Combinational Routing in Wireless Sensor Networks. *Wireless Personnel Communications* 97(1), 1075–1095.

23. Poongodi Chinnasamy, Siba Kumar Udgata, K. Lalitha, A. Jeevanantam. (2020) Multi-objective based Deployment of Throwboxes in Delay Tolerant Networks for the Internet of Things environment. *Evolutionary Intelligence*. doi: 10.1007/s12065-020-00474-w.

24. R. K. Dhanaraj, L. Krishnasamy, O. Geman, D. R. Izdrui. (2021) Black Hole and Sink Hole Attack Detection in Wireless Body Area Networks. *Computers, Materials & Continua*, 68(2), 1949–1965.

11

A Robust Image-Driven CNN Algorithm to Detect Skin Disease in Healthcare Systems

S. Suganyadevi, V. Seethalakshmi, and N. Vidhya
KPR Institute of Engineering and Technology, Coimbatore, India

K. Balasamy
Bannari Amman Institute of Technology, Erode, India

CONTENTS

11.1 Introduction

To detect objects in the image, image-processing methods including such noise removal will most certainly be utilized, associated with a low feature extraction to identify lines, regions, and probably spots with certain patterns. Single things, including such cars on the road, items on a belt conveyor, or cancerous cells on a glass slide, might be viewed as collections of these types. This seems to be an AI difficulty since an item might appear significantly different when viewed from different angles or under varied lighting.

DOI: 10.1201/9781003217435-11

Another problem is figuring out which features belong to which object and which are background, shadows, and other effects. These processes are usually accomplished instinctively by the visual system, but for a computer to approximate performance levels, good programming and a large amount of processing power are required. Controlling input in the form of an image with range of ways [1]. The introduction of some more advanced and powerful imaging techniques, telecommunications networks, and information sharing techniques has significantly changed how dermatologists analyze their patients. They can now carry out an assessment on healthcare 4.0, make a diagnosis, and plan a course of treatment using software designed specifically for this industry [2]. An image is usually represented as a two-dimensional array of brightness values, similar to those found on a photographic print, movie screen, slide, or television screen. A computer could either visibly or digitally assess an image.

In such a global operation, every one of the input picture pixels contributed to the output pixel value. Individually or combined, these methods are being used to improve, repair, or compression the picture [3]. An image can be improved by changing it to make the information contained more obvious, but also could be improved with making it more effective visually. One example is noise smoothing. Median filtering could be used to improve a noisy image with such a 33-pixel window. This implies that each pixel in the noisy image is captured, including the data of its eight nearest neighbors.

One more sort of upgrade is contrast adjustment, in which the worth of every pixel in the new picture is solely controlled by the worth of that pixel in the old picture; all in all, this is a point activity.

Healthcare systems in general should benefit greatly from healthcare 4.0 and IoT [4]. Here are a few highlights:

- Patient data analysis is simplified.
- Service that is controlled digitally.
- Medical imaging and surgical precision.
- Even when the patient is not in the hospital, their health is monitored in real time.

Healthcare 4.0 is a novel concept of the medical world that incorporates technologies, smart machines, and software such as Thing Worx. Figure 11.1 represents paradigm of healthcare 4.0. It can help in providing patients with a digital clinic-integrated surveillance system. It is capable of producing high-quality medical devices that are tailored to the needs of the patient. PC vision has since quite a while ago tried to perceive thing classes in genuine pictures. Because of impressive appearance varieties among object examples having a place with a similar class, this is adroitly dangerous. Besides, contortions brought about by setting mess, scale, and perspective contrasts can make even the indistinguishable thing example show up in an unexpected way [5]. Interclass likeness, which happens when models from unmistakable classes have all the earmarks of being very comparable, adds to the challenges. Thus, object class models should be sufficiently adaptable to represent class changeability, however, discriminative enough to isolate genuine article occurrences from swarmed photographs. An item class model's apparently disconnected rules make acknowledgment testing. The two points of acknowledgment tended to in this review will be image order and article recognition. Picture arrangement decides if an article class is available in an image, though object revelation finds every occasions of such a class in that picture. The significant commitment of this examination is a technique for entity-type recognition that main uses edge information to accomplish these points [6].

FIGURE 11.1
From healthcare 1.0 to healthcare 4.0

The advancement of our procedure is that we depict forms utilizing moderately straight-forward and nonexclusive line fragment and circle shape natives, just as an adaptable system for getting the hang of segregating crude blends. The line fragment and the circle are reciprocal natives in nature, with the line portion demonstrating straight form and the oval displaying bended shape. We picked a circle since it is quite possibly the most fundamental round shape while as yet being sufficiently adaptable to depict bended structures. These shape natives have various engaging qualities. First off, they grant conceptual and perceptually significant thinking like parallelism and nearness, dissimilar to edge-based descriptors. Moreover, not at all like form piece includes, these natives' stockpiling requests are unaffected by object size and might be effectively addressed with four boundaries for a line and five boundaries for a circle. Moreover, not at all like shape sections, which need correlations between individual edge pixels, coordinating between natives can be proficiently figured (e.g., using mathematical attributes). At last, on the grounds that mathematical characteristics can be effectively scale standardized, they make cross-scale coordinating with simpler Contour sections, then again, are not scale invariant, thusly one should either are according pieces, that produces cooperating (e.g., once edge pixels are attempted to pulled apart), or rearrange an image prior to disposing parts, that decreases image goal. Ongoing exploration has observed that line portions and circles have an inbuilt capacity to portray confounded structures and designs because of their overall qualities. While every one of these natives is less particular all alone, by joining them, we can make a blend that is adequately bigoted and oppressive [7]. Each joins a two-layer reflection of natives: a first layer of collection of natives (called token of shape) and a second layer of a learned overall number of tokens of shape. We don't force a blend to have the specific measure of token of shape; all things considered, we let it adjust to an article class normally and progressively. The metric influences a mix's ability to communicate shapes, with essential shapes requiring fewer shape-tokens than complicated shapes. Subsequently, to address an article class, segregating mixes of different intricacy can be utilized. This blend is learned by utilizing a thing class' distinctive shape, mathematical, and primary impediments. Mathematical limitations clarify the spatial association of shape tokens, while shape requirements depict the visual angle. The interrelationship (e.g., the XOR connection) among tokens of shape force primary cutoff points on elective stances/constructions of an item [8]. Currently on healthcare 4.0 AI and machine learning are assisting in skin cancer prevention and diagnosis.

In the advancement of healthcare 4.0, here are some of the important technologies used by the experts to diagnose the skin diseases such as Artificial Intelligent, Light Therapies, Telemedicine etc. And, for skin cancer, nanotechnology will help us fight against cancer, Tele dermatology, 3D Printing for Organ Shortages [9].

11.2 Related Work

The K-implies calculation is quite possibly the most fundamental solo learning algorithm for settling the notable grouping issue. The methodology follows a basic and clear strategy for ordering a specific information collection utilizing a decent amount of bunches (accepting k category) [10]. The focal concept is to make k centroid, one per each group. Since various areas produce fluctuated results, these centroids ought to be set with care. Therefore, the ideal choice is to orchestrate them as far separated as attainable. The subsequent stage is to relate each point in an information assortment with the centroid that is nearest to it. The principal stage is done and an early gathering age is finished when no focuses are extraordinary [11]. At this stage, we should recalculate k new subjective centroids for the bunches that came about because of the past stage. Following the production of these k new centroids, another limiting between similar informational collection focuses and the closest new centroid is required. There has been made a circle. We might take note of that the k centroids modify their area bit by bit until no further alterations are made because of this circle. As such, centroids are done moving. At long last, the objective of this method is to limit a goal work, which for this situation is a squared blunder work.

A progressive arrangement of picture divisions is an assortment of picture divisions of similar picture at various degrees of detail, with coarser degrees of detail divisions shaped by basic converges of better degrees of detail divisions [12]. For all divisions, the fragment or region boundaries are maintained at filled image geographical goal, which is an interesting property of progressive division. An object of interest in a progressive division can be addressed by many picture sections at higher degrees of specifics in the segment chain of command, which are then converged into such an encompassing area at lower degrees of particulars. The object of interest will be addressed as a solitary district fragment at some middle of the road level of division detail in case the division progressive system has satisfactory goal. One motivation behind the division progressive system's point examination is to decide the various levelled level at which the object of interest is addressed by a solitary tary locale section [10]. The item's ghostly and spatial highlights would then be able to be utilized to recognize it. The conduct of picture divisions at the progressive division level above and beneath the level at which the object of interest is addressed by a solitary locale can give extra signs to protest distinguishing proof.

The most essential method of image division is the thresholding method. This threshold method utilizes the high level image to convert from a grayscale to a double image (or a limit esteem). The most critical part of this strategy is choosing an incentive for the edge or qualities when numerous levels are chosen. One of the most broadly used methodologies in industry is the greatest entropy methodology [13]. Strategy of Otsu as well as K-implicates grouping, and recently, thresholding techniques for registered tomography (CT) pictures have been made. The essential thought is that, unusual for Otsu's strategy, the not really set in stone utilizing radiographs rather than the reproduced picture.

Bunch examination is a solid device for investigating and extricating valuable data from immense volumes of information, and it is a critical information mining strategy. The group calculation coordinates the data into bunches or classes, with objects within a group sharing a serious level of closeness while being totally different from those in different bunches. The trait esteems that depict the items are utilized to decide dissimilarities [14]. Distance estimations are as often as possibly utilized. Bunching, as a part of measurements and an illustration of solo learning, offers us with an exact and unobtrusive investigation apparatus got from the numerical view-implies calculation, which is a well-known segment strategy in group examination. The squared-mistake standard is the most by and large utilized bunching blunder basis, and it very well may be portrayed as follows:

$$Jc = (j=1)^m j - C(k=1)(nj) \times k(j) - C(k=1)(nj) \times k(j) - C(k=1)(nj) \times k(j) - C(k2) \quad (11.1)$$

where J is the amount of square-mistake for all items in the data set, C is the point in space that addresses a specific article, and Jc is the mean of bunch shows in equation 1. K-implies, which utilizes the squared-blunder standard, function admirably when the groups are conservative mists that are generally very much isolated from each other; however, it isn't great for tracking down non-arched structures or bunches of exceptionally different sizes. In any case, it isn't great for tracking down non-raised structures or groups of exceptionally different sizes. Besides, there are a few strategies to handle the issue where the calculation's presentation is profoundly impacted by the first starting conditions: the least difficult is reiteration with various arbitrary picks. To forestall becoming trapped in a neighborhood ideal, a few calculations utilize the recreation strengthen strategy. The idea is that various sub-examples from the dataset are grouped autonomously, and afterward these arrangements are bunched once more. At last, the refined starting community is picked as the arrangement with minimal measure of twisting among all arrangements. This paper presents another further developed K-implies calculation that depends on viable methods of multi-inspecting and once-bunching to look through the ideal introductory upsides of group focuses, tending to the reliance on starting conditions and the constraint of the K-implies calculation that applies the square-blunder model to quantify the nature of bunching. Our discoveries show that the new calculation accomplishes predominant dependability and beats the first K-implies in grouping results [15].

Edge-discovery is an all-around created field all alone inside picture handling. District limits and edges are firmly related, since there is regularly a sharp change in force at the area limits. Edge recognition strategies have thusly been utilized as the foundation of another division strategy. The edges distinguished by edge recognition are regularly disengaged. To cut or slice an item from a picture at any point, edge discovery and coordinates are main points that limits the need [14–15].

Bend proliferation is a typical picture-handling approach for object extraction, object following, sound system reproduction, and different applications. The fundamental thought hidden in this technique is to advance a bend towards the most reduced capability of an expense work, whose detail mirrors the main job and forces specific perfection necessities. Lagrangian approaches work by defining the shape dependent on an inspecting methodology, then, at that point, developing every component relying upon picture and inward terms. While such a method can be amazingly effective, it has various disadvantages, remembering choosing for an inspecting system, working out the bend's characteristic mathematical elements, adjusting its geography, and managing troubles in higher aspects. Osher and Sethian proposed the level set strategy to follow moving interfaces in 1988, and it stretched out across a few imaging areas in the last part of the 1990s. In an implied way, it tends to be used to proficiently resolve the issue of bend/surface/and so on proliferation. The key thought is to utilize a marked capacity to portray the evolving form, with the zero-level relating to the real shape. Then, at that point, utilizing the shape's movement condition, one can essentially ascertain a stream for the verifiable surface that, when applied to the zero level, will reflect the form's spread. The level set method enjoys a few benefits: it is certain, gives an immediate component to assess the mathematical properties of the developing design, can change the geography, and is inborn. Besides, they can be utilized to characterize a streamlining structure as proposed by Zhao, Merriman, and Osher in 1996. Along these lines, one can infer that it is an exceptionally helpful structure to address various uses of PC vision and clinical picture examination. Besides, examination into different level set information structures has prompted extremely effective executions of this strategy [16].

PCA is a numerical technique for changing over a bunch of perceptions of perhaps related factors into a bunch of upsides of straightly uncorrelated factors called guideline parts utilizing a symmetrical change. The quantity of unique factors is not exactly or equivalent to the quantity of essential parts. The main head part has the biggest conceivable change (i.e., it represents as much inconstancy in the information as doable), and each resulting part has the greatest difference conceivable under the imperative of being symmetrical to (i.e., uncorrelated with) the first parts. Provided that the informational index is together typically disseminated can the chief parts be guaranteed to be free. The general scaling of the first factors influences PCA. It is otherwise called the discrete Karhunen Loeve change (KLT), the Hotelling change, or right symmetrical deterioration, contingent upon the field of utilization (POD) [17].

11.3 Materials and Methods

Color characteristics and texture descriptors, as well as a Neural Network classifier, are used to classify skin diseases for use in a Computer Aided Diagnosis (CAD) system. Figure 11.2 depicts the suggested CNN architectural model, whereas Figure 11.3 depicts the proposed model's block diagram.

11.3.1 Local Ternary Pattern

LTPs (local ternary patterns) are an augmentation of LBPs (local binary patterns). In contrast to LBP, LTP doesn't use an edge steady to partition pixels into 0 and 1. All things being equal, it partitions pixels into three qualities utilizing an edge steady [18]. The result of limit is: Taking k as the edge steady, c as the worth of the middle pixel, and p as the worth of an adjoining pixel, the consequence of edge is shown in Equation (11.2).

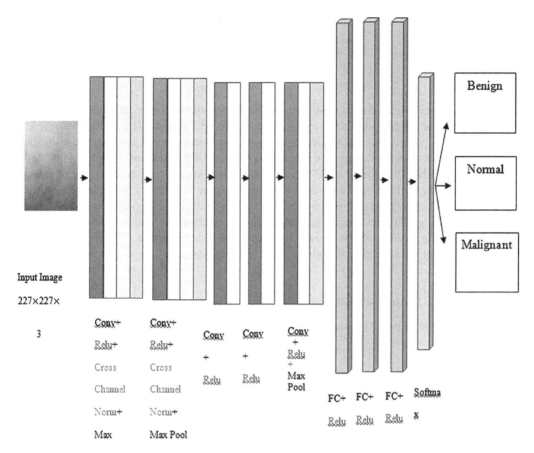

FIGURE 11.2
Proposed CNN architecture model.

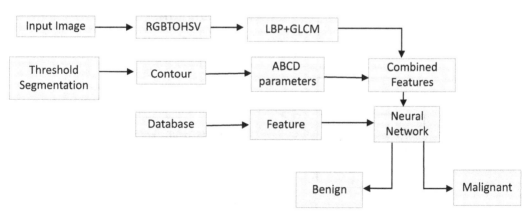

FIGURE 11.3
Block diagram of proposed model.

$$LTPU = \{0, \begin{array}{l} 1, if\ p > c+k \\ if\ p > c-k\ and\ p < c+k \\ -1\ if\ p < c- = k \end{array} \qquad (11.2)$$

Therefore, every one of the three-limit pixels has one of the three qualities. Subsequent to thresholding, adjoining pixels are joined into a ternary example. The ternary example is broken into two paired examples since processing a histogram of among those ternary qualities will have about an immense reach [19]. Connecting histograms yields a portrayal twice the size of LBP. Utilizing the LTP and marked piece augmentation, this work presents another procedure for highlight extraction that utilizes the focal pixel for include computation. The separated highlights are primary part of the underlying arrangement of learning pictures (preparing set). That once elements of the experiment images have been extracted, the image is characterized by comparing its element vector to certain other train vectors in the database using an artificial neural network (ANN) classifier.

11.3.2 Splitting LTP into Two LBP Channels

The accompanying Figure 11.4 shows the dividing LTP into two LBP channels.

11.3.3 Gray-Level Co-Occurrence Matrix

Utilize the dark comatrix capacity to make a grey-level co-occurrence matrix (GLCM). The graycomatrix work computes how regularly a pixel along with the force (dark level) esteem to be happened at a specific geographical association among the pixel with the worth j, bringing about a dim level co-event network (GLCM). The spatial connection between the two pixels is set up of course as the pixel of interest and the pixel to its nearby right (on a level plane neighboring); however, one can determine distinctive spatial connections.

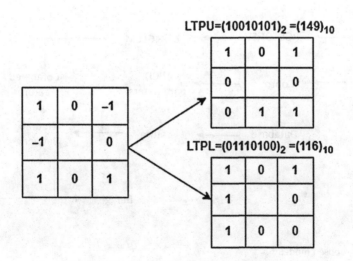

FIGURE 11.4
Splitting LTP.

Graycomatrix scales the info picture since the registering important to produce a GLCM for the full powerful scope of a picture is over the top. Graycomatrix diminishes the measure of power esteems in dark scale pictures from 256 to 8 naturally. The size of the GLCM is controlled by the quantity of dim levels. Utilizing the graycomatrix capacity's Num Levels and Gray Limits contentions, you might tweak the quantity of dim levels in the GLCM just as the scaling of power esteems. For additional data, see the graycomatrix reference page [20].

The geographic dissemination of dim levels in the surface picture can be uncovered utilizing the dark level co-event lattice. The surface is coarse as for the gave offset assuming that most of the passages in the GLCM are bunched along the askew, for instance. To show how graycomatrix computes the initial three qualities in a GLCM, consider the graph underneath. Since there is just a single event in the information picture when two on a level plane neighboring pixel have characteristics 1 and 1, and element (1,1) has a value of 1. As a result, GLCM has a value of 1. Because there seem to be two activities where two nearby pixels on a scale plane have the character traits 1 and 2, GLCM (1,2) incorporates the worth 2. Since there are no occurrences of two evenly contiguous pixels with the qualities 1 and 3 in the GLCM, component (1,3) has the worth 0. Graycomatrix keeps on handling the information picture, checking it for more pixel pairings (i, j) and saving the aggregates in the GLCMs-related components. The GLCM grid graph is displayed in Figure 11.5 [21].

To make a few GLCMs, utilize the graycomatrix work with a variety of counterbalances. Pixel associations of various bearing and distance are characterized by these balances. For instance, you can indicate four directions (even, vertical, and two diagonals) and four distances in a variety of balances. The info picture is addressed by 16 GLCMs in this situation. You can take the normal while ascertaining insights from these GLCMs. These counterbalances are determined as a p-by-2 cluster of numbers. [row offset, col offset] is a two-component vector that gives one offset to each column in the cluster. The quantity of lines between the pixel of interest and its neighbor is the column counterbalanced. The quantity of sections between the pixel of interest and its neighbor is called col offset. This model sets

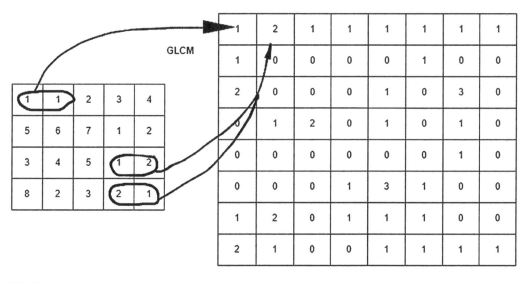

FIGURE 11.5
GLCM matrix.

a four-way offset with four distances for every course. Utilizing the graycoprops work, you might get various insights from the GLCMs whenever they've been made. These measurements give data on a picture's surface. Contrast, Correlation, Energy, and Homogeneity are measurements that give data about a picture [22–24].

11.3.4 Morphological Process

Morphological picture handling is a bunch of non-direct cycles that arrangement with the shape or morphology of picture highlights. Morphological tasks are appropriate to the handling of parallel pictures since they depend entirely on the summary requesting of bitmap esteem issues rather than their mathematical properties Dim scale pictures can likewise be exposed to morphological cycles in which the light swap capabilities are unknown and the absolute pixel values seem to be of no or little significance. Morphological methodologies utilize a little structure or format called an organizing component to examine a picture [21]. The organizing component is set in all accessible areas in the picture and contrasted with the pixels in its nearby area. A few tasks decide whether a component "fits" into the area, whereas others decide whether it "hits" or converges it: The testing of a picture with a primary element is displayed in Figure 11.6. Provided the probing of image with a structuring element in the info picture does a morphological procedure on a twofold picture produce another paired picture with a non-zero incentive for the pixel. A little double picture, that is, a little network of pixels having a worth of nothing or one, fills in as the organizing component: The grid aspects characterize the organizing component's size, while the example of ones and zeros characterizes its shape. The organizing component's starting point is regularly one of its pixels, however it can likewise be outside of it [16].

Neural organization models are forecast models that are approximately founded on the conduct of natural neurons. One of the incomparable PR wins of the 20th century was the decision of the name "neural organization." "An organization of weighted, added substance esteems with nonlinear exchange capacities" sounds much more energizing than "An organization of weighted, added substance esteems with nonlinear exchange capacities." Neural organizations, regardless of their name, are neither one of the thinking's

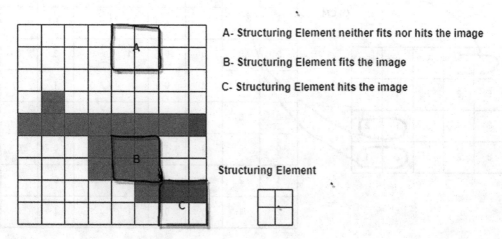

FIGURE 11.6
Probing of an image with a structuring element.

"machines" or "fake cerebrums." Total of 100 neurons make up a common counterfeit neural organization. The human sensory system, then again, is thought to have around 3×1010 neurons. We're as yet far from "Information." Frank Rosenblatt made the first "Perceptron" model in 1958. Rosenblatt's model had three layers: (1) a "retina" that scattered contributions to the subsequent layer, (2) "affiliation units" that joined contributions with loads and set off a limit step work that took care of into the result layer, and (3) the result layer that consolidated the outcomes. Tragically, in light of the fact that the neurons utilized a stage work, preparing faculties was troublesome or inconceivable. Marvin Minsky and Seymore Papert delivered a basic assessment of perceptrons in 1969, calling attention to various key imperfections, and interest in perceptrons blurred for some time [22]. At the point when David Rumelhart, Geoffrey Hinton, and Ronald Williams delivered "Learning Internal Representations by Error Propagation" in 1986, it reignited interest in neural organizations. They made a multi-facet neural organization with nonlinear yet differentiable exchange works that kept away from the downsides of the progression capacities utilized in the first perceptron. They likewise offered a sensibly decent neural organization preparing strategy.

Back engendering organizations and General Regression Neural Networks are two sorts of neural organizations. Multi-facet perceptron networks (otherwise called multi-facet feed-forward networks), Cascade Correlation Neural Networks, back propagation networks (BPNs), and General Regression Neural Networks are among the most usually used kinds of neural organizations executed by DTREG (GRNN). This organization has three neurons in the info layer (on the left), three neurons in the secret layer (in the center), and three neurons in the result layer (on the right). Every indicator variable has its own neuron in the information layer. When managing downright factors, N-1 neurons are used to address the variable's N classifications [17–20].

The input layer – It is given with a vector of indicator variable qualities (x1...xp). The info layer (or the handling that precedes it) normalizes these qualities so that every factor's reach is -1 to 1. The qualities are dispersed to every one of the neurons in the secret layer by the information layer. A consistent contribution of 1.0, called the predisposition, is given to every one of the secret layers notwithstanding the indicator factors; the inclination is duplicated by a weight and added to the total streaming into the neuron.

Hidden layer – At the point when the worth from each info neuron arrives at a secret layer neuron, it is increased by a weight (wji), and the weighted qualities are consolidated to get a joined worth uj. The weighted total (uj) is sent by means of an exchange work, which returns hj. The result layer gets the results from the secret layer.

Output layer – At the point when the worth from each secret layer neuron arrives at a neuron in the result layer, it is duplicated by a weight (wkj), and the weighted qualities are consolidated to get a joined worth vj. The weighted total (vj) is sent by means of an exchange work, which delivers the worth yk. The organization's results are addressed by the y esteems.

At the point when a persistent objective variable is utilized in a relapse study, the result layer contains a solitary neuron that creates a solitary y esteem. In characterization issues with clear cut objective factors, the result layer contains N neurons that produce N esteems, one for every one of the objective variable's N classes [17–22].

11.3.4.1 Back Propagation Networks

The designs of BPN as well as General Regression Neural Networks (GRNN) are comparable; however, there is a key distinction: When the true factor is all out, probabilistic organizations do arrangement, though nonexclusive backslide neural organizations carryon the relapse (backslide) when the objective variable is consistent. DTREG will naturally recognize the pertinent kind of organization dependent on the sort of target variable in the event that you pick a BPN/GRNN organization. The development of a BPN is shown in Figure 11.7.

All BPN networks have four nodes.

Input node – Every indicator variable is addressed by one neuron in the information layer. N-1 neurons are used for all out factors, in which N is the number of classes. By taking away the middle and separating by the interquartile range, the info neurons (or guiding going preceding the information node) standardize the quality of information. The standards are then taken care of to every one of the neurons in the secret layer by the information neurons.

Hidden node – Each case in the preparation informational index contains one neuron in this layer. Alongside the objective worth, the neuron keeps the upsides of the case's indicator factors. At the point when given the x vector of info esteems from the information layer, a secret neuron ascertains the Euclidean distance of the experiment from the neuron's middle guide and afterward utilizes the sigma esteem toward apply the RBF bit work (s). The subsequent worth is shipped off the example layer's neurons [19].

Design/summation node – For BPN and GRNN organizations, the following layer in the organization is unique. Every classification of the objective variable has one example neuron in BPN organizations. Each secret neuron stores the real objective class of each preparation occasion; the weighted worth result by a secret neuron is simply provided to the example neuron that compares to the secret neuron's classification. The qualities for the class that the example neurons address are added together (thus, it is a weighted decision in favor of that classification). In GRNN

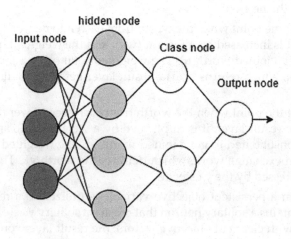

FIGURE 11.7
Architecture of a BPN.

organizations, the example layer contains just two neurons. The denominator addition unit is one neuron, whereas the numerator addition unit is the other. The weight esteems from every one of the covered neurons are added together by the denominator summation unit. For each secret neuron, the numerator summation unit includes the weight esteems duplicated by the genuine objective worth [20].

Decision layer – BPN and GRNN networks have separate choice layers. The choice layer in BPN networks thinks about the weighted actions in favor of each target class aggregated in the sample node and predicts an objective classification dependent on the biggest vote. The choice layer of GRNN networks isolates the numerator summation unit's worth by the denominator summation unit's worth and uses the outcome as the projected objective worth.

11.3.4.2 Back Propagation Algorithm

Think about an organization with just one genuine information, x, and the organization work F. The F'(x) subsidiary is processed in two phases:

Feed-forward – The organization gets the information x. At every hub, the crude capacities and their subordinates are assessed. The subordinates are kept in a protected spot.

Back spread – The result unit gets the steady 1 and the organization is turned around. The worth put away in the left half of the unit is increased by the amount of approaching data to a hub. The outcome is shipped off the unit's left side. The subsidiary of the organization work concerning x is the outcome acquired at the information unit [20].

11.3.4.3 Steps of the Algorithm

After arbitrarily choosing the organization's loads, the back-proliferation method is utilized to register the fundamental adjustments. The accompanying four stages can be utilized to breakdown the calculation: Feed-forward calculation, back proliferation to the result layer, back engendering to the secret layer, and weight refreshes are just a portion of the elements accessible. The calculation is halted when the worth of the mistake work has become adequately little. The accompanying Figure 11.9 is the documentation for three-layered organizations [21].

After self-assertively picking the association's heaps, the back-expansion strategy is used to enlist the basic changes. The going with four phases can be used to breakdown the computation: Feed-forward estimation, back expansion to the outcome layer, back inciting to the mysterious layer, and weight invigorates are only a part of the components available. The computation is ended when the value of the mix-up work has become close to nothing [20].

Back spread organizations are theoretically like K-Nearest Neighbor (k-NN) models, regardless of the way that their execution is altogether unique. The hidden thought is that a thing's expected objective worth will be like different things with comparative indicator variable qualities.

Accept that there are two indicator factors, x and y, for every model in the preparation set. As demonstrated in the picture, the models are plotted utilizing their x,y organizes. Expect that the objective variable is partitioned into two classes: positive (addressed by a

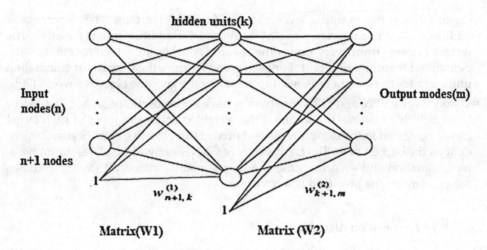

FIGURE 11.8
General structure of neural network.

square) and negative (addressed by a scramble). Accept that we're endeavoring to figure the result of another occasion addressed by the triangle, with indicator upsides of x=6, y=5.1. Would it be a good idea for us to make a positive or negative expectation about the objective? The triangle is actually situated on top of a scramble signifying a negative number. When contrasted with another runs, which are concentrated beneath the squares and to one side of focus, that run is at a strange spot. Subsequently, it's conceivable that the fundamental negative worth is an exception. The quantity of adjoining focuses assessed in this model influences the closest neighbor grouping. If 1-NN is utilized as well as simply the nearest position is used, the novel idea ought to clearly be ordered as negative, because it is situated on upper side of a previously established negative factor. Be that as it may, if the 9-NN order is utilized and simply the nearest 9 focuses are used, the impact of the encompassing 8 positive focuses may offset the nearby bad point. Figure 11.10 shows the impact of another point. The more prominent the distance between another point and the new area, the less effect it has [19]. Figure 11.8 shows the general structure of neural network.

11.3.4.4 Removing Unnecessary Neurons

One of the downsides of BPN models over multi-facet perceptron networks is their size, which is inferable from the way that each preparation column has one neuron. When using scoring to gauge esteems for new lines, the model runs more slow than multi-facet perceptron networks. DTREG contains a component that permits it to wipe out unnecessary neurons from a model after it has been constructed.

Eliminating undesirable neurons enjoys three benefits: it diminishes the size of the put away model, it decreases the time needed to apply the model during scoring, and it frequently improves the model's precision. It is an iterative procedure to dispense with pointless neurons. The model's mistake is apportioned utilizing leave-one approval, which eliminates each neuron in turn. The neuron that establishes the littlest mistake increment (or perhaps the littlest blunder reduced) is then erased from the design. The method is rehashed until the ending edge is reached with the excess neurons [20].

The "Model Size," a piece of the review report, exhibits how the blunder changes with various quantities of neurons when superfluous neurons are taken out. By choosing Chart/Model size, you can see a graphical portrayal of this. Limit blunder if this choice is picked, DTREG may erase neurons as long as the leave-one out mistake stays consistent or diminishes. It stops when it finds a neuron whose evacuation will make the mistake ascend over the setup least.

DTREG eliminates neurons until the leave-one out mistake is more prominent than the blunder for the model with all neurons assuming this choice is set. DTREG diminishes the most un-critical neurons until just the given number of neurons remain assuming this choice is set [21].

11.3.4.5 Contour Detection

Shape location alludes to a bunch of numerical procedures for perceiving focuses in an advanced picture, where the picture splendor suddenly changes or, all the more officially, where there are discontinuities. The sharp changes in picture brilliance are normally gathered into an assortment of bended line portions called edges. Step identification is the test of observing discontinuities in one-dimensional signals, and change recognition is the issue of setting aside signal discontinuities across opportunity. In picture handling, machine vision, and PC vision, edge discovery is a basic method, particularly in the fields of element acknowledgment and extraction. The objective of recognizing sharp changes in picture brilliance is to record huge occasions and changes on the planet's ascribes. Discontinuities in picture splendor are probably going to relate to discontinuities inside and out, discontinuities in surface direction, changes in aterial attributes, and variances in scene enlightenment given extremely broad suspicions for a picture creation model [22].

In such an optimal world, executing an edge locator to a picture would bring about a bunch of connected bends that demonstrate object borders, surface checking limits, and bends that compare to surface direction discontinuities. Applying an edge discovery technique to an image can diminish the amount of information that must be handled and, in this manner, sift through data that isn't as indispensable while keeping the picture's significant underlying characteristics. On the off chance that the edge discovery step is fruitful, crafted by breaking down the data content in the first picture might be altogether smoothed out. In any case, such amazing edges are regularly impractical to obtain from genuine pictures of unobtrusive intricacy. Edges extricated from non-paltry pictures are every now and again repressed by fracture, which implies that the edge bends are not associated, missing edge fragments, and bogus edge shots identified with fascinating events in the picture all of which convolute crafted by breaking down the picture data. One of the most essential strides in picture handling, picture investigation, picture design acknowledgment, and PC vision approaches is edge location. Point of view reliant or viewpoint free edges can be recovered from a two-dimensional image of a three-dimensional scene. The key characteristics of three-dimensional articles, like surface stamps and shape, are regularly reflected by a viewpoint autonomous edge. The calculation of the scene, for example, objects impeding each other, is frequently reflected by a point of view subordinate edge that differs as the perspective changes.

The line between a square of red and a square of yellow, for instance, is an ordinary edge. A line, then again, can be a minuscule number of pixels of a variable tone on a generally consistent foundation (as can be recovered by an edge locator). Therefore, there might be one edge on one or the other side of a line by and large [25–28].

Early shape discovery strategies utilized nearby estimations to measure the presence of a limit at a given picture area. Edges are distinguished by means of the Roberts, Sobel, and Prewitt administrators, which convolve a grayscale picture with nearby subordinate channels. No intersections of the Laplacian of Gaussian administrator are utilized by Marr and Hildreth. Edges are likewise displayed as sharp discontinuities in the brilliance channel by the Canny locator, which incorporates non-most extreme concealment and hysteresis thresholding stages [29]. Think about the picture's reaction to a group of channels of different scales and directions for a more itemized depiction. The Oriented Energy strategy, for instance, utilizes quadrature sets of even and odd symmetric channels. Lindeberg recommends a channel-based method with a scale determination process that is programmed. Shading and surface data are considered in later nearby methodologies, just as learning calculations for sign blending. Martin et al. make slope administrators for the splendor, shading, and surface channels, which they feed into a strategic relapse classifier to gauge edge strength. Dollar et al. present a Boosted Edge Learning (BEL) approach that looks to fabricate an edge classifier as a probabilistic helping tree from huge number of basic elements registered on picture fixes rather than depending on such hand-created highlights [30]. One advantage of this technique is that it could be feasible to oversee signals like parallelism and culmination during the order stage. By learning discriminative meager portrayals of neighborhood picture patches, Mairal et al. assemble both general and class-explicit edge locators. They gain proficiency with a discriminative word reference for each class and feed the reproduction mistake from every word reference into a last classifier as a component input. For these new nearby procedures, the wide scope of scales at which things can show up in the picture stays a test. Ren sees the worth in combining information from many sizes of neighborhood administrators created by him [31]. The limit classifier gets extra restriction and relative differentiation prompts portrayed as far as the multiscale indicator yield. The restriction prompt gathers the distance between a pixel and the closest pinnacle reaction for each scale. The connected differentiation prompt standardizes every pixel comparable to its nearby environmental elements.

11.3.5 Threshold Segmentation

The most fundamental methodology of picture division is thresholding. Thresholding can be utilized to make paired pictures from a grayscale picture. Thresholding is likewise conceivable with shading photos. One strategy is to set an unmistakable limit for every one of the picture's RGB parts, then, at that point, join them utilizing an AND activity. This reflects how the camera works and how the information is put away in the PC, yet it doesn't reflect how people see tone. Thus, the HSL and HSV shading models are all the more ordinarily used; notice that since tone is a round number, roundabout thresholding is required. Division is the most common way of partitioning an image into areas (or shapes) that relate to objects. We regularly attempt to portion districts by searching for shared attributes. Then again, we can track down shapes by searching for contrasts across districts (edges). Power is the most fundamental element that pixels in a district may share. Accordingly, thresholding, or the partition of light and dim locales, is a consistent procedure to section such areas [32]. Thresholding changes dim level pictures over to twofold by setting all pixels under a specific edge to nothing and all pixels over that edge to only one. (It doesn't make any difference how you manage pixels at the limit insofar as you're predictable.) If g (x, y) is a thresholded adaptation of f (x, y) at some worldwide edge T, then, at that point, g is equivalent to 1 if f (x, y) T and zero if f (x, y) T.

One of the main methodologies in picture division is the limit procedure. This strategy can be depicted as follows [17–23]:

$$T = T\left[x, y, p(x, y), f(x, y)\right]$$
(11.3)

The limit esteem is signified by the letter T which is expressed in Equation 3. The limit esteem focuses are x and y. The dim level picture pixels are addressed by p (x, y) and f (x, y). g (x, y) is a limit picture that can be characterized. Worldwide thresholding, local thresholding, traditional thresholding, iterative thresholding, and multistage thresholding are the few sorts of thresholding methodology. Thresholding at a global level: when the power dissemination among forefront and foundation objects is extremely unmistakable, the worldwide (single) thresholding strategy is applied. At the point when the qualifications among closer view and foundation things are inconspicuous, a solitary limit worth can be used to effortlessly recognize the two. Therefore, the worth of limit T in this kind of thresholding is only controlled by the pixel's trait and the picture's dark level worth. The Otsu approach, entropy-based thresholding, and other worldwide thresholding strategies are the absolute regularly used methodology. Otsu's calculation is a well-known worldwide thresholding procedure.

Conventional thresholding (Otsu's method) in picture handling, division is every now and again utilized as the underlying advance in pre-handling pictures to choose things of interest for resulting study.

Division methods can be used for the most part arranged into two structures, edge-based and district-based methodologies. Otsu's strategy is oftentimes utilized in design acknowledgment, record binarization, and PC vision as a division method. As a rule Otsu's strategy is utilized as a pre-handling method to section a picture for additional handling, for example, include examination and measurement. At the point when the histogram of the first picture incorporates two distinct pinnacles, one having a place with the foundation and the other to the forefront or sign, Otsu's strategy looks for an edge that limits the intra-class differences of the divided picture and can get great outcomes. The Otsu's edge is dictated via looking across the whole scope of the picture's pixel esteems until the intra-class differences are at their most minimal. The edge determined by Otsu's procedure is all the more essentially dictated by the class with the biggest fluctuation, regardless of whether it is the foundation or the frontal area, as characterized. Therefore, when the picture's histogram contains multiple pinnacles or one of the classes has a major difference, Otsu's methodology might create substandard outcomes. Thresholding iteratively (A New Iterative Tri class Thresholding Technique) another iterative strategy that depends on Otsu's strategy however varies from the standard utilization of the strategy critically. Likewise, with the regular application, we initially apply Otsu's way to deal with an image to acquire the Otsu's limit and the method for two classes separated by the edge. Then, at that point, rather than arranging the picture into two classes separated by the Otsu's limit, our technique partitions it into three classes dependent on the two determined class implies. The three classes are the frontal area, which has pixel esteems more prominent than the greater mean, the foundation, which has pixel esteems not exactly the more modest mean, and, most altogether, the "not set in stone" (TBD) zone, which has pixel esteems that fall between the two class implies. The strategy then, at that point, holds the past forefront and foundation regions unaltered and re-technique applies Otsu's to the TBD area, partitioning it into three classes similarly as in the past. At the point when the emphasis stops in the wake of accomplishing a foreordained condition, the last TBD district is separated into two classes: closer view and foundation, rather than three. The last frontal area

```
23x1 Layer array with layers:

   1   'input'       Image Input                   227x227x3 images with 'zerocenter' normalization
   2   'conv1'       Convolution                   96 11x11x3 convolutions with stride [4  4] and padding [0  0  0  0]
   3   'relu1'       ReLU                          ReLU
   4   'norm1'       Cross Channel Normalization   cross channel normalization with 5 channels per element
   5   'pool1'       Max Pooling                   3x3 max pooling with stride [2  2] and padding [0  0  0  0]
   6   'conv2'       Convolution                   256 5x5x48 convolutions with stride [1  1] and padding [2  2  2  2]
   7   'relu2'       ReLU                          ReLU
   8   'norm2'       Cross Channel Normalization   cross channel normalization with 5 channels per element
   9   'pool2'       Max Pooling                   3x3 max pooling with stride [2  2] and padding [0  0  0  0]
  10   'conv3'       Convolution                   384 3x3x256 convolutions with stride [1  1] and padding [1  1  1  1]
  11   'relu3'       ReLU                          ReLU
  12   'conv4'       Convolution                   384 3x3x192 convolutions with stride [1  1] and padding [1  1  1  1]
  13   'relu4'       ReLU                          ReLU
  14   'conv5'       Convolution                   256 3x3x192 convolutions with stride [1  1] and padding [1  1  1  1]
  15   'relu5'       ReLU                          ReLU
  16   'pool5'       Max Pooling                   3x3 max pooling with stride [2  2] and padding [0  0  0  0]
  17   'fc6'         Fully Connected               4096 fully connected layer
  18   'relu6'       ReLU                          ReLU
  19   'fc7'         Fully Connected               4096 fully connected layer
  20   'relu7'       ReLU                          ReLU
  21   'special_2'   Fully Connected               44 fully connected layer
  22   ''            ReLU                          ReLU
  23   'fc8_2'       Fully Connected               3 fully connected layer
```

FIGURE 11.9
Model summary of proposed CNN architecture.

and foundation are the consistent association of all the recently settled closer view and foundation locales. The new strategy is nearly boundary free aside from the halting standard for the iterative cycle and has insignificant added computational burden. Thresholding in stages (quadratic ratio technique for hand composed character): When thresholding penmanship photos with the accompanying rigid imperatives, the QIR approach was viewed as predominant: 1. The penmanship should be protected in the entirety of its subtleties. 2. The papers utilized may have a foundation that is brilliantly shaded or designed. 3. Different composing media, for example, a wellspring pen, ball point pen, or pencil, can be utilized to compose the penmanship. QIR is a two-stage worldwide thresholding technique. The calculation's underlying stage isolates a picture into three sub pictures: closer view, foundation, and a fluffy sub picture where it's hard to tell whether a pixel has a place in the frontal area or foundation. A, what isolates the closer view and fluffy sub pictures, and C, what isolates the fluffy and foundation sub pictures, are two critical boundaries that different the sub pictures. A pixel has a place with the closer view in the event that its power is not exactly or equivalent to A. A pixel has a place with the foundation assuming its force is more noteworthy than or equivalent to C. Assuming a pixel's force esteem falls among A and C, it has a place with the fluffy sub picture, and more data from the picture are needed to decide if it has a place with the closer view or the foundation [23]. Figure 11.9 represents model summary of proposed architecture and Figure 11.10 represents output of the model.

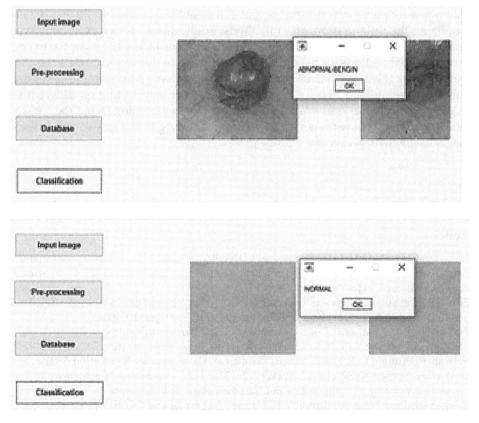

FIGURE 11.10
Classified output.

11.4 Results and Discussions

Each three of the examined algorithms were changed to some amount in order to enhance the learning achievement of the model. In this survey, VGG 16 network gained a most attention. The most significant source of modeling pain was the dataset's severe skew, with 4 times greater data for benign skin infections than for malignant skin infections. As a consequence, the average error while training and testing on the entire dataset was around 25%, that at first glimpse appears to be good; however, upon careful scrutiny, this 25% error is a direct consequence of the framework learning to forecast benign for all instances since the data set is skewed more toward benign moles.

11.5 Conclusion

Healthcare 4.0 demonstrates the vast capacity of producing recently personalized augmentations, as well as creative equipment and procedures for the medical field. Healthcare 4.0 produces high-quality, regulated medical equipment that are highly customized to meet the needs of the patient. This revolution embraces automation while also opening up new production possibilities in the healthcare globe. It establishes connectivity and data transfer by utilizing the unique production methods, applications, detectors, robotic systems, and other cutting-edge information techniques. Healthcare 4.0 has the potential to open up new avenues and directions for patient care in the future. In this work, CNN is used to classify skin diseases. It is used because of its quick training speed and simple configuration. More photos were utilized to train the network classifier, and testing on different sets of images were conducted to assess classifier accuracy. As a smoothing factor, the constructed classifier was tested with various spread values. According to the spread value, the CNN classifier is usable with an accuracy range of 94%.

References

1. Jiun-Wen Guo, Shiou HwaJee "Strategies to Develop a Suitable Formulation for Inflammatory Skin Disease Treatment". *International Journal of Molecular Sciences* 2021, 22, 6078. https://doi.org/10.3390/ijms22116078
2. Shuva Paul et al., "Industry 4.0 Applications for Medical/Healthcare Services". *Journal of Sensor and Actuator Networks* 2021, 10, 43. https://doi.org/10.3390/jsan10030043
3. Nazeer Hussain Khan, et al. "Skin Cancer Biology and Barriers to Treatment: Recent Applications of Polymeric Micro/Nanostructures". *Journal of Advanced Research*, June 2021, 36, 223–247.
4. Sathish, R., Kumar, D. R. (2013, March) "Proficient Algorithms for Replication Attack Detection in Wireless Sensor Networks—A Survey". In *2013 IEEE International Conference ON Emerging Trends in Computing, Communication and Nanotechnology (ICECCN)* (pp. 1–7). IEEE.
5. Yuka Asai, Paul Nguyen, Timothy P. Hanna "Impact of the COVID-19 Pandemic On Skin Cancer Diagnosis: A Population-based Study". March 31, 2021, https://doi.org/10.1371/journal.pone.0248492

6. S. Suganyadevi, V. Seethalakshmi & K. Balasamy "A Review on Deep Learning in Medical Image Analysis". *The International Journal of Multimedia Information Retrieval* 2021. https://doi.org/10.1007/s13735-021-00218-1

7. Ollo Roland Some, Malick Diallo, Damien Konkobo, Nassirou Yabre, Valentin Konse Gre, Issouf Konate, Sidy Ka "Inguinal Lymph Node Dissection for Advanced Stages of Plantar Melanoma in a Low-Income Country". *Hindawi Journal of Skin Cancer*, 2020, https://doi.org/10.1155/2020/8854460

8. K. Balasamy, S. Suganyadevi "A Fuzzy Based ROI Selection for Encryption and Watermarking in Medical Image Using DWT and SVD". *Multimedia Tools and Applications* 2021, 80, 7167–7186. https://doi.org/10.1007/s11042-020-09981-5

9. Mehwish Dildar, et al., "Skin Cancer Detection: A Review Using Deep Learning Techniques". *International Journal of Environmental Research and Public Health* 2021, 18, 5479. https://doi.org/10.3390/ijerph18105479

10. Julia Höhn, et al., "Integrating Patient Data into Skin Cancer Classification Using Convolutional Neural Networks: Systematic Review". *Journal of Medical Internet Research* 2021, 23(7), e20708, p. 1. https://www.jimr.org/2021/7/e20708

11. Samanthi Weerabahu and Ruwan Wickramarachchi "Combining Industry 4.0 with Lean Healthcare to Optimize Operational Performance of Sri Lankan Healthcare Industry". 978-1-5386-9500-5/18/$31.00 ©2018 IEEE. https://doi.org/10.1109/POMS.2018.8629460

12. Brian C. Baumann, et al, "Management of Primary Skin Cancer During a Pandemic: Multidisciplinary Recommendations". Published online June 1, 2020. https://doi.org/10.1002/cncr.32969

13. S. Suganyadevi, D. Shamia, K. Balasamy "An IoT-based Diet Monitoring Healthcare System for Women". *Smart Healthcare System Design: Security and Privacy Aspects* 2021. https://doi.org/10.1002/9781119792253.ch8

14. M. Arvindhan, D. Rajeshkumar, Anupam Lakhan Pal "A Review of Challenges and Opportunities in Machine Learning for Healthcare". *Exploratory Data Analytics for Healthcare* 2021, 67–84.

15. R. N. S. Karthick, R. S. Valarmathi, D. R. Kumar "Design and Analysis of Multiply and Accumulation Units Using Low Power Adders". *Journal of Computational and Theoretical Nanoscience* 2018, 15(5), 1712–1718.

16. Magdalena Ciążyńska, Grażyna Kamińska-Winciorek "The Incidence and Clinical Analysis of Non-melanoma Skin Cancer". 2021, 11, 4337. https://doi.org/10.1038/s41598-021-83502-8

17. Yu-Ching Weng, Hsiu J. Ho, Yi-Ling Chang, Yun-Ting Chang, Chun-Ying Wu, Yi-Ju Chen "Reduced Risk of Skin Cancer and Internal Malignancies in Vitiligo Patients: A Retrospective Population-based Cohort Study in Taiwan", 2021, 11, 20195, https://doi.org/10.1038/s41598-021-99786-9

18. Ngan Thanh Luu, Thanh-Hai Le, Quoc-Hung Phan, Thi-Thu-Hien Pham "Characterization of Mueller Matrix Elements for Classifying Human Skin Cancer Utilizing Random Forest Algorithm". *Journal of Biomedical Optics* July 2021, 26(7). https://doi.org/10.1117/1.JBO.26.7.075001.

19. K. Sathya, D. R. Kumar (2012, February) "Energy Efficient Clustering in Sensor Networks Using Cluster Manager". *2012 International Conference on Computing, Communication and Applications (ICCCA).*

20. K. Balasamy, N. Krishnaraj, K. Vijayalakshmi "An Adaptive Neuro-Fuzzy Based Region Selection and Authenticating Medical Image Through Watermarking for Secure Communication". *Wireless Personal Communications* 2021. https://doi.org/10.1007/s11277-021-09031-9

21. Tanzila Saba "Computer Vision for Microscopic Skin Cancer Diagnosis Using Handcrafted and Non-handcrafted Features". 2021. Wiley Periodicals. https://doi.org/10.1002/jemt.23686

22. Ritsuko Iwanaga, Brittany T. Truong, Jessica Y. Hsu, Karoline A. Lambert, Rajesh Vyas, David Orlicky, Yiqun G. Shellman, Aik-Choon Tan, Craig Ceol, Kristin Bruk Artinger "Loss of Prdm1a Accelerates Melanoma Onset and Progression". *Molecular Carcinogenesis* 2020, 1–12. https://doi.org/10.1002/mc.23236

23. S. Suganyadevi, K. Renukadevi, K. Balasamy, P. Jeevitha (2022) "Diabetic Retinopathy Detection Using Deep Learning Methods". *First International Conference on Electrical, Electronics, Information and Communication Technologies (ICEEICT)*, pp. 1–6. https://doi.org/10.1109/ICEEICT53079.2022.9768544

24. S. Ramakrishnan, T. Gopalakrishnan, K. Balasamy. "A Wavelet Based Hybrid SVD Algorithm for Digital Image Watermarking". *Signal & Image Processing An International Journal (SIPIJ)* 2011, 2(3), 157–174.

25. Laura Rey-Barroso, et al., "Optical Technologies for the Improvement of Skin Cancer Diagnosis: A Review". *A Review Sensors* 2021, 21, 252, https://doi.org/10.3390/s21010252

26. Rehan Ashraf, et al, "Region-of-Interest Based Transfer Learning Assisted Framework for Skin Cancer Detection", date of current version August 21, 2020. https://doi.org/10.1109/ACCESS.2020.3014701

27. K. Balasamy, D. Shamia "Feature Extraction-based Medical Image Watermarking Using fuzzy-based Median Filter". *IETE Journal of Research* 2021, 1–9. https://doi.org/10.1080/03772063.2021.1893231

28. Anna Choromanska Devansh Bisla, Russell S. Berman, Jennifer A. Stein, David Polsky "Towards Automated Melanoma Detection with Deep Learning: Data Purification and Augmentation". May 2019, 14, arXiv: 1902.06061v2[cs.CV].

29. Katelyn Urban "The Global Burden of Skin Cancer: A Longitudinal Analysis from the Global Burden of Disease Study, 1990-2017". https://doi.org/10.1016/j.jdin.2020.10.013

30. Mohd Javaid, Abid Haleem "Industry 4.0 Applications in Medical Field: A Brief Review". *Current Medicine Research and Practice*, https://doi.org/10.1016/j.cmrp.2019.04.001

31. T. Gopalakrishnan, S. Ramakrishnan, K. Balasamy, A.S.M. Murugavel (2011) "Semi Fragile Watermarking Using Gaussian Mixture Model for Malicious Image Attacks [C]". *2011 World Congress on Information and Communication Technologies*, 120–125.

32. Giuseppe Aceto, Valerio Persico, Antonio Pescape "Industry 4.0 and Health: Internet of Things, Big Data, and Cloud Computing for Healthcare 4.0". *Journal of Industrial Information Integration*, https://doi.org/10.1016/j.jii.2020.100129

12

Patient Identity Ailments and Maintenance Using Blockchain and Health Informatics

K. S. Suganya

KCG College of Technology, Chennai, India

R. Nedunchezian

Coimbatore Institute of Technology, Coimbatore, India

K. S. Arvind

Jain University, Bangalore, India

CONTENTS

12.1 Introduction: Background and Research Motivation

With the advent of digital era, healthcare institutions across the world have migrated from paper-based health records to electronic health records commonly abbreviated as EHRs. Across the world, EHR is constantly used in lieu with other similar terms such as electronic patient identity, electronic health data and electronic medical records. These terminologies

DOI: 10.1201/9781003217435-12

commonly represent patient records containing varying information such as patient's identity, patient's demographic information, patient's pathological information, patient's banking and citizenship information [1]. Digital universe, big data, growth of communication technologies such as 5G have resulted in the wide-spread and the large-scale development and maintenance of EHRs [2–5]. The growth of Blockchain as a provider for immutable, decentralized ledger has resulted in revolutionizing the fields of finance, supply-chain management, healthcare and many more. With the advent of self-sovereign identity from Blockchain, patient self-sovereign electronic health record (PSSEHR) system has become popular in healthcare industry. This has resulted in the development of patient-centered electronic health informatics, wherein which the patient acts as the major role of authenticating access to their health data for all stakeholders except in emergency situations.

Blockchain, which is the foundation for bitcoin cryptocurrency, is a decentralized, immutable ledger technology that consists of a time-stamped continuous transaction known as blocks that are connected using public key cryptographic principles [6, 7]. Because the blocks are connected and immutable, data that has already been stored cannot be tampered without affecting all the connected blocks which is maintained across a peer network with consensus mechanism. The blocks are made immutable, tamper-proof and anonymous by hashing it with a one-way cryptographic hash algorithm (e.g. SHA-256) [8]. Furthermore, it employs varying consensus mechanism to create, update and validate the transaction and add the blocks to the Blockchain for security and privacy [9, 10]. A Blockchain is a continuous growing list of records called as blocks that are cryptographically and securely linked together shared by the users in a distributed peer-to-peer network. There are three types of Blockchain namely public, private and permissioned. In public Blockchain, any users can perform the transaction and add a block to the Blockchain after reaching consensus among others. Bitcoin and Ethereum are the two popular platforms using public Blockchain. Private Blockchain is suitable for fully trusted closed system. Permissioned Blockchain is hybrid of public and private Blockchain. In permissioned Blockchain certain amount of authorized user can perform the transaction and add the block to the Blockchain after reaching consensus. Hyperledger fabric (HLF), Ripple and Multichain are some of the popular platforms build using permissioned Blockchain. Our proposed Blockchain network for PSSEHR is designed to addresses the following issues such as accessibility, interoperability, scalability, reliability, integrity, security and privacy problems in the legacy EHRs systems. Our PSSEHR takes advantage of Blockchain's intrinsic features to provide a viable EHR management system that addresses healthcare issues stated above. The permissioned Blockchain technology used in our PSSEHR is HLF [13], which offers a foundation for safeguarding interactions among the entities in the health chain network.

12.1.1 Background and Research Motivation

We recommend a decentralized EHR management in this paper to overcome the security and privacy concerns of sharing the patient EHRs instead of the legacy centralized EHR system which is currently existing. Our PSSEHR system addresses the following four issues by incorporating the following features:

- Privacy – An anonymous ledger-based Blockchain ensures the protection of patient's identity while sharing EHRs with healthcare experts.
- Security – PSSEHR employs proxy re-encryption scheme while sharing the information among the healthcare experts and also ensures auditability and data integrity with the help of immutable access to EHRs.

- Scalability – A decentralized scalable Blockchain network with certain overheads ensures better availability, transparency and accessibility of EHRs.
- Self-Sovereign Identity – The patient centric self-sovereign Blockchain enables the patient to share their health information to the stakeholder's of their choice with exception during emergency situations.

For our PSSEHR, we are using the HLF infrastructure to implement permissioned consortium-based Blockchain, namely the permissioned consortium type [14]. Consortium network is employed to cover the wide range of global hospitals with a private peer-to-peer network, wherein the inclusion of hospital requires the consensus among the other global hospitals. To avoid the 51% attack of Blockchain, we are employing permissioned consensus mechanism. Our chosen HLF is an open-source platform which employs Byzantine fault-tolerant consensus mechanism [15] for adding transactions in a block. The performance of this fabric is more because it has high throughput of more than 20,000 transactions per second from end to end with the help of parallelism and caching [16]. The components and flow in HLF are illustrated in Figure 12.1.

The primary motivations of this paper are listed below:

- Firstly, we are employing HLF to build this a self-sovereign patient-centric decentralized health record management system that uses Hyperledger composer. The proposed system also ensure reliability because of its robustness and no single point of failure and pseudo-anonymity to the permissioned nodes in the consortium Blockchain.
- Secondly, the major issue of scalability and performance efficiency is achieved by only adding the hash of EHRs on the Blockchain and storing the original EHRs

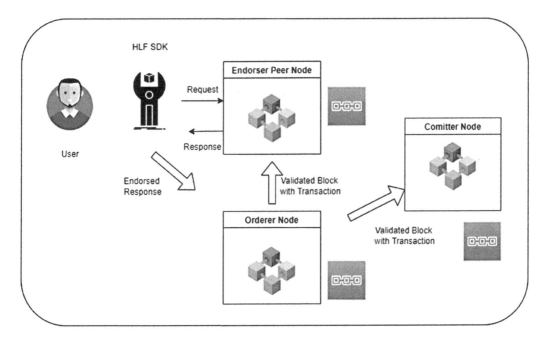

FIGURE 12.1
Hyperledger fabric components and workflow.

by encrypting it using proxy re-encryption and then storing it in a decentralized Interplanetary File System (IPFS) storage system. The system also ensures only valid transactions is hashed and added to the Blockchain by employing fault-tolerant consensus mechanism and the visibility of the original data is validated after gaining necessary privileges from the patient. To improve the confidentiality and integrity of the stored health records in IPFS, we are employing a strong and secure public key cryptographic encryption technique.

• Finally, PSSEHR develops a self-sovereign patient-centric decentralized health record management wherein which the patients have total control over their sensitive health information ensuring better security and privacy.

12.2 Hyperledger Fabric

HLF is a Blockchain framework designed for private corporate networks. Fabric is one of the Hyperledger projects hosted by the Linux Foundation and was originally created by Digital Asset and IBM. HLF gives developers the ability to create reliable apps using a modular design. It leverages container technology to host chaincodes, which is a smart contract analogue. Despite the fact that traditional Blockchain networks use consensus techniques such as Proof of Work to confirm transactions and safeguard the network, they nonetheless allow for participation by unknown parties. Members of an HLF network sign up with the help of a reputable MSP. An HLF network can decrease consensus overhead by focusing on a single private application and enforcing strict membership control: removing additional mining speeds up block generation, which leads to speedier transaction acceptance. A consensus in Hyperledger is just the verification of a block's transactions. A consensus also contains endorsement policies to ensure that all parties involved in the transaction are on the same page. Before we built our own solution based on the HLF Blockchain, we needed to understand the fundamental features of the Hyperledger network architecture [18]. This will help us better understand how the platform functions and what makes HLF unique and this is shown in Table 12.1.

TABLE 12.1

Hyperledger Fabric (HLF) Architectural Components

Component	Visual Representation	Functionalities
Organization and Consortiums		In a Hyperledger Fabric network [18], the key actors are organizations. In most situations, a coalition of organizations comes together to build the network. Their access rights are governed by a set of policies that the consortium agrees to while setting up the new network.

(*Continued*)

TABLE 12.1 (Continued)

Component	Visual Representation	Functionalities
Orderers		The HLF network's backbone is made up of Orderers. They make up the ordering service, which is a communication network that ensures that transactions are delivered fairly. A single node might be included in the ordering service for development or testing purposes. It might also be a multi-node system with defined failure tolerance. An ordering service offers clients and peers with a common communication channel, as well as a broadcast service for messages containing transactions. Within each channel, orderers are responsible for assuring atomic delivery of all messages or transaction consensus [18].
Policies and Configurations		In Hyperledger Fabric [18], policies range from fundamental administrative operations, channel construction and chaincode instantiation to complicated endorsement (validation) policies that specify which peers should validate each given transaction. When the network is first configured, the consortium agrees on policies. Network policies can be changed over time with the consent of all consortium members.
Peers		Peer nodes, or simply peers, are the most common representation of the network. Peers are an important part of the network since they are involved in practically every aspect of it. Each company may have one or many peers depending on their requirements. Each peer retains a copy of the ledger for each channel on their own computer and can execute chaincode instances locally. As a result, peer nodes are responsible for giving access to the ledger and chaincode of their channels to client applications [18].
Channels		A channel is a dedicated communication route between two or more peers. It's a logical structure made up of a group of peer nodes. All channel interactions are done through peers. Messages can be broadcast on a channel to all peers in that channel by network clients. All communications are sent atomically across channels. To put it another way, they send the identical messages to all connected peers, ensuring that messages are received in the same sequence. This type atomic communication is known as consensus. Each channel has its own Blockchain state, as well as a fully separate ledger. As a result, there are as many different Blockchains as there are channels. If a peer accesses numerous channels, each channel will have its own copy of the ledger [18].
Chaincode		Chaincode is the Hyperledger equivalent of smart contracts [18]. Users may design and upload bespoke business logic that interacts with on-chain data, just like any other smart contract implementation. Chaincode runs on a variety of peers and in a variety of channels. In order to view the ledger, not every peer must execute chaincode. Chaincode has a few distinguishing characteristics. Hyperledger Fabric, for example, allows you to control who has access to the network. Access to some smart contracts (or their functionality) may be limited. You also don't have to rely on the smart contract developer to verify that the contract's functionalities are safe because access restriction is built into the network. The native runtime for chaincode is another fantastic feature. Chaincode is developed in Go and runs independently on each peer node. When compared to networks with virtual computers, this provides extraordinarily high efficiency (Ethereum, EOS).

12.3 Proposed Patient Identity Hyperledger Architecture

For our proposed PSSEHR, we developed a private HLF channel with a distributed peer-to-peer consortium network as shown in Figure 12.2. The nodes in the peer network are hospitals who is sharing the same immutable Blockchain ledger. These hospitals allow their sub-departments within their organization to create separate autonomous channels with the same immutable Blockchain ledger in a nested manner. It is common knowledge that medical data often tend to be larger and cannot be stored directly in the immutable Blockchain ledger. As a result, these immutable Blockchain ledgers contain only the hash of the address of the original encrypted EHR stored in IPFS resulting in an offchain immutable Blockchain ledger [19].

The resulting hash value of the address alone is kept in the immutable Blockchain ledger in our PSSEHR systems. Consequently, the data become tamper-proof because of their immutable nature ensuring trust among the user to verify the validity of their EHR. The users of PSSEHR systems can be patients directly or indirectly through healthcare experts who assist the patient's or patient's relative in managing the EHR in our systems. These EHRs originally contain variety of information varying from patient's identity, patient's demographic information, patient's pathological information, patient's banking and citizenship information which is stored in the HLF IPFS whose address is hashed and stored with timestamps in the blocks of the ledger after reaching consensus among the peer nodes (Hospitals). These blocks also contain the healthcare experts request information, execution results, metadata and history which can be used for audit purpose to ensure data integrity in the future.

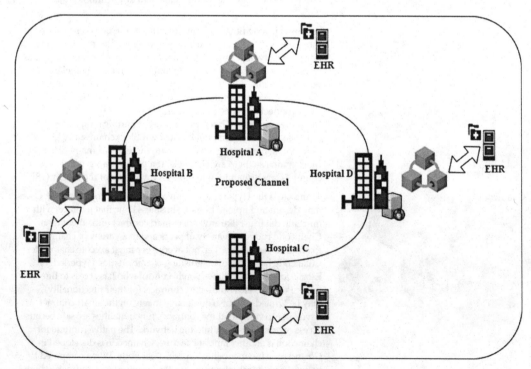

FIGURE 12.2
Proposed HLF channel.

The patient ID (pID) supplied by an HLF service provider is used in the private HLF channel for unique identification of each individual patients. As a result, these ledgers contain transactions with a pID, which is hashed in the following way after being concatenated with randomly chosen data called here as "randomsalt" as shown in Equation 12.1:

$$\$hash(randomsalt + pID)\$n\, \$randomsalt \tag{12.1}$$

This structure is similar to how the Linux operating system maintains their hashed passwords in the etc/passwd with salts (random mumber) for its users. "$" is used to separate nearby fields; "n" is the hash algorithm type which can be any one of the following hash algorithms: MD5, SHA-256 and SHA-512. Randomsalt is a 16-letter string of randomly chosen mixed alphabetic and numeric characters.

PSSEHR Systems Architecture is depicted in Figure 12.3. Our system architecture comprises Web Server, REST API Server, Hyperledger composer, chaincode and CouchDB, which formulates the HLF and IPFS for efficient storage. The users of this architecture are Peers, Orderers and Certificate Authority (CA) with a private HLF channel. We have used Angular web framework for developing the front end of our PSSEHR Systems connecting to the Composer Rest server, which interacts and visualizes the CouchDB state database from the HLF. The proposed system processes the admin and user request to the HLF via the Web and REST API server. The REST API server employs GET request and responses to interact and visualize the CouchDB state database and chaincode from the HLF. Hyperledger composer is responsible for creating smart contracts for ensuring self-sovereign immutable Blockchain ledger network.

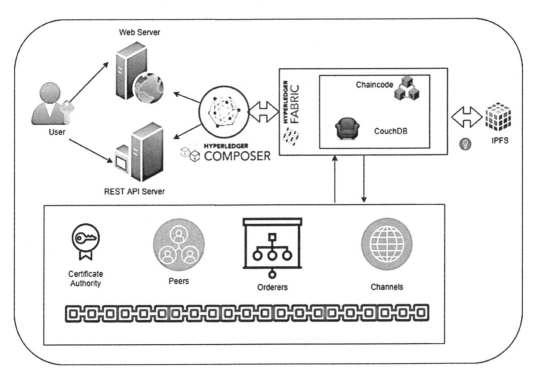

FIGURE 12.3
PSSEHR systems architecture.

Hyperledger fabric [18] is a permissioned Blockchain platform for developing self-sovereign immutable Blockchain ledger solutions that allow the users to create smart contracts known as chaincodes and used to validate data submissions by peer-peer network members by achieving consensus. The HLF framework commonly has two types of Blockchain platform: (1) an on-chain Blockchain that uses the Couch DB on-chain database and (2) an off-chain solution that uses IPFS to store data. Our PSSEHR Systems employ an off-chain ledger which uses IPFS as previously stated.

EHR is usually encrypted using symmetric key before it's uploaded to the IPFS with the patient's consent. Then, the used symmetric key is encrypted using the patients public key and stored along with the encrypted EHR. The reason behind the use of symmetric key to encrypt EHR is its capabilities to large data quickly rather than the asymmetric key resulting in a hybrid encryption technique. This form of hybrid encryption is a better performer than employing the normal encryption scheme. A proxy retrieves patient data from the relevant EHR and transfers it to the receiver in order to view it. However, if the recipient is not the patient, the data's encrypted symmetric key should be modified such that it may be decrypted by the receiver's private key. To accomplish this, we employ a P2B proxy re-encryption system as shown in Figure 12.4. This proxy re-encryption system ensures the patient produces the proxy re-encryption key by mathematically mixing their private key and the receiver's public key, as shown in Figure 12.4. This proxy encryption [20] is better than the default broadcast proxy encryption scheme used in the legacy Blockchain-based EHR.

The P2B proxy re-encrypts the symmetric key for the recipient after receiving the freshly created re-encryption key. The P2B proxy only knows the re-encryption key, and the symmetric key is not revealed to the proxy throughout this encryption scheme making it more secure. As a result, the data must be sent to the patient, who will encrypt it using the receivers public key.

The working prototype of our PSSEHR system is built on a permissioned HLF Blockchain to develop decentralized web applications for hospitals. This organization contains three peer nodes, a validating node, an ordering node and a CA node. To demonstrate system scalability, this may be extended to numerous peer nodes and several organizations on separate computers. To update the ledger, the application communicates with peer nodes and calls smart contracts.

The proposed PSSEHR network was constructed with three peer nodes using Docker Services on a local computer for demonstrative purposes, but it can be definitely in different networks or cloud environments in the real world. The organization's three peers are known as Node1 (N1), Node2 (N2) and Node3 (N3), and each has its own set of ledgers and smart contract copies. Hyperledger Composer uses a single channel to connect with other Hyperledger Composer peers. PSSEHR application A1 sends a transaction T1 to peers N1, N2 and N3 over the HLF channel in this network. The chaincode is placed on the peers after a transaction is completed. The application communicates with peers and uses chaincodes to query and alter the ledger. The transactions are saved as hash values in the Blockchain, which ensures the tamper-proof nature for our PSSEHR system to be tracked.

Supposedly, for a patient x health record consists of the current transaction hash value H#(x) and previous transaction hash value Hp#(x), and it makes up a block in the ledger. HTot(x) may be used to compute the overall workload of that block as shown in Equation 12.2.

$$\text{HTot}(x) = \text{Hp}\#(x) + \text{H}\#(x) \tag{12.2}$$

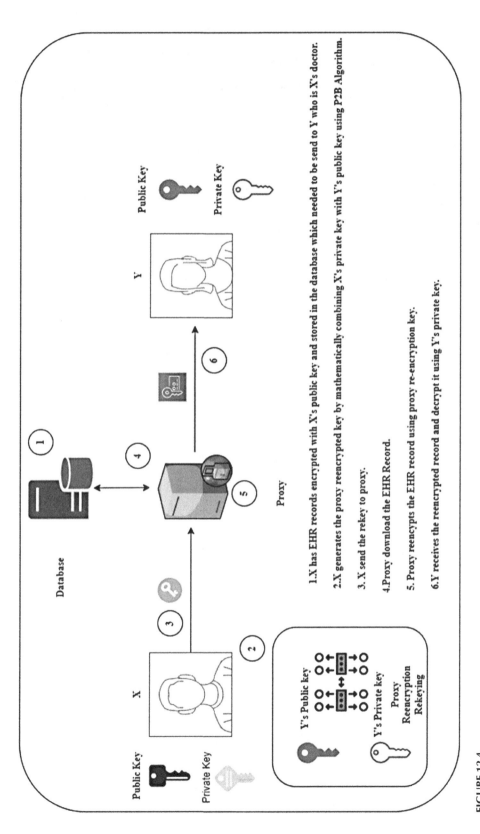

FIGURE 12.4
P2B Proxy encryption scheme.

12.4 Proposed Architecture Implementation

This section focuses on how the patients create and manage their EHRs in our PSSEHR system as well as how to grant/revoke access permission to their EHRs.

12.4.1 Registering the Users

In PSSEHR system, the process of adding/registering the users on the Blockchain is explained in the following: patients, healthcare experts such as doctors, pharmacists and medical officers may register and login to our system using their email address and password. The system comprises an administrator role who will add the blocks to the Blockchain after validating the transactions by following fault-tolerant consensus among their consensus voters. The patients and healthcare experts can update the EHRs with their login credentials along with their own public–private key pairs Xki, Xri. The password is hashed by adding a random salt and employing the popular SHA-512 hashing algorithm and stored for more security.

12.4.2 Adding EHR Record to the Blockchain

In PSSEHR system, the process of updating the patient's EHR by the healthcare experts is explained in the following: The healthcare expert should acquire the access permission from patient to access and update the EHRs of the patient. Then, the sensitive medical information can be added to the existing EHRs of the patient by encrypting them and updating them, respectively. In our PSSEHR system, we employ the option whereby the healthcare expert can add/update the patient's medical information to EHRs and encrypt them and store it in the IPFS using the patient's public key. The transactions resulting from healthcare expert access and EHRs modifications will be hashed and added to the Blockchain using smart contracts to ensure data integrity and trustworthiness.

12.4.3 Self-Sovereign Identity for the Patients

The patient maintains total control and ownership of the medical record by granting/revoking access permissions to the healthcare experts. In the proposed PSSEHR system, we make use of the XML rules to offer access and deny access permission to the Blockchain. Furthermore, the patient can grant/revoke access to EHRs to an authorized user who has been approved by consensus based on their role and permission type granted by the voter nodes. Moreover, the patient can also revoke the granted access to EHRs from a certain healthcare expert, and in that case, the right to view the EHRs might be revoked. For refined and controlled access to medical records in our PSSEHR system, this Blockchain incorporates permission rules based on role-based and rule-based access control methods. During patient request, the Hyperledger composer employs smart contracts to detect patient/healthcare expert's requests, validate patient/healthcare expert's requests, update EHRs and grant/revoke access permissions for their EHRs.

12.4.4 Retrieving the Record

In our PSSEHR system, EHRs can be retrieved by performing a series of valid transactions. The patient begins the process by uploading their public key encrypted medical data to

IPFS. The PSSEHR system provides a composite view to the healthcare experts who has access to the EHR with the help of session key Sk. To ensure more protection, these session key can be further encrypted using health experts public key Hpk. After medical treatment, the healthcare expert can update the existing EHRs by using the session key before saving it in the IPFS. The system in turn informs the patient about their change in the medical record and the system uses the session key to decrypt the updated EHRs. The patient can then accept the changes to their EHRs and encrypt them with their public key, commit the changes and add the modified EHRs to the IPFS. The system employs smart contracts to detect all the above transactions and encrypt it using hashing and upload the modification to the Blockchain to ensure data integrity and auditability.

Clients at each hospital can use our system's web-based application to seek access to the ledger or EHR. In a hospital or clinic, a web-based application is the front-end side application software. A hospital may have one or several peers, depending on their size, whereas a tiny clinic serves as a customer without a peer. Doctors at each hospital are expected to have their ECerts for identifying participants across the system. Web-based applications provide web-based user interfaces and vital interactive functionalities for system participants to communicate with one another. Patients utilize it to produce key pairs, which they use to register and enroll their identities in the system in order to get ECerts. Additionally, they may produce and communicate proxy re-encryption keys to the proxy. The client, on the other hand, utilizes this web-based application to generate a transaction proposal and send it to the Blockchain system for tasks like determining a patient's identification and producing, uploading and exchanging medical records, metadata and so on.

12.5 Security Analysis Using Use Case Scenarios

Some test cases have been investigated in order to confirm the prototype's functional capacity and evaluate its performance. Four case studies are examined in order to evaluate the proposed PSSEHR systems' performance in terms of security, storage performance and efficiency, privacy and scalability.

- Use Case 1: Enhanced Security
- Use Case 2: Efficient Health Records Storage
- Use Case 3: Improved Data Privacy
- Use Case 4: Better Data Scalability

12.5.1 Use Case 1: Enhanced Security

Firstly, the test case is successfully completed since the users' passwords are encrypted before being stored in the CouchDB of the HLF. Secondly, the EHRs are checked by performing encryption/decryption and hashing/verifying the hash values to ensure more level of security. Further, the patients EHR is encrypted/decrypted using their public–private key pair to ensure confidentiality. Further, the use of session key between the patient and the healthcare experts ensures more protection to the patient's EHRs using public key infrastructure and confirmed to be successful. The prototype was also put to the test to see if the session was kept alive, and it was found successful until the current session is kept alive.

12.5.2 Use Case 2: Efficient Health Records Storage

Firstly, the healthcare experts were tested against the updating of patients EHRs with patient's ailments and treatments. The result was found successful with authorized healthcare experts to upload the encrypted record to the decentralized IPFS storage of the HLF. Secondly, the system is checked against the authorized and unauthorized healthcare experts to give the access permission for the patient's EHRs respectively and found positive and negative result as expected. Further, the IPFS storage is also checked for unique identification of each EHRs without any indexing issues. Finally, the encryption/decryption is performed with suitable public–private key and session key to check its proper functioning and found successful.

12.5.3 Use Case 3: Improved Data Privacy

The proposed system makes use of a number of privacy-preserving methods. The role-based Secondly, the system is checked against the authorized and unauthorized healthcare experts to give the access permission for the patient's EHRs respectively and found positive and negative result as expected. and rule-based access control to access the patients EHRs is tested by using flooding visitors to the web application. The authorized visitors may access the application based on their roles, the initial instance is confirmed and successful. Further, the revoke/grant permission to EHRs for healthcare experts were tested and found successful and ensures data privacy and trustworthiness for the patient [11].

12.5.4 Use Case 4: Better Data Scalability

The PSSEHR system is based on a number of concepts that encourage scalability. The proposed system improves the efficiency by employing offline chain method of using IPFS for storing the EHRs and hashing only the address and metadata of the EHRs which greatly improves scalability A record of 500 MB was successfully uploaded to IPFS at a time, demonstrating the system's scalability. The proposed system was tested against the time taken to add/modify the EHRs and found efficient which is discussed in detail in the following section. As a result, it's safe to say that the system can manage a huge dataset with little delay [12].

12.6 Performance Analysis and Discussion

The proposed system successfully passed the security analysis against various use case scenario ensuring confidentiality, data integrity, accessibility, scalability and reliability. The patients can manage their own medical information without risking third-party interventions and trustworthiness. The proposed subsystem employs CouchDB, a Blockchain's state database that stores the patient/healthcare experts request. Patients were able to grant/revoke permissions seamlessly ensuring better security and privacy. Data storage with IPFS and public key cryptographic principles also ensured the data are safeguarded against unauthorized tampering [17].

Several tests have been conducted to analyze and assess the proposed Blockchain system's performance. To test the performance various transactions were carried out: (1) user and healthcare expert register/login, (2) EHR creation, (3) administrator creation, (4) voter creation, (5) consensus, (6) updating EHR, (7) session key generation, (8) public key

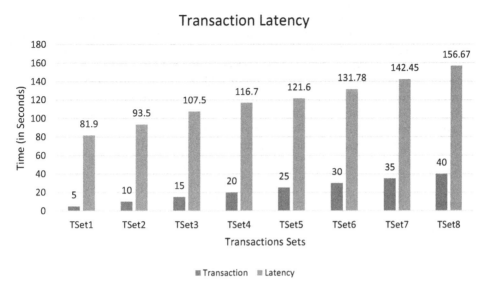

FIGURE 12.5
Transaction latency.

encryption, (9) intimation of EHR update to the user, (10) commit changes to the EHR, (11) grant permission to healthcare expert, (12) revoke permission to healthcare expert. The proposed system transaction latency was computed in the experiment, as shown in Figure 12.5.

The length of time it takes for a transaction to commit and litigate changes across all peer network is known as transaction latency. TL is the transaction latency, TC is the change confirmation time, and TS is the transaction submission time in seconds assuming there are n nodes in the proposed system which is represented in Equation 12.3.

$$TL = TC - TS \qquad (12.3)$$

Figure 12.5 illustrates the eight set of varying transactions discussed above were completed in various transaction sets ranging from 5,10,15,20,25,30,35, and 40 were conducted in the experiment. The first four transactions sets took an average transaction latency of 100 seconds to commit across the entire network of our proposed system whereas the remaining four transaction sets took an average transaction latency of 130 seconds to commit across the entire network. As a result, it is clear that the time it takes to complete transactions rises as the number of peers and transactions grows. As a result, more peers may result in higher latency.

12.7 Conclusion

Lastly, our proposed PSSEHR system can be extended for building global level EHR system. Our proposed system successfully passed the security analysis against various use case scenario ensuring confidentiality, data integrity, accessibility, scalability and reliability.

The patients can manage their own medical information without risking third-party interventions and trustworthiness. The proposed system efficiently stores the patient/healthcare experts request with better transaction latency than the legacy EHR system. Patients were able to grant/revoke permissions seamlessly ensuring better security and privacy. Data storage with IPFS and public key cryptographic principles also ensured the data are safeguarded against unauthorized tampering. We hope that our findings will make it easier for patients to locate their medical records when they visit other hospitals. We want to test our approach in a full –fledged hospital setting in the future and our future focus is on improving the transaction latency and security attacks against IPFS.

References

[1] Kruse CS, Mileski M, Vijaykumar AG, Viswanathan SV, Suskandla U, Chidambaram Y. Impact of electronic health records on long-term care facilities: Systematic review. *JMIR Medical Informatics* 2017; 5(3). https://doi.org/10.2196/medinform.7958

[2] Chenthara S, Ahmed K, Wang H, Whittaker F. Security and privacy-preserving challenges of e-health solutions in cloud computing. *IEEE Access* 2019;7:74361–74382.

[3] Cheng K, Wang L, Shen Y, Wang H, Wang Y, Jiang X, et al. Secure K-NN query on encrypted cloud data with multiple keys. *IEEE Transactions on Big Data* 2017;7(4):689–702. https://doi.org/10.1109/TBDATA.2017.2707552

[4] Li P, Guo S, Miyazaki T, Xie M, Hu J, Zhuang W. Privacy-preserving access to big data in the cloud. *IEEE Cloud Computing* 2016; 3(5):34–42. https://doi.org/10.1109/MCC.2016.107

[5] Masud MAH, Huang X, Islam MR. A novel approach for the security remedial in a cloud-based elearning network. *Journal of Networks* 2014; 9(11):2934.

[6] Nakamota S (2008) Bitcoin: A peer-to-peer electronic cash system, www.bitcoin.org, pp. 1–9. https://doi.org/10.1007/s10838-008-9062-0

[7] Amsden Z et al. (2019) An introduction to Libra, Libra association Facebook Inc., pp. 1–29. https://www.lawinsider.com/clause/see-libra-association-2019-amsden-et-al-2019-catalini-et-al-2019

[8] Chaum D (1984) A new paradigm for individuals in the information age. *IEEE Symposium on Security and Privacy*, Oakland, CA, USA, pp. 99–99. https://doi.org/10.1109/SP.1984.10025

[9] Haber S, Stornetta S. How to time-stamp a digital document. *Journal of Cryptology* 1991; 3(2): 99–111.

[10] Merkle RC. A digital signature based on a conventional encryption function. *Advances in Cryptology — CRYPTO '87 Lecture Notes in Computer Science* 1988; 293, pp. 369–378. https://doi.org/10.1007/3-540-48184-2_32. ISBN 978-3-540-18796-7

[11] Sathya K, Kumar DR. (2012, February). Energy efficient clustering in sensor networks using Cluster Manager. *2012 International Conference on Computing, Communication and Applications. 2012 International Conference on Computing, Communication and Applications (ICCCA).*

[12] Zhang E, Li M, Yiu SM, Du J, Zhu JZ, Jin GG. Fair hierarchical secret sharing scheme based on smartcontract. *Information Sciences* 2021; 546:166–176. https://doi.org/10.1016/j.ins.2020.07.032

[13] Androulaki E, Barger A, Bortnikov V, Cachin C, Christidis K, De Caro A, et al. (2018). Hyperledger fabric: A distributed operating system for permissioned blockchains. *Proceedings of the Thirteenth EuroSys Conference. ACM.* p. 30.

[14] Xu X, Weber I, Staples M, Zhu L, Bosch J, Bass L, et al. (2017 April 3–7). A taxonomy of blockchain-based systems for architecture design. *Proceedings of 2017 IEEE International Conference on Software Architecture (ICSA)*; Gothenburg, Sweden. pp. 243–252.

[15] Sousa J, Bessani A, Vukolic M (2018 June 25–28). A byzantine fault-tolerant ordering service for the hyperledger fabric blockchain platform. *Proceedings of the 48th Annual IEEE/IFIP International Conference on Dependable Systems and Networks (DSN)*; Luxembourg City, Luxembourg, pp. 51–58.

[16] Androulaki E, Barger A, Bortnikov V, Cachin C, Christidis K, De Caro A, et al. (2018 April 23–26). Hyperledger fabric: A distributed operating system for permissioned blockchains. *Proceedings of the 13th EuroSys Conference*; Porto, Portugal.

[17] Sathish R, Kumar DR. (2013, March). Proficient algorithms for replication attack detection in wireless sensor networks—A survey. In *2013 IEEE International Conference ON Emerging Trends in Computing, Communication and Nanotechnology (ICECCN)*, pp. 1–7. IEEE.

[18] Arvindhan M, Rajesh Kumar D (2022). Analysis of load balancing detection methods using hidden markov model for secured cloud computing environment. In: Deepak, B.B.V.L., Parhi, D., Biswal, B., Jena, P.C. (eds) *Applications of Computational Methods in Manufacturing and Product Design. Lecture Notes in Mechanical Engineering*. Springer, Singapore. https://doi.org/10.1007/978-981-19-0296-3_53

[19] Kuo TT, Kim HE, Ohno-Machado L. Blockchain distributedledger technologies for biomedical and health care applications. *Journal of the American Medical Informatics Association* 2017; 24(6): 1211–20.

[20] Maiti S, Misra S. P2B: Privacy preserving identity-based broadcast proxy re-encryption *IEEE Transactions on Vehicular Technology* May 2020; 69(5), pp. 5610–5617. https://doi.org/10.1109/TVT.2020.2982422

13

An Innovative Outcome of Internet of Things and Artificial Intelligence in Remote Centered Healthcare Application Schemes

Lalitha Krishnasamy
Kongu Engineering College, Erode, India

A. Tamilselvi
Chennai Institute of Technology, Chennai, India

Rajesh Kumar Dhanaraj
Galgotias University, Greater Noida, India

CONTENTS

DOI: 10.1201/9781003217435-13

13.1 Introduction

The world's population is increasing at an exponential rate, particularly in urban areas, where the larger the population, the greater the strain. Despite the fact that medical services and facilities are available in urban areas, and the number of such resources and facilities is growing every day, even though the adequacy level has not yet reached as expected, making the Government to struggle in all the ways. Health care in urban cities has improved as a result of better technology that are accompanied with the appropriate answers to the issues. It marks a new step in the evolution of e-health, with a variety of different sensors being added to provide a new way of monitoring system for the treatment of a variety of illnesses. The Raspberry pi ARM11 (BCM2837) is being used in the experiments, and this device is continuously creating a multidimensional way of attention in the treatment of different illnesses such as cardiac seizures, diabetes, and fever. [1] A constant signal is being recorded by the sensor, and they are then linked to the required communication through physical parameters, with wireless data received from the network being saved, processed, and analyzed to update and improve the quality of current health records. A physician can provide an accurate diagnosis for first aid advice based on accessible data records and decision support systems. If physicians are not available, today's devices can anticipate health issues, allowing for better first aid advice. According to the database's system, we can not only anticipate the arrival of new medications and medical equipment, but also monitor the impact of modern technology on the quality of life and health of all those who make a difference in the world. As a result, the cost per step towards a more precise prediction of the illness is reduced in the healthcare industry.

This article provides patients with an introduction to a financial model for technical services and invites them to consider philosophical issues. The actual medical sector [1] presents a significant barrier in terms of Internet of Things (IoT) implementation. The lives of Lorem's students have a variety of safety-enhancing impacts, and by lowering medical expenses, it contributes to that step as well as substantially improving the accuracy of predictive disease prediction. As shown in this paper [2], a technology sector, economic concerns for sick patient wellbeing, and open space difficulties when applying the IoT system in the actual world of common health care [3] are all discussed.

The following is a concise summary of the document's primary purpose:

- The IoT may be used to gather medical information about a patient.
- Conducting an analysis of the information gathered about the patient.

- Data mining will begin with particular data on sickness or disease, which will be used to define and define illness or disease, allowing for more effective decision-making.
- Making healthcare choices based on the IoT at any time and from any location.

13.2 Machine Learning Applications

Manufacturing, transportation, and governance have all been transformed by algorithmic learning and deep learning systems [3, 4] and machine learning [5, 6] in general. Over the last several years, DL has outgrown its current location in the state. Art is developing across a wide range of disciplines, including computer visualization, text analysis, and word processing, among others. ML/DL algorithms are being used extensively in this project. The sector (e.g., social media) has evolved into a technology that is amazing in comparison to our everyday life. The ML/DL calculating technique is currently being used in health care, which is beginning to have an effect. Large-scale technology has historically been a hindrance to the development of diseases. [4] The performance of ML/DL technology has been excellent. In a recent range of activities, and other relevant fields of research, significant progress has been achieved. Smart software helps Radiologists and doctors who will be assessing patients in the near future in the fields of pneumonia, lung cancer therapy and diagnosis, image reconstruction, and also brain tumor sections, to name a few. Figure 13.1 shows the machine learning clinical overflow.

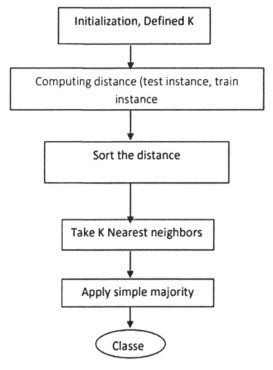

FIGURE 13.1
Machine learning clinical overflow.

In the current years, clinical care is one of the promising application fields for machine learning/deep learning models, and such models have already been developed. The technology has progressed to the level of human physicians in clinical pathology and radiation therapy as well as eye and skin disorders [5]. There are some advanced synchronization technologies like big data analytics, mobile computing, cloud, or edge computing are used to benefit from the expertise in machine learning models in healthcare applications that the company has. In addition to the technology and machine learning/deep learning, they provide excellent accuracy. Contributes to the evaluation of outcomes and intellectual solutions that are based on people. Additionally, it has a number of additional advantages, which include activation of the medical services in rural and low-income regions, and it contributes significantly to the modernization of healthcare technology [4, 5].

13.3 Related Works

Various researchers in the different field have suggested different models for the IoT in healthcare, in addition to predicting the various kinds of illnesses by using diverse methods. This section mainly focuses on the work that has been implemented and applied in the field.

Incorporate a mechanism for detecting physiological signs, such as an electrocardiograph (ECG), in the sitting area. Ballistocardiogram (BCG) employs a smart chair that constantly recognizes the same person. By providing classics, bio signals and a monitoring system may be utilized in the same manner that they were originally designed.

Almutairi and colleagues have suggested the M-Health system in which he used to gather the patients' real-time data from their mobile devices and store them to the network servers with Internet facility, which only allowed certain clients to view the data he collected. This data may be utilized since it is produced and obtained via the use of medical diagnostic of patients. A network of portable gadgets and body sensors that communicate with one another [1].

Berger and colleagues' Sensors for smart houses were used in the construction of the building. Hockey and its prototypes are also being tested by a network that monitors and tracks the movements of patients. The primary goal of their job is to test their system's behavioral patterns and determine whether or not they are capable of subduing and discussing the same thing in their work.

Chiuchisan and colleagues suggested a framework to prevent this problem. When an intelligent intensive care system threatens patients, the patient's family and physicians express their concerns about the technology. A person's health or bodily motions are incompatible with the environment in which they live.

Dwivedi and colleagues establish an organizational foundation for reassuring Clinical information must be supplied over the Internet in order for the EPR (electronic patient Internet) system to function properly. Developing a multi-level health information system is being proposed. Opportunity is a universal key combination that may be used everywhere. Infrastructure, smart cards, and biometric technologies are all being developed. Gupta, and so forth.

Gupta and colleagues proposed a model for model measuring and recording. The use of an ECG as well as other significant symptoms of the patient Raspberry pie is a delicious dessert that may be served to patients and their families in hospitals and other settings. Gupta, and so forth.

Intel has developed a technique that makes use of Galileo. There are different data and loads included in this development chart. Databases that doctors are able to and do use Patient's delivery discomfort should be minimized when they arrive at the hospital, and their health indicators should be checked on a regular basis [6, 7].

Magarelli and Rao developed a novel technique for determining the severity of the illness in a patient's medical record, which they believe is more accurate. These findings were reached via the use of a statistical technique based on the mining of disease probability threshold as well as to meet us. Essentially, their aim is to improve upon the 0 algorithm. Websites must be able to bear the weight of their own hyperlinks.

Sahoo et al. [10] investigated the healthcare system and a huge amount of patient details from a variety of reports in their study. They gained a better understanding of health attitudes in order to forecast the patient's or future health status. They make use of the voluminous of data from the cloud. There are certainly more methods to make advantage of the same analytics platform.

Taigi and colleagues investigated IoT health and its significance in society. Because he was unable to physically distinguish her from a fake, genuine option recommended cloud care. If we get authorization, we may transmit medical data with precise and reduced size in a safe and secure manner. Create a network of support for the patient and his or her family. Patients, hospitals, physicians, labs, and so forth are all included. In other words, the patient is responsible for the clinic for one month. Drug deficiency elimination and distribution are two important goals. Increase the safety and convenience of patients [9].

13.4 Background

The IoT platform was recently created for the healthcare system, with Wang and his colleagues for developing web apps that are compatible with particular medical equipment. Data retrieval based on data quality and communication quality Unified Design Methods for the Internet of Things (UDA-IoT) [2]. Information is the foundation of medical applications [13]. It is built on top of peer-to-peer (P2P) frameworks and IoT-enabled technologies for treatment in order to keep patients within the monitoring system's reach. AI syndrome provides test results for various scenarios on Real Web Communication, which were conducted by Kahiki et al. In the first instance, pay attention to dependable data performance. Using the sphygmomanometer, activate the Bluetooth switch on your phone. Systolic blood pressure (SBP), diastolic blood pressure (DBP), and influenza were all stored in SBP, an Android application intended to note such data. This makes it easier to transmit the information that has been saved by the application. It is possible to store mobile devices and information, as well as record conflicts and send messages to the general public.

When it comes to real-world applications, the major problem faced are real time architecture that supports all the ends. Portable electronic devices are used to build a customized gadget for the blind, ultra-devices are connected to the seat, and Bluetooth headphones are used to monitor the difficulties that users encounter while driving and out of sight. Another sensor for the blind [18] offers a complete communication system that gives the user with accuracy and readiness for the glove's long-term usefulness while being cost-effective. To overcome these restrictions, this paper offers a hypothetical cloud infrastructure system that may be utilized in different health-care systems under Internet-based circumstances [8].

13.5 Collection and Transmission of Information

The patient will be provided with disposable sensors. Sensors nowadays are made of leather and can be readily put in various areas of the body, making it easier to take accurate measurements. Physiological data is gathered through sensors implanted in the bodies of patients, and this data contains a variety of physiological characteristics. Then a tiny gadget is capable of being used for collecting this data and will be sent using the communication softwares [10]. Sensors are expected to be compact and lightweight so that they do not restrict with patient's ability to move and move freely. These sensors should be powered by tiny, low-energy batteries to save energy. The sensors should be able to operate constantly without the need for shipping and recharging. You should be able to transmit patient data from an accurate and secure location inside the health facility if the system components responsible for transmission are in place as shown in Figure 13.2. Bluetooth may be used for transmission purposes. Additionally, the information may be obtained by visiting the online health center and completing the collecting form [11].

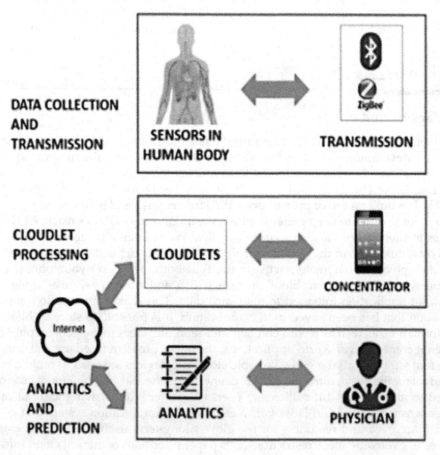

FIGURE 13.2
Data collection and transmission.

13.6 Record Establishment to Do Disease Diagnosis

To establish a patient record for disease diagnosis, certain processes need to be followed. The stages are as follows: Data collection and storage of sensor readings, analysis of cloud and stored data, and the current Cloud Health Checkup situation. Insanity is often characterized by unexplained activity in the body.

The frequency of seizures in the brain increases. Heart rate sensors may be used to monitor the rate of the heartbeat and the rhythm of the heart. Everyone experiences a heart attack, and its severity can be determined instantly. View the findings of the Raspberry Pi, the storage is expensive using the sensor interface. Also available is an appropriate screen or LCD display interface that may be utilized to access the value. Because of the sheer volume of big data, all of the information get gathered and the data has been sent to the cloud. Figure 13.3 explains the diagnosis that takes place in machine learning for health care.

Supports a number of open-source services and cloud platforms, including the Raspberry Pi and also Raspbian Jessi operating systems. When the platform is an open source, data gets uploaded to cloud storage by capturing the physical location of the data source.

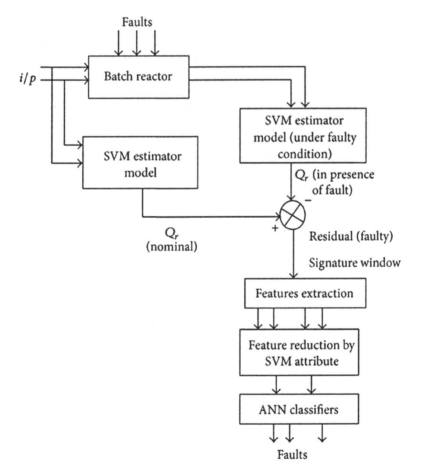

FIGURE 13.3
Machine learning diagnosing for health care.

Because any disruption is produced by habit, any accumulated values are subjected to scrutiny. The technique of machine learning computation and the values collected in a cloud are summarized for further investigation.

This system must be taught using model value prediction until it is accurate, which implies that large amounts of data must be used in the training process. The greater the amount of data used in training, the greater the accuracy. There should be training data collected from a large number of individuals in a variety of situations [10]. Furthermore, the database must include information that has been gathered and is required from individuals of all ages. People inherit both good and harmful data.

13.7 System Architecture

If you want to reintegrate your current wireless sensor in your condition monitoring system, you must improve your network (WSN). In the future, health centers will get more bodily information depending on the relative distance between sensors, which will allow them to avoid needless labor for a longer period of time. When concentrating on low-power usage, the following criterion should be established: How to cope with crises [6]. Other sensors may be activated at the same time in order to prolong the life of the dough. Because of low energy usage, there is a strong demand. Low-power communication protocol is a kind of wireless communication protocol. In comparison to IEEE 802.15.4, Chigby is accomplished via the use of a network connection, which increases battery life and extends battery life than Zigbee. The low-power consumption of an Energy Emission for Short Range Communication (PLE) connection is another kind of wireless connection that is very desired. Suitable for those with particular requirements programs such as health monitoring, home recreation, and sports are examples of this. For a lengthy period of time, you can put components using BLES jump, but this requires a significant amount of energy. In terms of the amount of bytes transmitted per ounce, this is a very tiny figure. The Raspberry Pi health care monitoring architecture is given in Figure 13.4. Leather has a lot of energy [12]. Furthermore, the protocol is a low-power wireless protocol. There is also access to the private portion of the network (6 lupine). Examples of connections of energy-emitting devices as specified by the WPAN Internet protocol suite [21].

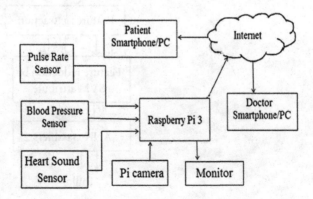

FIGURE 13.4
Raspberry Pi healthcare monitor architecture.

13.8 Cloudlet Processing

Smart phones are becoming more popular due to the enhanced capabilities that are accessible via LTE Wi-Fi. Smartphones with sensing systems, such as this one, are possible. Cloud storage would be adequate if the data gathered by concentration were kept indefinitely. When physicians need to access or evaluate claims in internal storage processing but do not have sufficient local resources to fulfil their requirements, this is a helpful tool. Patients will be able to complete medical records in a timely way as a result of this. When data is saved, Cloudlet offers access to data analytics 24×7 in a week. Improve the quality of your diagnostic information. Because health applications are often included in the Sun fly data, it is suggested that a cloud data system is a preferable option. Concentration and the presence of clouds are permitted. Finally, data collected from various devices are kept within the cloud's safe storage, and access to dispersed data might be possible via a decreased Wi-Fi interface, which is one of the main causes of data transfer delays in data set applications [22, 23].

There is nothing more to consider except the patient's present and anticipated state of health. When medical records are kept in the cloud, it is critical to safeguard the electronic patient information. Using proper privacy settings, you can prevent unwanted access to your data. You should also take precautions while moving data from an offline to an offline cloud. The cloud storage framework was safely implemented in order to cope with sensitive medical information; as a result, significant changes have happened in the creation, usage, storage, and interchange of medical data. The medical sector has improved its data management methods over the years, transitioning from traditional storage to digitalization of medical data [15].

13.8.1 Cloud Computing in Healthcare

The creation, use, storage, and interchange of medical data have all seen significant transformations in recent years. The medical sector has been improved a lot in terms of data management methods, having progressed from conventional storage to the digitalization of medical data.

The medical sector serves as an example for the application of cloud computing technologies in industries that have traditionally been more advanced than the contemporary era. Approximately 35 percent of healthcare businesses and more than 50 percent of data or cloud infrastructure companies took part in the study, according to a research by West Monroe Research. When compared to other sectors, the healthcare sector has proved to be far behind the times [11].

The extensive usage of cloud computing applied in the healthcare area extends beyond the data architecture's cloud storage to include a variety of other services. In order to simplify the impact, decrease healthcare expenses, and modify health programmed in order to enhance this result, healthcare professionals use this technology.

This article discusses how cloud computing is changing the medical sector. There are two benefits to moving to the cloud. It has widely proved that it is beneficial to both the medical personnel and patients. Cloud computing model is advantageous in the corporate world, because it allows suppliers to offer high-quality, customized assistance while also lowering operational expenses. Patients who are more reliant on immediate services get the same benefits from the healthcare industry. Patients' engagement with their healthcare plans is improved by the cloud [13, 14]. The utilization of medical data with the availability of remote access to this data liberates clinicians and patients while also removing obstacles to accessing treatment. Here's how cloud consulting can have an impact on the healthcare industry.

13.8.1.1 Cost Reduction

The heart of the cloud computing idea includes processing power in addition to the memory storage. Hospitals and healthcare providers are no longer required to purchase equipment and servers on their own behalf [16]. When it comes to cloud storage, there are no upfront fees to pay. The fact that you only pay for the resources that you really utilize results in significant cost savings. The expectations for company growth are shown in Figure 13.5.

Price for cloud computing units is often determined based on resource consumption, which means that you are paid based on the data storage amount and collected by the cloud service provider and, in certain cases, entered into the cloud service provider's system. A few stocks, such as Google Big Query, are available on a "all you can eat" basis, which means they do not limit the number of resources or time you can spend managing a job. When dealing with pricing model like this, it is essential to adhere to certain best practices, for example, avoiding the raw data processing, limiting the number of expensive operations, such as connections, to a bare minimum whenever possible, in order to maximize profitability. Using cloud storage to store company data and distribute the same to a voluminous of consumers is shown in Figure 13.6 and it is made feasible by adhering to a set of best practices [18], which allows the organization to make better-informed decisions.

13.8.1.2 Facilitating the Interaction

Interoperability is the goal of establishing the integration of data into the health system, regardless of where it comes from or where it is stored. Patients and information to assist in the planning and delivery of healthcare services are readily available as a result of the interoperability that has resulted in cloud usage [15].

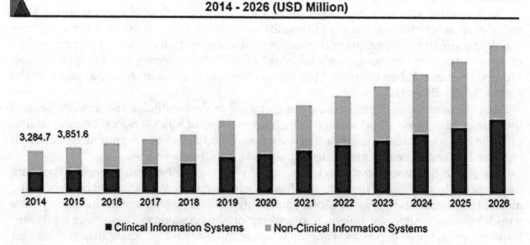

FIGURE 13.5
Revenue growth chart.

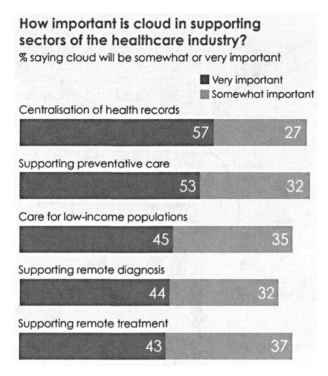

FIGURE 13.6
Adopting the cloud computing for health care.

In the healthcare industry, cloud computing makes clinicians to quickly collect patient data from various sources, share the data with key partners, and deliver prescriptions and also treatment regimens in a timely way. Because of this, experts are no longer need to travel long distances in order to evaluate situations and offer their views, independent of geographical limitations [19]. Cloud-based patient data storage facilitates interoperability across various sectors of the medical business, such as medicines, insurance, and payments, amongst others. This enables you to easily transmit data across various partners, thus increasing the speed of healthcare delivery mechanism and improving the overall process efficiency [20].

13.8.1.3 Access to Performance Analysis

Health data, both organized and unstructured, is a tremendous resource. Patient data from a variety of sources may be incorporated into the cloud to make it more relevant. Medical research will benefit from the use of big data and artificial intelligence analytical techniques to cloud-based patient information as like given in Figure 13.7. The processing of big data volumes is becoming more feasible as cloud computing capabilities become more sophisticated [14].

The examination of patient analytical data will result in the development of numerous individual patient care plans at the individual level of the patient population. This ensures that all of the patient's information are captured and that nothing is overlooked when prescribing medication. Excludes pertinent patient information from the database.

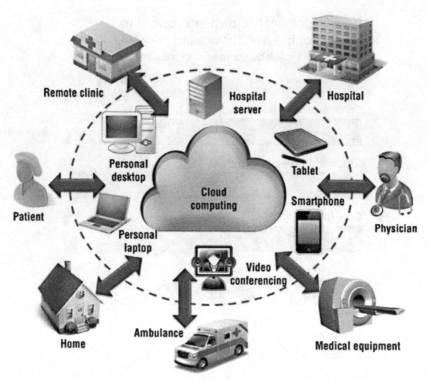

FIGURE 13.7
Cloudlet flowchart.

13.9 Proposed Methodology

In this work, we are admitted to a government hospital since there are no physicians accessible at all times to regulate blood sugar, blood pressure, heartbeat, and heat transmission to the body, as is the case in many other countries. A number of medicines are expected to be delivered using the technology developed by the team at work. It is possible to monitor different kinds of fever by measuring blood pressure, stress, and heart rate. To assess these limits, four different kinds of sensors are utilized: A blood glucose sensor, a high blood pressure sensor, a heart rate sensor, and a heat exchanger. They are all linked to a single module [21], which contains all of the sensors. ARM11 gene determines whether the patient is recognized by the recipient and processed at the time the patient opens their profile after receiving the microprocessor. It then begins to communicate with the patient via speaker and teaches them how to use medical equipment, as well as providing a video demonstration.

If the connection to the server is successful, disease management hub (DMH) will provide the unique microprocessor code that will be used for all subsequent connections around the stage. This standard is specifically designed to meet the clinical requirements of patients. For starters, the microprocessor goes via the visual system shown in Figure 13.5 to process the application. Among the sensors used in this study are four kinds of blood sugar, blood pressure, heart rate, and ARM11 speaker interfaces, as well as four types of sensors such as blood pressure sensors. Each sensor is utilized to track the movement of various bodily components. The camera is used to improve the look of patients or to build a face from scratch with the help of a computer. The speaker is used to reply to a law enforcement officer and to make a referral to the Department of Mental Health. Be cautious while watching videos or following medical advice [12]. MCP3008 is a technology used in analogue converters that allows for the usage of digital contrast sensors in conjunction with them. DMH is a device that transmits information from diabetics to a microprocessor that is connected to the Internet. The heart sensor, the blood pressure sensor, the blood glucose sensor, and the temperature sensor are the four kinds of sensors utilized in this study. It is these sensors that are linked to the Raspberry Pi ARM11 (BCM 2837) processing unit.

The employee is in charge of a wide range of responsibilities. Toto, the pressure sensor monitors the amount of the fluid in the body and transmits the information to the computer. When blood sugar levels are elevated, heart and healing heart temperatures are raised to high levels, and the results are sent to the client. All of the prices are determined in accordance with the sensors. Using the MCP3008, you may transform computed values received from the sensor into discrete numbers and transmit them to the channel manufacturers in any application where you utilize it. The image sensor and door settings for the pump have already been established. A connection between the Equipment Section and a program that provides a set of services between a physician and a patient may be established. They are a group of people developing a high-quality tool is essential in the management of various illnesses, which is referred to as sickness Site Management (DMH).

It uses the IoT idea to offer a distinct IP address when creating a patient database page. It is possible for patients to register with an IP address information in order to monitor their reading levels as directed by their physician. The last stage, in comparison, is to produce readings and transmit them to the patient's location through a Wi-Fi module. The Figure 13.8 depicts the proposed technology of adding sensors to extract the information from the surrounding.

In this case, the camera is linked to the equipment that is responsible for registering the patient's face or adding facial information to the statement. When it occurs, a comparison between the stored face and an existing face is performed. If a patient's face information is accessible, the picture opens a window with the patient's information [18]. It may be used to keep track of a patient's information. If no information is given, a column will display for them to enter their information, as if they were a brand new machine. A patient is diagnosed and the employee starts to interact with them as well as other members of the team. Monitoring is used to keep track of and engage with the illness on the site [24].

The staff ensures that all patients' health records are up to current with the doctor in the cervix. This is also accomplished via the WIFI module. The doctor is monitoring the information of all patients from any location and at any time, as well as the DMH value to be sent to medical and Ethernet. Another procedure has been developed for the physician to use in order to diagnose the patient information and deliver a gift to the patient. Allow the doctor to record their information so that he or she may establish a login ID and password for future usage on their behalf. Through the use of this login ID and password, the doctor gets access to the site. A source of protection [3] is provided by it. Recipe may be recommended to you by your doctor in either oral or written form. The audio input is received by the doctor via one of the microphones, and the patient hears it through the other microphone and speakers. In addition, the patient receives his or her own Health Cards and recipes through e-mail or SMS text message. They either listen to the doctor's advice or see the prescription on a monitor in front of them. This is how patients benefit themselves by getting their health care without depending on a nurse or other professional, and they can do it properly on their own recordings [9].

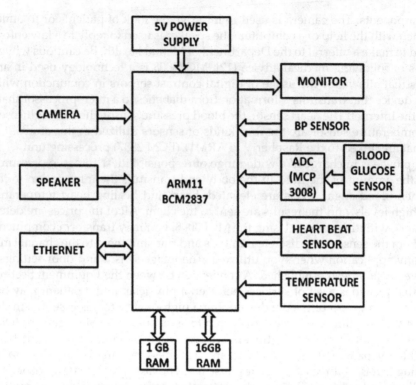

FIGURE 13.8
Proposed technology.

13.9.1 System Modules

1) Healthcare Monitoring Section
2) Emergency Alert and Notification Section
3) Health Status Predictor

13.9.1.1 Healthcare Monitoring Section

The IoT may be seen of as a continuous source of Car Internet Serving for the general public. Mobile phones are used to access the Internet [17]. Diverse sensors and sensors with different purposes are available [18]. With new technological developments, the IoT is having a significant effect on the system of health care. In addition, there is health care. Improve your health by learning about yourself, getting a diagnosis, and getting treatment. Protect you against sickness, disease, and the physical and psychological damage that people may do to one another. It has a positive impact on a large portion of the national economy. A combination of limited communication resources and the necessity of performance improvement has resulted in this situation. It is seen as an emergency situation rather than a support device.

13.9.1.2 Emergency Alert and Notification Section

A healthcare facility is a critical component of medicine, because it influences the time, availability, and precision of medical treatment. In addition, the requirement for success is dependent on the quality of the information gathered during the emergency call as well as the quality and accuracy of the information gathered during an emergency response situation. Information collected during two stages of ambulance monitoring is equally critical to the effectiveness of ambulance monitoring: emergency calls and transport. The majority of the information received during an emergency call is inaccurate, and the process of collecting, storing, processing, and retrieving information during an emergency call is completed in a reasonable amount of time [9]. Patients' medical records are often ignored by emergency room doctors, who instead depend on information obtained from the patient or their siblings. Patients rather than informed patients are the target audience for ambulance services, as a result. In medical applications, the network and wireless body technology (EOT) can gather accurate data because of their ability to transmit data wirelessly. This chapter discusses the difficulties associated with delivering emergency treatment, particularly in poor nations. A patient-centered information platform for the delivery of patient-centered information services is described and discussed. The majority of the research is focused on road accidents. The findings of the tests that were conducted are described in Table 13.1.

13.9.1.3 Health Status Predictor

Predictions may be made not just in the field of health care, but also in the broader community. Predicting the future is essential for achieving success in a variety of fields, from weather predictions to stock market outcomes as shown in Figure 13.9. Prediction techniques, on the other hand, are critical in a clinical context because they have the potential to save lives. Researchers may investigate the predictive qualities of specific biomarkers and

TABLE 13.1

Threshold Values

COMPONENT	BLOOD RANGE
Blood pressure	80–120 mm hg
Body temperature	36–37.5°C
Heart rate	60–100 beats/minute

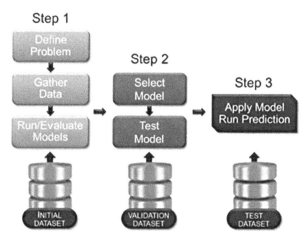

FIGURE 13.9
Healthcare prediction model.

patient features by using reliable prediction and prediction techniques, which will allow them to anticipate a wide range of clinical outcomes in the future (e.g., reprints, bed rest, patients illness risk, and so on). As a result, it should come as no surprise that forecasting health outcomes are essential not just for patients and their families but also for healthcare professionals and policymakers.

13.10 Implementation

The IoT is a computer process in which each physical item is outfitted with a sensor, microcontroller, and transmitter that communicate with one another, and it is constructed utilizing a protocol stack to accomplish this task. Communicate with one another as well as with your consumers. Multiple dispersed devices gather, analyze, and transmit medical data on the cloud in Internet-based health care, enabling a huge quantity of data to be collected, saved, and analyzed in a variety of different formats and by triggering contextual disruptions. Through the use of the Innovative Information Finding Model, anybody may get continuous and complete access to medical information from any location through the Internet. As a result of the limited battery life of all Internet-connected gadgets, the energy used to improve your health system is low.

This article describes the implementation of the Internet health system in hospitals, which makes use of the ZigBee mesh protocol to communicate. It is possible to check on the pathological parameters of hospitalized patients on a frequent basis throughout the deployment of the health system. For example, expert equipment that is subjected to frequent monitoring enhances the quality of maintenance and lowers the cost of maintenance while also actively participating in data gathering and analysis. Raspberry Pi is written in Python, and it communicates with a server on the Internet in order to gather health information. Patient identity and health status are required to access the information online. The software makes use of a variety of components:

13.10.1 Raspberry Pi

The IoT may be used to monitor health-related restrictions. According to this study, a patented method used to monitor stroke, body temperature, lung function, hypertension, and ECG is one of the most essential online criteria for training, and the Raspberry Pi is one of the most important [6].

13.10.2 Temperature Sensor

Using an electronic instrument to measure the natural environment and send precise information into computer records, temperature may be recorded, monitored, or sent to keep track of changes in temperature [6]. Heat exchangers are available in a variety of configurations. Infrared sensors are often used as heat transfer sensors.

13.10.3 Heartbeat Sensor

During the manual setup, the heart rate sensor is intended to extract the heart rate output and store it for later use. Whenever the pressure detector is activated, the continuous LED strap within does not change color in response to each pressure beat that occurs. This output is directly linked to the CPU, allowing it to measure the value of Beats per Minute (BPM). It works on the premise that light emitted by the blood flowing through the fingers of each person is utilized to illuminate the room [18].

13.10.4 Vibration Sensor

In the field of engineering, accelerometers are instruments that detect vibration or accelerate the structural structure of a structure. They are equipped with a transducer, which transforms mechanical power produced by vibrations or changes in electric current into electrical power, which is then transmitted [18].

13.10.5 BP Sensor

The cuff is inflated across the upper arm or wrist as a result of the oscillation stress. A significant amount of blood flows through the vein due to the damage done to the cuff during systolic pressure, which causes noticeable vibrations in the vein wall when lower pressure is applied to it.

13.10.6 Analog-to-Digital Converter

When an analogue scale (constant voltage) is converted into distinct digital values, the ADC is referred to as an analog-to-digital converter (ADC). This is particularly helpful when you need to analyze body sizes that are typically comparable across the board in natural settings. The ADC module incorporates the majority of PIC microcontrollers.

13.10.7 Global System for Mobile Communications Module

Global System for Mobile Communications (GSM) is a standard created by the European Telecommunications Standards Institute (ETSI), which was initially the group's specialist interface (ETSI). It was created to describe the second-generation (2G) digital cellular network protocols used by mobile phones, and it has since become the global default standard for mobile communications, accounting for more than 90 percent of the global market and operating in more than 219 countries and territories [6].

13.10.8 Camera Specifications

These papers detail the specifications of the product in order to guarantee that it is designed to meet the needs of the consumers. An extra camera for a USB class camera with a video function intended for laptop imaging, the AH5020B23-S1-2Z1 is an addition to the AH5020B23-S1-2Z1. CMOS sensor, lens, holder, support, printed circuit board (PCB), image processing channels, and an interface with access to digital video devices are the components that make up the system. It will be a trustworthy device that is integrated into a laptop and will transmit video data through the USB connection to the computer. Through the USB 2.0 interface, the AH5020B23-S1-2Z1 not only offers UXGA resolution (1600 × 1200) for still image creation applications, but it also provides a video stream for the end user to preview/record a movie. In YUY2 mode, it is capable of supporting VGA resolution (640 × 480) at up to 30 frames per second. The AH5020B23-S1 2Z1 is responsible for the construction of AE, AWB, and AGC for auto image management supported by

CMOS sensors. In addition to providing standard UVC UI (user interface) to make the end user excellent thin picture by ownership page, it also offers image quality control.

13.11 ML for Health Care: The Challenges

In this part, we examine the different difficulties that may emerge from the use of machine learning and deep learning systems in real-world healthcare applications.

13.11.1 The Safety Challenge

A great deal of renown in a controlled laboratory setting (which is standard practice in the ML community) is not evidence of salvation. ML/DL is a protected trademark. Determine the level of patient safety provided by the ML/DL system. To determine the level of patient safety provided by the ML/DL system, there should be continuous consideration of salvation everywhere with DL Lifecycle and the majority of regular doctor work dependent on this. It was previously common for millions of individuals to practice for the identification of uncommon, delicate, and concealed health problems, and it is still common today. If this option is enabled in order to guarantee the security of current artificial intelligence systems, coatings, external layers, edges, and subtle casing are required.

13.11.2 Personal Obstacles to Overcome

Privacy is a significant issue in the context of data-driven health. ML/DL system for Predictive Users (i.e., patients) expected healthcare service providers to adhere to the appropriate security measures in order to protect their private rights, such as their age, gender, and date of birth, as well as their personal health information. There are two kinds of potential privacy concerns, both of which must be disclosed. Make use of harmful information as well as private information (possibly by an unauthorized agent). Your level of privacy is determined by your characteristics and nature. Data was gathered, an environment was established, and patient demographics were analyzed. As a result, personal privacy is jeopardized. The use of the relevant technique (or tactic (s)) was condemned as a result. Patients may be harmed as a result of direct breaches. Information that should not be shared in order to avoid infringement and also personal information should be kept anonymous [10]. Individual identity is required. Additional to that, it is important to recognize and address privacy issues in this context. Data should be sent at the beginning of, and at each step of, data processing. A secure atmosphere for communication between different departments inside a hospital is essential.

13.11.3 Ethical Issues to Consider

As we move away from users in machine learning applications, much as we do in health care, it is more essential than ever to guarantee that ethics are followed. There must be clear measures made to understand this target group of consumers, and socio-economic factors make this feasible. Collect data in order to build an ML model. Additionally, be aware of how data gathering may be detrimental to a patient's health. In this case, respect for one's dignity is essential. Otherwise, if this is not taken into consideration, then the ML application will fail. The implications of using real-world situations will be severe. Except for the fact that operating system ethics are automatically provided in a reasonable manner, it is essential to have a thorough understanding of the VI system since the situation is confusing and difficult.

Reason to comprehend the difficulty is a good one. Health care is essential since it is the most important thing in the world. Problems require deductive reasoning, for example, "If so?" Until, for example, you could inquire as to what would happen if a doctor performed anything. Drugs are not substituted for the letter b. This is a problem that affects the whole country. Classical learning method that does not operate via it to respond; instead, they must examine lens data in order to answer. In the field of healthcare, learning is often dependent on experience. Inquire about practical issues using information and persuasive techniques. Data that is difficult to work with is a difficulty Model of construction reasons. There is no fundamental theory behind the DL model, and it is mostly exploited and linked connections are formed without regard for their functional relationship. For the most part, being a human cannot be regarded a limitation, and there are no prerequisites for making accurate predictions. In the field of prophetic health care, the lack of cause-and-effect connections may raise concerns about the validity of the conclusions derived from the findings of the DL Model. Furthermore, justice will be able to make better judgments since the cause will be applied via the prism of logic. To guarantee that the forecast is fair, it is necessary to estimate the efficacy of various factors like Output quality (e.g., Target class in multi-class classification) and other issues [18].

13.12 Conclusion

In order for specialists and physicians to build on this knowledge and draw fast and positive conclusions for patients, the suggested scheme has as its primary goal the provision of higher connected economic health services to patients via the deployment of the information cloud. The final model is loaded with the features that the doctor is searching for in a patient, regardless of where they are or when they are seen. So the appropriate expert would act against the healthcare victim in the clinic as linked economic assistance to ill nations, resulting in decreased hospital lines and direct consultation with doctors, which minimizes contextual dependency and allows for full use of the website in its entirety. The core strategic goal is to offer patients with a high-quality financial life connected with its services via a cloud of information on the network, which includes specialists, as part of its central strategic plan. Using this information, doctors may offer a patient with a fast and cost-effective solution that meets their needs. The final model is packed with choices that allow the doctor to test the patient from any location and at any time of day or night. Consequently, the IoT for traumatic health care would function as an economic advantage for ill individuals who wish to cross borders in hospitals and have direct consultations with physicians, while reducing the consistency of their family. This proposed solution would be cost-effective in terms of excellent health management in public hospitals since it would make full use of a web-based application.

13.13 Future Work

Reproduction has the potential to enhance even more aspects of the artificial intelligence system than it already has. Doctors and patients are in the same boat. Information gleaned from a person's medical history, the majority of patients have parameters and outcomes that are suitable. Data mining is used to look for templates all of the time, as well as for systemic connections in illness. The effects of changing the patient's health parameters may be anticipated using a model that is comparable to prior patients in the database, for example. If there is a pattern like this, we will be able to identify it quickly and it will be simple for physicians to recognize it. Medical experts have devised a method of resolving this dilemma.

References

[1] H. T. Sullivan, S. Sahasrabudhe. Envisioning inclusive futures: Technology-based assistive sensory and action substitution. *Futures* 87, 140–148, 2017.

[2] P. Saravanakumar, T. V. P. Sundararajan, R. K. Dhanaraj, K. Nisar, F. H. Memon et al., Lamport certificateless signcryption deep neural networks for data aggregation security in wsn. *Intelligent Automation & Soft Computing*, 33(3), 1835–1847, 2022.

[3] Himadri Nath Saha, Supratim Auddy, Subrata Pal. Health monitoring using Internet of Things (IoT). *IEEE Journal*, 69–73, 2017.

[4] Sarfraz Fayaz Khan, Health care monitoring system in Internet of Things (IoT) by using RFID. In *IEEE International Conference on Industrial Technology and Management*, pp. 198–204, 2017.

[5] Rajesh Kumar Dhanaraj, Lalitha Krishnasamy et al. Black-hole attack mitigation in medical sensor networks using the enhanced gravitational search algorithm. *International Journal of Uncertainty, Fuzziness and Knowledge-Based Systems*. https://doi.org/10.1142/S021848852140016X

[6] M. S. D. Gupta, V. Patchava, V. Menezes. Healthcare based on IOT using raspberry Pi. In *2015 International Conference on Green Computing and Internet of Things (ICGCIoT)*, pp. 796–799, October 2015.

[7] P. Gupta, D. Agrawal, J. Chhabra, P. K. Dhir. Iot based smart healthcare kit. In *2016 International Con-ference on Computational Techniques in Information and Communication Technologies (ICCTICT)*, pp. 237–242, March 2016.

[8] N. V. Lopes, F. Pinto, P. Furtado, J. Silva. IoT architecture proposal for disabled people. In *2014 IEEE 10th International Conference on Wireless and Mobile Computing, Networking and Communications (WiMob)*, pp. 152–158, October 2014.

[9] R. Nagavelli, C. V. Guru Rao. Degree of disease possibility (ddp): A mining based statistical measuring approach for disease prediction in health care data min- ing. In *International Conference on Recent Advances and Innovations in Engineering (ICRAIE-2014)*, pp. 1–6, May 2014.

[10] R. K. Dhanaraj, V. Ramakrishnan, M. Poongodi, L. Krishnasamy, M. Hamdi, K. Kotecha, V. Vijayakumar. Random forest bagging and X-means clustered antipattern detection from SQL query log for accessing secure mobile data. In D. K. Jain (Ed.), *Wireless Communications and Mobile Computing* (Vol. 2021, pp. 1–9). Hindawi Limited, 2021. https://doi.org/10.1155/2021/2730246

[11] Krishnan, B., Sai, S. S., Mohanthy, S. B.. Real time internet application with distributed flow environment for medical IoT. In: *International Conference on Green Computing and Internet of Things, Noida*, pp. 832–837, 2015.

[12] V Arulkumar, Charlyn Puspha Latha, Daniel Jr Dasig. Concept of implementing big data in Smart City: Applications, services, data security in accordance with Internet of Things and AI. *International Journal of Recent Technology and Engineering* 8(3), Vol. 8, 3, 2019.

[13] D. Azariadi, V. Tsoutsouras, S. Xydis, D. Soudris. ECG signal analysis and arrhythmia detection on IoT wearable medical devices. In: *5th International Conference on Modern Circuits and Systems Technologies, Thessaloniki*, pp. 1–4, 2016.

[14] A. Mohan. Cyber security for personal medical devices Internet of Things. In: *IEEE International Conference on Distributed Computing in Sensor Systems, Marina Del Rey, CA*, pp. 372–374, 2014.

[15] L. Y. Yeh, P. Y. Chiang, Y. L. Tsai, J. L. Huang. Cloudbased fine-grained health information access control framework for lightweight IoT devices with dynamic auditing and attribute revocation. *IEEE Transactions on Cloud Computing* 99, 1–13, 2015. IoT-Based Health Monitoring System for Active and Assisted Living 19.

[16] V. Arulkumar. An intelligent technique for uniquely recognising face and finger image using Learning Vector Quantisation (LVQ)-based template key generation. *International Journal of Biomedical Engineering and Technology* 26(3/4), 237–49, February 2, 2018.

[17] P. Porambage, A. Braeken, A. Gurtov, M. Ylianttila, S. Spinsante Secure end-to-end communication for constrained devices in IoT-enabled ambient assisted living systems. In: *IEEE 2nd World Forum on Internet of Things, Milan*, pp. 711–714 (2015).

[18] K. Yelamarthi, B. P. DeJong, K. Laubhan. A kinect-based vibrotactile feedback system to assist the visually impaired 2017.

[19] X.-W. Chen, X. Lin. Big data deep learning: Challenges and perspectives. *IEEE Access* 2, 514–525, 2014.

[20] M. Siekkinen, M. Hiienkari, J. Nurminen, and J. Nieminen. How low energy is bluetooth low energy? comparative measurements with zigbee/802.15.4. In *Wireless Communications and Networking Conference Workshops (WCNCW), 2012 IEEE*, pp. 232–237, April 2012.

[21] N. Bui, M. Zorzi. Health care applications: A solution based on the internet of things. In *Proc. of the 4th Int. Symposium on Applied Sciences in Biomed and Com. Tech., ser. ISABEL '11*. New York, NY, USA: ACM, pp. 131:1–131:5, 2011.

[22] K. Laubhan, M. Trent, B. Root, A. Abdelgawad, K. Yelamarthi. A wearable portable electronic travel aid for the blind. In: *IEEE International Conference on Electrical, Electronics, and Optimization Techniques*, 2016.

[23] M. Li, S. Yu, Y. Zheng, K. Ren, W. Lou. Scalable and secure sharing of personal health records in cloud computing using attributebased encryption. *IEEE Transactions on Parallel and Distributed Systems*, 24(1), 131–143, January 2013.

[24] V. Arulkumar, C. Selvan, V. Vimal Kumar. Big data analytics in healthcare industry. An analysis of healthcare applications in machine learning with big data analytics. *IGI Global Big Data Analytics for Sustainable Computing* 8(3), September 2019.

14

Electronic Health Records Storing and Sharing System Using Blockchain

Shailendra S. Aote
Shri Ramdeobaba College of Engineering and Management, Nagpur, India

Amit Khaparde
G. B. Pant DSEU Okhla – I Campus, New Delhi, India

Balamurugan Balusamy
Galgotias University, Greater Noida, India

Aayush Muley, Adesh Kotgirwar, Atharva Uplanchiwar, and Lalita Sharma
Shri Ramdeobaba College of Engineering and Management, Nagpur, India

CONTENTS

14.1 Introduction

In today's world of digitalization, in order to make the data access and maintenance effective and convenient most of the critical data is stored digitally. This digital management of data makes the process convenient, but also leads to some serious issues with respect to data privacy and security. In today's scenario, the global pandemic of 2020 had made us realize the importance of health. Today information related to one's health has become most crucial piece of data with respect to a particular human being, since may it be one's job or while travelling or getting benefit of a particular scheme healthcare information plays the vital role. But still in 21st century, the medical records of the person are maintained as a hardcopy in file with the person. In some cases, the records are stored digitally in the form of electronic health records (EHRs), but still the data is kept with the jurisdiction of a healthcare provider may it be stored on local server or on cloud. The patient himself does not has the authority or control over his own crucial medical data. This serious problem can be solved with a technology that is immutable, secure as well as transparent, and sustainable to cyberattacks.

This can be achieved using Blockchain. With the help of Blockchain we can create a decentralized application that stores data in most secure way, which gives whole authority of data to the patient, which maintains the expense proof of treatment as well as the medications bought from the chemists, and can also help a patient to claim insurance cover with respect to particular treatment with transparency. With the help of Blockchain not just the whole medical chain process is digitalized but also made secure with transparency due to decentralized nature [1].

14.1.1 Blockchain

Blockchain is the distributed ledger technology which stores the data in an immutable and transparent way with the help of decentralization and cryptographic hashing. Here data is stored in peer-to-peer network of blocks which has unique hash code and which makes it impossible to modify or hack the particular data. Since security with transparency can be achieved using Blockchain maintaining the integrity of the data it has become the most trusted source for the user and a lots of security problems can be solved using Blockchain. Blockchain does not have any central authority controlling because of which people has considered it as the most trusted source for storing their crucial information with encryption [2].

14.1.2 Types of Blockchain

Blockchain broadly consists of three types, which can be further categorized depending upon the applications of Blockchain:

1. *Public Blockchain*
   Public Blockchain is fully decentralized and allows the access to any user throughout the globe to participate in the network. All the transactions that take place on public Blockchain are transparent and can be examined by any user. One of the major aspect of public Blockchain is that no one has the control over the network.

2. *Private Blockchain*
   As the name suggests this Blockchain consists of the network of few listed individuals which are authorized to access the Blockchain. The transactions within the Blockchain are only visible to the users within the particular Blockchain. Since it contains the central authority controlling the access of the users, private Blockchain have more controlled system as compared to public Blockchain.

3. *Hybrid Blockchain*
   Hybrid Blockchain is the combination of private and public Blockchain. It combines the privacy benefits of private Blockchain with the security and transparency of public Blockchain. It provides more flexibility to the business with security [3].

14.1.3 Smart Contract

Ethereum Blockchain is the special type of Blockchain which allows one to create the real world decentralized applications on Blockchain, which can be used by an individual in his day to day life. The main heart of these decentralized applications which contains the main logic of transactions executed on the Blockchain is smart contract. They are basically programs written in solidity language which interacts and executes the transaction in Blockchain and manages the communication between various actors using the application through Blockchain network. It checks the conditions which are written in the logic of the program before the transaction. This smart contract is connected with the frontend in order to produce the end-to-end application.

14.1.4 Ganache

We have used Ganache, which provides the personal Blockchain, to deploy the DApp and to test the transactions happening between various actors during data storage and sharing. Ganache provides the personal Blockchain with 10 accounts and 100 ethers in each of them with each account having unique private key. We have used this personal Blockchain to migrate the smart contract and to test the execution of various functions through different accounts.

14.2 Proposed System

In order to make the healthcare data access, storage, and maintenance effective and secure we propose a Blockchain-based healthchain management system. This system is based on consortium Blockchain technology [3]. There are mainly four members who can access and maintain the data of the healthchain, giving full authority of data to the patient who is being treated. The system we have proposed is an Ethereum-based web application DApp, where people belonging to specific organizations can create the account and login. Through login each of the actor can perform specific functions with respect to the role of the person.

The four main actors who can access the system are as follows:

- Patient
- Healthcare Organization/Doctor
- Chemist/Pharmaceutical Organization
- Insurance Providers

The system focuses on giving the full authority of one's medical data securely with the person/patient and giving the person authority to share data only with healthcare organization or insurance company to whom he wants to share. Healthcare Organization can only have access to particular data of patient only if patient gives access and the data is stored in the decentralized network with respect to patient and not with the healthcare organization. The system also focuses on maintaining the expense information with respect to a particular treatment, in order to have a proof of price at what particular medicine or treatment had cost to the patient in an immutable storage.

The diagrammatic representation of all the functionalities with respect to each actor of the system is explained in Figure 14.1.

I. **Registering an user on the system**

In order to access the system, one has to register himself on the system and login to the account in order to access the functionalities of the system. The patient in the system is uniquely identified by his/her Aadhar card number. This ensures that there is no ambiguity of multiple account creation. The patient also need to update information about some specific precautions, blood group, and emergency contact number while registering. All the other three organizations are uniquely identified by a specific id which is generated by hash code. The healthcare individuals has to mention his practice type and area of expertise while registering which can be checked and verified by the patient.

II. **Updating and maintaining the treatment information**

When a patient approaches the healthcare organization for the treatment, then he/she can display his/her past healthcare information to the doctor by giving him/her the access. The data of the patient can be seen by doctor only when patient gives access. The basic medical information of the patient is known to doctor only in case of emergency. When the patient approaches the doctor for a treatment, the doctor generates a new treatment with respect to the particular patient having unique treatment id.

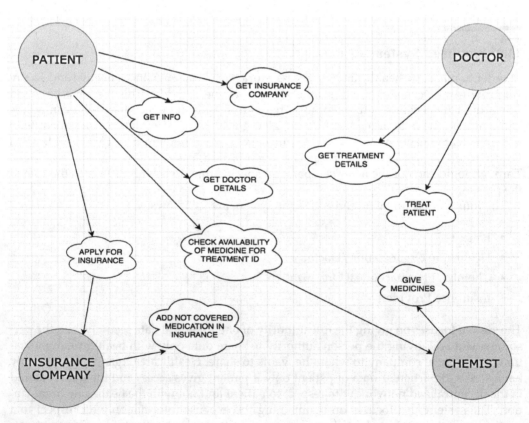

FIGURE 14.1
Functionalities of the system.

The data with respect to the particular treatment can only be updated by the doctor. The bills and other expenses with respect to the treatment are mapped to the particular treatment. The expenses of the medication from the chemist are also mapped to the particular treatment id. In order to claim the insurance cover, the patient can then give access of the data of particular treatment to the insurance company.

III. **Maintaining pharmaceutical records**
The pharmaceutical data with respect to particular treatment is stored securely with the patient. When the doctor issues some medicines for a particular treatment to the patient, he/she can check the availability of medicines with the chemists and if available then the expense of the medicines is mapped with the treatment. This eliminates the false price hike on medication by storing the medication expense proof in immutable ledger [4].

IV. **Claiming insurance cover**
A patient can get insurance and register for particular insurance policy by exploring insurance company. After the treatment, in order to get insurance cover, the patient can give access of the data of particular treatment to the insurance company and by analyzing the data and expenses the company can issue the cover. The insurance company can also been given the access to pharmaceutical data to add medication in the cover [5].

14.3 Methodology

The proposed system is Ethereum Blockchain-based Decentralized Web Application [6]. The main logical unit of the system is smart contract. This smart contract contains the logic of each and every set of conditions, which are needed to be checked in order to validate the transaction and store the records in Blockchain. The whole system is developed using truffle as development environment. This smart contract communicates the information to the frontend web application, which is developed using React-JS through which user can interact with the Blockchain [7]. The web application is linked with the personal test Blockchain of Ganache using the Metamask browser extension. The transactions take place when a function of a smart contract is invoked, these transactions charge ethers, and the ethers corresponding to the user account from whom the function is invoked are deducted. These transactions lead to deployment of data on the Blockchain.

From Figure 14.2, one can see the detailed study about how the application works and how does the information transfer happens between the various entities is shown in Figure 14.2.

From Figure 14.2, one can see the frameworks and tools used during the development of system and what work they are doing to manage the whole round system. Truffle is the major development tool used, which provides the platform to frontend, backend, and middleware of the system to interact. Truffle helps in integrating a compiled smart contract into end-to-end decentralized application. Truffle consists of the configurable built pipeline that supports the development and execution of decentralized web applications.

The backend of the system is the main logical unit of the application. It consists of a smart contract, which is written in solidity language. Solidity is the high-level, object-oriented programming language used for writing the smart contracts, which are used for developing the DApp using Ethereum Blockchain. We have used structures in solidity language to create the unique instance of patient, doctor, chemists, and insurance

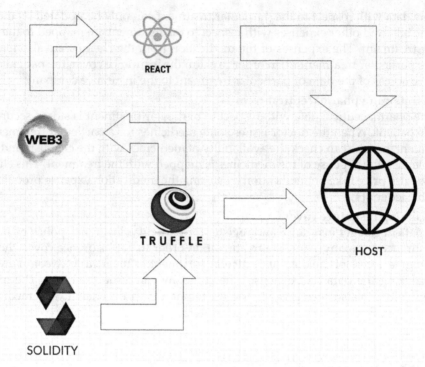

FIGURE 14.2
Information transfer flow.

organization. This structure consists of lots of instance variables, which have unique values for each and every user who is registered onto the system. This data of users using the system is stored in Blockchain by using map data structure by mapping user's instances by its unique identity. This smart contract written using solidity also consists of lots of functions with respect to the category of the user and it also consists of events which are triggered when any course of action is performed.

The frontend of the application is designed using React-JS, which is one of the best tools used for developing web interfaces of interactive applications. This user interface interacts with the backend smart contract using the tool or library known as web3.js. The data on web interface is send by web3.js to the backend solidity code and invokes the functions of solidity by using the data as a parameter. It also used to display the data in the Ethereum node on the web interface of the user.

In order to successfully use the DApp on the web browser one has to use the Metamask extension. This Metamask extension is used to store or link the accounts for the smooth usage of Blockchain-based application on the local system. Through Metamask one can link the local Ganache Blockchain accounts to the web browser and transactions which took place while using the application are smoothly executed.

14.4 Results

This is the main page to register and sign up via Metamask (Figure 14.3).

FIGURE 14.3
Home page.

Accounts for every actor were created using the Metamask (Figure 14.4).

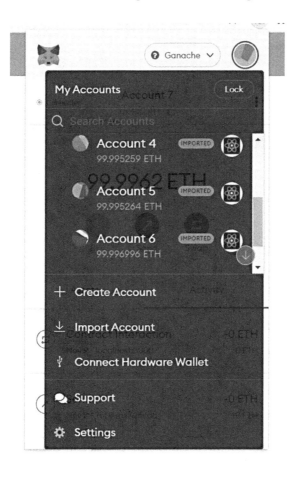

FIGURE 14.4
Meta mask accounts.

These are the functionalities for the corresponding actors of the chain (Figure 14.5).

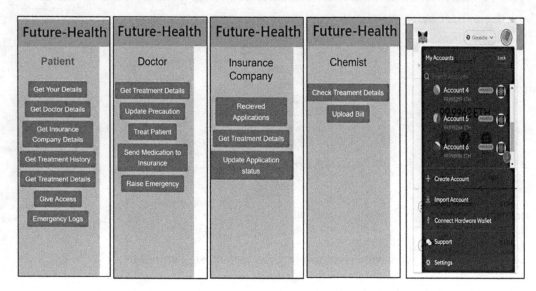

FIGURE 14.5
Functionalities implemented.

Working of **Get Your Details** functionality of the patient entity (Figure 14.6).

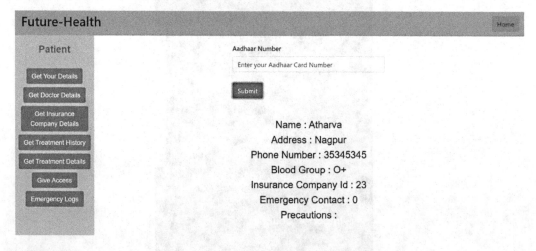

FIGURE 14.6
Get patient details.

Whenever there is a change in data in the blocks in the Blockchain a new block is created (Figure 14.7).
Whenever a contract is called a transactions are recorded in Ganache (Figure 14.8).

FIGURE 14.7
Block chain blocks recorded in Ganache.

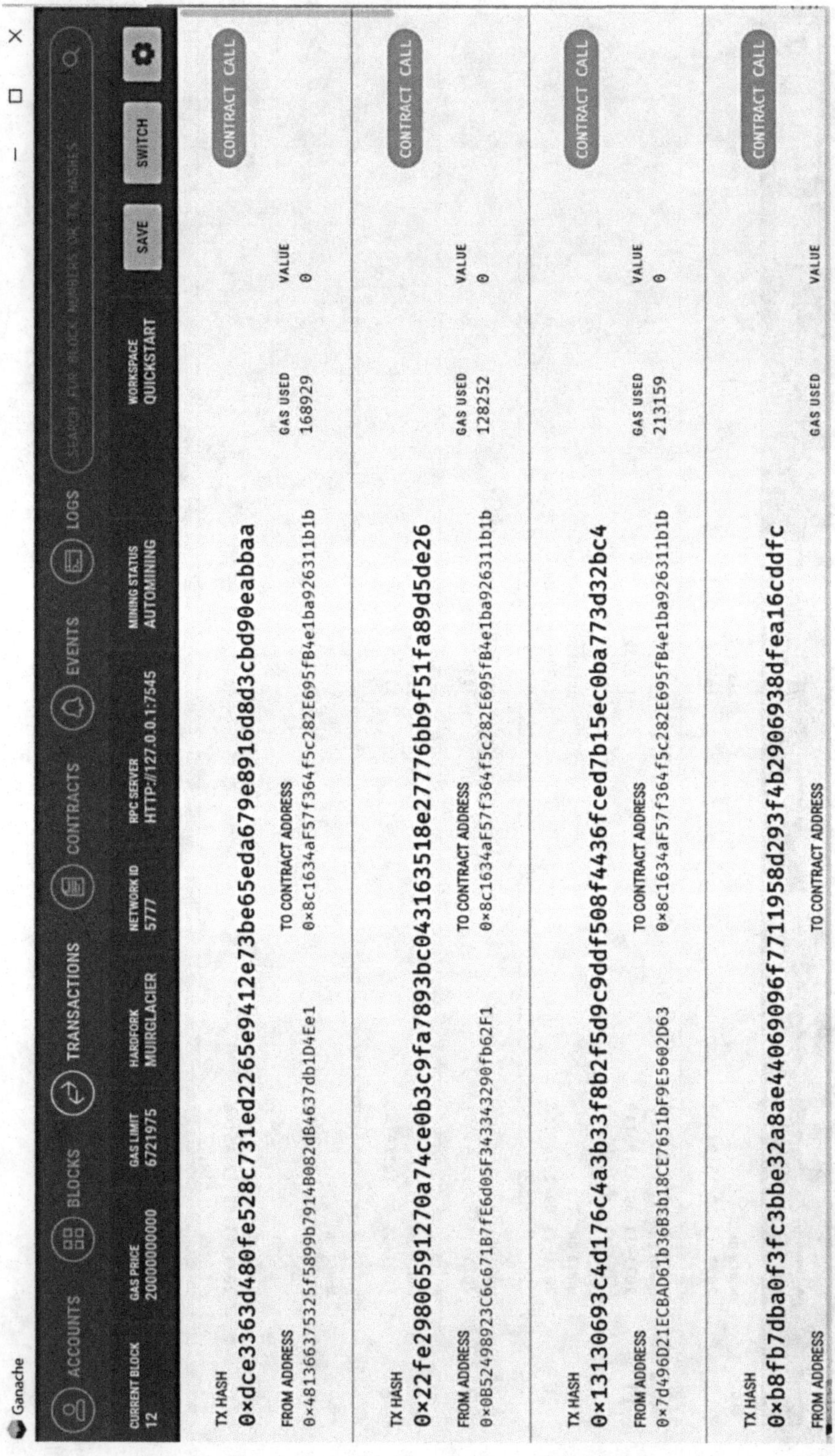

FIGURE 14.8
Transaction record in Ganache.

14.5 Conclusion

Using Ethereum Blockchain network we can deploy our application on Blockchain which constitutes smart contract as business logic.

With Blockchain a secure, decentralized, effective, fast distributed ledger system can be built. The entities present inside a chain can be represented using smart contract and the interactions between each entity can be validated. The transactions and data sharing between various entities of the system were tested successfully [2]. A cryptographic hash of preceding block is generated and stored because of that the validation becomes fast when another record is inserted. With the help of Ethereum Blockchain the secure storage and maintenance of EHRs were observed and the secure and trusted solution to the problems of healthchain ecosystem was proposed.

Blockchain can provide a revolutionary contribution in transformation of medical sector. It can reduce the malpractices, provide authorization to user, and prevent misuse of incentives provided by insurance company/govt [4]. We can extend the research by adding some more functionalities of authorized login, etc. This technology can be a significant change for country's medical sector. Identity authentication, asset register, and transaction certification are some of the features that can be achieved very easily by using Blockchain.

References

[1] Ekblaw, A., Azaria, A., Halamka, J.D., Lippman, A. A case study for blockchain in healthcare: "MedRec" prototype for electronic health records and medical research data. *Proceedings of IEEE Open & Big Data Conference* 2016; 13: 13.

[2] Ahram, T., Sargolzaei, A., Sargolzaei, S., Daniels, J., Amaba, B. Blockchain technology innovations. In: *IEEE Technology & Engineering Management Conference (TEMSCON)*, pp. 137–141. IEEE, 2017.

[3] Dhanaraj, R. K., Lalitha, K., Anitha, S., Khaitan, S., Gupta, P., Goyal, M. K. Hybrid and dynamic clustering based data aggregation and routing for wireless sensor networks. *Journal of Intelligent & Fuzzy Systems* 2021; 40(6): 10751–10765. IOS Press. https://doi.org/10.3233/jifs-201756

[4] Fan, K., Wang, S., Ren, Y., Li, H., Yang, Y. Medblock: efficient and secure medical data sharing via blockchain. *Journal of Medical Systems* 2018; 42(8): 136. doi: 10.1007/s10916-018-0993-7.

[5] Gatteschi, V., Lamberti, F., Claudio, D., Víctor, S. Blockchain and smart contracts for insurance: Is the technology mature enough? February 2018.

[6] Xhafa, F., Li, J., Zhao, G., Li, J., Chen, X. Wong, D.S. Designing cloud-based electronic health record system with attribute-based encryption. *Multimedia Tools and Applications* 2014 February 11; 74(10): 3441–3458. doi: 10.1007/s11042-013-1829-6.

[7] Kosba, A. Miller, A. Shi, E., Wen, Z., Papamanthou, C., Hawk: The blockchain model of cryptography and privacy-preserving smart contracts. In *Proceedings of the 2016 IEEE Symposium on Security and Privacy (SP)*, pp. 839–858, IEEE, San Jose, CA, USA, May 2016.

Index

Printed in the United States
by Baker & Taylor Publisher Services